Literature, Pedagogy, and Curriculum in Secondary Education

M. Martin Guiney

Literature, Pedagogy, and Curriculum in Secondary Education

Examples from France

M. Martin Guiney
Department of Modern Languages
and Literatures
Kenyon College
Gambier, Ohio, USA

ISBN 978-3-319-84830-3　　　ISBN 978-3-319-52138-1 (eBook)
DOI 10.1007/978-3-319-52138-1

© The Editor(s) (if applicable) and The Author(s) 2017
Softcover reprint of the hardcover 1st edition 2017
This work is subject to copyright. All rights are solely and exclusively licensed by the Publisher, whether the whole or part of the material is concerned, specifically the rights of translation, reprinting, reuse of illustrations, recitation, broadcasting, reproduction on microfilms or in any other physical way, and transmission or information storage and retrieval, electronic adaptation, computer software, or by similar or dissimilar methodology now known or hereafter developed.
The use of general descriptive names, registered names, trademarks, service marks, etc. in this publication does not imply, even in the absence of a specific statement, that such names are exempt from the relevant protective laws and regulations and therefore free for general use.
The publisher, the authors and the editors are safe to assume that the advice and information in this book are believed to be true and accurate at the date of publication. Neither the publisher nor the authors or the editors give a warranty, express or implied, with respect to the material contained herein or for any errors or omissions that may have been made. The publisher remains neutral with regard to jurisdictional claims in published maps and institutional affiliations.

Cover image © Tetra Images / Alamy Stock Photo

Printed on acid-free paper

This Palgrave Macmillan imprint is published by Springer Nature
The registered company is Springer International Publishing AG
The registered company address is: Gewerbestrasse 11, 6330 Cham, Switzerland

In memory of Louise Purves Guiney

ACKNOWLEDGMENTS

The research for this book was made possible by generous, ongoing support from Kenyon College, and by a grant from the National Endowment for the Humanities. Faculty members of the University of Paris III – Sorbonne Nouvelle welcomed me during the 2008–2009 academic year, when I began in earnest to research and reflect on the academic status of literature as a "general education" discipline. I am grateful in particular to Jean Bessière and Stéphane Michaud of the department of Comparative Literature, and to Jean-Louis Chiss, Emmanuel Fraisse, and Dan Savatovsky of the department of *Didactique du Français Langue Etrangère*, for allowing me to sit in on their seminars, meet their students, and spend long hours in discussion with them about the current debates over the literature curriculum in France. Emmanuel Fraisse also played an important role in the genesis of this book by encouraging me to investigate the teaching of literature in American secondary education, and inviting me to publish on the topic in the journals *Revue Internationale d'éducation de Sèvres* and *Revue de l'Association française des acteurs de l'éducation*.

I benefitted from the generous advice, encouragement, and depth of expertise of many other French specialists in the burgeoning field of literary pedagogy, including Pierre Albertini, Anne-Marie Chartier, Violaine Houdart-Merot, Martine Jey, and Isabelle de Peretti. Francis Jacques helped me to clarify the relationship between education and the free-market economy, on which much of my argument depends, and to find an outlet for early speculation on the topic in the *Revue de Métaphysique et de Morale*.

I have many colleagues in American Universities to thank as well. Gilbert Chaitin has provided support and inspiration, both in person and through his work, as has Dana Lindaman. Ralph Albanese has been a wonderful colleague and collaborator over the years, and I continue to discover new inspiration in his vast and pioneering work on the teaching of classical French literature in the nineteenth and twentieth centuries. His generous feedback on an earlier draft of my manuscript was invaluable. I am especially indebted to Leon Sachs, who thoroughly scrutinized each chapter with an unerring critical eye, and made countless suggestions for improvement, both large and small. If this book makes any contribution toward advancing the debate over the value of literature as a required subject in secondary education, it is due to the knowledge, inspiration, and moral support of these many great colleagues and friends, for which I am very thankful.

The *French Review* has published early versions of Chapters Four and Five: "The Literature Problem in the *lycée*: French Education Debates Today" *French Review* 85:4 (March 2012) 642–57; and "How (Not) to Teach French: *Psittacisme* and *Culture de Proximité* in Three Cinematic Representations of School" *French Review* 86:6 (May 2013), 1147–1159. The editor-in-chief, Edward Ousselin, has graciously given permission to incorporate material from these articles.

Finally, I am eternally grateful to my wife, Amy Mock, and to our daughters Zoe and Kate, for their patience, understanding, and the countless other ways in which they have supported me over the years.

Contents

1 Introduction: Literature as Academic Discipline During Hard Times ... 1

2 Aristocrats or Anarchists: Who Has Power over Literature? ... 35

3 The *Baccalauréat* Exam and the French Canonical Literary Exercise ... 61

4 Inventing and Defending the General Education of Literature ... 89

5 Literature in French Schools After 1968 ... 121

6 How (Not) to Teach: "Parroting" vs "Proximity" in Cinematic Representations of Literary Pedagogy ... 161

7 Harnessing the Neo-liberal Beast ... 191

8 Conclusion: The Future of Literary Studies in General Education ... 233

Bibliography 273

Index 295

CHAPTER 1

Introduction: Literature as Academic Discipline During Hard Times

LITERARY PEDAGOGY FOR ALL?

We begin with two questions. Should literature be a subject taught in school to a general population? If so, how should it be taught?

Only in the last century has secondary education become universal in developed countries, with the increase in the length of compulsory schooling and in the rate of completion of secondary education. Literature has been part of the secondary curriculum for centuries, but now that it is being taught to virtually everybody instead of to a privileged minority, it must justify its "general education" status. Teachers of literature, whatever part of the world in which they operate, have yet to find definitive answers to our opening questions. Soon, they may find that the responsibility for answering those questions is no longer theirs and has been taken over by businesspersons, politicians, and even students. Never before has the world seen as much access to general education, nor has there ever been as much pressure on general education to serve the material needs of society over spiritual ones. From primary education to the university, teachers around the globe face challenges from government agencies, families, and private enterprises, based on the perceived need for practical and economic benefits. As a result of this challenge, new centers of power in the educational landscape seek to hold teachers accountable for supporting economic growth and are eager to suggest ways they can be more effective. The European Union, the Organization for Economic Cooperation and Development, and the Bill and Melinda Gates Foundation are just some

© The Author(s) 2017
M.M. Guiney, *Literature, Pedagogy, and Curriculum in Secondary Education*, DOI 10.1007/978-3-319-52138-1_1

of the transnational organizations that have recently declared themselves to be in the business of education reform, often with a surprising degree of success.

What hope is there for literature, one of the few disciplines in the arts and humanities that is (still) required as part of general education in most countries, under the new regime of economic accountability? Literature will no doubt survive as an area of scholarly research, just as literature itself will continue to have a market presence as a commodity, as the economist Robert Topel suggested in his contribution to a conference on "Education and Economic Development" organized by the Federal Reserve Bank of Cleveland in 2004: "[E]ducation is itself often a consumption good, which, in turn, enables the consumption and enjoyment of human capital goods such as information, literature, and ideas" (48). To define literature as merely one "human capital good" among others does not, by itself, justify its status in general education. The domination of such economic definitions of value leads to a crisis of legitimacy for literary pedagogy, which fails to make a strong enough economic case for its continued support, not only by parents and students, but by taxpayers. If the crisis continues, such support as there is will gradually disappear, and the study of literature will become the academic equivalent of a niche market.

What are the consequences, if the crisis continues? How different, or worse, is a society in which literature is a high-end commodity and an esoteric field of research, rather than a general education discipline required of all students at the secondary and sometimes tertiary levels? Such questions are relatively new in the United States and much of the Anglophone world, but have occupied French debates over education since the nineteenth century, to a degree that is difficult for citizens of almost any other modern nation to comprehend. In part because literature has played an important role in the successful emergence of French secular nationhood from the shadow of Catholicism,[1] it has a much more secure status in general education than elsewhere. Arguments in justification of this status, like French literary culture more generally, are far more visible and consensual than in the United States. But literary pedagogy in France is not immune to the same market forces and calls for accountability that operate in the rest of the developed world, and the responses to such challenges have dominated academic and journalistic debate. If a solution to the crisis of literature in general education is to be found, it therefore requires a detour through the "crisis of French", a term that has stood for deeply entrenched conflicts over the purposes and methodologies of literary pedagogy in France for more than a century. In order to understand the relevance of the perennial "crisis" to the general education of literature today, one must begin with the history of the challenge to the educational institution posed by quantifiable standards of evaluation, a challenge that intensifies in periods of economic insecurity. We now turn to the specific place of literature in relation to the dominance of economic definitions of value, before returning to a discussion of the conditions that make the French experience exemplary.

LITERARY PEDAGOGY AND THE MARKETPLACE

If one has ever taught a literature course that students are required to take, in order to receive a secondary school diploma, for example, or as part of an undergraduate core curriculum, one has encountered resistance. So do teachers in other general education disciplines and, to some degree, such is to be expected. It is natural that people should chafe at limits to their freedom of choice, whether in education or any other aspect of their lives. In the case of literature, however, the resistance is intensified by a widely shared sense of injustice, based on literature's lack of obvious market value. Students ask: "What is the use of this class? How will it help me get a job?"[2] These are not questions to be dismissed lightly. Simply put, it is hard to teach literature when the people who pay to make education possible are worried about the future. Instead of "learning for its own sake", they want learning for the sake of reassurance. In September 2015, for example, President Obama unveiled the "college scorecard", a website designed to give prospective students statistical information on "college *opportunity, cost, and value*; and supports for students and families as they search for and select a college suitable to their academic, *career and financial goals*" (White House). I added italics to those words that most clearly address the anxious concerns of the contemporary consumer of higher education, who wants above all to graduate in a timely fashion, unburdened by excessive debt, and prepared for a well-paid and secure professional career.

These are reasonable demands. But where does literature fit in? Are there any objectively measurable "outcomes" of the study of literature that justify the time and money that it requires? These questions do not apply only to higher education. In secondary education, literature and other liberal arts subjects are not only taught, they are mandatory. All school districts in the United States continue to require students to take years of English classes in which literature still plays an important part. At the same time, every educational level (K-12 and higher) is expected to demonstrate cost-effectiveness, measurable outcomes, and attention to the financial "needs" and "goals" of the general population that increasingly are defined by students, parents, and public and private agencies, rather than by education providers themselves.

The White House is not only responding to public demand for accountability and access to a financially secure future, it is echoing what the business community has been saying for years. Forbes released its list of the top 50 colleges and universities in August 2015 with the following introduction:

> While the cost of U.S. higher education escalates, there's a genuine silver lining in play. A growing number of colleges and universities are now focusing on student-consumer value over marketing prestige, making this a new age of return-on-investment education. This pivot is the result of intense public scrutiny on the substantial cost of a degree vs. long tail worth.... (Howard)

The public has been focusing more than ever, Forbes tells us, on the ratio of cost to "long tail worth" (business jargon for long-term returns), and why not? Rational consumer behavior is rare enough that it should be encouraged whenever it occurs. Education is not an industry like most others, however, and we should not be surprised if it has so much trouble behaving like one. The contradiction between the outside pressure on the education establishment to behave like a commercial service provider, and its own claim to be exempt from market forces, is the subject of this book.

But where does this sudden "intense public scrutiny" on the "long tail worth" of education come from? To those of us who provide education, especially in literature, it feels as if a profession that has evolved over the centuries into an autonomous and ostensibly disinterested enterprise faces an unprecedented challenge. People who are not educators, but rather students, parents, and members of government agencies and business interests are influencing the future of education, not just in the United States but around the world. Among many causes of this change, one of the biggest is fear of economic uncertainty. In order to discuss where the general education of literature has been, where it is now, and where it might be headed in the future, it is first necessary to explore the sources of this fear that has caused a worldwide revolution in education, for better and for worse.

Citizens of economically developed countries suffer today from a range of collective anxieties that have roots in the previous century. Following the traumas of the Great Depression and World Wars, it is understandable that a strong yearning for economic security and political stability took hold, which led to the successful creation of transnational organizations such as the United Nations (UN) (chartered in 1945), the World Bank (created at the Bretton Woods Conference in 1944), the World Trade Organization (based on the General Agreement on Tariffs and Trade, first signed in 1948), and the Organization for Economic Co-operation and Development or OECD (which has its roots in the Marshall Plan of 1948). The birth of these institutions during the four-year period that immediately followed the darkest chapter in modern history has certainly contributed to global economic growth and even reduced the frequency and severity of armed conflicts.[3] Alas, effective cures often have unwanted side effects. The anxieties that organizations, like the UN and the OECD, were designed to repress, have returned under a different form. The new fears include the clash between local, rooted cultures and a free-roaming global, commercial culture, frequently identified as American[4]; the ideology of the unregulated free market or "neo-liberalism", also viewed as a tool of American expansion; and environmental decline fed by global warming, species extinction, and more.

The strategy of global economic growth as a bulwark against crisis is, it seems, itself a crisis. When the oil embargo of 1973–1974 revealed the limits of postwar prosperity, it became harder to ignore the killjoys who had always been skeptical of the new world order, and their nagging questions: Is the standard of living enjoyed by most of the citizens of industrialized nations, and growing percentages of those of developing nations, viable in the long term? Was Marx right to claim that market economies always privilege the few at the expense of the many? And finally, will the ultimate result of global economic growth be the extinction of the human species through environmental pollution and climate change? People have always feared poverty and war, but now they also fear the unintended consequences of the postwar strategy against poverty and war, as economist Mary Wrenn argued in her path-breaking article "The Social Ontology of Fear and Neoliberalism" (2014).

Compared to issues of such consequence, the future of literary studies in our society seems unworthy of attention. And yet, the future of "humanity" and the future of "the humanities" are related, and even interdependent. The relationship of literary study to economic and ecological forces has always existed. It has often been a symbiotic relationship, as when rising middle-class prosperity increased the demand for literary studies by democratizing the privilege of engaging in the disinterested life of the mind. According to classical tradition, one can say that broad-based economic growth increases the percentage of those who have access to the "liberal arts", in their original definition of education suitable for a free citizen. Conversely, when the middle class shrinks and economic inequality grows, as is the case today in many parts of the world, there is a corresponding increase in utilitarian demands upon the educational supply, and students flee from subject areas that do not lead to employment opportunities.

"General education", on the other hand, is in principle immune to the shifts in demand on the part of students, since it is required. Students cannot act as consumers when they have no choice. Virtually, all of primary education is "general", and in the United States, most of secondary education and at least some of higher education is as well. Literature is a general education discipline like math or history, which means that at various times during their careers students must try to learn it, whether they want to or not. Literature as general education can take many forms, from a tool for acquiring literacy in primary education, to a full-fledged academic discipline in its own right in secondary and tertiary education. While the decentralized structure of American education makes generalizations difficult, we can tell from high school English textbooks that there is a widespread expectation that students become familiar with literature from a young age and have to study it in high school in order to graduate. But why?

Part of literature's importance in education is that it provides shelter from the harsh laws of social exchange. That certainly has been the case in France, where contemporary novelist Pierre Bergounioux has provided an exemplary definition of literature as "counter-discourse" to the quantifiable values currently dominating the field of education:

> La littérature française fut l'effort de cinq siècles pour porter au jour la nature des hommes et des choses.... C'est pour être restés à l'écart de l'échange généralisé, de l'évaluation strictement monétaire que les êtres, les objets, les heures se sont présentés comme autant de mystères enivrants ou terribles....
>
> [French literature has been a 500-year effort to bring to light the nature of humans and things. Because they remained separate from generalized

exchange, from strict monetary valuation, living beings, objects, and time were presented as so many intoxicating and awe-inspiring mysteries] (171).

To Bergounioux and others, "humans and things", or at least their authentic value, exist only "separate from generalized exchange". To put it differently: the dynamics of the market substitute relative value for absolute value, thereby making the "nature" of all phenomena inaccessible to human consciousness. The world of exchange (which covers not only markets, but a wide range of human interactions) is a labyrinth of mirrors, and literature has the potential to save us from getting lost.

It is easy to be seduced by this idealistic notion according to which literature, and art in general, promises of a kind of secular salvation. Many defenses of the humanities rely on the argument that economic criteria are incapable of accounting for the "higher" values that legitimize general education, such as Martha Nussbaum's aptly titled book *Not for Profit: Why Democracy Needs the Humanities* (2010). The argument derives from money's power to reduce almost any object or action to a numerical value, including even human beings. Why should the absolute, nonmarket value that we ascribe to individuals not also characterize the products of human creativity?

The argument of literature's immunity from market forces is persuasive but encounters stiff resistance in the pedagogical context. Even if our education system were not constantly being challenged to produce measurable results in the form of higher test scores or more successful job applicants, a major source of resistance to the belief in its "higher value" would remain. Such stubborn resistance arises precisely because we are dealing here with a belief, rather than a fact. "Learning for the sake of learning" is a beautiful motto, but it is not as popular as many of us in the education profession might think. This is especially true when the learning in question is in a discipline that has little obvious purpose outside of itself, and even less relevance to a student's future career, as is the case with literature. Most people, I argue, do not accept "disinterested learning" at face value, especially when the subject being learned is the gratuitous, ostensibly priceless universe of artistic creation. As a result, those who want to make literature or art classes required for all students are met with a "faith gap". Many people accept that such disciplines are of universal importance, but most do not. Hence, arts programs are the first to be considered for elimination when high school budgets are cut, and the content of English classes tends to be advertised as "communication" or "composition" rather than literature. To what extent, if any, should society be concerned about the "faith gap" that separates part of the educational establishment from the rest of the population?

Answers to the question of whether to close the "faith gap" and more importantly, how to do so, will help determine the future of general education. Underlying the attempt to find answers, over the following chapters, is the assumption that preaching the absolute and universal value of literature, à la Bergounioux, is not enough. General education is not about converting people to a creed nor is it purely a matter of classical economics, by which one persuades students that it is in their material self-interest to study certain subjects. I intend to break with the litany of defenses of the "unquantifiable" value of literature and other humanities, by exploring a specific set of questions: why is literature considered a general education discipline, historically and in the present? What relationship does teaching literature have to the economy? What factors, in addition to economic anxiety, explain the resistance to studying literature on the part of students? Can and should society continue to require its members to study literature, just as it requires them to study history, science, and other core subjects? What is the connection between "literariness", the elusive distinguishing characteristic of literary discourse, and the teaching of literature as general education? Finally, are there methods of teaching literature as general education, that do not apply when it is taught as an elective field of specialization, and that may therefore justify literature's privileged status as a subject that every educated person needs to have studied? In other words, how does it embody propaedeutic, foundational knowledge, on the model of medieval higher learning, in which the *trivium* must be studied prior to more specialized knowledge, the *quadrivium*?[5] To begin, we need to look in more detail at the two extremes that define the "faith gap" afflicting the discipline of literature: between the pragmatic, market-based approach to general education, and its antieconomic, idealist "liberal arts" counterpart.

Economics, Education, and the Resistance to Literature

In hard times, often under parental pressure, not only do students gravitate toward educational offerings that promise economic security, such as applied sciences, business, and information technology, they push back against general education requirements in humanities disciplines and thus contribute to their relative decline. Simply put: why do I need to study Shakespeare when all I want is secure employment? It is no small irony that, when the humanities are in least demand in the free market of education, they are, in a sense, most needed, since they are the source of many of the most effective alternatives to an otherwise unchallenged economic standard of value.[6] "Man shall not live by bread alone" is scripture that can refer to the need for art and literature as well as for God and reminds us that these activities are not an escape from the world, but rather a critical engagement with it, a rebuttal to the ideologies of materialism and positivism that feed the demand for utilitarian education. The best known of the recent briefs in defense of the humanities, such as Anthony T. Kronman's *Education's End: Why Our Colleges and Universities have Given Up on the Meaning of Life* (2007), are very good at justifying the need for categories other than the measurable and the quantifiable. This book is different, not because I take issue with Kronman, Nussbaum, et al (I do not), but because I explore the possibility that there is a path to general literary pedagogy that recognizes rather than dismisses economic concerns and even uses them as a means to achieve an education that is as universally inclusive as the term "general" implies. Nobody has yet found a way to resolve the contradiction between "literary" and "general" in the discipline of "literary general education", and few have tried, at least outside of France. The solution may not yet be at hand, but recognizing the contradiction, and analyzing its history in the French school, is a necessary first step.

There are, of course, many ways in which literature and economics overlap. The subversive and even revolutionary role of art as the embodiment of an alternative conception of value that is not determined by supply and demand, and therefore resists commodification, does not liberate it from the tyranny of the market. The literary field itself has many of the characteristics of a market, and the form of literary consumption that occurs in the school is itself a captive market, subject to a high degree of regulation. The school accepts literary pedagogy's claim on resources such as class time, classroom space, and teaching staff; in return, the professionals responsible for the discipline of literature are not entirely free to determine its goals and methodologies. Like artistic production itself, literary pedagogy costs money, and those who control public or private funding demand a return on their investment. Under such conditions, even literary pedagogy, especially when it is mandatory, must account for its contribution to the material conditions (schools, staffing) that make education possible, by showing that it helps train better workers, who then become taxpayers and philanthropists. This is the economic vicious circle from which humanists have always fought to escape, with mixed results.

Certainly, there have been times when it looked as if the humanist fight to escape from the market had succeeded. For most of the second half of the twentieth century, financial capital provided ample support to cultural capital, by ensuring that a portion of the resources for education be reserved for "disinterested" academic pursuits such as literature and the arts. Capitalism has subsidized the general education of literature, just as it subsidizes museums, theaters, and musical ensembles that would languish at best if they had to compete in the open market. One does not send tax-deductible gifts to multinational "wealth creators" like Unilever or General Motors, since they are expected to take care of themselves (various forms of corporate welfare and trade protectionism notwithstanding). Similarly, public and private agencies that allocate funds to education do so on the understanding, still widely shared, that much worthwhile and even necessary educational activity is noncommercial in the sense that it does not have and should never have any direct bearing on economic growth. More and more, however, the belief that education should be protected from unregulated market forces is eroding, and not just in the United States.

"Core curriculum" and "general education requirements" are practices in public and private education that disproportionately benefit those disciplines that students are generally disinclined to choose of their own free will. In a free educational market, students enroll in subjects that they like (which could be anything, depending on the individual), or ones they think they need. Literature as an academic discipline would lose market share, if students who neither enjoy it nor consider it useful were not required to study it. Whatever power literature still has to attract students beyond its small natural constituency depends on two factors: the ability of the discipline to market itself in order to increase its consumer base, and society's willingness to subsidize the discipline by allocating the resources needed to impose it on students, sometimes against their will. Each factor, not surprisingly, comes with a long list of problems.

We now have defined three types of closely related links between the academic discipline of literary studies and financial capital. The first is

INTRODUCTION: LITERATURE AS ACADEMIC DISCIPLINE 11

antithetical: the ideal of "disinterested" education, which is a reflection of the perceived incompatibility of art with the law of supply and demand.[7] The second is sociological: cultural and financial capital are mutually dependent, since the production of wealth leads to its unequal distribution. The need to reproduce the conditions of production that benefit a particular social class, described in Chapter 23 of *Das Kapital*,[8] generates a kind of social hierarchy of taste, which literary study helps to perpetuate. The third is the most basic: education costs money, and those academic disciplines that make no obvious contribution to economic growth survive, and sometimes thrive, according to the size of the subsidy that public or private entities are willing to allocate. The subsidy, in turn, exerts a power over "unproductive" disciplines that pushes them toward proving their value as economic stimulants, that is, toward becoming productive. An example of this insidious *quid pro quo* on a global scale is the Program for International Student Assessment (PISA) test that I discuss in Chapter 7: transnational nongovernmental organizations (the OECD, in this case) advocate for a greater role of education in promoting economic growth. Through various means, including testing of students on a massive scale, that lead to immensely powerful and controversial rankings of national education systems, they acquire authority over the classroom. In order for a country to improve its ranking on the reading comprehension portion of PISA, it must conform to its standards. Interestingly, as we shall see, PISA does include literature as part of reading competency. The question is whether literature according to the OECD, an organization designed to solve economic problems, is significantly different from literature according to humanistic tradition in which it has been taught up until now.

Those who allocate public or private wealth subsidize a range of academic disciplines that otherwise would decline in importance, or even disappear.[9] The danger of subsidies is that they depend on the good graces of the underwriters, just as revenues of a private enterprise depend on the demand for its goods or services. Even though education tends to be publicly funded through taxes, rather than privately funded through profits, any belief that public education is better protected from market influences than private education has to confront the inconvenient fact that private schools and colleges in the United States generally do a better job of promoting the general education of arts and humanities than do public ones. Of course, one reason is that private secondary and higher education on the Eton-Oxbridge model plays a bigger role than public education in the reproduction of the conditions of wealth production mentioned earlier. The issue is not to recognize the obvious fact that the liberal arts continue to serve as a marker of class, but rather to debate the claim that their dissemination in *all* of society is a universal good that must be pursued, even at a great cost.

In the United States as well as other industrialized nations, the merging of private interests with the ostensibly universal mission of the educational enterprise has a long history, symbolized by auto executive Charles E. Wilson's claim that "what [is] good for General Motors [is] good for the country".[10] When members of the liberal arts establishment complain today about the "corporatization" of higher education, or the transformation of their schools into vocational centers, they often claim that private interests, allied with government agencies, wield illegitimate power over what are supposed to be autonomous, self-governing institutions. Local school boards in the United States, for example, are under pressure from government initiatives such as the *No Child Left Behind Act* of 2001 and the *Common Core State Standards Initiative*, combined with the *Race to the Top* federal grants, of 2009. In response to such pressure, often in the form of mandated testing that determines the allocation of funds, such as the linking of *Race to the Top* grants with adoption of the *Common Core* standards, the fear is that schools may overemphasize "STEM" disciplines[11] at the expense of the humanities and fine arts, or define reading comprehension purely as a practical rather than literary skill, reinforcing the belief that the main purpose of education is to promote economic growth.

THE ELITIST ORIGINS AND DEMOCRATIC PAST OF LITERARY PEDAGOGY

The tension between "useful" disciplines that contribute to economic growth over "disinterested" ones that do not, has existed since long before our time. The disciplines of "*belles lettres*" and "*beaux arts*" have frequently come under attack as privileges of wealth and class, in contrast to the (relatively) more democratic science fields, and pre-professional disciplines such as law and business. Perhaps because of the elitist tradition according to which instruction in those areas was reserved for the free citizens of classical antiquity, European aristocrats, and members of the *grande bourgeoisie*, its position in universal public education has always been a defensive one. Why, ask the challengers, should the general population be required to pursue an education that throughout history has been mostly a matter of privilege? Is literary study, since that is the specific discipline in question here, a general education requirement simply as compensation, even revenge, for those many centuries during which most people did not have access to it?

The answer to the last question is a qualified "yes". Before the advent of universal secondary education, literature, especially of the canonical, that is, classical (Greek and Latin) variety, was a luxury product, a status it has not entirely shed in the intervening years. But what explains its importance in the first place? In order to be in danger of being dropped from the general education curriculum, it had to be added at some previous point in time. In fact, not only had literary pedagogy always been considered a luxury reserved for an elite, so had education in general. High schools, colleges, and universities were until the last century exclusive institutions. Between 1900 and 1940, the percentage of the American population to graduate from high school by the age of 18 rose from a mere 7 percent to 49 percent, and to 75 percent by the end of the twentieth century (Lassonde). In 1940, barely 5 percent of the population completed at least four years of college, whereas today, approximately one-third of all Americans earn a bachelor's degree before the age of 30 (Snyder 8). The point is, while the secondary and tertiary curricula changed dramatically along with huge enrollment increases over the course of the twentieth century, certain parts of them did not. The idea that literature should be a required subject for the top 5 or 7 percent of the population made sense, even if only as a means of social, cultural, and economic reproduction. Surprisingly, as access to secondary and tertiary education improved, the principle that literature should be a required subject did not disappear. Since the nineteenth century, in France, the United States, and much of the developed world, *the "privilege" of studying literature in school gradually became a "right".* One of the aims in the coming chapters is to explore how and why literature became a "right", and whether such a status can survive the contemporary demand that education help lower unemployment. As Senator Marco Rubio said to the TV cameras while campaigning for the 2016 Republican nomination, we need "less philosophers and more welders".

The status of literature as general education has many explanations. One needs to identify those explanations and determine which of them, if any, are valid. One explanation is simply that literature has been taught to the greatest possible numbers because modern, industrialized nations could afford it. For much of the previous century, literature teachers successfully resisted challenges to their legitimacy thanks to economic growth and the consequent prosperity of high schools and universities. Even as returning soldiers flocked to higher education under the G.I. Bill, badly needing to start peacetime careers and to receive an education consistent with their material needs and ambitions, colleges and universities could afford to subsidize liberal arts disciplines that did not directly answer those needs, funneling veterans into "great books" programs and other subjects once regarded as irrelevant to a general population. Painful as it is to admit, most teachers of literature have been living on a type of welfare for the last 70 years, and the public tolerance for all forms of public subsidy is running out.

Now that the era of relative abundance is over, many institutions are reducing and even eliminating programs, while emphasizing the material rewards of a secondary diploma or college degree over immaterial ones. University language and literature departments in the United States, for example, face a double threat: of being reduced on the one hand to academic niche disciplines that cater only to the tiny number of students who desire to become experts, and on the other hand, to a "service" role of providing marketable linguistic and cultural skills to enhance the employability of future professionals. The defenders of literature, in a panic, argue for the practical value of such fields for general education, that is to say their "relevance" in the broadest sense, as the Modern Language Association did in its 2009 *Report to the Teagle Foundation* that gave a long list of practical reasons for increasing the numbers of majors in language and literature.

If literature classes were not required as part of general education, it is likely that far fewer students would enroll. After all, 100 percent of high school graduates have studied literature, but less than 5 percent of college students choose it as a major (MLA *Report to the Teagle Foundation* 16). Even taking into account the fact that the number of majors available in college is far higher than the number of subjects taught in high school, this suggests that literature classes would be fewer and further between, if secondary education operated more like a free market. Other general education subjects such as math are not exactly popular, and no doubt would also have far fewer students if they had to compete for enrollments, but it does not follow that they suffer from the same crisis of legitimacy that literature does. In fact, math has the unusual handicap of being the first academic discipline associated with a debilitating mental condition, "math anxiety", identified in 1972 (Richardson and Suinn). In spite of the irrational fear it elicits in a large segment of the population, however, most people accept that math helps to develop cognitive skills and has myriad practical applications in society, while they do not extend the same credit to literature.

The fact that literacy rates today are at a historic high does not have much effect on literary education. When it comes to reading literature outside the school, there is statistical evidence that it is in decline. A recent (2012) British survey on reading among school-age children states that "[w]hat was initially believed to be a phenomenon of reading migration from print to digital, has in fact turned out to be an increasing trend to consume information in ways that do not involve reading or writing text in any way, and to embrace instead video/image-based communication" (quoted in Lirca 1). The *National Endowment for the Arts* report called *Reading at Risk* (2004) reached similar conclusions, although the follow-up report, *Reading on the Rise* (2009), provided a more optimistic assessment. Literature's decline becomes a rallying cry in polemical works such as Mark Bauerlein's *The Dumbest Generation: How the Digital Age Stupefies Young Americans and Jeopardizes Our Future* (2008). Since most students read less, do not recognize the study of literature as a useful form of cognitive development like math, nor see it as producing benefits transferrable to other disciplines or to professional opportunities, there is little public support for its continued "gen ed" status, or much probability that students would chose it as an elective. It is not enough to make a philosophical or practical argument for the value of literature as a pillar of general education if its consumers, the students themselves, are not on board.

The issue is simple: student resistance to the general education of literature would diminish if they believed that the requirement is justified. In a demand-based environment, lack of student commitment threatens to further marginalize our profession, since administrators are less likely to protect curricular requirements that students openly resist. In a "pure" competitive market, such as the one for carbonated soft drinks, the nature of the product is determined by consumer demand, or what consumers can be persuaded to demand (which raises the vexed question of whether markets respond to a demand or create it, an economic conundrum to which we will return). Less pure is the market for classical music or Shakespearean theater, both of which depend on public subsidies or "protectionism" and therefore face their own existential threat. Quite a few people are predisposed against protectionism or anything that smacks of commerce regulation, no matter the intrinsic value of the product. It is just such interference in the dynamics of the free market that angered opponents of the Affordable Care Act, including Supreme Court Justice Antonin Scalia who compared the "individual mandate" to purchase health insurance to a legal obligation to purchase broccoli.[12] If one does not believe that health care deserves protection from pure market forces, then one is unlikely to believe that literary study does.

In this book, I will address directly the problem of "demand" as applied to education, instead of denying any relevance to the term by hiding behind the veil of education's "disinterestedness", or of its inviolability by materialistic, market-based values. Now that we have reached the point of public resistance, both against the financial costs of education, and against the ideology of its purported immunity from market forces, the slogan that it is "not for profit" can only go so far.

A quick example will illustrate our profession's dependence upon student support for general education requirements. At my alma mater, the University of Massachusetts, students for decades have had to take a minimum number of credits in the Humanities division, including one literature class. Though my professors referred to the "gen ed" classes they taught to a classroom or auditorium full of mostly pre-professional majors as "service courses", they also enjoyed the challenge of reaching out to a general student population and realized that such courses allowed their departments to thrive, creating demand for discussion sections led by their graduate students. Without exception, they took these "service courses" very seriously, first as a way of convincing a broad segment of society of the value of literary study, secondly as a way of securing their departments' status in the university. How many other institutions, especially public ones, continue to value literature enough to make it a requirement? Not SUNY, Albany, which has only a broad humanities requirement and is notorious for having eliminated several literature majors in recent years, including French (though to their credit, they maintain an undergraduate language requirement, while Massachusetts does not).[13] Unless a case can be made that most students should experience literature and that even majoring in literary studies is not an upper-class privilege but a reasonable and useful option for any student, the warnings will come true: fewer students will study our disciplines, and many of them, having read the writing on the wall, will do so primarily for pragmatic reasons, such as acquiring communicative proficiency (in their own language as well as others) in order to increase their marketability.

Indeed, the trend is to enlist economic arguments in defense of the humanities. In 2009, a conference, "Meeting the Current Challenges: the Humanities and Employability, Entrepreneurship and Employer Engagement" took place in London under the auspices of the Centre for Languages, Linguistics, and Area Studies for the purpose of "[d]emonstrating that the study of the humanities creates economic, social and cultural value has particular poignancy in the present economic climate". This strategy of adopting the vocabulary of neo-liberalism in defense of humanities subjects may backfire, however. Already, we see the following scenario being played out: administrations demand linguistic proficiency at the expense of cultural knowledge (as if the two were unrelated), under the assumption that it has measurable benefits in today's globalized economy, and will consider courses in literature (as opposed to ones in composition and language, filled with literature though such courses may be) ripe for elimination when forced to make cuts to their instructional budgets. Defending the "market value" of the humanities by arguing that the interpretive and communicative skills they require will help students become more successful entrepreneurs, executives, and employees is no doubt important. One must be careful, however, not to present secondary outcomes of humanistic education as primary outcomes: we must not confuse the tangible economic benefits of humanistic disciplines with the *raison d'être* of those disciplines, which is to be found within them, and not in the world of economics. But how do we convince the world and that most important constituency of all, our students, of this non-relative "value" that exists separately from any market?

There is no shortage of attempts to do exactly that. Eloquent defenses of the humanities, not only of their ability to foster economic growth (the "Humanities and Entrepreneurship" conference mentioned earlier), but to provide such growth with an ultimate goal outside of itself, abound in the pages of the *New York Review of Books* and its ilk, and in polemical essays accessible mainly to people who already have benefitted from liberal arts education (in addition to the aforementioned titles by Martha Nussbaum and Anthony Kronman, recent contributions to this genre include works by Fareed Zakaria and Paul Jay). Such essays, along with documents such as the American Association of Colleges and Universities reports: *College Learning for the New Global Century* (2007) and *Making the Case for Liberal Education: Responding to the Challenges* (2006) are major statements, fraught with a sense of urgency and should be read by all those who care about the future of our profession. Just like the 2009 London Conference, however, there is one respect in which these efforts fall short: their intended audience includes policy makers, business leaders, academics, and other groups, but there is one vital constituency to which the above-mentioned essays are not addressed: students and parents. Those for whose benefit education exists in the first place generally do not read about the crisis of the Humanities in books, or the *Chronicle of Higher Education*, or even the *New York Times*. Yet it is the choices students make, and the experiences they have in the classroom, that will ultimately decide our future. We must now turn our attention away from the altar and attend to members of the congregation, many of whom are in attendance only because they have no choice.

The classroom is one of the most important spaces in which the attack on and defense of non-market-based value is acted out. The failure of literary theorists to agree on a definition of literariness has unintentionally contributed to a recurring malaise in the teaching profession. Symptoms of the malaise fall into two main categories: literature attracts a smaller percentage of university students than in the past, and professors are also more divided concerning the content and methodologies that are appropriate to our discipline. In 1966, according to the Modern Language Association, 7.47 percent of bachelor degrees awarded by American universities were in the discipline of English, and 2.94 percent were in foreign languages (which at the time was almost exclusively a "foreign literature" major). In 2004, the numbers were 3.74 and 1.05, respectively (United States Department of Education survey statistics, quoted in MLA, *Report to the Teagle Foundation on the Undergraduate Major in Language and Literature*, 17). Within living memory, therefore, literature accounted for more than 10 percent of the majors in higher education, compared to well under 5 percent more recently. Some of the decline, of course, is demographic: a far higher percentage of the overall population attends college today than in 1966, and the new student populations tend to be more focused on career training than on the liberal arts (the actual *number* of students specializing in literature and languages has declined only slightly over the same period). Our profession cannot help blaming itself for its failure to benefit from the increase in numbers of students, however, and justifiably so. Given the fact that literature is a required subject for all high school students, should not college professors be more successful in attracting them to our classes? In short: what is it about our discipline that turns people off?

That question has received a lot of attention over the years. When theorists of literature turn their attention from problems of reading to problems of teaching, it is often in order to address a "crisis". More than 25 years ago, Harvard University Press published an anthology titled *Teaching Literature: What is Needed Now*, implying the existence of a problem (the teaching of literature "needs" something), and its urgency (it must be solved "now"). The problem has not gone away. "General education" in the Humanities suffers the same fate as "basic research" in the sciences. People have become increasingly skeptical of the claim that society is best served by supporting scientific inquiry in a purely disinterested way, through public rather than private financing. Private funds are invested in order to produce immediate returns, which is why Big Pharma, for example, may be more interested in developing marketable drugs that treat the symptoms of cancer than in finding a cure for the disease, a far riskier and longer-term gamble. Is a similar short-sightedness squeezing literature out of general education to make room for linguistic skills demanded by "job creators"? But while one can point to the long-term benefits of basic scientific research and argue that such benefits are ultimately greater than the more commercial, short-term applications discovered by privately funded research, what are the equivalent benefits of the similarly disinterested study of literature? Reading poems and novels will never lead to the discovery of a cure for cancer or even of a palliative treatment, so why should we continue to support such activities with ever-decreasing household incomes and public treasure? If even basic research and its many proven, measurable contributions to society are under threat, can there be any hope at all for the survival of literary pedagogy? To find out, one needs to return to the fundamental question behind the very notion of teaching literature. The first question is not whether literary pedagogy inhibits social mobility by preserving an unequal distribution of cultural capital, or encourages mobility by providing more students with better professional skills, but simply: what is literature, and what distinguishes it as an object of study from other types of discourse?

LITERARINESS, THE INDISPENSABLE FOUNDATION OF LITERARY PEDAGOGY

The Russian formalists first produced a definition of "literariness" as a function of language that is separate from goal-oriented communication. One consequence of this distinction is that most linguistic functions can be objectively evaluated according to the degree of success they attain, whereas literariness cannot. In other words, the metaphor of language as a system of exchanges among people, on the model of economics, falls short as a way to describe literary texts, which seem to exist independently from the mundane concerns of what Stéphane Mallarmé called "the language of the tribe".[14] Of course, such a definition of literariness risks falling into the trap of essentialism, an ideological tool that promotes the belief that truth exists outside the confines of history. Such an exalted definition of art, like religion itself, reassures the bourgeoisie that its particular class interests are universal, and many have indeed accused those who believe in artistic autonomy of political naïveté or bad faith. That being said, the idea that art and commerce are antithetical is powerful, especially as it developed in France during the nineteenth century. When Pierre Bourdieu discussed the autonomy of literature (e.g., in *The Rules of Art: Genesis and Structure of the Literary Field*, 1992), the idea of its immunity to economic concerns was crucial. I argue that it is also one of the reasons why there is so much opposition, especially in France, to linking literary pedagogy to nonliterary concerns, such as developing communication skills that might have practical and even commercial applications.

The history of the concept of literariness, and the difficulty of relating it to an economic model, will play a major role in this book. Indeed, while the term "literariness" has eluded attempts at definition in spite of the groundbreaking efforts of Roman Jakobson and his colleagues, the division between practical and literary language continues to be fundamental to any discussion of literary pedagogy. That is because, as we will see repeatedly in the following chapters, the unending controversy over literary pedagogy can almost always be described as an argument about whether the literary function of discourse can be *useful*, in a specific way that other functions of discourse cannot. To put in its simplest form, the debate pits "literarians" against "utilitarians". The neologism "literarian" applies to those who subscribe to Roman Jakobson's theory, in his famous essay "Linguistics and Poetics" (1960), of a poetic function of language that cannot be reduced to practical considerations:

> [T]he message as such, focus on the message for its own sake, is the POETIC function of language. This function cannot be productively studied out of touch with the general problems of language, and, on the other hand, the scrutiny of language requires a thorough consideration of its poetic function. Any attempt to reduce the sphere of the poetic function to poetry or to confine poetry to the poetic function would be a delusive oversimplification. The poetic function is not the sole function of verbal art but only its dominant, determining function, whereas in all other verbal

activities it acts as a subsidiary, accessory constituent. This function, by promoting the palpability of signs, deepens the fundamental dichotomy of signs and objects. Hence, when dealing with the poetic function, linguistics cannot limit itself to the field of poetry. (69–70)

Jakobson describes two very important characteristics of literariness, or what he calls the poetic function, as distinct from the five other linguistic functions he identified: referential, emotive, conative, phatic, and metalingual (66–9). The first is that the poetic, which is also the literary, focuses on "the message for its own sake". There is no *exchange*, or social relationship that pertains exclusively to the poetic function, while there is for all other linguistic functions. That is another way of saying that literature as such functions in relation to itself and not to the world, a scientific expression of the "art for art's sake" credo. Putting literature in relationship to the world is therefore to deemphasize the poetic function, the "dominant" characteristic of a literary text, and to risk a fatal betrayal of the legitimate foundation of the discipline. However, the poetic function is a "subsidiary, accessory constituent" of *all* verbal activities. From this, one can conclude that according to Jakobson there is no such thing as a "pure" literary text, since the poetic function is a dominant, but not an exclusive, characteristic of literature (and some literary texts are more poetic than others). Conversely, there is no such thing as verbal activity that is utterly devoid of literariness, since one cannot produce an utterance that does not display some degree of the poetic function; that would be as absurd as to say that one can produce an utterance devoid of form. In fact, there are many utterances that are not literary because of the context in which they occur but that are very literary in their use of some aspect or aspects of the poetic function, such as the campaign slogan "I like Ike" (70).

Whether Jakobson's essay approaches the goal of a scientific definition of literariness is a fascinating question but goes beyond the confines of this study. For us, its importance lies in the ability to define literariness as a separate characteristic of human discourse, and yet one that is not exclusive to literature *per se*. It opens the way toward a reconciliation between: the "literarians", those who believe it is a violation to teach literary reading as a skill applicable to other human activities, such as getting a job, or to consider literary texts as commensurable with nonliterary texts, such as office memos or sales agreements; and the "utilitarians", who by and large do not share such inhibitions. In his insistence that linguists must deal with literature as a separate linguistic function, but one that also occurs outside the recognized sphere of literature itself (outside of Bourdieu's "literary field"), Jakobson grants to literature and literary studies the credentials they need to stand independently among all other human activities and academic subjects, at the same time as he identifies some relative degree of literariness in virtually *any* linguistic utterance. By doing so he goes a long way toward justifying the role of literature in general education. Since literariness is ubiquitous, it just might be necessary for every human being to be consciously aware of it, and to study it, as a matter of course.

It follows from the above that the teaching of literature is actually the teaching of literary reading, which is a mode of reading that foregrounds the literariness of a text, regardless of the text's *degree* of literariness. Such is in fact the conclusion of Mircea Marghescu in his influential 1974 book *Le Concept de littérarité* [The Concept of Literariness]:

> Le message désigné comme étant littéraire sera lu automatiquement, par réflexe culturel, d'une manière différente qu'un message appartenant à un autre groupe de textes. La spécificité de la littérature ne pourra être trouvée qu'au niveau d'un régime littéraire dont le fonctionnement est distinct du fonctionnement linguistique aussi bien que d'autres fonctionnements sémantiques. C'est ce régime spécifique qui pourra être appelé à juste titre: Littérarité.
>
> [The message designated as being literary will automatically be read, due to cultural reflex, differently from a message belonging to another group of texts. The specificity of literature will only be found at the level of a literary order the function of which is distinct from the linguistic function as well as from other semantic functions. This is the order that one will legitimately call: Literariness.]
>
> (112)

Marghescu paves the way here for the reception theories of Hans Robert Jauss and Wolfgang Iser, well before the "Constance School" of literary criticism became influential in France. The concept of a "literary order" prevents one from vainly trying to identify literariness as an intrinsic property only of certain kinds of text, since it is only convention, and not some ontological distinction, that makes us approach a poem differently from, say, a shopping list. A shopping list, after all, can be a poem under certain circumstances (if it is published in an anthology of poetry, for example, or carved on a 17-foot tall slab of granite as in the case of a recent sculpture, "Memorial", by David Shrigley), and anything that can be read cannot avoid being poetic (to some degree), a fact that poets have often exploited to good effect (see the discussion of William Carlos Williams's "This is just to say" in Chapter 7): since literariness is almost everywhere, *almost any human expression can be considered literature*, an insight that will play an important role in the remainder of this study. The reader who is conscious of the literary order and its infinite manifestations in spoken and written utterances *is* herself the means by which "literariness" comes into being. The questions to consider are whether the purpose of literary pedagogy is to develop such a consciousness in the general population, and if so, why?

Literariness according to this view is indeed an end in itself and becomes manifest precisely when texts resist interpretation are ambiguous and enigmatic, *as is almost always true of all texts*. Returning to Jakobson's colleagues among the Russian formalists, Viktor Shklovsky's "*ostranenie*" or "defamiliarization" is a variation on this theme of the uniqueness of literary discourse, which does not prevent it from appearing in the most unholy and unexpected places. The ubiquitous nature of literariness has the additional advantage of dissolving the boundaries between highbrow and lowbrow, between "legitimate" and "illegitimate" culture, or between that which normally is allowed to be taught in a literature class and that which is not. All utterances are interrelated on a literary continuum: histories, contracts, owner's manuals, shopping lists, pop songs, etc. "Literariness" is a characteristic that can at best serve to hierarchize texts, perhaps placing Shakespeare's plays on a higher end of the scale than Marvel comics, but that cannot be invoked to justify the claim that *Hamlet* is incommensurable with *The Incredible Hulk*. The main difference between the two is that a schoolchild in America (and many other parts of the world) is much more likely to be already familiar with the Hulk than with Hamlet which, pedagogically speaking, is an advantage that Stan Lee's creation has over Shakespeare's. The literariness of *The Incredible Hulk* is far more accessible to the student for the simple reason that he or she already has, in some sense, experienced it. *Hamlet*, by contrast, is a dark fortress. The vast difference in accessibility that distinguishes the "culture of proximity" that secondary school students already know, and the "taught culture" that dominates the literature curriculum, has only recently emerged as a subject of scholarly research.

Regardless of what texts one chooses to teach, the purpose of education, for the utilitarian, is an interested one: literature enhances reading and writing proficiency, making one a more productive (and higher earning) member of society; for the literarian, literary culture provides meaning that *homo economicus* cannot conceive of. In either case, the choice of text matters. The preceding example introduces an important dimension of the literary pedagogy debate: the dreaded "culture wars". Today, the term has a very specific meaning in American academia. One associates it with fights over the curriculum, such as those over the required Western Civilization course at Stanford University in 1988. Many trace its history to the post-WWII population explosion, when consumers of higher education demanded courses that would either help them move up the social ladder or that would be "relevant" to their individual experiences and cultural backgrounds, rather than "universal" according to the classical Liberal Arts tradition. The debate has pitted liberals against conservatives, relativists against absolutists, minorities and women against white males. I suggest that it is also economic, not just in the sense of social class, but according to the opposition of "interestedness-disinterestedness". Those who believe in literariness as a radically distinct function of language tend to fall in the "conservative" camp, not because of their political beliefs (many in fact are on the left), but because they believe that literature is not defined, nor should it be taught, according to utilitarian principles. Those who do not separate literature from more prosaic functions of language will be more inclined to accept that it is fine to teach *The Incredible Hulk* in English class, because doing so does not alienate students who have yet to be initiated into "high" literary culture, and who may never be. Some, whom I consider to be truly in the vanguard of literary pedagogy, regard popular culture as a tool that allows students to start their apprenticeship at an accessible point of a continuum that may lead them one day to study *Hamlet* voluntarily, instead of under the gun (the "gun" being graduation requirements, grades, and test scores). As students become more and more linguistically proficient, they might come to understand and appreciate canonical literature, but the stated ambitions of general education tend to be more modest, limited more and more to the ability to excel at job interviews, write clear and persuasive memos and, more idealistically, to see through the deceptive rhetoric of politicians and advertisers. In 1990, the *National Council of Teachers of English* adopted the following supremely pragmatic mission statement: "The Council promotes the development of literacy, the use of language to construct personal and public worlds and to achieve full participation in society, through the learning and teaching of English and the related arts and sciences of language" (www.ncte.org/mission, July 14 2010). Can and should the NCTE, and the entire educational enterprise, put greater emphasis than it does on literature as an end in itself?

The question of whether literariness is compatible with communication, exchange, and other utilitarian functions or is defined in opposition to them, is crucial for literary theory, and even more so for literary pedagogy. In literature's status both as a cornerstone of mandatory general education in secondary education and as merely one among all specialized academic disciplines at the university level, the question of legitimacy is paramount. In order to be part of general education, literary study must provide students with something that no other discipline provides, and there must be a consensus that its value is important enough to be imposed on the population at large. Similarly, for literary studies to exist as a specialized academic discipline at the university level, it must accomplish something of intellectual value that no other discipline can. Are the questions of literature's legitimacy as part of general education, and of its legitimacy as academic discipline related? Are they the same?

We must explore the idealistic hypothesis that in the process of creating and evaluating justifications for the teaching of literature, one can better understand the phenomenon of literariness itself,[15] which is simply a version of the legitimacy question applied to writers rather than to teachers. The production of literature and the teaching of literature (one form of its "consumption") are not simply components of a diverse and dynamic "literary field". They are linked in a deeper, moral sense, in that each derives its legitimacy from the structural impossibility of any other human activity (e.g., the visual arts, and the teaching thereof) to achieve the same ends. Literature belongs to general education, for reasons that are identical to those that justify its existence as a distinct mode of artistic creation, and the practice of teaching it should reflect that identity.

"Should" is the correct word, because the theory and practice of the teaching of literature, as of so many other activities, are frequently at odds. If the premise that the teaching of literature depends for its legitimacy on its specificity, or that which no other academic subject can provide, then we must conclude that the uses of literature in a classroom for nonliterary purposes, such as linguistic proficiency, moral education, or historical insight, while they may be very worthwhile uses of time within an educational context, do not satisfy the definition of "teaching literature". Even a cursory glance at most schools and universities, in the United States and abroad, present and past, reveals a gap between the practice of teaching literature and the goals and principles that grant it legitimacy. In cases where literature is part of the general education curriculum, it is often without explicit recognition of the legitimating principle that it be a different form of human inquiry and expression than other fields such as history, psychology, or music, and why such a form of inquiry and expression deserves priority.

Why France?

The subtitle of this book, "Examples from France", is more than a simple reflection my own area of research. There are many reasons why France is an ideal source of material for the nexus of general education, economic policy, literariness, and cultural relativism outlined previously, several of which have already been mentioned. They include the dominance of a symbolist, "pure", and antieconomic conception of literature and art that, in spite of its origins in a specific post-romantic historical moment, has continued to exert enormous influence on the course of French literature, and also on its teaching, from the mid-nineteenth century to the present. Unlike the United States, where the general education of literature has always been part of a larger pedagogical project known since the 1940s as "language arts", France has a tradition of separating literature from its broader linguistic context that makes the philosophical stakes in the debate over its purpose as a part of general education gratifyingly clear.

The exceptional degree of autonomy and prestige attached to literature within French cultural politics is one of the reasons for the revolution in literary studies in the latter part of the twentieth century. If Jakobson argued for the pervasiveness of literariness across all utterances, French theory produced even more radical claims regarding the textual and therefore literary characteristics of non-linguistic phenomena as well. Semiology, psychoanalysis, structuralism all converge in their claims that a world that is apprehended through language also is apprehended *as* language. Literariness, following such a claim, no longer is a means of representing the world and becomes constitutive of the world, insofar as it emerges into human consciousness.

Claims on behalf both of literature's autonomy from mimetic and moral functions and of its ubiquity as an underlying principle of cognition are very much a French invention, at least since Baudelaire's attack on the literary establishment's failure to understand the universal relevance of its own medium, such as in his writings on Edgar Allan Poe. It also explains why, until recently, the idea of literary pedagogy as a simple subset of a larger discipline such as "language arts" was inconceivable. Literature in France is not simply a particular function of language, it is language revealed in its glorious, disinterested autonomy. That is why, when reforms to literary pedagogy in 1999 spoke of literature as, among other things, a means to "understand the world" and to "train the citizen" rather than as an end in itself, the negative backlash on the part of academics and intellectuals was forceful and uncompromising. Chapter 5 describes the reforms, originally recommended by a commission led by distinguished scholar Alain Viala, and their subsequent violent reaction by writers and critics that has created an impasse that persists to this day. "No 'language arts' in France!" might be the rallying cry of the resistance; but can a general education of literature remain cut off from questions such as practicality, self-interest, and social integration? Is it possible to sustain a "literature for its own sake" conviction when one is attempting to justify, and to construct, a literary pedagogy for all? The tension between such radically different interpretations of the role of literariness as a cornerstone of general education will come under examination in the following chapters.

Thanks to the intensity of the struggle for the establishment of free, secular, and mandatory education before and after the 1905 law of separation between Church and State, the sheer volume of material on the evolution of the role of literature in general education in France is overwhelming. Finally, the reemergence of the debate at key moments in French history, such as May 1968, the more recent battles between former President Nicolas Sarkozy and the literary-educational establishment, or the French government's reaction to the results of the PISA test since it was first administered in 2000, provides a kind of laboratory for identifying and evaluating arguments that are relevant for teachers of literature regardless of where, and what educational level, they teach. For all of these reasons, France presents a clearer, starker, fuller version of the complexities of a deceptively simple pair of questions, already posed at the outset: should literature be a subject taught in school to a general population? And if so, how should it be taught? The examples may be French, but the conclusions will apply to every society that engages in reflection over the principles and methods of education. It is urgent that literature teachers in the United States at the secondary and tertiary level learn from France's problems, because doing so will help to resolve our own crisis of relevance.

In presenting French illustrations of the debate over literary pedagogy, some of which occurred in the late nineteenth and early twentieth centuries, others of which are contemporary, I do not follow a strict chronological order. Chapter 2 begins with the "*Princesse de Clèves* Affair", an episode in the aforementioned war of words between Nicolas Sarkozy and the intelligentsia that perfectly illustrates many of the problems touched upon in this introduction, including the relevance of literature to economic concerns, elitism and the reproduction of cultural capital, and the self-governance of the educational profession. Sarkozy's professed (and possibly strategic) disdain for canonical works such as *La Princesse de Clèves*, and for higher culture in general, brings to mind the large percentage of students who are bored in their literature classes. But does that mean that they are condemned to be forever ignorant of literature's benefits? Ironically, the dunce, the dropout who fails miserably at the tasks demanded by the school, may be far closer to understanding literature's benefits than the "straight A" student, as the militantly anti-elitist poet Jacques Prévert implies in one of his most famous poems, "Le cancre" ("The Dunce"). Through Prévert we arrive at Baudelaire's literary esthetics as expressed in his prose poetry, demonstrating the specificity of the poetic function of language as theorized by Jakobson and therefore helping to create a potential foundational principle both for literature as an autonomous enterprise, and for its role as an academic discipline.

Chapter 3 is a detour into a much earlier controversy, the evolution in the early twentieth-century French school of the "canonical school exercise" from its earlier guise as the creation by the students of a literary text that imitates classical models, to its more recent status as a commentary *on* literary texts, both from the classical and French canons. The shift from "writing literature" to "writing about literature", from "*savoir-faire*" to "*savoir*" or from skill to knowledge, is a paradigmatic instance of the substitution of "pure" literature with the universally accessible tools of argument and positive knowledge, and the emerging viewpoint that literary pedagogy can only be justified as general education if it leads to nonliterary and even practical ends. The chapter begins with historical background on the origins of French literary pedagogy, including the Jesuit order's instructions to secondary school teachers, the *Ratio Studiorum* of 1599. Not only did this document continue to influence education until well into the nineteenth century, it serves to illustrate some of the reasons why the articulation between literary practice and literary education has always been problematic. The late-nineteenth-century reforms of literary pedagogy in France are among the first attempts to move beyond the principles set forth by the Jesuits, culminating in the invention of the "modern canonical literary exercise", enshrined in the ritualistic secondary school outcome assessment that is the *baccalauréat* exam in French literature. The best analyses of these attempts are the work of two contemporary historians of literature and education, Martine Jey and Violaine Houdart-Merot.

The often-maligned founder of literary history in France, Gustave Lanson, played a visionary role in this transition. His many critics deplored the contamination of literary pedagogy due to its emergence as a general education discipline, comparing it to the scientific rationalization of labor theorized by Karl Marx and Emile Durkheim and adapted to industrial production by Frederick Winslow Taylor. Chapter 4 centers on the founding of the modern French university system at the end of the nineteenth century and the many attacks on "la nouvelle Sorbonne" that ensued, most famously those of the Catholic socialist Charles Péguy, and "Agathon", the pen name chosen by the reactionary polemicists Henri Massis and Alfred de Tarde. By insisting on a scientific approach to literature as well as to history and the fledgling discipline of sociology, the faculty of the Sorbonne created a new foundation for the general education of literature that continues to influence classroom practices, while their enemies played an equally paradigmatic role.

The political tone of the debate over the democratization of literary pedagogy increased sharply 60 years later when a portion of the French professorate, inspired by the revolution of May 68, formed an association devoted to teaching French literature as a means of liberation. Chapter 5 examines their manifesto, forged during a meeting in the chateau of Charbonnières in 1969, which continues to inform the editorial philosophy of the most influential French journal on the teaching of literature in secondary education, *Le Français Aujourd'hui* ("French Today"). A fascinating mixture of pragmatic and idealistic statements on the value of literary pedagogy, the *Charbonnières Manifesto* still serves as a rallying cry for reform, and a lightning rod for those who believe that to link literary study to socioeconomic concerns is nothing short of sacrilegious. If Charbonnières reflected a period of revolutionary idealism that found little immediate response in classroom practice, that is not true of the equally innovative, though less radical reforms to the teaching of literature based on recommendations from an official committee chaired by literary critic Alain Viala in 1999. France is still, almost twenty years later, in the "post-Viala" era of argument and counterargument set off by his recommendations. The modest goal of empowering students and reaching out to the cultural and social practices that they bring to the classroom has been tied to multiculturalism, communitarianism (two words with strong negative connotations in much of French society), and even to concrete policies regarding the cultural assimilation of immigrants such as the ban on Islamic headscarves in public schools.

In Chapters 6 and 7, I move away from simply describing and analyzing the French crisis of literature in general education, and start looking at possible solutions. It is not a coincidence that, at the same time as the Viala reforms sparked a new wave of acrimonious debate and self-doubt among the stakeholders of French education, the school began to appear more and more in the mainstream media, including cinema. Sometimes these representations of the school are unabashedly nostalgic, as in the two remakes of *La Guerre des Boutons* (*The Button War*) released almost simultaneously in 2011; the adaptation of René Goscinny's and Jean-Jacques Sempé's internationally famous series of vignettes on 1950s school life *Le Petit Nicolas* (2009); and the acclaimed documentary *Etre et avoir* (*To Be and To Have*, 2002). Popular films about the school have clearly invited themselves into the debate over the future of literary pedagogy. Three much less nostalgic but equally well-known examples, each representing the teaching of literature to underprivileged middle school students from immigrant backgrounds, hint at a range of possible solutions to the crisis: *L'Esquive* (*The Dodge*, distributed in North America under the title *Games of Love and Chance*, 2004) by Abdellatif Kechiche; *Entre les murs* (*Between the Walls*, distributed under the title *The Class*, 2008) by Laurent Cantet; and *La Journée de la jupe* (*Skirt Day*, 2009) by Jean-Paul Lilienfeld.

Chapter 7 focuses on a phenomenon mentioned earlier in this introduction, the influence on the educational policy of outside agencies, particularly those that are part of the globalist promotion of economic growth. The PISA test of reading comprehension, math, and science skills, developed and administered by the OECD, exerts enormous power over educational policy in the 65 countries in which it is currently administered. The above-mentioned *Common Core Standards*, for example, are in part a response to the mediocre results that a representative sample of American 15-year olds achieved on the PISA test. France is even more strongly influenced by the PISA results, according to which it ranks near the middle of all participating nations (almost as low, as it turns out, as the United States). One has every right to be suspicious of the encroachment of the OECD on national educational policy and to be concerned about the possible distortion of liberal arts principles that its reading comprehension section might cause. But first we must try to understand what the reading test entails. Given that PISA's power will only continue to grow in the years to come, it is at least somewhat reassuring that, at least for now, literature constitutes a significant part of the test. As we know, assessment is one of the biggest drivers of educational policy. Does the recognition of literature's importance by the OECD correspond to a recognition of its value by society more generally? Can it become the starting point for a new direction and renewed mission for the general education of literature? We will return to the questions asked at the start of this introduction, but with more knowledge of how they have played out in the French context, and a better sense of conceivable answers, not only in France, but every part of the world where literature is taught.

NOTES

1. For more on the institution of the modern, secular French nation through literary pedagogy, see my book: *Teaching the Cult of Literature in the French Third Republic* (Palgrave Macmillan 2004).
2. Variations on these questions can occur in almost any educational context but were reported to be especially frequent by participants in the March, 2016 *American Comparative Literature Association* seminar: "Teaching (to) Diversity in Two and Four Year Colleges" organized by Dominique Zino and Tiffany Magnolia. The demand that education serve the material and professional needs of students has long been one of the greatest challenges faced by most Liberal Arts disciplines and is growing stronger.
3. In his book *Winning the War on War: The Decline of Armed Conflict Worldwide* (2011), Joshua Goldstein credits the United Nations with having succeeded in its peacekeeping mission much better than most people assume.
4. The identification of the word "global" with the word "American" is a paradox that will play an important role in this study. Anti-Americanism derives in part from the belief that the dominance of American culture is proof of its unique compatibility with two of modernity's great scourges: the subordination of art to commerce, and the absence of deep historical and geographical roots that enable a culture to travel so effortlessly across national borders.

5. The medieval *trivium* was, in fact, literary. It consisted of language (grammar, logic or dialectics, and rhetoric), while the subsequent *quadrivium* consisted of number (geometry, arithmetic, music, and astronomy). As we will see in Chapter 3, the crisis in literary pedagogy is in part due to the decline of rhetoric as a prerequisite for higher learning.
6. Anthony T. Kronman's *Education's End: Why Our Colleges and Universities Have Given Up on the Meaning of Life* (2007) is an excellent example of such "counter-discourse" in which the absence of "meaning" represents the spiritual void in modern education.
7. The ideology that art exists outside of the market, or that it is necessarily tainted when economic considerations come into play, of course has only prevailed during certain specific periods and in certain places. It does not occur for most of the history of art, in which patronage, a variation of market forces, dominates, nor does it pertain to mass-marketed popular culture, not to mention the extreme cases of successful artist-entrepreneurs such as Andy Warhol, Jeff Koons, or Damien Hirst. The ideological opposition to the relationship between art and commerce, I will argue, is one of the reasons why the debate over literary pedagogy, and the status of the humanities more generally, tends to repeat itself indefinitely without reaching a resolution.
8. The relevant quote from Marx is as follows: "The labourer...constantly produces material, objective wealth, but in the form of capital, of an alien power that dominates and exploits him; and the capitalist as constantly produces labour-power, but in the form of a subjective source of wealth, separated from the objects in and by which it can alone be realised; in short he produces the labourer, but as a wage labourer. This incessant reproduction, this perpetuation of the labourer, is the sine quâ non [*sic*] of capitalist production" (818). In order for the process of transforming labor into capital and vice versa to continue, it is not enough for there to be laborers and capitalists; there must be self-perpetuating laboring and capitalist classes, with very limited permeability between the two, such that the exploitation of labor by the bourgeoisie can continue. Such is the function of ideology, which presents the results of class differences as the cause of those differences. Literary education does a perfect job as ideology, since it creates the illusion that owning cultural capital is one of the causes of wealth, and not its result. Pierre Bourdieu and Jean-Claude Passeron used statistics on French society to illustrate this argument in *Les Héritiers* (*The Inheritors*, 1964) and *La Reproduction* (1970) among other works.
9. See Martha Nussbaum.
10. Spoken during his 1953 Senate confirmation hearing as Eisenhower's Secretary of Defense, when asked if his business background would conflict with his public responsibilities.

11. This popular acronym for "science, technology, engineering and math" is important for us for two reasons. First, it was invented during a meeting initiated by the United States government held at the National Science Foundation for the purpose of finding a solution to the low number of scientists emerging from American schools. Second, the meeting itself was in response to a shortage in the number of qualified candidates for jobs in the rapidly expanding technology sector. It is therefore an example of the influence of both government and private enterprise on educational policy, rather than the local self-governing structure on which educational policy in this country is traditionally based.
12. "How Broccoli Landed on Supreme Court Menu", *New York Times* Business Section, June 13, 2012.
13. See under "General Education Requirements" on the websites of both universities.
14. The phrase appears in the 1877 poem "Tombeau d'Edgar Poe" (The Tomb of Edgar Allan Poe), one theme of which is the inability of members of society to recognize the genius in their midst, because the poet's relationship to language is radically different from their own. Mallarmé used the fact that Poe died penniless in the gutter to accuse the world of only being able to recognize and reward contingent, relative value, and not the authentic, eternal value of art. Wealth therefore accrues to those who debase language by subordinating it to their economic aims, while it eludes those who respect its sacred purpose. For Mallarmé, like Baudelaire before him, the fact that Poe produced his work in America, a nation ostensibly founded on the cult of money, underscores his life's tragic meaning.
15. Such is the strategy, for example, of Gerald Graff in *Professing Literature* (1987): that the study of the institution of literary pedagogy is a way to better understand literature itself.

CHAPTER 2

Aristocrats or Anarchists: Who Has Power over Literature?

THE *PRINCESSE DE CLÈVES* AFFAIR AND THE CULTURAL ARISTOCRACY

Over the last ten years, Madame de Lafayette's 1678 literary masterpiece and forerunner of the modern novel, *La Princesse de Clèves*, has been in the news in France a lot more often than one might expect. Its sudden relevance began very precisely on February 23, 2006, in Lyon after a speech by then Minister of the Interior Nicolas Sarkozy. Speaking to members of his political party during his campaign for the presidency, he made fun of the fact that the recruitment exam for entry-level public servants contained a question on *La Princesse de Clèves*:

> Dans la fonction publique, il faut en finir avec la pression des concours et des examens. L'autre jour, je m'amusais, on s'amuse comme on peut, à regarder le programme du concours d'attaché d'administration. Un sadique ou un imbécile, choisissez, avait mis dans le programme d'interroger les concurrents sur *La Princesse de Clèves*. Je ne sais pas si cela vous est souvent arrivé de demander à la guichetière ce qu'elle pensait de *La Princesse de Clèves*... Imaginez un peu le spectacle!
>
> [In the public sector, we have to get rid of the pressure of competitive exams. The other day I was having fun, you have to have fun anyway you can, by looking at the [civil service] exam for the position of administrative officer. Some sadist or imbecile, choose one, put in the program that candidates should be questioned on *La Princesse de Clèves*. I don't know if

you've often had the opportunity to ask the woman at the ticket counter what she thought about *La Princesse de Clèves*. Just imagine the sight!]

The content of the statement – that only a sadist or an imbecile would ask candidates for a job selling train tickets or handing out brochures what they think of a standard work of the classical literary canon[1] – was as shocking to members of the intellectual class as its dismissive tone. In a single remark, Sarkozy managed to insult: rank-and-file public employees, whose opinions on the novel could only be a sorry "sight"; women, by the use of the feminine *guichetière* for the hypothetical unsophisticated civil servant; and most egregiously, the memory of Madame de Lafayette herself and the literary culture for which she stands.

His comment was interpreted in the media as proof of a hidden agenda: the attack on any aspect of public education that is not designed to promote full employment. Literary culture led the resistance against neo-liberalism, and the French classroom, at all educational levels, became the front line. But of all the things Sarkozy said and did during his time in office and leading up to it, does his *Princesse de Clèves* remark truly deserve so much scorn? Leaving aside the unfortunate sexist and classist connotations of the word *guichetière*, he may well have a point: familiarity with the 350-year-old novel is arguably not a predictor of future job performance for anyone except a teacher of French literature. France may well have the only government in the world that requires public employees not only to demonstrate "general culture" in addition to job-specific competence, but to speak authoritatively about ancient icons of literary patrimony.

As Americans, it is easy for us to share Sarkozy's scorn. After all, how likely is it that a random federal employee could converse about *Moby Dick*? And more pertinently, do the French recruitment criteria for public service even achieve the desired effect? In other words, when a person does engage a French public employee on his or her knowledge of patrimonial culture, is the "spectacle" as ludicrous as Sarkozy implied it would be? Maybe, maybe not. But the underlying issue is important to anyone who cares about the role of culture in general education. Throughout history, educators have warned against the dangers of the exclusively vocational education that Sarkozy implicitly promoted. The Liberal Arts were invented for the disinterested moral and intellectual development of the privileged classes, and in our post-revolutionary democracies, these privileges have ostensibly been extended to all citizens. Modern societies in every part of the world recognize the importance of such an education, of learning for its own sake, and not simply as a means to acquire life skills and material prosperity. Perhaps nowhere in the curriculum of institutions of education is this value more evident than in the requirement to study that most useless of subjects: literature. And there are few countries where the teaching of literature has traditionally been more strongly imposed upon the general population than France.

As the campaign for the 2007 presidential election heated up, Sarkozy became a punching bag for members of the left-wing intelligentsia such as Christine Lapostolle, who wrote an editorial in the daily newspaper *Libération* of November 21, 2006 titled «*La Princesse de Clèves au Kärcher*[2]»:

> On peut se représenter le raisonnement qui... sous-tend [ces remarques]: qu'est-ce que les jeunes (sous-entendu à plus forte raison des banlieues) peuvent comprendre à cette vieille élucubration XVIIe? Quel intérêt y a-t-il à leur faire connaître un tel roman ? A quoi cela servira-t-il sur le marché du travail?
>
> [One can imagine the reasoning behind [these remarks]: what can young people (implying primarily those from the *banlieues*) possibly understand in this old rant from the seventeenth century? What possible purpose is there in getting them to know such a novel? What use will it be for them on the job market?]

The literary critic and author Pierre Assouline posted on his blog for *Le Monde* on December 10, 2006, under the title "*Qui veut tuer la Princesse de Clèves?*" ["Who wants to kill *La Princesse de Clèves?*"]:

> Est-il besoin de rappeler que *La Princesse de Clèves*, modèle d'intelligence et de finesse dans l'analyse, est la matrice de la littérature moderne? A ce titre, ce livre fait partie du bagage culturel de tout honnête homme de notre temps, fut-il [*sic*] attaché d'administration, voire même, *horresco referrens* [*sic*], guichetier!
>
> [Is it necessary to remind one that *La Princesse de Clèves*, a model of intelligence and analytical grace, is the matrix of modern literature? As such, this book is part of the cultural baggage of every self-respecting man today, were he an administrative officer, or even, *horresco referens*, a ticket clerk!].

Lapostolle played the race card in her editorial quoted earlier. She claimed that Sarkozy was not simply declaring literary culture to be superfluous. By using the term "*sous-entendu*" (meaning something understood without having been said[3]), she accuses him of implying that underprivileged youth from the immigrant community, for which the term "*banlieue*" is a metonymy, are not only unconcerned with such literary monuments, but intellectually incapable of appreciating them. Lapostolle may have overinterpreted Sarkozy's remark by bringing in race with her use of the terms "*banlieue*" and "*kärcher*", reminding readers of his famous promise to clean out France's housing projects with a power washer ("kärcher", see note two) and their connotation of disaffected and delinquent youth of African origin, but her point is widely shared: that it is at best condescending, at worst racist and classist, to say that patrimonial culture, while it may "belong" to everyone, is in fact accessible only to a minority.

Ironically, it is precisely the same elite minority that Assouline addressed in his blog post, even while making the point that every "*honnête homme*", by which he meant every upstanding citizen, using a term associated with seventeenth-century French moralists, has the right and even the duty to carry Madame de Lafayette's novel as part of their cultural baggage. But he undermined his point, perhaps intentionally, by using the Latin phrase "*horresco referens*", a phrase from the *Aeneid* meaning "I shudder as I recount (the story)". The rhetorical strategy Assouline adopted by quoting a famous phrase from Vergil is a "*signe de connivence*": not in the sense of the English cognate "connivance", or complicity in the commission of a criminal act, but rather a more benign type of "complicity": signaling one's common membership in a select group of initiates. It is the literary equivalent of a refined and most of all discreet style of dress and manners that can only be the result of generations of taught culture, and which therefore separates the true aristocrat from the bourgeois wannabe. In this case, "*connivence*" takes the form of the gratuitous use of a Latin phrase from the classical canon. The readers of Assouline's blog on literature already belong to the exclusive group of people who read *Le Monde*, the daily paper of the new aristocracy: the members of the left-of-center intellectual elite. Many of them (but by no means all) will recognize the phrase and derive from their recognition a sort of pleasure that comes from knowing that one belongs to Stendhal's "Happy Few". The use of Latin in this context, as in so many others, serves *no other purpose* than to exclude the uninitiated, like a masonic handshake, or two men wearing the same prep school necktie discreetly acknowledging each other in a crowd. Assouline's allusion, like so many that one comes across in high-brow media outlets, is completely opaque to members of the population who, during their educational careers, did not acquire enough "baggage" to even bother to read his blog, much less understand his style (or, for that matter, Madame de Lafayette's).[4] Even though Assouline's argument is for inclusivity (the right of everyone to have access to literary culture regardless of social class), his entire rhetorical strategy promotes exclusion: quoting Vergil in the original, referencing the neoclassical paradigm of the *"honnête homme"*, even the term *"finesse"* with its aristocratic connotation of hereditary refinement. There was a time when the function of secondary education was to reinforce social separation and hierarchy. Today's inclusive (general) education, especially in France, has yet to fully free itself of its elitist antecedents. It is not surprising if students respond negatively to what is, in essence, a code that serves to exclude those who do not intuitively grasp its mechanism.

LITERATURE AS *"CONNIVENCE"*, OR HOW TO RECOGNIZE ONE'S OWN

The role of literature as a "secret handshake" or sign of recognition among an elite group, such as Assouline's use of Vergil's phrase in the example cited earlier, is important enough to merit further discussion. Already, it should be clear that such snobbery is at the opposite extreme of the subject of this book, literature as general education. The ability to quote Latin or Greek has for centuries been a useful marker of class distinction, a kind of reverse slang.[5] In an era like ours, when even highly educated people may well possess at most "small Latin and less Greek", *any* reference to high culture, whether music, literature, or art, serves the same function. Consider the headline from the French daily newspaper *Libération* on October 7, 2008: "La Guerre des trois aura bien lieu" [The War of the Three Will Indeed Take Place]. Even some native speakers of French undoubtedly had difficulty deciphering that cryptic headline. The first and easiest difficulty is that *"trois"* [three] is the homonym of *"Troie"* (Troy). So it is a pun on *"la Guerre de Troie"* [the Trojan War]. But then it becomes more complicated. The words *"aura bien lieu"* [will indeed take place] refer antithetically to Jean Giraudoux's 1935 play, *La Guerre de Troie n'aura pas lieu* [*The Trojan War Will Not Take Place*]. Though Giraudoux's play is a canonical text, there are plenty of people in France and the French-speaking world who are either unaware of its existence, or for whom the words of the title are at best a nearly forgotten and not very pleasant school memory. Finally, what is "the War of the

Three"? For French people following current events, that is the easiest part to decipher and, in fact, the only *real* meaning of the entire headline. The French Socialist Party was preparing its annual convention, at which its next leader was to be elected. Three politicians were vying for the job, and up until that day there had been rumors that one or more of them might pull out, but that turned out not to happen. Hence, the "War of the Three" (candidates for position of party leader) was indeed going to take place (at the upcoming convention). Why is this now-forgotten newspaper headline worthy of attention? Because it is a perfect example of *"connivence"* based on shared literary culture. It was not enough to be up to date on French socialist party politics in order to understand the headline; one also had to be aware of the Trojan War (fairly easy), and of Giraudoux's play (less easy). But what is most important for our purposes is the *meaninglessness* of this pun *cum* literary allusion: knowing Giraudoux's play, an adaptation of Homer that was one of several notable artistic contributions to the pacifist movement in France leading up to World War II, is of absolutely no benefit for understanding the subject of the news article beneath the headline, which dealt with the minutiae of socialist party politics. It is a gratuitous allusion that served only one purpose: to make those who recognized both the pun and the literary reference it contains feel a smug sense of superiority over those who understood it only partly or not at all. It is a prime example of the misuse of literary culture to which the general education of literature can and should serve as an antidote.

After Sarkozy won the 2007 election, he continued to antagonize the intellectual class by cultivating the public persona of an unsophisticated everyman. Shrewdly pretending to dig himself deeper into the hole, he referred in public several times to his distaste for canonical literature in general, and for *La Princesse de Clèves* in particular. A professional organization of historians, the *Société Internationale Pour l'Etude des Femmes de l'Ancien Régime*, kept a running account of each incident on its web page. Even his short-lived plan in late 2009 to transfer the remains of Albert Camus to the *Panthéon*, which appeared to be his play for cultural significance in the time-honored tradition of the French presidency, only exacerbated the conflict. Camus's daughter and the guardian of his estate, Catherine Camus, had approved the proposal. Her brother Jean, however, publicly opposed it, basing his argument on Albert Camus's disdain for state-sponsored honors, and more importantly, on a refusal to grant Sarkozy any kind of cultural legitimacy, a stance shared by the majority of the cultural media elite. One member of the large anticapitalist wing of said elite, Michel Soudais of the newsweekly *Politis*, voiced a common opinion when he called the proposal "*une profanation obscène*" [an obscene desecration].

The failed transfer of Camus's remains is of interest to us for at least two reasons. First, Camus was a brilliant choice for Sarkozy in his fight against the guardians of inherited culture, since the writer's prose style resulted from a conscious attempt to purge literary and philosophical language of its elitist character. Such is the function of the systematic (though not total) avoidance of literary verb forms, such as the simple past tense and imperfect subjunctive, in his most famous novel *L'Etranger* (*The Stranger*, 1942), characteristics that make it a godsend for teachers of French as a second language. Secondly, by arousing once more the collective ire of the literary intelligentsia, Sarkozy aligned himself with his electorate, a kind of "silent majority" of the culturally underprivileged, those who are fed up with the literary and linguistic *connivence* that has forever permeated the discourse of France's political and cultural elites. Through all these controversies, Madame de Lafayette's novel became a symbol of resistance against the invasion of the school system by free market ideology and globalization (or just vulgarity), a kind of literary *Croix de Lorraine*. The backlash even included the production of two films: an adaptation of the novel called *La Belle personne* (*The Beautiful Person*, Christophe Honoré, 2008) and a documentary *Nous, princesses de Clèves*, (*We, Princesses of Clèves*, Régis Sauder, 2011). Both films are set in a high school, to remind viewers that we are talking here about arguments in favor of "literary general education", the relevance of inherited culture to the daily lives and urgent concerns of adolescents. In the adaptation, the plot of the novel gives a high-cultural sheen to the cliché of teenage lust, and in the documentary, students from underprivileged backgrounds read the novel for their French class and demonstrate how it enhances their lives. Clearly, much more than educational policy was at stake: in an attempt to understand the affair from an American perspective, *The New Yorker* magazine even suggested that it contributed to Sarkozy's loss of the presidency to François Hollande in 2012 (Zerofsky).

Unfortunately for Sarkozy's critics, the size and power of their resistance may not have been adequate to the task at hand. Here is an illustration of the problem: one of the many protests against the educational reforms and budget cutbacks during Sarkozy's presidency was a marathon public reading of *La Princesse de Clèves*, organized on February 16, 2009 by students and faculty of the University of Paris in front of the same

Panthéon that would become the focus of the Camus affair a few months later. The event accidentally illustrated the dilemma of those who defend the notion of high culture for the masses. By some measures, it was a successful protest: the marathon reading was repeated in other cities over the following days and weeks, and sales of the novel jumped as a result of the media coverage. On the other hand, the crowd in front of the *Panthéon* that day was sparse, only about 100 according to the newsweekly *Marianne* (Roels). Many of the passersby, far from being enthralled by the reading out loud of Madame de Lafayette's prose, clearly found the whole *mise en scène* ridiculous. But the group of academics, actors, and yes, even some public employees and office workers, pressed on until the end, protecting the flame of classical culture against the headwinds of efficiency and commercialism.

As the above-mentioned examples illustrate, the reaction against Sarkozy's self-professed boeotianism was passionate and rested upon a few deeply held assumptions: that the value of great literature is self-evident (Assouline: "Is it necessary to point out...?") and that teaching it to the poor, the marginalized (Lapostolle: "young people...from the *banlieues*") is one of the best ways to free them from oppression. Another implicit assumption underlies all the others: great, past works of literature, and of culture in general, *must* be taught in schools to *everyone*. Such general education is not simply a perfunctory or symbolic process of placing children in the proximity of great works; the school must make students *responsible* for assimilating this cultural legacy. Even a person aspiring to a low-level position in public service such as *"guichetière"* (which has now become the symbol of all jobs in France requiring minimal education), in order to live a fulfilling life, should be expected to answer questions on the content and meaning of a text such as the *Princesse de Clèves*. The usual reasons are both idealistic – high culture is a fulfillment of one's human potential, and affirms membership in a spiritual community – and practical – reading and interpreting great literary works hones communicative skills *better* than any other exercise.

In the United States, the idea that one might be required to show familiarity with a canonical work of literature in order to work for any public or private entity in any capacity (except literature teacher and a few other rare birds) is of course ludicrous. We, like the former French president, find it plausible that a person can perform tasks that require skills of speaking, writing, and even critical thinking without ever having read, much less appreciated and understood, a single work of great literature. But are we right in thinking so? Was Sarkozy – so often characterized by the French left-wing media as an American at heart – sacrificing some universal value that France has traditionally protected from modern expediency, when he ridiculed the public service exam back in 2006? The answer to these questions depends on one's opinion concerning literature and general education. If one truly believes that literature, consisting not only of contemporary or popular texts, but of ones that are both linguistically and culturally complex and archaic, must be understood *to some degree* by all citizens, then one is in the camp of the *lafayettistes*. A traditional corollary of such a belief is that the greatest value of general education does not lie in any practical outcome, but in helping students lead a more meaningful life. Anybody can *choose* whether to read literature, and can have his or her reasons for deciding one way or the other. The *requirement* to read literature, however, is an entirely different matter. By such a requirement, society is in effect telling the individual: "this is something you *need* to know; like other general education disciplines, including math, history, and science, literature has benefits that simply cannot be reserved for the happy few who are already inclined, by nature or by upbringing, to enjoy it, benefits that are all the more valuable since they cannot be measured or compared". Sarkozy evidently was pleased to admit that his own literary education brought him no benefits, which obviously did not prevent him from succeeding, though many would say that his disdain for literature proved that his political ambition was accompanied by moral failure. Clearly, he represents the constituency of those who resent having to read literature in school, and probably would not do so, or would only read more accessible texts, had *La Princesse de Clèves* (and similar canonical works) not been required. Should one generalize from his case and simply abandon literary pedagogy to the category of elective academic options, both at secondary and at tertiary levels of education? Conversely, do such attacks as Sarkozy's, in their confident equation of value with wealth and power, only illustrate the need for more general education of literature, not less?

In France, Sarkozy's statements have the power to shock, though not nearly so much outside the confines of the educated elite: there is no evidence that his declining popularity among the broader French voting public was related to his comments about literature, and he has managed a remarkable political comeback since losing the presidency to François Hollande. Cultural elites insist that if the French people were not under fear of economic catastrophe, then they would less readily sacrifice cultural values for utilitarian ones. However, despite the impression conveyed in the media that the *Princesse de Clèves* affair was the symptom of a national crisis, very little evidence exists that most French people cared what their president had to say about it. Elizabeth Zerofsky's above-mentioned speculation in the pages of *The New Yorker* that it contributed to Sarkozy's defeat in 2012 is not supported by opinion surveys or other kinds of sociological inquiry. Faced with the possibility that a majority of the public is indifferent to the literary culture of political leaders, one must ask whether such indifference might extend to literary culture in general. To what extent, in other words, does teaching literature to a general population resemble preaching in the desert? And to the extent that it does, what has to change in order to attract the attention and enlist the commitment of more students to the specific benefits, practical or not, of literary reading? If literary pedagogy works, then the percentage of readers of literature in the population should match, or at least approach, the percentage of people who have completed general education. Since the latter group is now close to 100 percent of the population of most developed countries, and the former group is dramatically smaller (see statistics on the literature market in Chapter 4), one must conclude that literary pedagogy fails, at least as far as general education is concerned. Should efforts be made to improve it? A more basic question is: should the general education of literature even be preserved? Is its (relative) failure proof that the transformation, over the last century, of literary study from a privilege to a right was a historic mistake? The issue may not simply be of how to improve the teaching of literature to a general population, but of how (and whether) to save it.

The abyss separating the participants in the Madame de Lafayette reading-marathon from the flummoxed members of the Parisian crowd is not simply due to socioeconomic factors, or the clash between timeless values and temporal ones; bad education is also to blame. Many citizens of the developed world, while they have studied literature in school, did not have a good experience doing so. They failed their literary education or, more likely, their literary education failed them. Their struggles with Shakespeare and Austen, or Molière and Madame de Lafayette, just never paid off. It is a myth that all literature teachers are immune to such trauma in their formative years. No less a figure than Stephen Greenblatt, one of the world's foremost authorities on Shakespeare, confessed that "[m]y first encounter with Shakespeare – [in] eighth-grade English class – left me cold" (Greenblatt 60). Gerald Graff devoted an entire chapter to his own imperviousness to literature that lasted until his junior year in college, in *Beyond the Culture Wars: How Teaching the Conflicts Can Revitalize American Education* (1992). Such failed encounters with canonical texts in school is either an indictment of the very principle of literature in general education or, if the rate of failure can be significantly reduced through better teaching, of the assumptions and methodologies on which it has traditionally relied. One should not expect, of course, that a young person's first encounter with Shakespeare will always be successful. It is a rare teacher who can make even the majority of her students respond positively to an artifact of inherited culture, with all of its challenges related to historical context and esthetic form, from the outset. The problem occurs when the resistance that characterizes the first encounter persists throughout the process. No doubt Stephen Greenblatt warmed up to Shakespeare fairly quickly, perhaps even before the end of his eighth-grade English class, just as Gerald Graff did in college. One should not have to be a Stephen Greenblatt or Gerald Graff in order to benefit from literary general education, although the possibility that neither person would have become a world-class scholar had he not been forced to read literature in school should give one pause. There are always students whose resistance never seems to weaken, however, whether the class is on literature or some other subject, and no pedagogy is universally successful. Success may simply be a matter of increasing the likelihood that more students will overcome their specific resistance to literature and view it as a viable general education subject, even if they do not grow up to become professional literary critics. Faced with student resistance, the teacher is in a bind: literature must be taught (if it is justifiably a part of the general education curriculum); literature cannot be taught (if the resistance to literature is never fully overcome).

JACQUES PRÉVERT'S DUNCE: THE STUDENT WHO TEACHES HIMSELF

Is literary general education therefore doomed to fail? Is literature itself, and the true learning thereof, incompatible with the institution charged with teaching it? Surely, no genuine discussion of the subject can proceed without acknowledging the fact that much of the population, unlike Greenblatt and Graff, never overcome their initial resistance. As with any pedagogy, one must also ask if failure is even more common than it appears, to the point of being the default outcome of general education.

Even students who earn good grades and high test scores, in more than a few cases, may well have failed to learn in meaningful way. In fact, it may be that such traditional indicators of successful learning tell us very little about the growth in theoretical and practical knowledge of literariness.

To illustrate this last point, let us examine what most pedagogues consider to be one of the biggest obstacles to learning: the "problem" of the "bad student". As suggested earlier, it is often hard to tell whether those who earn that label failed their education, or their education failed them. The failures of literary pedagogy follow their own patterns, while failures in math or science have theirs, but all involve boredom and alienation, a failure to appreciate the higher purpose for which the tools of the discipline (in literature, the ability to read and write) are designed. Some people experience all education as unbearably oppressive and cannot be persuaded otherwise. Even if we were not that kind of student ourselves, or do not want to admit it, we can remember classmates who stubbornly refused to play by the rules of the educational process, the "dunces". Whatever the subject, whether in primary or secondary school, they could not wait for the end of the school day (week, year), and barely made it to graduation, if at all. But what if "dunces" were not the obstacle to literary pedagogy, but a key to its success? Are such students, with whom many feel at least some small degree of affinity at various points in their education, recuperable? Maybe it is the "bad student" who lives in each one of us, more or less buried under outward acquiescence to pedagogical assumptions and expectations, who is in fact an indispensable part of the learning process.

The work of mid-twentieth-century poet Jacques Prévert provides us with a case in point. He devoted most of his career to demystifying the creative act, and thereby the entire institution of literary production and consumption. In literary history, Prévert stands at the intersection of "low" and "high" culture, having pursued a strategy of accessibility in his work that set him apart from the avant-garde to which he had once adhered. His literary populism, while it condemned him to a marginal status in the modernist pantheon at the same time as it nurtured his status as a celebrity,[6] makes him especially relevant to a discussion of literature and general education, since his reputation for accessibility would seem to make "teaching" his work unnecessary. Indeed, his poems are often cited in elementary French textbooks, yet rarely appear in literature classes in secondary or higher education. Prévert seems to have anticipated his "expulsion" from the literary sanctum when he wrote a paean to the victims of pedagogical oppression titled "Le cancre" [the dunce], published in his collection *Paroles* [words] from 1946. The poem's hero is a boy who, when called to the front of the class, rebelliously refuses to answer any question or obey any command, breaks into laughter, and finally seizes control of the blackboard. It begins simply by describing a routine example of child-like recalcitrance in the face of pedagogical oppression:

> Il dit non avec la tête
> mais il dit oui avec le cœur
> il dit oui à ce qu'il aime
> il dit non au professeur
> il est debout
> on le questionne
> et tous les problèmes sont posés
> (75)

Here is Lawrence Ferlinghetti's translation, published in 1958:

> He says no with his head
> but he says yes with his heart
> he says yes to what he loves
> he says no to the teacher
> he stands
> he is questioned
> and all the problems are posed
> (15)

In the second half of the poem, the "dunce" transforms from a negative to a positive character. Prévert has made the radical suggestion that the school not only fails in its mission, it is so inimical to literariness itself that the worst students are the ones who stand a chance truly to understand and even embody it. The "dunce" in this case is not a reciter of poems, nor a reader of poems, therefore, but a poet himself:

> soudain le fou rire le prend
> et il efface tout
> les chiffres et les mots
> les dates et les noms
> les phrases et les pièges

et malgré les menaces du maître
sous les huées des enfants prodiges
avec des craies de toutes les couleurs
sur le tableau noir du malheur
il dessine le visage du bonheur.
(75)

Ferlinghetti's translation:

sudden laughter seizes him
and he erases all
the words and figures
names and dates
sentences and snares
and despite the teacher's threats
to the jeers of infant prodigies
with chalk of every color
on the blackboard of misfortune
he draws the face of happiness.
(15)

So here we have a twist on Sarkozy's hypothetical, literarily challenged "*guichetière*", who had to have studied Madame de Lafayette's novel in order to get a job selling train tickets. Far from being indifferent, hostile, or impervious to literature, the "*cancre*" is superior to other students in regards to the elusive quality of literariness. Unlike all the "prodigies" who excel only at following the rules of the game, he dares to seize control of the pedagogical tools almost out of the teacher's hands: the blackboard, eraser, and chalk. As a result, failed pedagogical production, the refusal to answer, becomes successful artistic, and even poetic production.

On the continuum between those two extreme figures of the student, the idealistic and anarchistic "dunce", and the practical and submissive "prodigy", is where the general education of literature takes place. Needless to say, the "prodigy" is the ideal student whom the system rewards, whereas the "dunce", who may be far more representative of the general education population as measured by his or her degree of resistance to literature, is simply ignored. Prévert's attack on the school destroys one of its most cherished assumptions: that in its ideal form, literary pedagogy facilitates the individual's empowerment outside of the confines of economic servitude. In practice, according to the poem, pedagogy functions as a covert means of oppression by training the individual in practical skills and rote memorization so that he or she can more easily disappear into society. One can recognize the Marxist sympathizer Prévert's belief that the school, by betraying its ostensible mission as a tool of personal empowerment, fulfills its latent ideological role as a producer and sustainer of oppression. There is no doubt that the "good student" is a dupe, a future producer and consumer of goods, of the kind that capitalism needs in order to perpetuate the conditions of production. The fundamental contradiction between "good" and "bad" modes of learning spotlights the urgent need for deeper reflection on literature as a general education discipline, and hints at the possibility that only the "dunce" has the potential to learn how to create, rather than consume. Prévert confronts us with two radical hypotheses: first, that the resistance to learning, instead of leading to failed learning, instead leads to a deeper, truer learning; second, that successful literary pedagogy does not turn students into consumers of literature, but rather producers. The dunce begins by resisting (his refusal to answer); then, he rebels (he erases the blackboard and commandeers the chalk); finally, he creates. In doing so, he reveals what every student has the potential to accomplish, provided that he or she can muster the courage to salvage the literariness that can be attained only if one rejects the pedagogical relationship. One must consider the radical possibility that the school, precisely because it is inimical to literariness, provides the conditions in which actual literary production can occur, if only by reaction. In very simple terms: maybe literature emerges out of the resistance against the school's tendency to reduce literary texts to something other than literature, and all good writers are (or were) "dunces".

Prévert's classroom is such a rich representation of the paradoxes of literary pedagogy that it requires further explication. The "bad student as hero" motif is a modernist cliché of Western literature, especially the *Bildungsroman*, which often includes scenes of scholarly disaster.[7] It plays on the romantic myth of absolute individualism, the superiority of the autodidact. The dunce is in fact a savior of his classmates, if they are only willing to recognize him as such, helping them avoid the "sentences and snares" of education, all of those tactics that promise liberation and deliver oppression instead. These include simulacra of art, such as samples of prose and poetry from the pedagogical canon that serve as a tool for training the student in grammar, memory skills, morality, or whatever goal the educational system chooses to substitute for the liberating potential of the works it claims to teach. One can imagine that the question the dunce refuses to answer, the "problem" that is "posed", is a command to recite a poem, the most common reason for which a student might be called to the front of the class in a French school before the end of the twentieth century, though of course he might also be asked to comment on a text, or interrogated on some other subject. The combination of numbers, words, and dates covering the blackboard suggests that we are witnessing an impossible, simultaneous lesson on *all* aspects of the curriculum: literature, history, geography, arithmetic and science, united by the technique of rote learning and parroting, common to all.

The laughter of the dunce substitutes for the expected, ritualistic answer to the teacher's question, whether it was an order to recite the words of a poem, solve a math problem, or some other mechanical task that foreshadows the alienated labor that he will someday perform. The expression "*fou rire*" means "uncontrollable laughter", which Ferlinghetti translates adequately as "sudden laughter", but "*fou*" also suggests "mad laughter", of the sort that might come out of the mouth of a fool, a jester, or the Pythia herself. Laughter is an involuntary act, is voiced and yet wordless. Like Walt Whitman's reference to the equally nonverbal "barbaric yawp" in *Leaves of Grass*, it becomes a metaphor of pure poetic speech that successfully escapes any attempt at interpretation or paraphrase because it is beyond language as we *use* it.

Prévert's poem is about a schoolchild who, by refusing the institutional definition of the literary, reveals himself to be the genuine guardian and practitioner thereof. Let us examine more closely his uncontrollable laughter and his erasure of the blackboard, followed by his drawing of a "face of happiness". Like graffiti on the walls of a public bathroom, his hijacking of the blackboard is a prohibited form of expression that authorities call, not coincidentally, "defacement" (in French, "*défiguration*"). His drawing of a face "defaces" or desecrates the secular altar of the blackboard. The substitution of an image (a face) for numbers and words, like the laughter that precedes it, alludes to the unattainable (and romantic) goal of poetry as linguistic transcendence. It harks back to prealphabetical writing, the glyph or ideogram, which in turn evokes pre-Babelian language, the *Ursprache*. By scrawling on the blackboard, the dunce uses the implements of writing (chalk and slate) to produce a figure ("the face of happiness") even as he "disfigures" the writing surface by treating it like a wall to be covered in, that is to say defaced by, graffiti. His transgressive drawing/defacement thereby produces a kind of ideogram, humankind's first form of writing, which is also its first step toward literature, the text, the object of institutionalized literary study. In French, the word "*visage*" evokes its synonym "*figure*": both refer to the human face, but "*figure*" also means "image", as in English. The modest scene of a classroom becomes the theater for the illustration of art's uncompromisingly anti-institutional origin as well as of the subsequent production of art with the colored chalk, thereby exposing via contrast the tragic incongruity of a poem imprisoned inside of a textbook, or recited uncomprehendingly by a docile student.

Prévert's heroic, "bad" (or recalcitrant) student has many literary cousins. In many a *Bildungsroman*, the theme of youthful rebellion is only the starting point of a complex indictment of the very principle of formal education. From the sacred space, it was intended to be, school has become a prison, a foreshadowing of Hell. Founded in order to help purge society of the many scientific varieties of madness on which the legitimacy of power depends, the carceral environment is thus inherently unsuited, in these works, for the role of transmitter of culture. Because the school is the sanctuary for nothing except perhaps reason itself, it literally *cannot* teach literature, but only a simulacrum thereof; an anthologized, rationalized text, but not the poem itself.

Teachers understandably resist being compared to tyrants and define their role as one of empowerment, not oppression. The pitiful teacher in Prévert's poem has to cope with the anarchist behavior of his worst student, but the dunce is saying "no" to the system, more than to the person who represents the system in the classroom. The tragic irony of education is that it is a socially conservative institution, yet one that is founded on the principle of individual empowerment. But it is urgent to point out that the contradiction inherent in the school does not justify the cynical accusation that it is some sort of fraud, or the argument that its mission should be scaled back to only answering the demands of the free market. The classroom must somehow be a space that accommodates, and even provokes the dunce's barbaric vandalism, without disintegrating into irrelevance. To repeat: literature cannot be taught, and yet it must be taught.

CHARLES BAUDELAIRE'S VANDAL AS EXEMPLARY POET

The Beckettian aporia in the previous sentence is the unstable foundation of our discipline. Every day, students rebel overtly or covertly against the teacher's questions and commands, like Prévert's dunce, albeit usually without the laughter. The dunce laughs because he is a holy fool, that is to say an artist, while the schoolchild who is not mad or brave enough to be a dunce merely yawns and sighs (and sometimes texts). "Mad laughter" is redemptive, since it marks the young student as an artist, compelling him to cover the "blackboard of misfortune" with color. This final image in Prévert's poem of a sudden, irrational, and colorful act of creative destruction (defacement) is strikingly similar to Baudelaire's prose poem "Le Mauvais vitrier" ("The Bad Glazier") in *Le Spleen de Paris*, published posthumously in 1869. The kinship between the two texts helps to address the dilemma of literary pedagogy, and the biggest challenge of literary theory in general: to define "literariness", the quality that ostensibly situates the field of literary production and founds literary studies as an autonomous discipline. "The Bad Glazier" provides the beginning of an answer to that same challenge, one that will prove influential in the subsequent history of literary pedagogy in France.

From the start, Baudelaire adopts the first person, self-referential perspective that characterizes many of his works and that helps convey the sense that we are reading a personal esthetic manifesto. Close to the end of the text, the narrator-poet hears the cry of the glazier in the street far below his garret, and summons him upstairs, as if his window needed fixing. After struggling up the narrow staircase, the glazier shows his wares to the poet, who explodes with the famous invective:

> Comment? vous n'avez pas de verres de couleur? des verres roses, rouges, bleus, des vitres magiques, des vitres de paradis? Impudent que vous êtes! vous osez vous promener dans des quartiers pauvres, et vous n'avez pas même de vitres qui fassent voir la vie en beau!

Here is the translation of the passage by Louise Varèse, published in 1970:

> What? You have no colored glass, no pink, no red, no blue! No magic panes, no panes of Paradise? Scoundrel, what do you mean by going into poor neighborhoods without a single glass to make life beautiful!

Whereupon the narrator shoves the unhappy glazier down the stairs, and when he emerges back into the street, drops a flowerpot on him from the garret window, knocking him over and destroying every piece of his merchandise.

The comic, gratuitous act of breaking the panes of glass with a flowerpot is carefully dramatized by Baudelaire, in the paragraphs leading up to the climactic scene, as a variation on Edgar Allan Poe's "Imp of the Perverse". He presents it as a variation on the sudden uncontrollable urge, in an otherwise passive, submissive, and anonymous member of the crowd, to flirt with chaos, like the example he gives of the man who deliberately lit a cigar next to a barrel of gunpowder, or another who started a forest fire "just to see". But the narrator-poet is not the mad agent of pointless mayhem. His perversity has an ulterior purpose, the creation of art. The glazier's panes of glass are transparent, which makes them apt images for the practical, communicative functions of language, and by selling his wares, he is kin to the school teacher. The language normally taught in school, like the panes of glass, is a neutral and transparent medium, a mere commodity to be bought and sold in the course of social relationships indistinguishable from commercial transactions. For the teacher, it is indeed important that students achieve communication by believing in the myth of a natural bond between signifier and signified, and learning to agree on the meanings of words and phrases.[8] The problem is that the conditions necessary for communication are different and even incompatible with those for literature, at least from a Baudelairean perspective.

Informed by the linguistic ideology of the school, the oppressive pedagogical process that forms the backdrop of Prévert's poem is analogous to the wares of the bad glazier. It is the opposite of the poetics of Baudelaire, whose anger at the glazier stands for his aristocratic contempt for all the moralists, philosophers, and other pedagogues who insist on straightforward, evident, unambiguous meanings, in other words: who believe that the purpose of art is to have a purpose other than art. For the same reason that the language of the school, chained to its mimetic mission, provides no means with which to transform misery into bliss, ugliness into beauty, the artist destroys. He destroys by erasing the lesson on the blackboard, and by breaking the transparent glass panes that cannot sufficiently transform the world as it appears to the naked eye. The narrator-poet's destruction of the communicative, "transparent" function of language is actually an act of creative madness, a lesson in the nature of art, in this case, of literature. Colored glass is poetic language, and its effect is radically different from the illusion of reality produced by its colorless cousin. Baudelaire exacerbates, in a sense, the realist versus symbolist opposition that became a journalistic cliché later in the century, when Jules Huret interviewed Emile Zola, Stéphane Mallarmé, and others in an attempt to turn their philosophical differences into a sort of competition for the right to define the meaning and purpose of literature.[9]

Fortunately, the division of language into two sorts of glass, one clear and the other colored, is merely a construction. Like the distinction between "high" and "low" art, "legitimate" and "illegitimate" culture, the one between "transparent" and "opaque (colored)" language is false. The language of primary school (the setting of Prévert's poem) cannot be purely functional, nor can the "literary" language that is the ostensible object of literary study, associated with secondary school be purely artistic, an end in itself. The false dichotomy of realism versus symbolism in Jules Huret's book confirms this. Of course nineteenth-century realism is just as literary as nineteenth-century symbolism. The nature of words does not change depending on who is using them, and for what purpose. Whether one's intentions are to represent the world or to escape from it, the result is the same: it is not the world that one discerns through the glass that matters, a vision of the monochrome city[10] that is bound to be more or less tinted, since absolute transparency is itself an illusion. What matter are the panes of glass themselves. The modernist turn in painting, contemporaneous with Baudelaire's poetics, pointed to a similar conclusion. Baudelaire witnessed and chronicled its birth, and predicted its increasing obsession with the materiality of the artistic medium: paint, canvas, and the act of joining the two. In a much later permutation of Baudelaire's metaphor of the colored panes of glass, it is the individual brushstrokes of Monet's late paintings of the Rouen cathedral that constitute the artwork, not the cathedral itself, which remains inaccessible in its noumenological unknowability.

Baudelaire was interested in what makes art artistic, and as a literary author, in what makes literature literary, an attitude that does give him a certain advantage, when it comes to the founding of the academic discipline of literature, over the pseudoscientific desire for objectivity of naturalism, and the positivist assumptions of the pedagogical establishment of his time.[11] "The dunce" echoes Baudelaire's uncompromising insistence that society always denies language its artistic status by claiming that it can and should be a "transparent" medium for communication. Whatever literariness is, he teaches us, it has nothing to do with the utilitarian functions of language, with our daily attempts to render the world "as it is", in other words to communicate, as if agreement on the true meaning of any discourse were even possible. It is precisely this disinterested view of literature, the symbolist dream par excellence, that general education tends to avoid. It is also, unfortunately, the closest we have to a valid foundation for literary studies as an autonomous discipline, since the communicative dimensions of literature, while important, do not differentiate it clearly from nonliterary discourse: disciplines that use language (which is to say all disciplines), tend toward the verbal equivalent of the unlucky glazier's transparent panes of glass, in order to produce science, history, philosophy, law... the list is long. And when language inevitably occurs in one of these fields in a manner that evokes Baudelaire's colored glass, for example a rhyming slogan ("I like Ike") or a well-crafted figure of speech in a scientific paper, it only proves that literariness is to be found *everywhere*. It is, in fact, the best evidence we have that teaching literature in itself, impossible as that may be, is nevertheless of universal relevance, a necessary complement, at the very least, to the disciplines taught under the rubric of "communication" or "composition". All glass panes, in other words, are tinted to some degree (which is literally true as well, since pure transparency does not exist in nature), and every human being must use them, no matter how much we may in specific cases wish our words to be a transparent medium of description, narration, thought, argument, and so on.

Not all bad students are poets, but everyone is a dunce to some degree. Ones that reject every single rule of the game, such as Prévert's "*cancre*", whether they are latently artistic or incurably bored, are the exception. Most students are willing to find some value in the educational process, or understand it as a game to be played; in either case, they are open to persuasion.[12] Literature, however, is often an exception to this uneasy truce between teachers and students. We already know that outside of the school and university, people seldom read literature.[13] Attempts to make the universal value of literary reading apparent in the classroom, according to the evidence available, are falling short, and literary pedagogy faces a double crisis, of legitimacy and of methodology.

In order to reach the majority of students who, like the former French president, have no prior inclination in favor of literature, we have only a limited range of choices. One option is to abandon any attempt to teach literature to students who do not freely choose it among the range of elective subjects offered to them. At the other extreme, we can simply require all students to read and understand a certain number of more or less complex and archaic works from the canon of world literature, whether they want to or not. Between these two options, neither of which is likely to guarantee the future viability of the profession, there are many alternatives. France, a country that has supported the principle of universal access to literature more strongly than others, and currently faces an acute identity crisis due in part to the failure of its established literary pedagogical model,[14] is a kind of laboratory for proposing and testing those alternatives.

In the pages that follow, we will explore the fate of literature as a general education discipline in France, both historically and in the present. In the process of doing so, many pages and even entire chapters will look at the issue of the general education of literature in the abstract, or in relation to American pedagogical practices, such as "Humanities" general education requirements in high school and college, or the "Common Core Standards". As stated in the Introduction, it is urgent that literature teachers in the United States at the secondary and tertiary level learn from France's problems, because doing so will help to resolve our own crisis of relevance. We need our discipline to remain a pillar of general education if it is to survive, and we must learn to attract more students to the Liberal Arts, of which literature has always been a cornerstone. We can and must re-found the discipline of literature in a manner that, at the very least, recognizes its paradoxical dual role as the guardian and transmitter of a sacred corpus on the one hand, and on the other hand, as a means of teaching "communication" skills that will turn students into better citizens and, yes, even wage earners and entrepreneurs. While both roles, transmitting culture and creating productive citizens, have always been part of the literary pedagogy profession, they exist in a state of tension, if not contradiction, that has largely remained unexamined.

One of the keys of the paradox is the fact that in order to assimilate art, it is not enough to study it; one must also practice it. As we will see, however, a viable literary general education involves more than adding creative writing to the curriculum, which is why I have undertaken to explore the problem by examining how it has been debated at various moments during the history of literature as general education in France. France's own re-founding of the discipline is still a work in progress, but no other country has worked longer on the process, or proposed more solutions. The examples mentioned earlier, taken from electoral politics and literary texts, already provide an illustration of the exemplary value of French debates over the value, purpose, and methods of literary pedagogy for the general population. This is their story.

Notes

1. In order to make his point about the futility of literary study for the general population, Sarkozy took some liberties. An "*attaché d'administration*" is more of a mid-level administrator than a "*guichetière*", or ticket clerk. It might not literally be the case that in France, one has to be able answer questions on literature in order to get a job selling tickets; but one does have to do so, apparently, if one wants a job *supervising* people who sell tickets. The question that remains is whether any public employee, no matter the pay grade, who is not a teacher of French, should have to demonstrate such a high degree (or any degree) of literary competence, and why.
2. The French public recognized Lapostolle's reference to "Kärcher", a brand of pressure washers (also sold in the United States), as a quote from another infamous public statement by Sarkozy, also made while he was Minister of the Interior. After the riots in the Paris suburbs in November 2005, he threatened to address the criminality among young men of African descent the way one might solve the problem of mold on patio furniture: "On va nettoyer au Kärcher la cité." [We'll clean up the projects with a power washer]. In a separate statement following the riots, Sarkozy famously referred to the rioters as "*racaille*" or scum.
3. "*Sous entendre*" means "to imply" that which cannot be understood except by means of a secret code. We call this a "dog whistle", for example: expressing doubts that Barack Obama was born in the United States, instead of openly accusing him of being a Muslim or complaining about his race. As with Sarkozy's speech, the problem is that such a strategy provides deniability. Did Sarkozy really imply that French literature, in addition to being useless, is beyond the capacity of youth from the "*banlieues*", who are of African origin, to understand? Was he using a racist dog whistle while choosing explicitly to ridicule the lowly female ticket seller? It is impossible to know for certain.
4. The fact that Assouline misspelled the word "*referens*" and forgot the circumflex accent on the imperfect subjunctive *fût* while committing an act of high-culture *connivence* is very funny, but we should probably cut him some slack since it is only a blog post.
5. I use the term "slang" not in the generic sense of demotic speech, but rather in the sense that French *argot* evolved in part as a secret code that protects its speakers, not from the hoi polloi, as classical languages and literary references do, but from the police. Slang and erudition share the same function, that of a semiprivate dialect that excludes undesirables, whether of a higher or lower social class.

6. Prévert was the rare poet whose works were commercially successful, not just as poems, but also in other media, such as their adaptation into hit songs recorded by popular artists such as Yves Montand. Most of his very large audience knows him as a screenwriter, especially for some of the most famous films directed by Marcel Carné, including *Les Enfants du paradis* (*Children of Paradise*, 1945). His ability to combine a reputation for artistic achievement with popularity makes him especially relevant to a discussion of the (in-)accessibility of the pedagogical literary canon.
7. Just to remain in the French tradition, examples of formal schooling's disastrous effect on the hero include Voltaire's *Candide* and the first two volumes of Jules Vallès's *Jacques Vingtras* trilogy, *L'Enfant* (The Child) and *Le Bachelier* (The Graduate). Gustave Flaubert's *Madame Bovary* also has a scene of scholarly disaster, but in the tragicomic rather than heroic mode. The novel begins in a secondary school in which the young Charles Bovary, Emma's future husband, is humiliated by the teacher and his peers. He is the "*cancre*" as antihero, and as such provides a useful counter example to Prévert's schoolchild-as-artistic genius.
8. See Renée Balibar's *Les français fictifs. Le rapport des styles littéraires au français national* (*Fictitious French: The Relation of literary Style to National French*, 1974) for an account of the separation of French language by the school system into a transparent, "national" speech for primary education, and an opaque, literary speech, the status of which is granted official recognition in secondary education.
9. Jules Huret, *Enquête sur l'évolution littéraire* (based on interviews with contemporary writers conducted in 1891).
10. The beauty of Paris is something on which almost everybody agrees, but it has very little to do with color. On most days, the city is a kind of arrangement in grey and beige. During the early years of Haussmannization that Baudelaire witnessed, the city was becoming even more monochromatic as its mosaic of neighborhoods and architectural styles was being destroyed, a fact that probably helped the poet choose colored glass as an image for the artistic medium. In addition to the contrast, it provides with the anti-esthetic dimension of modern urban architecture, colored glass symbolizes the Baudelairean intersection of art and religion, or more accurately the usurpation of religious values by art. Stained glass windows act as supernatural prisms, turning sunlight, the rays of which pass through prosaic clear panes of glass without transforming the world, into sacred images. According to the symbolist esthetic, especially when taken to its logical extreme in Baudelaire's adopted persona as Satanist, those sacred images are in fact secular ones, deriving their power not from God but from the artist.
11. See Ferdinand Buisson's *Dictonnaire de Pédagogie* as well as Pierre Larousse and Emile Littré's complementary lexicographical enterprises.

12. I am speaking of course of the middle class, suburban American education of my own experience. Students in underprivileged areas are much more likely to be alienated from the educational pact that binds teachers and students. This problem, which is increasingly prevalent in France's high-minority, high-unemployment neighborhoods, is obviously a far greater crisis than the one in literary pedagogy. Still, disaffection from literary study, whether caused by socioeconomic marginalization or other factors has always been part of education, and is getting worse.
13. In addition to the above-mentioned National Endowment for the Arts reports, *Reading at Risk* (2004), and its more optimistic update of American reading habits titled *Reading on the Rise* (2009), see Zill and Winglee: *Who Reads Literature?* (1990) for an outdated but still relevant discussion of literary competency in the United States.
14. There will be plenty of opportunity to examine the shortcomings of the French educational apparatus in later chapters, but to those readers who might be surprised to hear that French schools are experiencing a crisis of mediocrity not very different from American ones, the *New York Times* has published an insightful op-ed piece by Peter Gumbel in its September 11, 2015 edition: "The Stranglehold on French Schools".

CHAPTER 3

The *Baccalauréat* Exam and the French Canonical Literary Exercise

Over time, literary pedagogues have developed what I call "canonical literary exercises", the tasks that students must accomplish to demonstrate their successful assimilation of the goals that the literature curriculum is designed to attain. Whether oral or written, these exercises are simultaneously instruments of pedagogy and of assessment. In France, these exercises have been codified in the *baccalauréat* exam, an institution that has no equivalent in North America and is substantially different, at least in its literary version, from other European tests such as the British A Levels or the German *Abitur* with which it is often compared. To understand literary pedagogy in French secondary education, it is important to understand the "bac", its history, its present status, and the principles of assessment on which it is based.

THE PROBLEM WITH TESTING

The study of literature, like any general education discipline, involves more than practicing for an exam or some other form of certification or assessment. Ideally, years spent inside and outside of the classroom practicing reading, discussion, and writing about literature constitute literary study, and a steady regime of comprehensive evaluation by teachers, called "*contrôle continu*" in France, verifies the diverse range of achievements of each student. In reality, however, such continuous monitoring of the daily work of reading, writing, and speaking that arises organically from the regular interaction of students and teachers is in competition with forms of evaluation that originate outside of the classroom. Just as literature itself is frequently reduced to extraneous, nonliterary factors, such as its capacity to transmit ideas and information, the aims and methods of literary pedagogy are not necessarily defined by teachers, but rather by entities that are not, in principle, authorized to do so. The academic freedom of teachers, which has traditionally served as the foundation and protection of their authority, can be undermined by high-stakes assessment, the form and content of which are determined by nonteaching agencies both public and private. The governing bureaucracy under which general education takes place, and the social, economic, and political powers that provide its legitimacy, thereby limit the pedagogical role of the teacher, in order to satisfy the hunger for what we now call "outcomes assessment": the Holy Grail of a reliable, even scientific measurement of disciplinary achievement. Although the term "assessment" has only recently come to dominate the lexicon of American education, the concept of an objective standard of measurement to which it refers, and to which students are held accountable regardless of their individual circumstances, needs, and aptitudes, is universal.

In order to discuss the impact of centralized methods of evaluation on the general education of literature, it is important to explain what these methods are. In the United States, boards of education at the state and local level often engage in standardized testing, such as the *New York State Regents Exam*, in a supervisory role that is comparable to the way in which government education agencies operate in many countries. At the national level, up until now, assessment has largely been the responsibility of the private sector, from nonprofit organizations such as the College Board, to multinational enterprises such as Pearson PLC, the largest publishing house in the world. The biggest exception to the domination of private enterprises in nationwide testing is the National Assessment of Educational Progress, administered by the Department of Education. Such tests, regardless of the supervising agency, aim for the objective quantification of knowledge and skills. In the testing of English, this means vocabulary, grammar, rhetoric, and reading comprehension. The primary means by which the tests measure literary skills at all grade levels are the multiple-choice questions on passages and short texts that include fiction, literary nonfiction, and poetry. College aptitude tests, such as the SAT and ACT, now also include optional essays in order to assess higher-order language skills. The more sophisticated, discipline-specific instruments such as the *Advanced Placement Exam in English Literature*, also include open-ended essay questions that cannot be considered purely objective, since there is no single, correct answer; however, since the AP and similar exams are only given to students who have taken optional high-level classes in the relevant discipline, they do not count as "general education" assessment. Nevertheless, even when general education tests include nonobjective measures such as essay questions, they maintain a reputation as being reliable quantifiers of students' disciplinary achievement and readiness and have served to measure "institutional effectiveness" in the United States for over a century.[1]

The history of extra-institutional testing reveals that it actually fulfills two roles. One is the simple verification that pedagogical practices do, in fact, achieve predetermined disciplinary goals. The other is less benign and not necessarily intended. It occurs when outside assessment becomes so powerful that it no longer verifies the attainment of teacher-developed disciplinary outcomes, but rather imposes its own standards and goals. This leads to the well-known "teaching to the test" syndrome that undermines academic freedom by determining personnel decisions, funding, and students' access to higher education. Even when testing does not directly affect the evaluation of teacher performance or the size of school budgets, it stands to reason that teachers whose students are tested by an outside authority will be tempted to adopt the goals and values of the test as their own. The struggle over assessment that pits teachers against public and private agencies, inside against outside, is one of the major contributors to the crisis in the general education of literature.

In the United States, the "*Common Core State Standards Initiative*" and the testing apparatus it enables at every grade level, as well as old standbys such as the SAT, SAT II and the Advanced Placement exam, all include literature among the subjects they evaluate. Together they exercise a growing influence over the classroom practices of teachers and students. In Chapter 7, we will examine a test that has even more power because of its global reach: the *Programme for International Student Assessment* or PISA, administered by the Organization for Economic Cooperation and Development, the results of which have impelled many government agencies to make profound changes to their educational policies. The *Common Core State Standards*, for example, were created by the National Governors Association partly as a way to address the relatively poor performance of American students on the PISA exam[2] and include an extensive series of recommendations and curricular models for the teaching of literature, designed in part to practice the kinds of reading skills that the OECD considers important. Such developments will increase the already considerable distance separating North American methods of assessing literary reading from French ones, especially the famous *baccalauréat* exam that simultaneously marks the end of secondary education and the start of tertiary education. And yet, as we will see, the "*bac*" is under assault by many of the same pressures from the OECD and other agencies that have only recently emerged on the educational landscape.

THE LITERATURE *BACCALAURÉAT* TODAY

In France, external measurement of institutional effectiveness via standardized testing plays a much smaller role in the general education of language and literature than in the United States[3]; instead, attention has traditionally focused on the "open-ended" exercise, especially the literary essay and the oral "*explication*" at the middle and high school levels. The grand patriarch of this style of general education testing is the literature portion of the *bac*, which now serves as a rite of passage at the conclusion of the penultimate year of secondary education for the majority of the population.[4] With its oral and written components evaluated by actual teachers of French literature in the *lycée* (high school) rather than computers, it has also come to symbolize the refusal to submit to a scientific, objective, yet superficial and mechanical measure of academic achievement. The *bac*, as it is commonly known, is more like a performance, for which the various oral and written exercises practiced in secondary schools are the rehearsal, and of which the teachers themselves are the judges.

The literature portion of the *bac*, called *épreuve anticipée de français* [preliminary exam in French], is part of a much larger set of exams spread out over two years, that combine general as well as specialized education assessment. The focus and content of the exams vary not only according to the type of *lycée* one attends ("general", the most popular one; "technological"; or "professional/vocational"), but also according to one's specialization. The way it works in practice is that students have to sit for a number of exams at the end of each of the last two years of study. For example, students in the "S" (science) track of the *lycée général* must take exams that verify their general education knowledge and skills in humanities subjects, such as history, literature, and philosophy, as well as in the specific subjects relevant to their area of specialization, such as physics, mathematics, and biology. Students in the "L" (literature and languages) track will take the oral and written *épreuve anticipée* in French literature at the end of the penultimate year (called *première*) along with students in the other tracks, but unlike these others they will sit for another, more advanced literature exam at the end of their final year (called *terminale*). Students in the "ES" (economy and society) or "S" (science) tracks also take the oral and written exams in French literature at the end of *première* but take exams only in other subjects the following year. A written exam in philosophy is also required at the end of the year of *terminale* in all the tracks of the *lycée général*, as well as of the *lycée technologique*, which means that France has the unusual distinction of considering philosophy to be a general education subject (Eduscol, "Baccalauréat général").

Unlike American high schools, French *lycées* do not have the authority to grant diplomas, which are the responsibility of the government.[5] The Ministry of Education therefore develops and administers an examination apparatus at the conclusion of every educational level that doubles as a certification process that teachers and administrators control, in their role as civil servants. The *bac*, rather than the official school transcript, still constitutes the official *lycée* diploma, and to obtain it one must achieve an average grade of ten or higher (out of twenty) in a minimum number of general education as well as specialized subjects. So, just what is this all-important exam that elicits much public awe and hostility in France, often at the same time?

Today, a student having just completed the second year of the three-year sequence in a *lycée général*, the closest French equivalent to an American high school, will undertake the French literature *bac* over two days, as explained by the Ministry of Education on its "Eduscol" web page titled "*Baccalauréat général série littéraire*". The oral portion of the exam normally lasts just under one hour. In a room, the student meets a teacher from a different school than the one he or she attends, so as to eliminate the risk of bias on the part of the examiner. The examiner chooses a short text or excerpt from a list of works that the student has studied in class during the previous year and presents him or her with a general question or problem based on the text. The student has 30 minutes to prepare, then gives a ten-minute presentation that includes a number of ritualistic requirements, such as reading the text aloud, providing relevant historical and biographical information, and giving a structured argument based on the examiner's question. A ten-minute discussion follows, during which the examiner asks further questions. Each ten-minute oral performance is scored on a scale of one to ten, and the combined total constitutes the student's grade. Ten out of twenty constitutes a passing grade, and any student who scores sixteen or above is considered to have excelled, receiving the additional accolade of "*mention très bien*" [highest distinction].

The written exercise takes four hours and consists of two parts. The first is a series of one to four short-answer questions on one or more literary texts, either fragments from narrative or dramatic works, or entire poems, that are provided on the exam form itself. The second part of the written exam is a more substantial essay, and despite the countless reforms undertaken since the "French composition" was instituted in the middle of the nineteenth century, it is still very similar to the traditional canonical exercises of (many) years past. Students have three options: a "commentary", or interpretive essay on one of the excerpts or poems from part one of the exam; a "dissertation" or argumentative essay on a broader literary topic; or a more open-ended, "creative" piece.

As an illustration, let us look at the tasks for the written portion of the *bac* distributed to all general *lycée* students in the "L" track (literature and languages) on June 19, 2015. In part one (short answers), they were shown three poems and a prose passage on the theme of travel, from periods ranging from the eighteenth century to the present, and were asked to compare the different "conceptions of travel" in the texts. In part two, the interpretive "commentary" option prompted the students to write an essay on the second of the three poems that had been provided, "Les Voiles" [The Sails] by Alphonse de Lamartine. The second option, the "dissertation" or argumentative essay, asked the following question: "Pensez-vous que la poésie soit une invitation au voyage ? Vous répondrez à cette question en vous fondant sur les textes du corpus ainsi que sur les textes et œuvres que vous avez étudiés et lus." [Do you think poetry is an invitation to travel ? Answer the question using examples from the corpus (i.e., the four texts provided in part one), as well as texts and works you have studied and read.] Finally, the "*écriture d'invention*" or "creative" option was as follows:

> Deux lycéens confrontent leurs points de vue sur le rôle du voyage pour nourrir l'inspiration poétique: l'un estime le voyage indispensable, l'autre lui oppose que l'on peut faire œuvre poétique sans avoir voyagé. Imaginez ce dialogue, au cours duquel chacun de vos personnages développe des arguments qui s'appuient sur les textes du corpus, sur ceux que vous avez étudiés en classe et sur vos lectures personnelles.
>
> [Two high school students contrast their points of view on the role of travel as a source of poetic inspiration: one considers travel to be indispensable, while the other claims that one can create a poetic work without having traveled. Imagine this dialog, during which each of your characters develops

arguments based on texts from the corpus (the four texts given in part one), on ones you have studied in class, and on your own reading.]

(Eduscol, "Epreuve anticipée de français, série L")

Part one is scored on a scale of one to four, part two on a scale of one to 16, and the combined total out of 20 is the grade for the written portion. As with the oral, a grade of 16 or above carries the "*mention très bien*", the coveted accolade of "highest distinction".

Most educators will look at the above descriptions with justified admiration for the ways in which they support some of the most cherished values of the liberal arts tradition. The exam questions force students to think independently and allow for a wide range of responses, drawing on positive knowledge, reasoning skills, artistic sensitivity, and fluency both in speaking and writing. One might express certain reservations as well, pointing out the close similarity of all of the prompts for the writing exercises, for example, or the fact that the ritualistic constraints that students must respect throughout the process, especially on the oral exam, decrease the potential for individual expression. Furthermore, while the "creative" exercise might provide students with a better opportunity to display their literary talent than the other two essay options, only a rare few will manage to avoid producing at best a cliché, and at worst, a caricature of two earnest adolescents engaged in a pretentious intellectual debate. When compared to the banality and mechanized rigidity of standardized multiple-choice tests, however, such objections fade into insignificance. The bottom line is that students must wrestle with difficult texts, covering various time periods, genres, and non-canonical as well as canonical works. A more important problem is the fact that the *bac* as a whole is an extremely expensive and labor-intensive enterprise, especially when one considers that there are oral and written exams in virtually every discipline, divided over the final two years of the *lycée*. The administration and grading of the exams are packed into the short time period between the last day of school and the start of summer vacation, to which one must add the "*rattrapage*" sessions, the retakes of the exams, administered later in the year for students who failed on their first attempt. The burden on the taxpayer, the questionable relevance of the literature exam as a certification of general education, as well as the high stakes of a diploma that is increasingly viewed as indispensable for occupational integration,[6] are some of the reasons why some people want to eliminate, or at least drastically streamline, the entire process. The *bac* today is less admired, and more reviled than in the past.[7]

The voices calling for the elimination or radical reconfiguration of the *bac* are growing louder but so far have not been effective. Given the expense and stress associated with the exam, along with accusations of declining standards and arbitrary grading practices, one may wonder why. Part of the explanation is no doubt the sentimental attachment to a national ritual with roots that are more than two centuries old. Another argument in favor of preserving the current process that is more relevant to our purposes is that its very complexity prevents it from becoming a mechanized, superficial assessment of quantifiable skills and knowledge, like standardized tests.[8] Complexity actually helps to protect the process against charges, common in American testing, that it lacks integrity or reduces general education to the acquisition of information. There is indeed a stark contrast between the image of computers processing millions of multiple-choice answers, and the one of flesh and blood teachers spending an hour each with dozens of students during the oral portions of the *bac*, and then spending long days poring over a large stack of *commentaires, dissertations,* and *exercices d'invention.* It is analogous to the contrast between a fully automated assembly line, and a workshop where skilled craftspeople produce handmade objects. On the other hand, any teacher knows that grading student essays can easily become an alienating, mechanized routine. The pressure of a government-imposed deadline, the repetitiveness of the exercises, and the massive scale of the enterprise all conspire against a truly individualistic appreciation of each student's performance; one grader might discern a unique voice in a student's essay and give it a high mark, whereas another might not, and give the same essay a low one. This is just one of many variables that contribute to a phenomenon known as "the lottery of the *bac*", studied by the sociologist of education Pierre Merle in *Les Notes: secrets de fabrication* [Grades: Trade Secrets]. By giving groups of identical *bac* essays to different teachers and studying their grading processes, Merle proved that two different teachers can award to the same essay grades that differ by as many as 11 points. Since the score is out of 20, 11 points can easily be the difference between a low "fail" (five) and "highest distinction" (16). Such wide discrepancies are exceptional, but Merle discovered that no less than 40 percent of a large sample of social science *bac* essays in his experiment showed grading disparities of at least five points, a result that makes standardized testing suddenly look a lot better.

Even the rule that teachers can only evaluate students from other schools gives one pause. Is it not better to know personally the students whose essays one is evaluating, and already be aware of the unique abilities that might give value to their work, and which a stranger might not recognize in a single reading? True, the anonymity of the process guards against the possibility that teachers might be influenced in their grading by the students' ethnicity, gender, or social background, but getting to know students over time, and becoming familiar with their work, can provide teachers with precious information on how best to evaluate them. An even deeper question hovers over the entire culture of summative evaluation of students, whether the *bac* or the SAT: is this kind of assessment, that originates from outside the confines of the classroom, better carried out cheaply and objectively by machines, or inefficiently and subjectively by people? Or does it even need to occur at all?

What we are really comparing, by juxtaposing the "*bac*" with American-style forms of assessment, are what education theory calls the "testing and measurement" and "mastery" paradigms. The former seeks objective quantification as a means of evaluating learning, while the latter is holistic, multi-dimensional, and descriptive. Standardized tests tend to fall under the "measurement" paradigm, whereas the "mastery" paradigm might rely on portfolios, oral interviews, and other more complex, subjective, and (one hopes) sensitive instruments. Peter Ewell, one of the leaders in the field of educational assessment, wrote that the two paradigms not only represent "a clash between ... quantitative 'scientific' investigation and qualitative 'developmental' observation" but also between methods that "consciously divorce the process of investigating student attainment from the act of instruction in the name of objectivity" and ones that consider student attainment and the act of instruction "inseparable" (6–7). If one follows Ewell's logic, then despite the fact that the motivation for assessment almost always arises from a source exterior to the classroom, such as a school administration, government agency, or even the private sector, it can nevertheless adhere closely to the educational practices of actual teachers and students. The term "organic" frequently arises in discussions of qualitative, as opposed to quantitative assessment methods, and it describes the "*bac*" far more accurately than it does quantitative methods such as the SAT or PISA tests. Clearly, it favors the inner realm of the classroom, over the outer realm of social and economic exchange, and strives to judge the student's "true" intellectual achievement as opposed to his or her ability to perform objectively measurable tasks, such as the communication of information.

In the realm of general education, especially of literature, the reconciliation between interior and exterior forces is an overriding concern.

Often, the exterior forces are perceived to threaten the interior ones with corruption or dissolution. "Communication", which is essential to social and professional integration, is a "lower" function of language than the literary. The reduction of literature to a vehicle for something outside of literature, such as a moral lesson, or a means of developing one's rhetorical skills, offends the Baudelairean sensibility. But when literature is taught, the separation between a pure, undefiled literariness and the fallen world of everyday speech immediately becomes problematic. The walls of the school simply do not function symbolically or practically like those of a temple, and various forms of testing are evidence of this failure. The French tradition of the literature *bac* has, to a large degree, accomplished the seemingly impossible by maintaining the integrity of literary pedagogy, without cloistering it impermeably. It emanates from outside (the public agency of the Ministry of Education) but is administered and scored by human beings who are also, for the most part, teachers; it evaluates each student holistically, through literary readings both oral and written, yet does so paradoxically by means of an assessment that certifies whether the student is prepared for certain types of employment, as well as for university study; it recognizes the value of a non-utilitarian sensitivity to literature, while also measuring a student's logical and rhetorical skills. Assessment is a feature of education that has only grown more and more in recent decades, and the pressure to use it in order to measure a person's, or even a nation's ability to thrive in the global economy, is fierce. Chapter 7 of this book examines such pressure, and the threat it poses to the strictly literary foundations of the discipline of literature. The present discussion of the literature *bac* is one of several hypotheses I explore in order to try to move beyond the standoff that has now opposed the "literarian" and "utilitarian" approaches to the discipline for almost as long as it has existed.

Of course, while the literature portion of the *bac* has the merit of straddling both sides of the pedagogical divide, it is far from being a perfect compromise. Aside from the alienating process to which French teachers are subjected every year during the dreaded "exam season", there are at least three more factors that undermine the distinction between American-style standardized testing and French-style open-ended testing. The first is that the legitimacy of the results of the *bac*, like those of any exam, depend on the claim that they are in fact "objective". Receiving an "eighteen" or "nineteen" out of twenty on any portion of the French literature *bac* is therefore, in terms of perception, not much different than scoring a perfect 800 on the SAT reading exam.[9] Both reduce individual, unique profiles of skill and knowledge to a single number, as if one was measuring the students' body temperature or blood pressure, rather than creating a "holistic" or "organic" account of his or her educational attainment. The second is that both testing methods exert a disproportionate amount of influence on pedagogical practices, making it difficult for teachers to decide by themselves on the best way to address the infinitely variable needs of their students. The third is that general education in France, like general education all over the world, is increasingly subjected to international rather than national norms. New assessment methods such as PISA make international comparisons possible and are much closer to the American model in design, as we will see in Chapter 7. Now that the authority of the "canonical literary exercise" epitomized by the *bac* is under attack, from the left and from the right, both nationally and internationally, it is important to see what value it has had and might continue to have, as a general education practice.

The influence of testing performed by outside agencies on the educational process has always presented a dilemma. What begins as a bureaucratic verification that public funds are being invested efficiently, turns into a case of the tail wagging the dog: the verification process becomes, in effect, the new mission on which classroom practices depend. Such a dynamic occurs even more readily in France than in the American system, where local school boards stand as a barrier to universal normative pressures. Educational practices in France are made uniform at the macro level by national government policies, and at the micro level by the content of certification tests devised and administered by the Ministry of Education at various junctures in the educational continuum, such as the *brevet*, taken at the end of middle school, all the way to the *agrégation*, the prestigious recruitment contest for *lycée* professors.

Since the literature *bac* is a tradition that goes back to the First Empire, it is important to examine a few relevant aspects of its history. Prior to doing so, one needs to remember a few principles. First, the "wag the dog" aspect of any such powerful evaluation tool creates a barrier against local and individual initiative in matters of education, which adds considerably to the challenge of recognizing, and adapting to the students' individual needs and aptitudes. Secondly, the assumptions that underlie the development of the test, and the ways in which it is carried out and evaluated are often different; in other words, one must not only look at the test, but also at the responses by students to the questions, and the evaluations by the examiners, in order to understand its impact on the classroom. Finally, although testing is just one aspect of education, it continues more than ever to be a major force in the development of goals and methodologies. When discussing the future of literary pedagogy one must be critical of the influence of testing, whether or not it represents an encroachment by nonacademic interests, such as the promotion of "marketable skills" by the private sector, and one must not underestimate its power. The French literature *bac*, in spite of its reputation as a model for the disinterested evaluation of literary skill and knowledge, has never been immune from the kinds of charges made against the *Common Core Standards* or the SAT.

First, I will examine one of the antecedents of the French "canonical literary exercise" in the Jesuit pedagogical tradition, before moving on to its complex and contradictory evolution since the late nineteenth century. This story has been told very well in two major books on the subject: Violaine Houdart-Merot's *La Culture littéraire au lycée depuis 1880*, and Martine Jey's *La Littérature au lycée, invention d'une discipline (1880–1925)*, both published in 1998. However, we first need to understand what paradigm the literary pedagogy of the Third Republic was trying so hard to replace.

Rhetoric, Religion, and the Birth of the French Literary Exercise

If the discourse of "crisis" as applied to literary pedagogy is both more frequent and strident in France than in the United States, it is due in part to the historical fact of the persistent centrality of literature in secondary and higher education over many centuries. Evidence of its status includes the rhetorical instruction of the Jesuits that had such a strong influence on neoclassical French writing, an influence that has never completely disappeared, at least as a symbol of linguistic and artistic purity, and of the power of tradition.

There are many ways in which the distant past of literary pedagogy in North America parallels the French experience, in particular the fetishism of the Greek and Latin corpus, of which contemporaries on both continents were well aware. In *Professing Literature* (1987), Gerald Graff quotes the 1883 Phi Beta Kappa address of Charles Francis Adams appropriately titled "A College Fetich", in which he lambasts "'the great-impalpable-essence-and-precious-residuum theory' of the classics" (30), according to which "endless memorization and recitation of grammatical and etymological peculiarities" (28) of exemplary texts emblemized literary knowledge. Simply undergoing the process of learning to repeat and to parse such texts was, like religious practice, a strong enough outward sign of enlightenment that actual belief (or understanding) were not necessary. And the absence of any attempt to apprehend the literariness of the texts beyond memorization and imitation meant that, by graduation, the number of students who could honestly profess a love of literature was no higher than when they began their education.

The similarity between the French and American experiences is striking and helps to explain the persistence of the claim that literariness operates in the classroom as a process of revelation rather than gradual acquisition of skills and knowledge, and is therefore unlike any other subject in the general education curriculum. The difference between the two cultures is also great, however. In France, reforms to the teaching of literature in the late-nineteenth century faced a steeper challenge in a society that still conceived of literature in the same way as scripture, as a text that is fundamentally alien to everyday discourse and experience, in part because scripture is both foreign and ancient, whereas the unmediated familiarity with the text of the Bible in American Protestant denominations, most of which were affiliated with specific colleges and universities, facilitated the transition to a demystifying pedagogy that was no longer incompatible with the scientific agenda of the modern university (see Graff *passim*). A century or so later, this difference resulted in a huge gap between the two cultures, with American high schools placing literature within the larger discipline of "language arts" with all the practical, goal-oriented connotations of the term, whereas the French *lycée* still regards itself as a site for the transmission and dissemination of the "impalpable-essence-and-precious-residuum" of literature. Both institutions, I argue, currently suffer because of a lack of understanding of the other, opposite approach. American schools are ill-equipped to view literature as more than a "language art" that, at the most, prepares one for a more productive life (and at the least is nothing more than an indulgence), whereas French ones find themselves trapped in a defensive posture, unable to convert a majority of their students, who no longer even pretend to respect taught literature, to the belief that the alienating properties of literary texts are worth overcoming.

The association of literature with faith is due only in part to the difficulty of reading, to the "leap of faith" required in order to invest effort into understanding literary texts for the first time, especially those that are most alien to the students' own culture. In both societies, as well as the rest of the Western world, it is also due to the fact that literary education was carried out for centuries almost exclusively in religious institutions. The Jesuit order was one of the few to have developed a specific curriculum and methodology for literary pedagogy. Their system was based on the imitation of Greek and Latin texts and codified in the *Ratio Studiorum* of 1586 (definitive edition, 1599). The value of examining the distant origin of French literary pedagogy in Jesuit rhetoric is that it provides a historical basis for the focus of the discipline on inherited, canonical works from a past that seems to transcend temporality. In addition, the *Ratio Studiorum* promotes a method of instruction based on imitation that, while appearing to place students in the position of "authors" by requiring them to produce literary texts, actually constrains their freedom to such an extent that the written and oral exercises they produce are usually little more than a ritualistic simulacrum of literary production.[10] As such, it is neither an example of "teaching by doing", nor a scientific investigation of the nature and function of literariness. This double failure of Jesuit pedagogy to turn most students either into writers or into expert readers has not, however, prevented it from acquiring enormous prestige, nor from contributing to the continued insolubility of the crisis in literary general education.

The rhetorical exercises of the Jesuits were constrained by the imitation of ancient authors, and observance of the principles of *eloquence* codified by Quintilian. The more interpretive "explication" exercise, which emerged in the literature classroom during the nineteenth century, belonged to the genre of commentary. Both survive in France today: rhetoric in the form of the creative, open-ended "*exercices d'invention*" that have a distant kinship with the rhetorical principles of "*imitatio*", "*inventio*" and "*dispositio*"; and commentary, in the form of the oral or written analysis of a short text, a poem or an excerpt from a longer work. Though complementary, these two types of pedagogical exercise derive from radically different conceptions of the purpose and value of literary education, contributing to the never-ending "crisis of French", traditionally understood as the students' lack of linguistic proficiency, their unfamiliarity with literary history, and increasingly low rates of literary reading in society.

The term "rhetorical instruction" in literary studies carries a number of meanings. The one relevant to our topic is the Renaissance definition of the "humanities" as personal familiarity with classical texts in the original language, a definition that has persisted in France where the term "*les humanités*" still refers primarily, if no longer exclusively, to the study of Latin and Greek,[11] rather than the pluridisciplinary meaning it has in English. In the *Ratio Studiorum*'s meticulous description of the curriculum of the Jesuit school, mastery of language and of rhetoric based on the study of ancient texts, especially oratory, is a prerequisite for the study of other subjects, such as philosophy and science, just as the *trivium* prepares for the *quadrivium*. As historian Georges Leroux pointed out, the separation of form and function into separate stages of literary pedagogy simply reflected the history of Renaissance humanism up to that point: "D'abord les langages, ensuite l'expression et la persuasion, enfin les savoirs: on pourrait résumer ainsi la philosophie du *Ratio Studiorum*. Cette structure représente elle-même un héritage de la Renaissance, et en particulier du régime d'études de l'Université de Paris". [First (classical) languages, then expression and persuasion, finally knowledge: that is how one could summarize the philosophy underlying the *Ratio Studiorum*. This structure itself is a legacy of the Renaissance, specifically of the curriculum of the University of Paris] (Leroux 38). As the *Ratio Studiorum* states, in the section on the class of rhetoric:

> The scope of this class is not easily defined. Its purpose is the development of the power of self-expression. Its content spans two major fields, oratory and poetry, with oratory taking the place of honor.
>
> ... It may be said in general that this class is concerned mainly with the art of rhetoric, the refinement of style, and erudition.
>
> ... Erudition is to be sought in the study of historical events, ethnology, the authoritative views of scholars, and wide sources of knowledge, but rather sparingly according to the capacity of the pupils. (72-3)

Expression, both written (poetry) and spoken (oratory) were the primary goals of this education, with erudition "to be sought...sparingly" and occupying a secondary position. One must be careful, however, to understand "expression" in the very limited sense of "imitation", both as representation of nature and rhetorical appropriation of the classical model (Houdart-Merot 1998, 14n.). Further on, "erudition" is again identified as a poor relation within literary studies: "Erudition should be introduced here and there as a means of stimulating intellectual interest and relaxing the mind. It should not be allowed to distract attention from concentrated study of the language" (80).

Such strong demarcation between rhetoric and erudition, form and substance, still dominated nineteenth-century French literary pedagogy. In fact, there was a revival of Jesuit schools in the first half of the nineteenth century, after the Jesuit order was re-established by Pope Pius VII in 1814. The consequent updating of the *Ratio Studiorum*, published in 1832, only reinforced the literary foundation of their curriculum, reaffirming the sequence defined by classical languages, followed by the study of rhetoric, before the acquisition of positive knowledge. Literature in the vernacular, which is to say national literature, was finally recognized, but only under the category of positive knowledge, along with science and history, that followed the assimilation of classical languages (Leroux 43). The first modern "crisis of French" at the turn of the twentieth century is a result of the conflict between two visions of literary education: the assimilation of literariness through the mastery of language (Latin and Greek grammar, rhetorical strategies, written and spoken eloquence), versus erudition and commentary. The opposition is also between skill and memorization, between "talent", or the rare ability to express in one's own words and sensibility the elusive and ennobling quality of literariness, and the presumably much more widely shared capacity for simple hard work.

Jesuit education as codified by the *Ratio Studiorum* became the model against which Republican literary pedagogy began to define itself in the late nineteenth-century (Compère and Chervel). The belief that Jesuit education-supported aristocratic values was only partly based on fact: it rested as well on the strategic self-representation of public French secondary education as an attempt to become the opposite of existing pedagogical practice, as being applicable to all citizens, and therefore requiring an entirely new set of goals and methods. Although most students in Catholic secondary schools at the time were not aristocrats by birth, the social status of their families meant that the vast majority of them were the heirs to aristocratic cultural values. By learning Greek and/or Latin, and imitating classical writers and orators, it was assumed that these students were not acquiring knowledge, even less the skills necessary for the exercise of a profession, but simply the tools with which to express their naturally superior intellect and sensibility. The contradiction inherent in this prototype of literary education is obvious: the claim that education makes manifest the superiority that gentlemen had over the rest of the population (we are talking about the education of males exclusively, since the *bac* officially became open to females only in 1924[12]), must hide the fact that it was the education itself that created the superiority, and not the accident of birth. The history of literary general education is also, however, the history of repeated attempts to shatter the myth of aristocratic superiority, especially insofar as Jesuit-inspired literary pedagogy seemed to support it.

There are at least two ways of attacking the role of humanities as justifying class privilege. One is to say that the upper classes are no more adept at mastering classical rhetoric, taste, and erudition than other members of society, and that consequently one must give everyone the opportunity to learn them. An ancillary to this argument is that great works of "high" culture are not limited to social elites and are accessible, through education, to all. This antielitist principle is widespread in France, as illustrated by the militant collective *"Sauver les lettres"* [save literature] whose web page contains the slogans: "Sauver la culture classique, non comme un bagage distinctif, mais comme un trésor d'humanité à faire partager à tous" [to save classical culture, not as distinguishing (cultural) baggage, but as a human treasure to be shared by all] and "Sauver l'idée d'un 'enseignement élitaire pour tous', comme horizon à atteindre [to save the idea of an "elite education for all" as a horizon to be reached]. A second way to shatter the myth is to affirm, following Bourdieu and Passeron's *The Inheritors* (1964), that classical, rhetorical mastery and erudition, as well as their modern French equivalents, are not the real substance of literary knowledge, but only an arbitrary, time-consuming, difficult set of skills, the main purpose of which is to create an unbridgeable gap between the privileged and non-privileged classes. According to the second argument, it is a mistake to try to make the traditional "humanities" of classical rhetoric accessible to all. Instead, one must replace it in the general curriculum with a genuinely democratic pedagogy, for example by teaching the knowledge and interpretation of literature written in the student's native language, while declaring wit and classical erudition to be the secondary vestiges of an otherwise buried past. While very few French pedagogues would go so far as to say that "classic French literature" is as irrelevant to general education as the teaching of Greek and Latin composition, many recognize that the problem of access to "high" literary culture, even in the national language, continues to be one of the most daunting challenges of the profession. Even during the first half of the nineteenth century, canonical French literature started to become insurmountably alien to many students:

Dans leurs classes, ou dans les jurys d'examen, les professeurs de l'Université s'aperçoivent que la langue des auteurs du XVIIe siècle n'est plus immédiatement accessible, même pour les milieux cultivés ou relativement cultivés où elle ne semblait pas poser de problème jusqu'à la fin du XVIIIe siècle.

[In their classes or as members of exam committees, university professors noticed that the language of seventeenth-century authors was no longer immediately accessible, even to [students from] well-educated or relatively well-educated backgrounds, whereas it did not seem to pose a problem prior to the end of the eighteenth century.] (Compère and Chervel 18)

Teaching Shakespeare in American secondary schools is no different: the language may be "English", but of a type that has gradually become alien, as the vernacular has evolved. Michel Leroy addresses precisely this problem in his book *Peut-on enseigner la littérature française?* [is teaching French literature possible? 2001]. He expands upon the argument that a redefinition of "culture" is necessary that no longer reflects aristocratic values, opening the difficult issue of how, and even whether, one can teach inherited culture alongside, and perhaps even through works of contemporary culture.

The "crises" that recur wherever and whenever the teaching of literature is in danger of losing its status as a component of general education, or of losing "market share" as students opt for other disciplines, often are caused by the structural tension between rhetoric and erudition, skill and knowledge, and the vast range of standards in each of these categories. At times, the profession focuses on the challenge of democratizing (which is not the same as "dumbing down") the cultural values traditionally associated with privileged classes, taking the form of a complaint such as: "Why do my students refuse to share my faith in the inherent value of famous literary texts?" At other times, the profession ignores the crucial question of "faith" in an inherited and therefore aristocratic model of culture. If the focus instead is on the need to make literature "relevant" by any means necessary, for example as a means to achieve practical goals, the most important question becomes: "How do I persuade my students that it is in their best interest, personally and professionally, to acquire the skills of interpretation and communication that only literary studies can provide?" What both questions share is the democratizing urge: nobody today seriously argues that literature should be the private reserve of a cultural elite. The only disagreements, and they are many and profound, concern the reasons and methods for loosening the aristocratic grip on "taught" culture.

The Decline of Rhetoric in the History of French Literary Pedagogy

We now focus on the teaching of literature in the *lycée* during a period that has been especially well explored by historians of French education: the transition, during the second half of the nineteenth century and well into the twentieth, from a pedagogy based on Latin (and, to a lesser extent, Greek) literature and rhetoric, to one based on French literature and "erudition". The timeline of this transition is defined by the *baccalauréat*, since in France, the exam has had a particularly important effect on the pedagogical agenda, whether in its current form as described previously, or in its previous incarnations. In the process of examining the evolution of the *bac*, however, it is important to keep in mind that it is not just the content of the exam itself that matters, but how students are trained and evaluated; in other words, the practices as distinct from the regulations, decrees, *circulaires* (memos), and "official instructions" that emanate from the Ministry of National Education. As we will see, research shows that the practice of teaching often lags behind or even directly contradicts the principles enunciated at the top (Houdart-Merot 1998); when it created the new models for literary pedagogy in the late nineteenth century, for example, the ministry understandably wanted to present change as a *fait accompli*, when in fact it was largely still wishful thinking. Such a discrepancy between policy and its implementation, between theory and practice, was no doubt caused by the weight of tradition, which is a form of inertia, but also by a more active refusal to abandon the techniques inherited from the rhetorical tradition.

The following history of the *baccalauréat* is based on the previously-cited books by Violaine Houdart-Merot (1998) and Martine Jey (1998), and the monumental contributions to the history of literary pedagogy in France by André Chervel (1999, 2002, 2006). It illustrates the difficulty, and only partial success, of the shift away from the Jesuit rhetorical model. When it was first administered in 1809, the literature *bac* consisted entirely of an oral exam in Latin based on classical authors; it therefore tested one type of historical knowledge, but also a kind of literary skill, insofar as students were evaluated on their ability to mimic the authors whose texts they had studied. One has to imagine students using the Latin that they had learned by imitating ancient oratory: paraphrasing and sometimes describing, but not commenting on, the texts on which the examiners questioned them. As the century wore on, more analytical and interpretive skill was required, in addition to linguistic mastery and memory: beginning in 1821, students had to answer questions about the rhetorical devices of given texts; in 1830, the first written exam appeared alongside the oral performance and was the ancestor of the "canonical exercise in literary study" that exists today. Students had to write an "amplification", in Latin, of a Latin text, a hybrid rhetorical exercise combining mimesis (imitating and paraphrasing Latin models) and commentary (explaining the meaning of a text by identifying its themes, explaining its rhetorical devices, and so on). "Amplification" is also the primary rhetorical technique of the sermon, a reminder that the ancestors of the canonical literary exercise belong to the ecclesiastical as well as to the classical tradition (Houdart-Merot 1998, 16).

In 1840, the *version* exercise appeared, a translation or paraphrase in French of a Latin or Greek text. Finally, in 1853, the true ancestor of the modern canonical literary exercise was born: the *composition française*, also called *explication*. Why such a change, at this time? For one simple reason: the minister of public instruction Hippolyte Fortoul in 1852 established a new, predominantly scientific track in the *lycée* to complement the one that already existed. Prior to this groundbreaking though short-lived "bifurcation" of humanities and science, *lycée* education had been primarily literary (Jey 79). Since it was impossible to fit an ambitious science curriculum into a schedule that was dominated by Greek and Latin classes, the new section simply switched the emphasis from classical to French literature, granting enhanced status to the latter discipline by reducing the number of hours devoted to the former. *The invention of the canonical exercise in French literature therefore coincides with the reinvention of secondary education as a scientific as much as a literary enterprise.* The very notion of a scientific, non-classical humanist pedagogy became a major force for reform, as Clément Falcucci wrote in a landmark 1939 study *L'humanisme dans l'enseignement secondaire en France au XIXe siècle* [humanism in French secondary education in the nineteenth century]. The other context in which French literature was more important than Greek and Latin was the education of young girls who, because they were not required to learn classical languages, received far more instruction in the national literature than their male counterparts (see note 12, Rebecca Rogers's groundbreaking 2005 work *From the Salon to the Schoolroom: Educating Bourgeois Girls in Nineteenth-Century France*). From early on, therefore, the teaching of French literature in France was tainted by the suspicion that it was less rigorous, both more practical and more feminine, and therefore less literary, than the teaching of classical literature. The association with science was also reflected in the new methodologies: the fact that "erudition" went from least to most important component of literary study aroused suspicion that the discipline had regressed from being "literary" to being (merely) "scientific". The invention of *enseignement spécial* by Minister Victor Duruy in the 1860s, a new secondary track for future businessmen and technologists who did not need to pass the *bac*, and in which French therefore also replaced Latin, made things worse: the more French literature was being taught in secondary school, the more people viewed it with suspicion.

Even after the *lycée* gradually and reluctantly made room for French literature in its curriculum, the change from Latin rhetoric to French commentary took a long time. The French "composition" was at first merely a transposition of the traditional "amplification" exercise, based on a French rather than Latin literary text, and therefore prone to an inherent contradiction: the amplification of a Latin text involved translation, and therefore interpretation; it was not at all clear what a French amplification of a French text was supposed to be, other than a mere rewording, paraphrase, or other form of repetition. Such exercises had a self-evident purpose in Latin that seemed completely lacking in French. In response to this realization, the work of translation of the classical text was replaced by contextualization: the French text, because it is a fragment of a larger piece and/or an author's complete work, must be "explicated" by placing it in relation to the context from which it came, a task that is still the essential starting point of the *explication* exercise to this day (Massol 68–9).

But contextualization is still an exercise in erudition rather than interpretation, much less self-expression, and the designers of the canonical literary exercise felt that more was needed to replace adequately the Latin paradigm. The creation of secondary general education in French literature presented the pedagogical establishment with an opportunity: by writing in French, students could finally be considered *authors* rather than imitators. For the past 150 years, much of the debate has centered on the radical and disorienting revelation that students can, and maybe should, be granted authority in every sense of the term. Long before Jean Piaget, Maria Montessori, Paulo Freire, and others disrupted the teacher-student hierarchy, a similar revolution broke out in the field of literary pedagogy, though it remains, as we will see, an unfinished project. The promise, however, was visible to all: Fortoul's invention of a new type of French literature exam within the new science track in the *lycée* was accompanied by attempts to solve the dilemma of justifying the change from Latin to French through memos and special instructions. The 1852 instructions that accompanied the French-heavy science track, for example, defined *explication française* as an analysis by the student of "la valeur des mots...propriété des termes, leurs rapports, leurs acceptions...liaison des idées...quelle forme leur donne le raisonnement ou l'imagination, quels sentiments elles éveillent" [the value of words, appropriateness of terms, their relationships to each other, their usage, the connections between ideas, the shape given to them by reason or imagination, which feelings they elicit] (quoted in Jey 79–80). Only the reference to "ideas" and "feelings" gave an indication of what the student was supposed to write about; the work on terminology, usage, and appropriateness all traditionally belonged to the category of work necessary to decipher a text in an ancient language. At best, the new French exercise seemed too easy, and at worst, redundant. Clearly, the authorities had more work to do, and the educational reforms of the Third Republic, at the end of the nineteenth and start of the twentieth centuries, were the result.

The *amplification (composition) latine* was replaced by the *composition française* in the watershed year of 1880 that saw the official end of the long process of monopolization of education by the state. In 1890, the *composition française* changed to become a commentary on or explication of French literary texts, rather than an amplification, as it had been since 1853, and was finally given equal status with the Greek or Latin exercises that had survived the earlier reforms (Jey 82). The composition was supposed to solve the problem of paraphrase or repetition simply by forbidding those techniques, and replacing the author's text with the student's text. The instructions and related documents from the ministry during the 1890s explicitly and consistently forbade "*amplification stérile*" and "paraphrase", and encouraged individual judgment in the form of "*un discours critique et sincère*" ["a sincere and critical discourse"] (quoted in Houdart-Merot 49). At long last, with the word "sincere", the idea of modern self-expression as opposed to classical imitation emerged as a pedagogical goal in literary education. Debates over the degree to which self-expression *actually* occurs, or should occur in the work of students, continue up to the present day.

This change in definition of the term *composition française* (which later evolved into *la dissertation*, a term from higher education designating an essay that is focused on literature exclusively), naturally raised the question: what is the student's text made of, what is its content, if it is no longer simply a rewording of the original, as in the Latin exercises? On what authority is a mere *lycée* student supposed to produce "*un jugement critique et sincère*", in other words, to speak in his[13] own name, and not in the name, or style, of the author being studied? Lack of faith in the validity of individual student expression presented a challenge. Partly, it was the universal challenge of all literature teachers: how can the student speak from a position of authority? In addition, it reflected an epistemological crisis: if the necessity of writing commentary on a classical text is due to the opacity of the language, then the relative clarity of the modern vernacular presents a problem. Therefore, the fact that it is harder to master Latin than one's native language, but also the idea that literary value itself is ultimately beyond explication, enigmatic, and opaque, whereas the French language is by nature clear and self-evident (Jey 75), are some of the factors in the continuing quarrel between "ancients and moderns", and between "literarians" and "utilitarians".

Partly in order to provide students with the authority to comment on texts, literary history was officially added to the curriculum in 1885. Although it was removed during the sweeping reforms to the *lycée* of 1902, its long-term effect on literary study in France, as we know, was profound (Houdart-Merot 32). Gustave Lanson, whose influence on the creation of the modern canonical literary exercise during his career at the Ecole Normale Supérieure and the Sorbonne cannot be exaggerated, recommended that the ministry institute the "*commentaire écrit*" [written commentary], an explicitly interpretive rather than explicative exercise, as one of the options available to candidates for the *bac* starting in 1895, precisely in order to solve the contradiction of requiring a "French amplification" based on the classical model (Jey 101). During the brief period of time during which these reforms occurred, the reaction by professors and professional critics to the introduction of literary history in the curriculum ranged from passionate advocacy to virulent rejection, as literary studies experienced one of the many attempts to make it a "science" rather than an art.

The professors and critics responsible for the academic discipline of French realized that literature as general education presented a brand new challenge. It had traditionally been their task to justify the discipline of literature on its own terms: the institution of literature and its ever-changing corpus of texts exists; therefore, we need to learn, and teach others, to become readers. Its legitimacy is no different from that of the systematic teaching of music and art. By the 1880s, however, the teaching of literature had come up against a new challenge: to take an academic discipline designed to train a small cadre of experts (future literature teachers), or to provide social distinction to the upper classes, and "make it relevant" to a much larger group: not only the growing ranks of *lycéens*, but the even larger ranks undergoing some other form of general secondary education.[14]

In the spirit of replacing the rhetorical tradition with one more appropriate for a growing (though still very small and exclusively male) population, 1880 saw the elimination of the exercise in Latin verse, the genre that had provided Rimbaud with his first taste of poetic fame when he earned first prize in the national *Concours académique* of 1869 for his epic poem "Jugurtha" (Lindaman 115–8). Because composition of French verse was not considered pedagogically viable, poetry lost its status as the literary genre par excellence: students from then on only wrote in prose (Houdart-Merot 30). Of course, it is debatable whether the ability to translate Latin and Greek texts into French, and even to compose texts in those languages, is the best "literary" education. What is not debatable is that in the transition from classical languages to the vernacular in the literature classroom, a vast amount of what people understood to be the essence of literature, an early version of "literariness" which in the nineteenth century depended largely on the text's difficulty, was lost. Not only did students cease to compose literary texts, even if those had been limited to the genre of pastiche (such as Rimbaud's "Jugurtha"), they required "content" for the new types of essays they were required to write. What could that content be, if it was not a crude version of the self-identified "impressionistic" literary criticism that was fashionable during the *fin de siècle*, such as that of Ferdinand Brunetière and Jules Lemaître (see Chapter 4)?

Notes

1. The American Association of Colleges and Universities in 2007 published a useful history of the "outcomes assessment" movement, *A Brief History of Student Learning Assessment: How We Got Where We Are and a Proposal for Where to Go Next*. It reveals that standardized testing began around 1900, long before the start of the current debate on the economic value of education. This first phase of general education quantification culminated, between 1928 and 1932, in a massive experimental assessment of thousands of Pennsylvania high school and university students in literature, history,

English, science, math, and intelligence (I.Q.), financed by the Carnegie Foundation (Shavelson 6).
2. See *Strong Performers and Successful Reformers in Education: Lessons from PISA for the United States* (233–7), in which the OECD recognizes the Common Core as a strategy for improving the performance of American students on the PISA exam that it designs and administers.
3. There is some standardized testing in France administered at the end of elementary school and the end of middle school, as part of the government's statistical studies on education (see *Repères et références statistiques sur les enseignements, la formation et la recherche* [Statistical reference points on teaching, training, and research] 2013). In general, though, French students do not have anywhere near the familiarity with such testing formats as do American ones.
4. In 2015, according to the French Ministry of Education, 77.2 percent of students in the appropriate age group sat for the *baccalauréat* exam. The 22.8 percent who did not do so mostly were enrolled in various kinds of vocational training, such as apprenticeships. The *lycée* itself is now divided into three separate tracks: "general" or pre-university (49 percent of the total *lycée* enrollment), "technological" (20 percent), and "professional" (31 percent). Students enrolled in the latter two pre-professional tracks still must undergo a literature exam as part of the *bac* in their penultimate year. (http://www.education.gouv.fr/cid56455/le-baccalaureat-2015-session-de-juin.html)
5. Since 1880, partly as part of the strategy to diminish the educational role of the Catholic Church, the French Republic has had a monopoly on the authority to issue diplomas of higher education (*"le monopole de la collation des grades"*, *Code de l'éducation*, article L613-1). Because the *bac* is considered to be the first in the series of university degrees, it can only be issued by the government.
6. Any anxiety that American high school students feel when taking the SAT, ACT, or even AP exams is small compared to the fear most French students have of the *bac*, even the relatively easier versions of today. Psychologically, there is at least some balance once the testing is over: American students in their final year are more likely to face debilitating stress over the college admissions and financial aid process. In France, once the *bac* is in hand, going to university is a relatively straightforward process, and while financial challenges exist, especially for students who do not plan to live with their parents, tuition fees are trivial. On the other hand, French universities experience higher student attrition rates over the first two years than American ones. There is no greener grass on either side of the fence, it seems.
7. On the left of the political spectrum, for example, is sociologist Michel Fize and his book *Le Bac inutile* [The Useless Bac 2012], who argues for

replacing the exam with "*contrôle continu*", or grades earned throughout the student's career. That is roughly how the American system works if one removes standardized national tests, which more and more colleges no longer require for admission. On the right, philosopher Thibaud Collin advocates a return to the past, complaining that because a large majority of the population now takes the *bac*, about 90 percent of whom pass, it has become "une grande tartufferie quasi soviétique" [a giant, quasi-soviet hypocrisy] ("Faut-il supprimer le baccalauréat ?" [should one eliminate the *baccalauréat*], *Le Figaro*, June 17, 2014). Of course, it is precisely because the *bac* is no longer an elitist institution that it can truly be considered part of general education, and in spite of these attacks, it shows no sign of going away soon.

8. The written portion of the College Board's *Advanced Placement* test in English literature is very close to the literature *bac* in its level of difficulty, and even in the kinds of tasks it requires. In the 2012 exam, students had to write three essays based on the following prompts, each prompt followed by a poem, excerpt, or list of works: (1) "In the following poem by Sir Philip Sidney (1554–1586), the speaker addresses the subject of desire. Read the poem carefully. Then write a well-developed essay in which you analyze how poetic devices help to convey the speaker's complex attitude toward desire." (2) "Carefully read the following excerpt from the novel *Under the Feet of Jesus* by Helena María Viramontes. Then write a well-organized essay in which you analyze the development of Estrella's character. In your analysis, you may wish to consider such literary elements as selection of detail, figurative language, and tone." (3) For their third essay, students are given a list of literary works and asked the following: "Choose a novel or play in which cultural, physical, or geographical surroundings shape psychological or moral traits in a character. Then write a well-organized essay in which you analyze how surroundings affect this character and illuminate the meaning of the work as a whole." (*AP® English Literature and Composition Free-Response Questions*). The biggest difference between this and the written portion of the *bac* is that the College Board recommends 40 minutes per essay, and the *bac* allows four hours for the short answer(s) plus one essay. Of course, the AP exam is taken by a relatively small minority of high school seniors, whereas the *bac* is mandatory for all *lycée* students.

9. Those familiar with French secondary education often point out that the top grade, 20 out of 20, is almost never awarded. That is still mostly true, even though every year a few dozen students manage to pass the *bac* with an *average* grade in *all* subjects of 20. Today, one's average can even be higher than twenty, thanks to a complicated system whereby a fraction of the grade received on an optional subject test can be added to the student's average in all the required subjects. Thus, if a student's average is already 19 or 20,

which places him or her in the top tenth of one percent overall, the optional subject grade can increase the average to a number slightly higher than 20. (http://www.education.gouv.fr/cid80074/les-options-au-baccalaureat-general-en-2013-tres-peu-d-impact-sur-la-reussite.html). The fact that this happens so rarely, however, contributes to the long-held belief that the test is never a mechanical measure of achievement: the grades on the *bac* and the scores on the SAT, though both are numbers, at least appear to reflect entirely different standards of measurement, one subjective and human, the other objective and mechanical.

10. Some may argue that, although imitating Latin and Greek authors does not constitute literary creation, it is nevertheless an excellent form of training for future authors. Indeed, most members of the pantheon of French literature up to the mid-twentieth century spent a portion of their school years on such exercises, which no doubt had a determining influence on their style. There is a large body of scholarship on the relationship between "classical" secondary education and literary production, whether on the French neo-classical period (Paul Bénichou, *Morales du grand siècle* [*Man and Ethics: Studies in French Classicism*]), the reactionary anti-modernist movement in literature (Gaëlle Guyot, *Latin et Latinité dans l'oeuvre de Léon Bloy* [Latin and Latinity in the works of Léon Bloy]) and even on anti-establishment figures such as Arthur Rimbaud (Romain Jalabert, "Le latin dans l'œuvre de Rimbaud" [Latin in the Works of Rimbaud]). One must remember, however, that we are talking about general education: the fact that many French writers of the past had been influenced by the Latin compositions they created in their youth is interesting, but does not prove that such pedagogy was of benefit to their contemporaries who did not become literary authors, much less to the French population at large that is required to study literature today.

11. See for example the interview of Marc Fumaroli in the conservative daily *Le Figaro* of March 31, 2015: "Les humanités au péril d'un monde numérique" [classical languages under threat from a digital world].

12. The education of girls and young women was a separate institution. Even after the *bac* was officially opened to women in 1924 (there had been isolated instances of women passing the exam prior to that year), the segregation of schools by gender continued until well after the cultural revolution of May 1968. The story of female education and its relation to the issues discussed here is found in Rebecca Rogers's work, including the landmark study *From the Salon to the Schoolroom: Educating Bourgeois Girls in Nineteenth-Century France* (2005). One very important aspect of female education is that even before the French Revolution, girls had far less exposure to classical languages than boys. The earliest secondary curricula in French literature were therefore mostly developed for female education.

As a result, for many years expertise on national literature was more common among women than men, a fact that did not make the job easier for those who tried to make the study of French equal in prestige to the study of Greek and Latin.

13. I use masculine pronouns when referring to *lycée* education prior to 1924, the year when girls were officially allowed to study for the *bac*, even though there had been individual cases of girls taking the *bac* since the mid-nineteenth century.

14. The tiny, yet growing population of young men who attended the *lycée* was part of a much larger secondary school population. The secondary education levels in which the teaching of literature also grew in importance, mostly French as opposed to classical, were the years of *collège* immediately prior to the *lycée*; the institution of *enseignement spécial*, a Latin-free, pre-professional and practical alternative to the *lycée* instituted by Minister Victor Duruy in 1865; and the *cours primaire supérieur*, a continuation of primary education that was accessible to a much larger population than the social elite. Last but not least, a significant portion of the female population had its own system of public secondary education, established by Camille Sée in 1880. Each of these alternatives had its own exam apparatus that influenced the content of the curriculum the way the *bac* did for the *lycée*.

CHAPTER 4

Inventing and Defending the General Education of Literature

THE 1902 REFORMS AND THE FIRST GREAT CRISIS OF FRENCH

The reinvention of literary pedagogy based on French explication rather than Latin composition peaked in 1902 with reforms to the *baccalauréat* recommended by Alexandre Ribot,[1] a centrist politician who thereby became one of the founders of the general education of literature, as opposed to literary pedagogy for the elites. The reforms separated the exam into four tracks, with varying emphases on science, literature, and modern languages. One of those tracks allowed students for the first time in history to take the exam without undergoing a single "*épreuve*" [test] of Latin. Partly, as a result of this revolutionary change, the designation of the penultimate year of the *lycée* as "*année de rhétorique*" [year of rhetoric] was discontinued. The reform symbolized the Republic's attempt at democratization, at taking literature out of the hands of an elite and placing it at the center of the process of civic instruction. As Michel Leroy points out in *Peut-on enseigner la littérature française?* [can one teach French literature? 2001], the democratization of literature became a conflict between "*goût*" [taste] and "*érudition*", "un effet paradoxal de la victoire des Modernes sur les Anciens, et donc de la reconnaissance d'une littérature française" ["a paradoxical consequence of the victory of the Moderns over the Ancients, and therefore of the recognition of French literature"] (8). For the first time, the idea of viewing literary study no longer as a marker of social distinction, but rather as one of the foundations of general education, was taken seriously at the highest levels. The year 1902 marked the first major defeat of the rhetorical tradition in the form of a challenge to the legitimacy of "taste", the mysterious ability to make qualitative judgments on a work of art, in favor of the more objective, and therefore more easily teachable, realm of facts. Using scientific concepts in the study of culture, however, immediately brought to light problems both political (the attack on the ideology that culture is the exclusive province of the elite) and philosophical (the question of what constitutes literariness itself):

> Comment fonder cet enseignement... que l'on vient d'inventer? sur l'histoire, la science dominante... à la Sorbonne et qui empiète, dans le secondaire, sur l'enseignement d'histoire de la littérature, au risque de voir le monument littéraire traité en document? sur la philologie, suspecte d'influence germanique, et d'ailleurs trop éloignée des possibilités des jeunes élèves ?... Rien d'étonnant si... on parle déjà de crise.
>
> [How does one found this discipline that has just been invented? On history, the dominant science at the Sorbonne, and which encroaches on the discipline of literary history in secondary education, at the risk of seeing the literary monument treated like a document? On philology, suspected of being a Germanic influence, and anyway deemed out of reach of the abilities of young students? It is not surprising that one already speaks of a crisis.]
> (Leroy 208)

The crisis therefore opposed the rhetorical approach of the Jesuit tradition and the new, historical approach (associated with the Sorbonne, Gustave Lanson, and perhaps even more closely with his disciples, such as Gustave Rudler and Daniel Mornet, who are often blamed for giving *Lansonisme* a bad name). In addition to the 1902 reforms, symbolic changes to the institutional setting of literary studies had recently exacerbated the conflict, including the establishment of the new French university system in 1896 upon scientific principles modeled on the German tradition, an event that many considered a legacy of France's defeat in 1871 and therefore a further sign of national shame. While the percentage of the population taking the bac was not to increase above single digits until well after 1945, the shocking removal of the obligatory Latin exam was seen as an inappropriate response to the increase in numbers of students. It lowered the standards of instruction in two ways: firstly, by dispensing with the challenge of Latin and secondly by replacing literary sensibility with positive facts. Adding to the erosion of standards, the

Ministry of Instruction decided in 1907 to allow certain students who had not passed the *bac* or even been to a *lycée* but had simply a "*brevet supérieur*", to enter the new university system, further legitimizing the "modern" tracks in which teachers and students experimented new methodologies (Massol 67).[2] These events were considered part of an intentional decline in quality orchestrated to allow for easier access to higher education comparable, in the United States, to the revolution in higher education sparked by the G.I. Bill.

The ensuing reaction has a familiar ring to anyone involved with education over the last 50 years: accusations of "dumbing down", of declining standards, of the substitution of a timeless, sacred canon by an infinitely variable literary production tied to ever-changing historical conditions. The transition implied in the invention of the discipline of literary history was from the general to the particular, from the universal to the national, from the abstract to the concrete, from the theological to the scientific; it opposed critics against historians, rightists against leftists, and even, as stated above, the *Ecole Normale Supérieure* against the Sorbonne. The extent to which this debate can itself be abstracted from the history of the Third Republic and speak to contemporary concerns will help shed light on the question of whether the recurrent "crisis" in the teaching of literature is inherent in literary pedagogy itself.

Officially, the discourse on literature, supported by positive knowledge defined as historical knowledge, replaced the literary exercise defined as the mimetic rendering of an exemplary text. How did teachers and students respond? In other words, how successful was the transition from a literary practice to a practice that is largely nonliterary, from *amplificatio* and *inventio* to *eruditio*? Determining pedagogical practice at any given time is harder than studying educational policy and the reaction to it of scholars and critics, as it can only be done by examining actual student work. I will now return to Violaine Houdart-Merot's work on literary pedagogy in the *lycée*, and an important discovery she made about the evolution of the discipline: that it was far more radical in theory than in practice. She discovered the persistence of the literary exercise conceived as a form of literary writing, long after it had been officially replaced beginning in 1880 by an emphasis on reading. Indeed, for most of the nineteenth century, educators viewed the act of reading literature with suspicion. "*Lecture cursive*", meaning reading longer works in their entirety instead of concentrating on short texts and excerpts, and "*lecture privée*", meaning reading literature outside of the school, had no pedagogical status, and "culture" was defined as historical knowledge (17); before 1880, alternatives to Latin and Greek were largely relegated to *enseignement spécial* (the alternative, "practical" secondary track instituted by Victor Duruy in 1864), or the brief period of Fortoul's "bifurcation" of *lycée* tracks between literature and sciences in 1852 (mentioned in Chapter 3), that gave science students more freedom to complete their literature requirement in French. After 1880, things changed: as mentioned earlier, Jules Ferry elevated the "*composition française*" to the same rank as "*composition latine*" and eliminated the exercise of Latin verse composition.

Examining actual student work from the French literature portion of the *bac* as well as the even more selective *Concours général*,[3] Houdart-Merot discovered that the methodological revolution of the final decades of the nineteenth century occurred at the level of public policy, but not in the classroom. She gives numerous examples of the resistance to change, such as the fact that the radically new emphasis on literary history expressed itself as an old-fashioned "cult of admiration" in which, against all directives from above that require sincerity and exercise of individual judgment, the student practices what Gustave Lanson called "*psittacisme*" [parroting], the automatic repetition of recognized interpretations (see Chapter 6). Building on the ornithological metaphor of *psittacisme*, Houdart-Merot quotes Georges Darien's novel *Le Voleur* (1897), in which the narrator describes an essay topic he was given while practicing for the *bac*: to demonstrate the truth of the claim that "Bossuet [est] un aigle, et Fénelon [est] un cygne" [Bossuet is an eagle, and Fénelon is a swan]. The obvious way to receive a high grade would be to enthuse about the majesty and authority of Bossuet's oratorical style in contrast with Fénelon's equally admirable yet simple elegance, in order to justify the clichés that had attached to each one over the centuries and had come to replace any serious engagement with their texts. Darien's reaction: "Plumages!" [an apt translation might be "Horsefeathers"!] (quoted in Houdart-Merot, 36).

In other examples of student work, literary history takes the form primarily of biographical information on the author, but not on the far more comprehensive study of periods and genres advocated by the Sorbonne. Why? Because, armed with such personal information, students can more effectively produce the canonical "epistolary" literary exercise, the purpose of which is to pretend to be the author and to write in his or her name (38). The word "imitation" was banished from the official instructions and the descriptions of the exercises themselves, but not its practice. As late as 1923–1925, the official instructions from the Ministry still measured the value of literary texts according to their status as "un modèle de composition [pour l'élève]" [a model for the student's composition] (44), meaning that students must avoid reproducing the content of the original literary text, at the same time as they must emulate its style. In practice, the open-ended creative composition exercise was rarely either critical or sincere; it bore a close resemblance to the exercise of the *version latine*, the translation/summary/amplification of a text, minus the translation, since it is all in French. (53) "[M]ême des sujets qui, de prime abord, semblent être des sujets d'analyse, sont traités en fait selon la logique de l'amplification" [Even topics that at first glance seem suitable for an analytical treatment are in practice treated according to the logic of amplification] (55). Shifting her attention from the students' writing to the professors' comments, Houdart-Merot writes that "Les remarques concernant la construction du devoir l'emportent...sur les critiques touchant au style ou à l'expression écrite" [Comments on the construction of the exercise outnumber those on its style or on the written expression] (56). "[L]'aptitude à 'disposer' son développement fait partie des compétences requises de l'enseignement du français" [the ability to organize the development of the exercise is one of the required skills in French instruction], a standard that continues to prevail well into the twentieth century (58).

Amplification, the most common exercise of the rhetorical tradition that was being replaced, continued therefore to dominate the teaching of literature. "[I]l n'y a...d'invention, ni au sens de la rhétorique classique, dans laquelle la recherche des arguments se fait à l'intérieur d'un catalogue...ni au sens des Instructions de 1880, pour lesquelles il s'agit de trouver les principales idées par soi-même, puisque l'exercice de composition consiste à développer une thèse préexistante à partir d'éléments donnés d'emblée" [There is neither invention in the sense of classical rhetoric, according to which one searches for arguments in a catalog, nor in the sense of the official instructions of 1880, according to which it was necessary to come up with arguments on one's own, since the composition exercise consisted in developing a preexisting hypothesis using elements already provided] (60). *Elocutio* was subordinate to *dispositio* because it was assumed to have already been learned: in other words, linguistic competence (grammar, vocabulary, and even style) were considered preliminary and even, in a sense, pre-literary: *dispositio* was the measure of success on the written portion of the *bac*, and therefore of literariness. In whatever form, rhetoric continued to dominate: "dans tous ces devoirs sont perceptibles des traces importantes d'un savoir-faire rhétorique, alors que toutes ces copies ne relèvent pas de l'enseignement classique avec latin" [in all of these exercises one can discern significant evidence of rhetorical skill, despite the fact that all the examples of student work do not pertain to classical instruction in Latin] (64). In other words, even students who had never studied Latin – most females, for example, and the students of *primaire supérieur* and *enseignement spécial* who were not preparing the *bac*, were nevertheless evaluated as if they had done so, according to the mastery of classical rhetoric founded on mimesis. Houdart-Merot gives a sense of these standards of evaluation: "la culture littéraire n'est pas évaluée seulement à travers les exemples littéraires donnés ou les connaissances factuelles, biographiques ou historiques qui pourraient servir d'arguments, mais aussi à travers le style du candidat et sa capacité à reprendre des formes littéraires ou des figures de style assimilés grâce à la lecture des écrivains" [the literary culture (of a student) is not evaluated only according to the use of literary examples or the level of factual knowledge, but also according to the candidate's style, and his or her ability to imitate literary forms or stylistic devices assimilated through the reading of authors] (67). The official instructions condemned plagiarism, writes Houdart-Merot, "mais pas toujours les professeurs" [but professors did not always do so] (69). Standards of literariness inherited from the Jesuit tradition, understood as mimesis both in the sense of restricting the literary canon to works that claim fidelity to the outside world, and imitation of classical style, continued to define literary studies in the *lycée*, long after the Ministry had declared them irrelevant.

Why did literary pedagogy retain for so long the characteristics that one can trace back to the *Ratio Studiorum*? Part of an answer lies in common sense. Resistance to change was simply part of a natural process, and educational reform takes time. Teachers do not radically change methods in mid-career. No doubt that all is true. But there is another argument that helps explain why the old methods persisted and in some ways continue to influence French literary pedagogy to this day. The practice of modeling one's own oral or written discourse on canonical texts was broadly recognized as a way of teaching literature that was itself literary. Resistance to history, as the most visible form of opposition to the principles of republican education, was so strong because the old rhetorical techniques, inasmuch as they did not rely on erudition, critical thinking, or positive knowledge, were self-evidently literary. The assumption at the time, still common today, was that the discipline of literature could legitimately exist separately from other disciplines, such as history, *only* if it was itself *literary*. Imitation of classical texts is an apprenticeship in the practical application of that which distinguishes literary texts from everyday speech, beginning with the fact that they are in a language other than French. But what "literariness", if any, survived in the reformers' desire to replace Latin verse with French commentary?

By 1890, when the theoretical groundwork for the positivist reforms of 1902 was being laid, it was not simply the Catholic, conservative attachment to Jesuit rhetoric that posed a problem. The very reasonable argument that the teaching of literature should result in an active understanding of literary value, through the acts of speaking and writing, clashed with the democratic and demystifying impetus of the educational establishment, resulting in a "culture war" that rivaled, and in some ways reproduced, the battles surrounding the Dreyfus Affair (Chaitin 17-44). We now turn to the effects of this conflict between the preservation of value on the one hand, and its democratization on the other.

GUSTAVE LANSON, HENRI BOUASSE, AND THE PEDAGOGY OF PRAGMATISM

In 1909, when the reactionary resistance against the shift from a literary (mostly rhetorical) teaching of literature to a nonliterary (mostly historical) one was at its peak, Gustave Lanson gave a speech at the National Museum of Pedagogy in which he patiently explained why it is necessary to find nonliterary methods of teaching literature in response to a new crisis: the increasing number of students from families that did not subscribe to pseudo-aristocratic culture, and who rejected the notion that learning Latin, or even classical French literature, had intrinsic value.[4] Hard as it is for us to believe, the secondary schools of the *Belle époque* contained students who, though still representing a tiny and privileged fraction of the general population, no longer identified with aristocratic standards of cultural legitimacy. Lanson began his speech with demographics. When the *bac* was first administered in 1809, he said, there were 50,000 students in secondary schools, a tiny fraction of whom went on to actually take the exam; in 1909, there were 170,000 enrolled, including a much higher proportion of candidates to the *bac*. Because education minister Alfred de Falloux in 1850 had established "freedom of instruction", which meant the right of private (mainly Catholic) education to continue to exist, the competition between government and the clergy in secondary education was destined to continue, even after the 1905 law establishing the separation of Church and State. Acknowledging this historical reality, Lanson said that the Church had a major advantage in the area of literary pedagogy: its students, who came from upper-class, conservative Catholic families where they practically absorbed the French and classical literary traditions like mothers' milk.

> [N]ous avons gardé les enfants de la bourgeoisie aisée... des protestants, des israélites, un certain nombre de catholiques libéraux, un certain nombre d'étrangers, mais un très grand nombre des familles les plus cultivées nous ont échappé.... [Nos élèves] sont autrement intelligents... [d'une] intelligence droite et saine, mais fruste, toute positive et pratique.
>
> [We have retained the children of the wealthy middle class...some Protestants, some Jews, a few liberal Catholics, some foreigners, but a large number of the best educated families have eluded us. (Our students) are intelligent in other ways, with a direct and healthy intelligence, yet crude, completely positive and practical.] (9–10)

Students with a social background that made them adept at imitating classical texts, or even exercising independent literary judgment (as opposed to *psittacisme*) mostly remained in Catholic schools, and the *lycée* must learn to live without them; in fact the *lycée* seems no longer to be truly French, with its motley population of protestants, Jews, and foreigners, and bereft of the Catholic upper-class students steeped in the French cultural tradition, a situation that Lanson mentions but, to his credit, presents not as a problem so much as a fact, leading perhaps to an opportunity. Today we would look at his analysis differently, and avoid the distinction between two types of intelligence based on social class and religious affiliation. Yet while it is true that nothing distinguishes the level of intelligence of the students of the *lycée* of 1809 from that of the students of 1909 (contrary to Lanson's statement), it is also true that the latter group's willingness to believe in, or simply to enact, certain pedagogical rituals had declined. The question Lanson raised is as relevant today as it was then: how do those responsible for the discipline of literature teach, when students no longer play the game of pretending to be writers or critics of literature? Do economic principles apply, and the supply adapt itself to the demand? What is our responsibility to literature, what is our responsibility to students, and can one reconcile the two? Lanson recognized that "Literature for the sake of literature" was an outmoded and narrow legitimation, suitable for an aristocratic and pre-professional pedagogy, not for literature as general education. "Old-fashioned" rhetoric needed to cede ground to something else, an evolution that did not necessarily imply the expulsion of literariness from the school but might actually prepare for its return in a more accessible and practical form.

The visionary, progressive dimension of Lanson's contribution to literary pedagogy has been overlooked by historians and literary critics, with rare exceptions (see Jey 2008 and Deguy). Nor was he alone in his crusade: pragmatic analyses of the crisis caused in literary pedagogy by the growing disparity between *offre* [supply] and *demande* abounded during this period, such as the one by Henri Bouasse, a famous physics professor from Toulouse who published a vitriolic attack on the conservative resistance to change in the teaching of French titled *Bachot et bachotage: étude sur l'enseignement en France* (1910).[5] One might be surprised to find a physics professor involved in a debate over the teaching of literature, but as we are about to see, the nature of his argument justifies his interest in the topic. It is significant that Bouasse's contribution to the field of physics consisted of his unique ability to explain the *practical* applications of physics in a 45 (!) volume series titled *Bibliothèque scientifique de l'ingénieur et du physicien* [scientific library of the engineer and the physicist]. In fact, his considerable influence on the field was limited by his persistent and short-sighted skepticism toward the revolutionary innovations of relativity and quantum theory, which had only recently begun to emerge (Locqueneux). As a die-hard positivist, he failed to appreciate the developments in his own field but was primed to be very sympathetic to reformers in the field of literary studies. In his polemical pamphlet on the French literature *bac*, he blamed the professors and teachers who resisted the 1902 reforms for the same lack of pragmatism that he identified (mistakenly) as the biggest weakness of Planck, Einstein, and their followers. Bouasse espoused therefore an extreme version of the same pragmatism that Lanson and his colleagues defended but from a viewpoint on the other side of the scientific-humanities divide.

At times, Bouasse directs his satiric arsenal not only against the conservatism of his literary colleagues, but against literature itself. For example, he claimed that he would never take a book with him when traveling by train. Instead of reading, he would always stare out the window, regardless of the landscape, "le pays serait-il morne comme la Hongrie, désolé comme un schott saharien. Comment saurez-vous qu'il est monotone ou désolé, si vous ne le regardez pas de longues heures pour que sa monotonie vous pénètre, pour que sa désolation vous consterne ?" [even if the landscape were as drab as Hungary, desolate as a dry lakebed in the Sahara. How would you know it was boring and desolate, if you didn't watch it for hours, so that its monotony would penetrate you and its desolation appall you?] (110) Bouasse promotes in hyperbolic style the cause of radical positivism, according to which a direct experience of the world, no matter how dull, trumps any sort of reading (we'll leave aside the question of whether looking out the window of a moving train counts as "direct experience"): "la moindre vérité découverte par son propre travail est préférable à des monceaux de vérités enseignées" [the smallest truth discovered through one's own effort is preferable to mounds of taught truths] (108).

At a later point in his argument, Bouasse showed that however biased he may be in favor of empirical observation, he held no grudge against literature itself, as long as reading it is a matter of free choice rather than submission to arbitrary, time-honored rituals. He recounted the following anecdote which views the absurdity of the French system of education from a foreign perspective:

> [U]ne juive de Varsovie [est] venue en France pour acquérir le diplôme. A l'écrit du bachot on lui demande de choisir trois auteurs dont l'intimité égayera ses vacances. Les candidats mâles se précipitent sur Bossuet, sur Voltaire et sur Hugo, atténuant Voltaire par Bossuet, laïcisant Bossuet grâce à Voltaire. Notre jeune fille choisit Goethe, Macauley et Brandès, tout simplement parce qu'elle les avait lus et les aimait...elle eut un deux.
>
> [A Jewish woman from Warsaw came to France to obtain her diploma. During the written portion of the *bac*, she is asked to choose three authors whose intimacy will enliven her summer vacation. The male candidates for the exam throw themselves on Bossuet, Voltaire, and Hugo, rendering Voltaire less radical with Bossuet, making Bossuet less religious thanks to Voltaire. Our young woman chose Goethe, Macauley and Brandès, simply because she had read them and liked them...she received a grade of two (out of twenty).] (129–30)

"Sincerity" and "freedom" are indeed neglected values in this story, which incidentally proves that female candidates could take the *bac* under certain conditions, even before it officially opened up to both genders in 1924.

In another anecdote intended to illustrate the bankruptcy of literary pedagogy, Bouasse argued that the young Polish Jewess's experience was not as bad as what happened to his own nephew, a scientist like himself, during the oral portion of the French literature *bac*. The naïve young man made a dangerous confession to his examiner, a literature professor from Toulouse whom Bouasse does not hesitate to name: Moutonnard. When Professor Moutonnard asked the nephew a question about the orator-cleric Bossuet, he replied that he never much liked him (probably finding his work "as drab as Hungary"), and received a grade of "zéro pour prix de la franchise" [zero (out of 20) as a reward for honesty] (132). Perhaps he would have done better if the examiner had asked about Voltaire instead.

Of course we don't know whether Bouasse's anecdotes are true, and if they are, what else the young Jewess from Warsaw wrote, or Bouasse's nephew said, when both of them sat for the French literature *bac*. Maybe their failing grades were well deserved, though one has to admit that the claim that they were penalized for ignoring the ritual constraints of the exercise is plausible. The topic the young woman chose was the ancestor of today's "*écriture d'invention*" or creative option, an open-ended question that candidates are allowed to select in lieu of the narrowly constrained commentary on a specific text. The task probably appeared on the examination more or less as follows: "Choose three authors whose works you would like to take with you on summer vacation, and explain why". She made the mistake of thinking that an "open topic" implied that she was free to give an honest answer, so she chose her three favorite authors. Not only was it a mistake to choose a German, an Englishman, and a Dane instead of three French authors, but even had she chosen French ones, she still probably would not have done what the other (male) candidates did, according to Bouasse. Knowing the rules of the game, they limited themselves to the short list of legitimate, patrimonial authors, as if nothing else were appropriate for long days on the beach or in the mountains, and submitted those conventional choices to a time-honored ritual: if you choose a free thinker like Voltaire, you must choose an orthodox Catholic like Bossuet to counterbalance him, and vice versa. The fact that the official instructions ask that candidates express "sincere critical opinions" does not mean that one can admit out loud that one finds a canonical author boring. Bouasse, more than Lanson, but nevertheless in a Lansonist mode, rejects the claim that literary pedagogy can simultaneously remain literary (rhetorical or critical) and claim relevance for general education. The discipline must reach out of itself, connect with (and even subordinate itself) to other fields of inquiry, and most importantly of all, acknowledge people's pre-existing relationship to literature, if it is to be a required topic (even though in 1910, preparation for the bac was a general education requirement that still affected less than 3 percent of the male population).

THE "QUARREL OF THE SORBONNE" AND THE RETURN OF RHETORIC

For the advocates of literary history, it was a question of bringing scientific rigor to literary studies so as to grant the discipline a place in the new scientific university in the nationalization of French higher education in 1896. Parallel developments occurred in the United States, such as the founding of the University of Chicago in 1891 – this was indeed an international phenomenon. They also sought to put an end to the "impressionistic" school of literary criticism that founded its legitimacy on the rhetorical training of the classical curriculum taught in the *lycée*, epitomized by Ferdinand Brunetière who at the time was a dominant figure in the *Ecole normale supérieure*, in the general education of literature (with his popular *Manuel de la littérature française*), and in the literary press (*Mercure de France, Revue des deux mondes*, and others). Another sworn foe of the Sorbonne was Jules Lemaître, whose *Impressions de théâtre*, a collection of his theater criticism published in ten volumes between 1888 and 1898, reinforced the desire to elevate "impressionism" to the level of legitimate critical method. The problem with the individualist or "impressionist" school of criticism was that it defined literary interpretation as an art form; to make "impressionism" the basis for passing the *bac* made about as much sense as requiring all *lycée* students to demonstrate artistic talent, a proposition that may not be as illogical as it sounded at the time. It may well be that the late nineteenth-century turn against subjective criticism in literary pedagogy, while it was a well-intended move toward democratizing secondary education, was a major source of the crisis of the discipline that endures to this day.

Against the tradition of the talented amateur who engages in a subjective exercise of close reading, the "*Nouvelle Sorbonne*", the flagship of the revitalized and expanded French university system of 1896 onward, sought to impose a scientific approach in order to mediate between the reader, the text, and the author; it was based upon the recasting of the discipline of history (represented by Charles Seignobos, Charles-Victor Langlois, Gabriel Monod), the creation of the discipline of Sociology (Emile Durkheim), and the annexation of literary studies by those same two dominant fields (Gustave Lanson and his disciples). The invention of these disciplines is an integral part of an archeology of knowledge characteristic of higher education during the last decades of the Third Republic, beginning in the 1890s. The controversial aspect of the new pedagogy centered on the new historical methods in the literature department or *faculté de lettres* on the model of the *faculté d'histoire* which itself, in an unusual occurrence of symmetry, had recently been purged of the "literary", unscientific, and hence "impressionistic" historiographical tradition that had dominated the nineteenth century, from Jules Michelet to Numa Denis Fustel de Coulanges. Just as history went from being a literary genre to being a science, in other words, literary studies followed the same trajectory, first in the university, then in secondary education.

The confusion surrounding the battle over the *Nouvelle Sorbonne* arises from the fact that it was not simply a matter of replacing literary analysis in the University (and later, in secondary education) by history, but rather of using history as a tool for literary analysis, which is a far more complicated question. Lanson's role in the revolution of literary studies was misunderstood as an imposition of university-level historical research upon, and even against, humanistic literary studies, whereas Antoine Compagon suggests that it was actually an attempt to merge the new university with the traditional role of the *lycée*: "La complémentarité naturelle de l'histoire littéraire, chose du supérieur, et de l'explication française, chose du secondaire, toutes deux tendent harmonieusement vers la dissertation, comme la chose littéraire par excellence depuis que la rhétorique n'est plus." ["The natural complementarity of literary history, belonging to higher education, and French (literary) explication, belonging to secondary education, both converge harmoniously toward the dissertation, the literary exercise par excellence, since rhetoric no longer exists"] (89). Lanson's caution in limiting history to a subordinate role in literary analysis was not always shared by his disciples, a fact that gave "*Lansonisme*" a dogmatic and antiliterary reputation that set the stage for the counter-revolution of the "*nouvelle critique*" led by Roland Barthes in the 1960s. Henri Peyre led a small movement in defense of Lanson in 1965, just as the famous quarrel between Barthes-and Raymond Picard was reaching its peak, by presenting some of Lanson's texts in anthology form: *Essais de méthode, de critique et d'histoire littéraire*. In the early 1900s, however,

Lanson's methods, which had not yet hardened into what later become known as *Lansonisme*, were under attack from a very different direction, by a culturally reactionary, mostly but not exclusively Catholic faction, that called for a return to pre-1880 literary pedagogy, including the repeal of the 1902 reforms.[6]

Charles Péguy was one of the first to lead the charge, representing a culturally conservative (yet still socialist), Catholic, and very popular viewpoint; he attacked the atheism of the new historiography that presumed to find truth exclusively through empirical means, in a series of polemical articles republished as *L'Argent* and *L'Argent suite* [*Money*, and *Money, Continued*] in 1913. As the title implies, *L'Argent* is a broad indictment of modern capitalism, but one that takes education, rather than industry, as its target. Péguy's blend of socialism and Catholic mysticism compelled him to imagine a golden past when workers fulfilled a sacred destiny, epitomized by the builders of great cathedrals: "les ouvriers ne servaient pas. Ils travaillaient.... C'est le principe-même des cathédrales" ["workers did not serve (were not useful). They worked. That is the very principle of cathedrals." (1105).[7] The problem today is that workers "*servent*", that is, "are useful", reduced to fulfilling a narrow task that is meaningless by itself, but useful for the purpose of industrial efficiency. Work was sacred before it was defiled by owners and speculators who stripped it of its moral dimension. The integrity of work was destroyed by mass production, by its transformation from an end in itself into a means to produce wealth; workers no longer enjoyed the moral purity of producing the best possible object out of love of craft. Péguy was alluding, among other ideals, to the peasant values of his parents, who represented the survival of a pre-industrial and pre-capitalist values in the midst of modernity.

But if Péguy was angry at capitalism for having turned workers into meaningless parts of a larger, spiritually sterile process, he saved his strongest ire for the academics whom he considered the theorists and apologists of this particular decadence. Instead of history finding its inspiration in literature, which was a manner of redeeming itself, in the above-mentioned tradition extending from Michelet to Fustel de Coulanges, it now saw itself as scientific, in other words as materialistic: nothing is true that cannot be derived from verifiable observation, which in history, now beholden to these positivistic ideals, meant the scientifically valid interpretation of the all-powerful "document". If it were not bad enough that materialism, under the guise of scientism, has corrupted historians' work which now "consiste à démontrer que les héros et les saints n'existent pas" [consists in proving that heroes and saints do not exist] (1160) – hence, the demystifying aspect of the new university at odds with the literary – it has also infected the teaching of literature. It is useful here to point out that critic Antoine Compagnon in *La Troisième République des lettres* (*The Third Republic of Literature*, 1983) warned us against perpetuating a false caricature of Lanson. Lanson's reputation as the one most responsible for the crisis in literary pedagogy was created in large part by these reactionary attacks, in which his method was reduced to stating only historically verifiable truths about a literary text, when in fact Lanson, simply wanted to purge interpretation of its excessive subjectivism, particularly in secondary education.

Péguy was at the start of a long tradition, extending at least until the 1960s, of presenting the "new" literary history of Lanson and his disciples as a simple capitulation when faced with the challenge of expressing the literariness of a text. He accused Lanson of being the agent of the historians and sociologists of the Sorbonne and their materialist and Germanic demystification of saints and heroes (heroism and sainthood representing, for traditional historiography, what "literariness" represents for the "impressionistic school" of criticism):

[L]a querelle de la Sorbonne... est la querelle même des héros et des saints contre le monde moderne, contre ce qu'ils nomment sociologie, contre ce qu'ils nomment psychologie, contre ce qu'ils nomment science. Et une chaire en Sorbonne sera toujours pour celui qui déclare que les saints étaient tous à mettre à Charenton.

[The quarrel of the Sorbonne is the very quarrel of heroes and saints against the modern world, against what they call sociology, what they call psychology, what they call science. And a professorship at the Sorbonne will always be for the one who claims that all of the saints should be committed to Charenton (a famous mental institution).] (1273)

Péguy's attack against scientism in literary studies (and ultimately against the whole notion of "social sciences" as it was being developed) is reflected in the most famous assault against the "Nouvelle Sorbonne", led by Henri Massis and Alfred de Tarde, two former students of the *Ecole Normale Supérieure* who in 1910, under the pseudonym "Agathon", wrote a series of articles in *L'Opinion* that were later republished as *L'Esprit de la Nouvelle Sorbonne: la crise de la culture classique, la crise du français* [*The Spirit of the New Sorbonne: the Crisis of Classical Culture, the Crisis of French*] (1911).[8]

The main point on which Massis and Tarde based their attack dovetails with Péguy's argument in *L'Argent* and rests on the same educational reforms. They argued that literary studies, like any other academic discipline, are above all a form of labor. Regardless of the context in which it occurs, labor should be the expression of an individual, on the model of an artist creating a piece, rather than a collective workforce producing a commodity. The moral corruption of workers by modern industrial separation of labor is in the process of infecting intellectual and artistic workers as well. Péguy's reference to the builders of cathedrals is an especially suitable image for education, since it rehabilitates a pre-capitalist form of labor that harmoniously merges the individual and the collective. The artisan building the cathedral is anonymous, and disappears into the crowd, and yet his work has no corrupting and alienating effect. It is subordinate to transcendent rather than materialist aims and therefore serves as a metaphor for the institutional study of literature. The classroom is the space in which labor occurs, but on the model of cathedral-building. The new, corrupt literary methods, by contrast, constitute "[des] tâches menues et spéciales" [narrow and specialized tasks] (15), reflecting the relatively recent adoption by the manufacturing industry of Frederick Winslow Taylor's *Principles of Scientific Management*, in which a worker no longer produces a commodity from the ground up, but rather is responsible only for one small part of the manufacturing process. Specialization of labor is a capitalist invention that had already been identified by Marx as contributing to the alienation of workers from the act of production. Massis and Tarde were far from being Marxists, however, and thus were not able to develop this argument directly. Instead, they identified Emile Durkheim as not only one of the founders of the Nouvelle Sorbonne, but as the creator of a new and pernicious philosophy of collective as opposed to individual identity through two works in particular: *La division du travail social* [The Division of Labor in Society] his doctoral dissertation of 1893, and *Les règles de la méthode sociologique* [The Rules of Sociological Method] of 1895.

Durkheim's early sociological treatises focused on collectivism of labor, whereas traditional socialist theory was based on collectivism of wealth (Compagnon 1983, 138). Massis and Tarde attacked the Sorbonne in the same way that Péguy did, by associating it with the excesses of capitalism – of course, fascism also proposes a critique of capitalism, and Massis and

Tarde pointed out that many of their allies, especially their former classmates of the *Ecole Normale Supérieure*, include socialists, and indeed all colors of the political spectrum. They claimed that according to the new discipline of sociology, people are defined by their function within the larger collective. Similarly, students of literature, who once were craftsmen or even artists in their own right, have become assembly-line workers. Although Massis and Tarde do not mention them explicitly, the management theories of Frederick Winslow Taylor, or "Taylorism", had become influential worldwide at the turn of the century, and his system of dividing industrial labor into specialized tasks, which was to have such a decisive influence on Henry Ford's assembly line, already was being blamed for the de-skilling and dehumanization of the industrial worker.[9] Just as in factories, Massis and Tarde argue, skilled labor in universities was becoming less and less relevant. "[L]e talent est moins prisé, en Sorbonne, que l'habileté d'un ouvrier à l'usine" ["Talent is valued less, at the Sorbonne, than skill (akin to that) of a factory worker."] (77). This quote requires close attention, because it seems to imply that the university has forsaken talent, associated with artistic inspiration, for skill, associated with craftsmanship. But Massis and Tarde, by referring specifically to *usine* [factory], indirectly express the absence of any genuine "skill" whatsoever: the university in fact no longer requires either talent or "*habileté*" [skill] on the part of its students. By substituting material and historical minutiae for the esthetic questions of the previous era, the student and critic both fail in their moral responsibility: to appreciate, and therefore to judge the ultimate value of the work.[10] The goal of Taylorism, after all, is a rationalization of the production process from beginning to end, with engineering on a large-scale replacing individual craftsmanship and design, so as to require a totally unskilled (and therefore cheap and plentiful) workforce. The artisan, who has much in common with the artist (and literary critic), is being replaced by the assembly line worker, who has nothing in common with either. Lanson and his cohorts have replaced "le labeur personnel, bien plus exigeant et ardu [par] le labeur anonyme et facile" ["personal labor, far more demanding and difficult, (with) anonymous and easy labor"] (152). Making "talent" a prerequisite for literary study, of course, pushes the "coaching" role of the teacher in the direction of "scout" rather than "trainer", which directly contradicts the purpose of general education to benefit everybody. But then, as secondary school teacher Paul Crouzet wrote in 1910, the *bac* is supposed to be the first stage of university study, not the last stage of secondary education: "Si...en plus des méthodes scientifiques, il ne faut pas du talent et de la culture générale, l'enseignement supérieur devient vraiment trop à la portée de tous." [If in addition to scientific methods, one must not also have talent and general cultural knowledge, then higher education truly becomes too much within the reach of everyone] (301).

The metaphor of industrial production continues its course. The authors concede that the new methods are within the reach of a greater number of people. How could they not be, since the ultimate goal of the assembly line is to rationalize labor, dividing it into so many individual parts that no skill is required? "*Les médiocres*", which is to say those students who formerly were cast aside whenever they failed an exam or could not master the intricacies of Latin syntax or prosody, are able to remain viable under the new methods, which is a much more efficient use of students viewed as a workforce, as a human capital. Economically, this makes sense, according to Massis and Tarde, except for one thing: the product of specialized labor is inevitably inferior to the product of non-specialized labor; the goals of the enterprise conform themselves to the average, instead of demanding that the average conform itself to the goals of the enterprise, resulting in "l'anéantissement mystique de l'individu dans l'ensemble" ["the mystical annihilation of the individual into the collective"] (168 n.). It is clear that "mystical annihilation of the individual" does not have the positive connotation that Péguy gives to the equally anonymous cathedral-builder, but is instead an almost neo-romantic, rearguard attempt to preserve the myth of the artist-as-demiurge.

As if aware that their argument was taking an anti-industrial, reactionary, almost Luddite direction, Massis and Tarde eagerly pointed out that some of their strongest support has come from the ranks of businessmen and industrialists. If the captains of industry, for whom the benefits of Taylorism are quite obvious, deplore recent changes in education, it proves that literary studies must be protected from the modernization that increasingly pervades society. For just such an example of Latin's compatibility with modernity, they chose the Northern English city of Birmingham, that had long been synonymous with unfettered industrialization, just as more recently it has been synonymous with postindustrial decay: "Les directeurs d'écoles industrielles de Birmingham, notamment, exigent que tous leurs élèves apprennent le latin jusqu'à 14 ans, et le continuent deux années encore dans la division moderne." [The administrators of industrial schools in Birmingham, in particular, require all their students to study Latin until age fourteen, and to continue to do so for two more years in the modern track.] (177) The schoolmasters of Birmingham did not want their future industrial workers to study Latin, of course, but this passage refers to secondary education, which did not apply to the working class. They wanted secondary school students, who were later to become engineers and managers, to learn Latin for purely utilitarian (one might as well say "Anglo-Saxon") reasons, in contrast to disinterested ones: utilitarian, because Latin was considered necessary by the Birmingham industrialists so that engineers and executives would be able to think and communicate more clearly. But Agathon's real *coup de grâce* appears in a footnote appended to the above sentence: "Dans le pays le plus utilitaire du monde, en Amérique, on réclame à grands cris les humanités.... Le latin est, en effet, considéré par eux comme la meilleure gymnastique intellectuelle" ["In the most utilitarian country in the world, America, people loudly demand the humanities (i.e. Greek and Latin). They consider Latin to be indeed the best form of intellectual exercise"] (178 n.).

Thus, on the surface, we have a perfectly traditional and even banal appeal to classical studies as the best kind of mental discipline for students who were to become managers, rather than unskilled workers. In other words, it benefited individuals who needed to learn the skills for future tasks that still retained a holistic character. But why choose England and the United States to illustrate this argument? Not, as one might suppose, in order to model French practices on those of other countries. The entire force of those two examples rests upon the implication that even nations that have surrendered definitively to the challenge of industrialism and commercialism have not sacrificed classical literature in their general education curricula. The value of *les humanités* is so great and self-evident that the most spiritually corrupt societies in the world dare not eliminate them. But France has done exactly that, failing to create an exception for literary studies in order to protect it from the contaminating effect of industrial capitalism, especially in its extreme versions: the Northern English and the American. It is easy to assume that there is some practical reason why Birmingham requires its secondary schoolchildren to learn Latin, but in fact there is none. Or if there is, the reason is so weak that it can easily be dismissed. Can such study really help a shop manager or an engineer communicate more effectively, especially with a workforce that has only an elementary-school, Latin-free education? Is it such a great mental exercise that no other discipline, not even math, can better enhance one's mental faculties? The answers are no, and no. Paradoxically, the reference to an ostensible respect for Latin in the "Anglo-Saxon" world serves only to remind the reader of how corrupt and spiritually deprived it is compared to France. The familiar specter of French anti-Americanism rears its head in a debate that, on the surface, does not seem to involve America at all. As is still the case today, fear of cultural decline is linked to fear of (American) modernity, in which efficiency of communication, modeled on the capitalist model of production and consumption, replaces transcendent, "disinterested" values.

L'Esprit de la Nouvelle Sorbonne is unusual in the annals of polemical literature in that it contains an appendix consisting of several rebuttals that had appeared in the press, some written by members of the Sorbonne faculty itself. The authors wanted the reprints of their articles to appear in book form in the original context, so to speak, so that the reader could judge who is right. One such rebuttal is by the historian Ernest Lavisse, who conceded that *"la crise du français"* does indeed exist – students write and speak worse than they used to – but its extent and gravity are greatly exaggerated (209-10). In any case, there is nothing the university establishment can do to remedy it, because teaching students to write and speak well is the purpose of the *lycée*, and if that objective is not being met, it is unreasonable to ask the university to pick up the slack. Like virtually all aspects of the debate over "la Nouvelle Sorbonne", Lavisse's words resonate loudly in our own context. In the United States, but also in Europe and many other parts of the world, there are studies confirming the lack of basic knowledge displayed by college graduates that raise the same question: if foundational skills are not being taught in secondary school, does that leave universities without any responsibility, or are remedial classes – among which, arguably, one could include beginning foreign language classes – part of their mission?

But Lavisse makes another point that is even more pertinent today: "Je voudrais montrer que c'est une illusion de croire que le talent s'enseigne, et demander à ceux qui ont sans cesse à la bouche le mot de culture générale, s'ils n'entendent point par là leur culture à eux, qui pourrait bien être une culture très particulière" ["I would like to show that the belief that talent can be taught is an illusion, and to ask those who constantly spout the words general culture whether they really mean by that their own culture, which may be a highly idiosyncratic one."] (221). This surprising appeal to multiculturalism (in 1910!), implying that the classical values championed by Massis and Tarde cannot claim any special privilege over others, left the two reactionary militants speechless; whether because they found the argument too ridiculous to warrant a response, or because they were genuinely confounded, it is impossible to say.

Ernest Lavisse, to repeat, was a historian, with a very strong interest in secondary education. His schoolbooks on French history dominated the market during most of the twentieth century. But what about the discipline of French literature? One of the responses to Massis and Tarde from the literary disciplines came not from Lanson, as one might expect, but from Emile Faguet, who occupied the Chair of French poetry at the Sorbonne. His position in the debate was nuanced, another sign that the "*crise du français*" was a complex issue that did not clearly follow political or disciplinary boundaries. Faguet was frequently in conflict over the question of literary methods with Lanson, who viewed him as insufficiently committed to the reformist cause (Compagnon 1983, 92). Lanson's disciple Gustave Rudler identified Faguet as a member of the talent-dependent "impressionistic" school of criticism that defends "[l[e droit de faire des grâces de style sans rien savoir" [the right to produce felicities of style without knowing anything] (43).

Given the preceding comment, it is not surprising that Massis and Tarde preferred debating Faguet than the more orthodox proponents of the new pedagogy. But Faguet was no pushover either. At first, he seems to adopt the conservative view, continuing Lavisse's argument that the "*crise du français*" is a problem for the *lycée* and not for the university to solve, and arguing for the restoration of the Latin requirement on the *bac*. Given that French writing skills having declined in the years following the decline of Latin,[11] Faguet agrees that the two phenomena are related: "post hoc, ergo propter hoc" (236). But to counter the mistaken impression that Massis and Tarde may have had an ally within the walls of the Sorbonne, Faguet made the following astonishing claim, that would shock the French intelligentsia today almost as much as it did in 1910: "la crise du français n'est pas une crise, c'est une décadence; c'est une décadence définitive et sans retour, compensée par des progrès qui ont eu lieu dans un autre ordre de choses. On n'écrira plus le français, voilà tout." ["The crisis of French is not a crisis, it is a decadence; a definitive decadence without a cure, one that is counterbalanced by progress in other domains. One will simply cease writing French"] (240). If Lavisse's cultural relativism in the passage quoted earlier was shockingly ahead of its time, so was Faguet's pragmatic resignation to a future devoid of high cultural standards, in which the loss of French writing and speaking skills will be counterbalanced by gains in other domains, presumably having to do with technology, scientific progress, and economic growth. He displayed, no less than did Lavisse, an uncanny ability to anticipate the debates over education taking place today. For Faguet, the fact that students were less able to express themselves in their native language was perhaps compensated by increased proficiency in modern languages, greater knowledge of science and technology, and so on. Gustave Allais (no relation to the humorist Alphonse Allais), a French professor at Rennes and a prolific historian of literature, went much further when he wrote that future French people, finally free of the tyranny of Latin, will express themselves in "une langue dédaigneuse des mots, des fleurs...sèche, nette, probe et brève..." [a language that disdains wit and flowers (of rhetoric), that is dry, clear, honest, and brief] (502) – in a word: transparent (exactly what Baudelaire feared in "The Bad Glazier", discussed in Chapter 2). The value of Agathon's work is therefore not so much in its reactionary arguments (although its economic critique of divided labor is still relevant), as in the radicalness of the responses it elicited, many of which challenge the spiritual authority of literary culture head on.

Today, some say that despair over a decline in reading, writing, and general education shows an inability to appreciate the value of our students' greater visual sophistication, their comfort with technology, and their ability to adapt to new forms of knowledge. Indeed, to repeat Faguet's words: "*la crise du français n'est pas une crise*". The crisis of French is not a crisis. In fact, there are no crises of literary pedagogy, but only an unending debate over a privileged culture that may or may not be worth preserving; over secondary and higher education's responsibility to the masses; and over the competition among different varieties of skill and knowledge. Is Allais's wish for a new, honest and concise French language, devoid of classical rhetoric, a dream or a nightmare? The current debate over the general education of literature is a sign that we are still searching for the answer – a current debate that has a surprising amount in common with the struggle of French literature to establish itself as a discipline over a century ago.

Transmitting the Cult of Literature as Literary Culture

Problems such as the one described earlier could not easily be solved by creative classroom practices initiated by teachers and students because of the barriers to grassroots reform, many of which still stand. The centralized structure of French education since the nineteenth century means that decisions are made at the top and constitute a national political matter, unlike in the United States, where education is mostly under local control, and national debates over its content and methodologies migrate upward from the trenches, rather than downward from the general staff. An even more appropriate metaphor for the structure in which educational policy is devised and implemented than the military one is that of religious authority. In the early nineteenth-century, when education was largely the responsibility of the Church, both institutions shared the same bureaucratic body, the "ministère des affaires ecclésiastiques et de l'instruction publique" [ministry of ecclesiastical affairs and public instruction], an alliance that continued sporadically until 1895 (education.gouv.fr "Repères, histoire et patrimoine"). The Gallicanism of the Bourbon restoration that conflated national religion and national education reinforced the structural similarity of the institutions of Catholicism and education in French society, even long after the return of republicanism.

Centralized authority that functions centrifugally is anathema in the United States, especially in the realm of educational policy. Controversies such as the one over the teaching of evolution occur first in state and local boards of education and only become national debates after the fact: it took a local dispute between parents and their school board to create a legal barrier against the teaching of intelligent design, in the famous 2005 case Kitzmiller v. Dover (Pennsylvania) School District. In France, it is difficult for these kinds of curricular issues to originate at the local rather than the national level, partly because policy initiatives tend to travel from the top down. When Lanson and the "nouvelle Sorbonne" historians and sociologists tried to introduce science into literary pedagogy, it was therefore a subversive move on their part: students trained in positive knowledge and rational commentary would become active agents rather than passive recipients of an educational process that would function according to a centripetal model. But their revolution never succeeded, in part because of the persistence to this day of a top-down, centralized structure. The consequent lack of student agency, that Lanson and others deplored, simply reproduced at the local level an *ex cathedra* vision of authority that still operates, for better and for worse. For better, since it serves as a barrier against the hijacking of educational policy by private political and religious interests, and for worse, as it postpones indefinitely the dream, shared by Lanson, Allais and Faguet, of empowering students by teaching according to the ideology of a "transparent French language" that emerged during the educational debates of the French Revolution. Preserving literature as a "cult" rather than a tool of personal empowerment prevents Allais's prediction that pedagogy will one day valorize "language that disdains wit and flowers (of rhetoric), that is dry, clear, honest, and brief" from becoming true, again for better and for worse. For better, as it protects literature from subordination to, or replacement by, the utilitarian goals that Allais and Faguet viewed as the future of general education; for worse, as it perpetuates the practice of uncritical, quasi-religious adoration of literature from a distance.

The student empowerment formulated by the reformers of the "nouvelle Sorbonne" has been a principle in French educational policy for well over a century, but with limited success. In part, this is because the financing of public (and most private) education, as well as decisions on curricula, methods, and the training and hiring of teachers are largely the responsibility of the government and its largest agency by far, the Ministry of National Education.[12] Not only is education the largest public function in terms of resources, but the discipline of French language and literature at the primary, secondary, and tertiary levels attracts more media attention than any other, creating a synergistic alliance between political power and cultural identity of which the school is the nexus. One consequence of this synergy is a high degree of popular investment in an ideal and therefore unchanging linguistic norm, and the consequent valorization of mastery over the norm. Learners of French on their first trip to France are often surprised, usually grateful, and sometimes irritated at how often native speakers will correct their grammar, pronunciation, and vocabulary. In the United States, persons struggling to speak English might be praised, they might encounter xenophobia and told to go back to where they came from, or they might be ignored, but generally they will not be corrected. This is due at least in part to the fact that our schools do not (or more precisely, no longer) instill the idea of a single, inalterable linguistic norm in which everyone owns a stake. As a result, linguistic variations and even grammatical mistakes such as the phrase "between you and I" rarely offend, or if they do, the victim of the offense is labelled a snob, a pedant, or worse.

As far as attitudes toward literature are concerned, as distinct from the linguistic idealism described above, there is also a difference between the two countries, though not as great as one might think. While it is true that sales of literary works are proportionally larger in France than in the United States,[13] it does not follow that reading literature is a common activity throughout the French population. The percentage of avid readers in the French population may be relatively high compared to many developed nations (in a 2009 survey, 20 percent of respondents reported reading at least one book per month[14]), but that leaves a large majority of citizens who either read few works of literature or none at all. In light of such a statistic, one is tempted to say that the general education of literature has failed. On closer examination, however, a more complex picture emerges, that helps explain the failure of attempts to demystify the teaching of literature, from Lanson to the present.

Just as French bureaucratic power and cultural patrimony operate in a manner analogous to a centralized, hierarchical religion, literary practice in a society can resemble certain forms of religious practice. For example, it is useful to compare the minority status of literary readers in France with the relatively marginal contemporary status of the traditional rival of the Republic in the sphere of education: the Catholic Church. According to the website of the French Church, 61 percent of the population identifies as Catholic (down from 87 percent in 1972), but only 33 percent of infants are baptized, and less than 5 percent of the population attends Mass.[15] The large difference in numbers between "practicing" and "cultural" Catholics has a counterpart in the world of literature: those who read often, versus those who, even though they may recognize an elevated status for literature in society, do not. The 2009 survey quoted earlier showed that 64 percent of the population had read fewer than five books over the previous year, and almost half of that group read no books at all.[16] The percentage of the population that reads between zero and five books a year (whether literature or not[17]) is almost identical to the percentage of French people who are "cultural" but nonpracticing Catholics.

Why compare readers to Catholics? The purpose of juxtaposing two unrelated cultural practices, reading and religious observance, is to make a point about the inability of literary general education to create a majority of "lifelong readers" in the general population, which has parallels with the Church's inability to turn "cultural" into practicing Catholics. Both cultures, the literary and the Catholic, predominantly consist of people who identify with the culture but are only passive members, who may acknowledge its importance, yet without participating in any meaningful way through actual religious practice, or through reading. France is not only a nation made up largely of nonpracticing Catholics, which is a fairly well-known fact, it is also a nation where literature is widely valued by most of the population, yet actually practiced (that is to say read) by a much smaller group, a counterintuitive fact that Priscilla Parkhurst Clark explored in an important book, *Literary France* (1987).

We have seen that despite its high rates of literacy, the practice of reading in France is not exceptionally widespread. The French consume books at about the same rate as Americans, albeit with a much stronger preference for literature over nonfiction. The issue on which I want to focus is not the rate of consumption of literature, however, but rather the anomaly of a nation that espouses literary culture, as a basis for national identification, more strongly than its rate of literary reading suggests. To put it simply: a French person is likely to have heard of Gustave Flaubert, but not to have read his work, whereas an American is even more likely not to have read *or* heard of Herman Melville. As Priscilla Parkhurst Clark wrote in the above-mentioned *Literary France*, books "are perhaps the least of what literary culture is about" (15). I further claim that the phenomenon of widespread nonactive identification with a religion can help illuminate the similar phenomenon in the realm of literary culture. The neologism "literarian" introduced in Chapter 2 referred to those people, many of them literature teachers, who believe in the absolute value of literariness and resist its subordination to practical, measurable pedagogical outcomes; I now want to expand the meaning of the term to include those who place a high value on literary culture, even though they do not actually read, analogous to people who identify with, but do not actually practice, the Catholic religion.

We have already established that approximately one third of French people read five or more books a year and that 20 percent read at least one a month, which suggests that a large minority of the population regularly practices some form of literary reading (see IBISWorld, Statista, and TNS-Sofres). Since half of the trade books purchased in France are in the fiction category, or about twice their proportion in the United States, one can presume that French people read more literature than Americans, even though the total market in trade books per capita is about the same. One can deduce from those figures that there is not much difference in the total amount of reading, but rather in the kind of reading. Comparable percentages of the French and American populations read little or not at all, and are therefore equally estranged from text culture. The major difference between the two nations on this issue is therefore not the amount of reading (though "literary" as opposed to "general" reading is marginally higher in France), but in the much greater French engagement with para-literary phenomena. Such phenomena include all the streets, squares, libraries and schools named after canonical authors, the public monuments to their memory, the references to literary works and authors in the popular media, and so on, all of which contribute to a national "cult of literature". Another example is that one of the traumas caused by the introduction of the Euro was the realization that France would no longer have any portraits of national figures, many of them writers, on its currency. In the early 1960s, the lowest denomination bill, the five-franc note, bore a portrait of Victor Hugo. People started referring to the lowly bill as a "*misérable*".[18] How many other countries would incorporate literary culture into everyday speech in such a way? The long-running television talk show "*Apostrophes*", in which host Bernard Pivot chatted with literary authors and academics, was famously popular among the French viewing public, which of course did not have to read or even buy the books in order to watch. Clearly, the entertainment value of "*Apostrophes*" appealed to a much larger number of people than those who actually read the books by the star intellectuals who appeared on their TV screens every Friday night.[19] All of these phenomena point to the existence of a social role of literary culture that far exceeds the practice of literary reading, whether inside or outside of the school.

To pursue the Catholicism analogy further, one can say that the certification of French literature teachers is like the ordination of priests. In both cases, only a small number of individuals follow their vocation, but they minister to a flock that would ideally include the entire population; in the case of the general education of literature, which has succeeded in replacing Catholicism as the de facto national religious practice, of course, it *does* include the entire population. Church attendance may have declined dramatically in the last 150 years, but school attendance, which is mandatory, cannot; and while those who do attend Church can legitimately be called practicing Catholics, regardless of the faith that may or may not be in their hearts, those who attend literature classes against their will are not genuine readers unless they carry on the practice outside of the school. Their classwork and homework, while it necessarily involves some engagement with literary texts, may well be a minimal, reluctant acquiescence to the teacher's demands, if not an outright rejection of them on the model of the "dunce" in Prévert's poem discussed in Chapter 2, rather than a voluntary "practice".

How far does the religious analogy go? Teachers often desire to spread a certain kind of "faith", and literature has many of the characteristics of a religion, including even the ideology of a text, or texts, providing access to one type or other of transcendence. It is therefore possible to teach literature in a "seminarian" spirit, both as general education and as academic discipline, but is it wise? There are at least two objections to this model for the teaching of literature, one theoretical and one practical. The theoretical objection is that by founding pedagogical practices on a system of belief that cannot be tested by empirical observation, one separates them from the scientific model on which modern education founds its legitimacy. One returns to the monastic origins of the medieval university, when it was a school of theology, before its second foundation on the broader model of classical liberal arts (the *trivium* and *quadrivium*) around the thirteenth and fourteenth centuries. While it is possible to conceive of the training of literature teachers as answering a vocation, and therefore to assume, on the part of literature majors at the B.A, M.A., and Ph.D. levels a certain degree of faith in the value and even truth of literary texts, I argue that such a faith-based stance, while perhaps necessary and inevitable in the training of future professors of literature, is inappropriate for the teaching of literature as general education. The cult of literature is not the same as the study of literature, and while it is remarkable that faith in a non-quantifiable, non-demonstrable "literariness" is so pervasive throughout French popular culture, the only real benefit of that fact from the perspective of literary pedagogy would be the degree to which it enhances the quantity and quality of literary reading that goes on. A literary culture largely divorced from the practice of reading makes literary pedagogy more secure as a general education subject, but functions neither as its foundation, nor as its goal.

The difference between the two kinds of education, specialized and general, is freedom. Academic specialization is an instance of freedom of choice, given that students choose literature as their area of specialization based on subjective as well as objective criteria. In the case of general education, which is mandatory, freedom does not play a role, at least not at the outset. Most students forced to study Shakespeare in high school do not share with their teachers the natural love out of which vocations are born, which is not to say that vocations are not at times revealed and cultivated by mandatory "core" courses – in fact, such occasional revelations are one of the major arguments for the existence of such classes. After all, if I am not forced to take math, or art, I may never discover my affinity for one of those subjects (though by that argument, there should be many more general education disciplines – how many more philosophers would there be if it was a required subject in high school, as in fact it is in the *lycée?*). But as gratifying as it is to have students discover an affinity of which they may have had little or no prior awareness, such cases do not by themselves provide sufficient justification for the presence of literature in the general curriculum, since they occur in a small minority of the student population (less than five percent of college students major in literature, according to the already-cited *MLA Report to the Teagle Foundation*). "Literariness" from the pedagogical perspective is therefore something other than the idea of ineffable value that underlies the seminarian approach; "literature" as academic discipline must provide something that no other academic discipline provides, but that value must be understood in a relative sense, that is to say scientifically. The cult of literature, even in a society like France where it is widely acknowledged to be part of the social fabric, and permeates popular culture, is not an adequate basis for its inclusion in the general education curriculum.

The presence of literature within the general education curriculum has never been seriously challenged in France, as long as there has been a system of public schools. Where there has been a problem is in the disagreement over its justification, and the methods that such a justification legitimizes. The next chapter identifies both old and new elements in the "crisis of French" brought to light during the cultural upheaval of May 1968, in order to increase our understanding of the present state of the discipline in France, and its exemplary value for anyone who holds a stake in the general education of literature in the world today.

NOTES

1. The conclusions of Ribot's "commission on public instruction" are summarized in his important work *La réforme de l'enseignement secondaire* (1900), which was one of the first official attempts in France to make public education, including literary pedagogy, responsive to the social conditions of a broader cross section of the population. As such, it is a direct precursor to the 1999 reforms that brought on very similar reactions, as we will see in the next chapter.
2. The *brevet* was the diploma certifying completion of the "*primaire supérieur*" track, the traditional, less prestigious alternative to the *lycée* for students who continued their education beyond the obligatory age of twelve. It still exists today as the "*brevet des collèges*", or certificate of completion of middle school.

3. The *concours général*, formerly *concours académique*, is a contest open only to students selected by their schools as among the "best of the best". It was in the *concours* for "Latin verse composition" that Rimbaud won first prize in 1869, as mentioned earlier in this chapter.
4. The work of historian Marie-Madeleine Compère gives the best explanation for the persistence of the "cult of Latin" in literary pedagogy, that still exists to this day.
5. "*Bachot*" is the slang word still in use today, along with "*bac*", to refer to the *baccalauréat* exam; "*bachotage*" is the activity of cramming for the exam.
6. The politics of this movement varied considerably, as the examples developed here show: Péguy was from the left, "Agathon" from the right. Though it is an oversimplification, it helps to see the debates over the teaching of French in the 1900s as dividing society along similar fault lines as the Dreyfus Affair, from which the country was still recovering. Péguy, both a Dreyfusard and a foe of the "Nouvelle Sorbonne", is one example of an exception to this pattern.
7. The meaning of the verb "*servir*" in this context is not "to serve", or not only that, but rather: "to be used or to be useful (*servir à quelque chose*)".
8. This very influential polemical work displays affinities with Maurras and *l'Action Française*, and Massis indeed later joined the fascist movement (though Tarde did not). To Péguy and Agathon, the two most famous critics of the *Nouvelle Sorbonne*, one should add the names of Gustave Le Bon and Pierre Lasserre, whose contributions to the debate were especially influential (see Bibliography). Both authors are discussed at length in George Weisz, *The Emergence of Modern Universities in France, 1863–1914* (1983). Massis and Tarde were the primary foes of Emile Durkheim according to the account of sociology's early struggles for legitimacy by Wolf Lepenies, *Between Literature and Science: The Rise of Sociology* (1988).
9. Taylor's theories on the rationalization of industrial labor started to have a profound impact even before his first book, *Shop Management*, appeared in 1903. His most influential work, however, is *Principles of Scientific Management*, published in French translation in 1911, the same year it came out in the United States. The two men writing as Agathon would certainly have been aware of the phenomenon of Taylorism, and it is not surprising that their book, which can be read as a backlash against the growing mechanization of labor, appeared at roughly the same time as Taylor's.
10. I am grateful to Leon Sachs for reminding me of the moral as well as political and social dimensions of the esthetic arguments put forward by Massis and de Tarde.
11. The belief that the quality of oral and written expression declined in society after Latin ceased to be a requirement for all candidates of the *bac* was widespread in the early twentieth century (e.g. Henri Bergson 1923), and

still exists in some circles today (e.g. Jacqueline de Romilly 1993, and Marc Fumaroli 2015). Historians of education have thoroughly exposed the mystical connection between Latin (and Greek) and French as an amazingly persistent and popular myth, arguing for example that the alleged "decline of French" among members of the scientific elite in the early twentieth century became an issue long before the students who no longer had to take Latin had even finished their studies, and it therefore could not have been a factor. Gustave Lanson himself pointed out in 1910 that fears of the decline of French style due to the absence of Latin in the required curriculum were a bit premature, given that the students who joined the Latin-free science track in 1903 would not become engineers until 1916 at the earliest (Jey 1998, 201). In spite of the lack of historical evidence, Latin's aura as an antidote to bad French seems destined to endure.

12. The current budget for the Ministry of Education is the largest of any French government agency at more than 65 billion euros (not counting an additional 23 billion for higher education and research, which only recently have come under its jurisdiction) (http://www.education.gouv.fr/cid82613/projet-de-loi-de-finances-2015.html). That is more than twice the budget of the French Ministry of Defense, which stood at 31.4 billion euros in 2015 (http://www.defense.gouv.fr/sga/le-sga-en-action/budget-finances-de-la-defense/budget). By way of comparison, the United States defense budget currently stands at 496 billion dollars (http://comptroller.defense.gov/Portals/45/Documents/defbudget/fy2015/fy2015_Budget_Request_Overview_Book.pdf, 7), about sixteen and a half times larger than France's, while the budget of the Department of Education, admittedly much less powerful than its French equivalent, stands at 68.6 billion dollars (http://www2.ed.gov/about/overview/budget/budget15/summary/15summary.pdf, 5), or about 10 percent smaller than France's. Because the size of the French population is approximately one-fifth of the American, one can say that its public education budget per capita is close to five times larger (but its defense budget by the same calculation is then about one-third, instead of one-sixteenth, of the American one).

13. Precise comparative sales figures for literature in France versus the United States indicate that in 2010, 2.53 billion books were sold in the United States, about one quarter of which are literature, excluding the educational market (http://www.statista.com/statistics/240088/total-book-sales-of-the-us-book-market-by-quantity/), versus 451.9 million in France, of which almost half are literature, excluding the educational market (http://www.statista.com/statistics/420733/book-sales-france/). According to those figures, the size of the book market is about the same in each country relative to the population, but the market share for literature in France is about twice as large.

14. These figures come from a 2009 survey conducted by the TNS-Sofres agency and first published in *La Croix*, the French Catholic daily newspaper.
15. http://www.eglise.catholique.fr/conference-des-eveques-de-france/guide-de-leglise/leglise-catholique-en-france-et-en-chiffres/371402-statistiques-de-leglise-catholique-en-france-guide-2013/.
16. These figures also come from the survey conducted by TNS-Sofres in 2009.
17. While the statistics on reading do not differentiate between literary and nonliterary works, at least half of the overall market in France is in fiction, as already mentioned. Literary genres such as poetry and drama would be included under the "fiction" category.
18. There is little trace of this particular slang use of the word "*misérable*" that survives, but those who lived in France before Victor Hugo was replaced by Louis Pasteur on the five franc note might remember.
19. During the time it was on the air, from 1975 to 1990, "*Apostrophes*" regularly drew an extremely large weekly audience by French standards, of between 1.3 and 2.3 million households, a total viewership well in excess of one tenth of the entire population. While the program undoubtedly had a substantial influence on sales of featured authors, known as "*l'effet Pivot*" [the Pivot effect], the numbers of people who bought a book after seeing its author on the show was never more than a tiny fraction of the overall viewing audience. It is also difficult to assess the effect, if any, of "*Apostrophes*" on the book market in general. A similar conclusion can be drawn in regards to the "*Oprah Winfrey Book Club*" in the United States (Painbéni 38).

CHAPTER 5

Literature in French Schools After 1968

THE SECOND GREAT CRISIS OF FRENCH

While teachers of literature in North America have faced declining interest among students, charges of irrelevance, decreasing resources, and other symptoms of crisis, few of us are aware that our discipline is (once again) in crisis in France as well, and that a similar decline in student interest is one of its biggest problems. The previous chapter described an earlier crisis, roughly from 1890 to 1910, known as the "*querelle de la nouvelle Sorbonne*", sparked by the refounding of the university on a new paradigm of scientific research, and by the increased access of a broader cross-section of society to literary general education. I argued that the transition from classical rhetoric to commentary on French literature, the colonization of literary studies by the discipline of history, and the backlash from critics who regarded these changes as a form of Taylorism and betrayal of literature's higher purpose, contributed to a state of conflict that continues to this day. This chapter examines the paradigm in a more recent context, and how the contemporary theory and practice of teaching French literature in France has changed as a result.

The "French model" is especially relevant because it presents the debate in sharper contrast, compared to its Anglophone counterpart. In the United States, for example, the challenge to the authority of classical languages as symbols of "true literature" was never as politically charged as in France, where literature in the vernacular was enlisted by the Republic in order to provide it with a moral authority that rivaled that of the *Ancien Régime*. In addition, as Gerald Graff has convincingly demonstrated in *Professing Literature: an Institutional History*, the transition from the memorization of classical literature to the scientific study of vernacular literature occurred in the very limited realm of nineteenth-century American higher education, affecting less than 2 percent of the population, and did not become a major factor in broader general education before Robert Maynard Hutchins instituted the "great books" curriculum at the University of Chicago in the 1930s (162–5). The power exerted in France by a "cult" of literature and the "culture" of literature that supports it (see end of previous chapter), simply has no real equivalent in the Anglophone world; and yet it is precisely the existence of these phenomena in France that reinforces the claim that literary pedagogy cannot be reduced to transmitting a practical skill. In other words, there is a "cult" of literature that is implicit in the defense of its role in general education in such works as *Why Literature?* (Cristina Bruns 2011), *Why Reading Literature in School Still Matters* (Dennis Sumara 2002), *Why Literature Matters in the 21st Century* (Mark Roche 2004), and other recent essays that take as their starting point the argument that the decline in literary general education, and literary reading in general, is a matter of great concern. In France, the "cult" is explicit and omnipresent, and we saw in the previous chapter how clear the lines of conflict became, from the very onset of institutional efforts to demystify literature through general secondary education. At the opposite extreme of the literary cult is the absorption of literary studies, at the primary and secondary levels, into a multidisciplinary "Language Arts". That demystifying process had occurred by the mid-twentieth century in the Unites States, whereas France has only recently begun to attempt to dissolve the border between literature and language, under what Dan Savatovsky calls "*littéralangue*" (2008, 192). The idealistic (French) emphasis on literature "in itself" contrasts with the relativistic (American) one on literature as one of the many uses of language; sacralization contrasts with secularization. The difference in emphasis, however, does not change the simple fact that pedagogical practices in both educational systems emanate from sacred as well as secular conceptions of the discipline; as such, teachers of literature everywhere stand to learn from the French model, especially its long history of engagement with materialist, pragmatic, and even commercial pressures.

What are the origins of the current "crisis of French"? To begin with, the landscape of secondary and higher education has changed considerably since the early twentieth century, and even since the 1960s. The concern, shared over a century ago by Gustave Lanson and his colleagues at the Sorbonne that literary pedagogy had to be reinvented because candidates to the *bac* exam were approaching 2 or 3 percent of the male members of an age group, many of whom were not members of the predominantly Catholic upper classes, seems quaint when compared to the situation today. Quite simply, the post-World War II era brought back the "culture wars" of the turn of the twentieth century, and did so with a vengeance (see Chartier and Hébrard). Unless one happens to specialize in French educational history, however, one might be hard pressed to answer the question: how, and to what extent, has initiation into French literature in France really changed over the years?

In France today, the entire population follows the same curriculum until the equivalent of ninth grade, according to the egalitarian principle of the *collège unique*, the common middle school curriculum implemented in 1975. Following middle school, about two-thirds of all students enroll in a *lycée général* or *lycée technologique*, and many of the rest enroll in the more vocationally oriented *lycée professionnel*. About 20 percent of students either do not attend a *lycée* or, if they do, fail to obtain the *bac*, sometimes after several attempts ("L'éducation nationale en chiffres"). From these figures, one can conclude that literature is a mandatory subject for the vast majority of the school population between the ages of fifteen and eighteen, especially those in *lycée général* who, as described in Chapter 3, elect one of the three broad curricular tracks: Economics and Social Science (ES), Literature (L), or Science (S).

The percentage of students in the "L" track has declined steadily. It now accounts for about 16 percent of the students enrolled in *lycée général*, the only type of institution in which it is an option, compared to more than a third of all *lycée* students a few decades ago (Todorov 2007, 31).[1] Not only are fewer French students opting for literature as their major curricular focus when they specialize for the *bac*, as well as when they undertake university studies, but also the very status of the discipline as a cornerstone of general education is under fire. The *épreuve anticipée de français*, described in Chapter 3, continues to reign as the most important general education portion of the *bac*, administered a full year before the rest of the exam, but its status is no longer secure. In France today, journalists, teachers, parents, and academics question more and more the educational goals and methods of implementation of such a requirement, in an atmosphere of intensifying controversy.

The literary pedagogy practiced in France is not only quite different than in the days of Gustave Lanson, the *programmes*, or directives that traditionally define pedagogical content and methods, have changed dramatically just since the late twentieth century. The classic *Lagarde et Michard* series of anthologies has long been replaced by textbooks that bear almost no resemblance to their famous predecessor and its narrow, homogenized version of French literary history.[2] It is true, however, that the changes in France have in general been less transformative than those that have occurred in the teaching of French literature outside of France. For example, the French educational system still struggles to acknowledge fully the revival of previously undervalued female authors such as Françoise de Graffigny or Claire de Duras; to grant equal status to Francophone world literature (even as it has been increasingly well-received by the French public); and to recognize the literary, artistic, and pedagogical value of the extraordinary Franco-Belgian tradition of comics and graphic novels. French departments in the Anglophone world, in contrast, have mostly done so already.[3]

Just as American specialists of French and Francophone literature tend to perceive the literature curriculum in France, with some justification, in terms of an idealized and static past, its methods exist in our awareness as time-honored, ritualistic, and intimidating "canonical" exercises described in Chapter 3: the *explication de texte, commentaire, composition* and their variants, the origins of which we associate with Lanson and other founding fathers from over a century ago.[4] But there have been changes since Roland Barthes's famous attack on *lansonisme* in *Sur Racine* (1963), and the French educational establishment spends considerable efforts analyzing and reinventing itself through university departments of *Didactique du français*, specialized institutions (formerly known as *Ecoles Normales*, then *Instituts Universitaires de Formation des Maîtres* or IUFM, and now *Ecoles Supérieures du Professorat et de l'Education* or ESPE, each change in nomenclature accompanied by a shift in institutional priorities), and the administrative apparatus of the Ministry of National Education.

The previous chapters explored several examples of resistance to, and even barriers against fundamental pedagogical change, including: the extreme importance in French society of a shared literary culture; the institutional sacralization of literature that separates individual texts from their historical and social origins, imbuing them with intrinsic value; and a widely shared suspicion, across the political spectrum, of market-based theories of value subsumed under the catchall term "neo-liberalism".[5] In spite of these eminently "Franco-French" concerns, I believe the status of literary studies in the *lycée* is also relevant to those of us who teach literature in the Anglophone world, because we face a similar problem: the increasing distance separating teachers of inherited literary culture and their students. In France the problem is even more apparent, because the powerful tradition of transmitting an "inherited" culture, already alien to the population of public school students who do not automatically subscribe to aspirational bourgeois values, is now strongly resisted as well by a growing population of students of non-European background. The question of how to make literature accessible to the French teenager of African origin from the *banlieue*, is also the one of how to make it relevant to the American high school or college student from almost any social background, since the link between literary culture and social status, just like literary culture in general, is much weaker in the United States than it (still) is in France. The problem is not only one of increased cultural diversity: in France, one can no longer assume that cultural assimilation implies familiarity with, or even openness to, inherited national culture. The cult of literature, in other words, is in crisis. As in the United States, white middle-class children in France are not necessarily more receptive to literature than those from more socially and culturally marginalized communities, as Dominique Pasquier has demonstrated with statistical surveys in her book *Cultures lycéennes* (2005). It appears that the literature curriculum has even less impact on students' reading habits outside the school walls than in the past, even as it is taught to an ever larger percentage of the population.

Teachers of literature are familiar with student resistance, under the guise of challenge to the dominant culture, desire for financial security, or both: "The literary culture you teach is not my own, therefore I reject it"; "How will this help me find a job?"; "What skills will I learn that I can apply to my life?"; or simply "I don't understand these texts, and you are wasting our time trying to teach them to me". The elimination of entire university departments of modern languages in North America and the decline of the literature option on the *bac* are related, and not simply because they are the result of reduced budgets and increased consumerism; they are the consequences of the inability to make a strong enough case that literature and language are more than specialized academic disciplines, and that they are part of general education. In a sense, literature teachers must accomplish two very different goals: "sell" their discipline in a market-like environment in which students exercise freedom of choice, and argue that it deserves protection from the market, that populating our classrooms by enforcing "gen ed" requirements is not simply a way to preserve our jobs.

The role of literature teachers as "marketing executives" for the discipline comes into play only when a critical mass of recalcitrant students is reached. Because the increase in the size and cultural diversity of the *lycée* population occurred over a long period of time, it is hard to pinpoint the moment when the teaching of literature could no longer succeed in justifying itself as something closer to a religious ritual than an academic discipline. The 1960s, however, are the time period when the educational and professional opportunities guaranteed by the *bac* truly became the rights of the many rather than the privilege of the few, an undeniable triumph of social progress. The impact of Pierre Bourdieu and Jean-Claude Passeron's study of the relationship between social class, cultural practices, and educational success (*Les héritiers: les étudiants et la culture*, 1964) on a French teaching profession already primed to see its role as one of empowering the economically and culturally disadvantaged, was enormous. It contributed to a euphoric sense of revolutionary possibility, including the events of May 1968, and also influenced the radical reappraisal of the goals, methodologies, and legitimacy of literary pedagogy that echoes Lanson's campaign to turn literary pedagogy toward the inculcation of practical skills through the manipulation of language, rather than simply teaching devotion to a sacralized corpus of texts.[6] I now turn to the pioneering post-1968 era that led to many changes in the teaching of French; it laid the groundwork for a major revision to the national literature curriculum that occurred thirty years later, and that concludes this chapter.

LITERARY PEDAGOGY AS SOCIAL LIBERATION IN THE "CHARBONNIÈRES MANIFESTO"

Public school teachers since before the start of the Third Republic have traditionally identified with left-wing politics, especially through professional associations and unions. The reasons for such a political preference among the profession are many: the fact that public education throughout the nineteenth century was viewed as an attack on the Church; the scientism and philosophical materialism that dominated pedagogical theory, especially since the early Third Republic; hope in the school as an engine for social mobility; and many more. By the 1960s this tendency had only grown stronger, and the profession was more than receptive to the growing demand for alternative economic and societal models. In the wake of Bourdieu and Passeron's foundational study *Les Héritiers* mentioned above (1964), Paulo Freire's first book on liberation pedagogy came out in France in 1967 (*L'Éducation: pratique de la liberté* [*Education, the Practice of Freedom*]). In a sign of the times, teachers of French, who were particularly conscious of the importance of their discipline in cultural politics formed the "*Association Française des Professeurs de Français*" [French Association of Professors of French] or AFPF in 1967 (later changed to its current title, "*Association Française des Enseignants de Français*" [French Association of Teachers of French] or AFEF[7]). In 1968, they founded what continues to be the dominant journal in the field of French pedagogy, focused primarily on secondary education: *Le Français aujourd'hui* [French Today]. The February 1970 issue of this journal contained a twenty-page document, *Le Manifeste de Charbonnières*, the result of a three-day meeting of members of the AFPF in the château of Charbonnières in September 1969.

The *Manifeste* is very much a relic of its time, expressing a degree of militancy with which far fewer members of the AFEF would identify today. Nevertheless, it continues to be blamed for having inspired many of the pedagogical practices that are currently under attack in the name of preserving literature's elevated status. Its reliance on economic determinism, and the imperative to consider the material conditions of the students, have produced the ironic result that anti-market, 1960s radicals unintentionally paved the way for the neo-liberal intrusion into educational policy that we witness today. Even if the manifesto were not mentioned so often by today's critics, its role as a rallying point for an entire generation of French teachers, and its resonance among the current generation of reformers, make it a foundational document. It begins with a clear statement of the profession's role as a means of socioeconomic liberation, as opposed to acquiring marketable skills within the capitalist system:

> Notre action pédagogique pour la liberté, l'authenticité, l'épanouissement des hommes ne saurait...être dissociée du contexte économique, social et politique ou elle s'inscrit. L'école ne doit ni s'illusionner sur son pouvoir, ni se replier sur une formation qui préparerait exclusivement à la vie professionnelle.

[Our pedagogical action in favor of mankind's freedom, authenticity, and fulfilment cannot be separated from the economic, social and political context in which it occurs. The school must have no illusions regarding its power, nor must it fall back on training that prepares one exclusively for professional life.] (2)

The refusal to participate in "training that prepares one exclusively for professional life" is at first simply another version of the belief that literature, and art in general, occupy an autonomous realm that is free of the corrupting influence of the market. Nicolas Boileau and Jean de La Fontaine would have agreed that instruction in French language and literature should, *noblesse oblige*, be divorced from any concern for making a profit or earning a living. But the authors of the Charbonnières manifesto were not echoing such aristocratic disdain for material concerns, quite the opposite. As Marxists (since many, if not most AFPF members in 1969 identified as such), they believed in the economic determinants of all human activity, including not only the teaching profession, but artistic production as well. Literature and its teaching are indeed inseparable from the "economic, social, and political context" in which they occur, yet at the same time teachers opposed cultural transmission that served the purpose of integrating students into the capitalist system. The dream of 1968 was to reconcile historical materialism with freedom from the tyranny of the market; to deny art its transcendent claims, while using it as a means to achieve a socialist egalitarianism.

The manifesto proposed a third way, an escape from the stalemate between "literarians" who view the discipline as a sacred construct, and "utilitarians" for whom literature is simply a potentially useful and remunerative function of language. In the idealism of the counterculture, life had the potential to be a product of material circumstances as well as a spiritual emancipation, a rejection of market forces that did not require any Baudelairean exile from society. Can literature legitimately regain its privileged status as a pillar of general education if one replaces "utilitarian" goals with revolutionary ones? That is what the founding members of the AFPF were trying to accomplish. The manifesto provides us with a working hypothesis that literature is part of general education, but only inasmuch as it provides a materialist solution to cultural alienation and passivity.

The elimination of the language-literature distinction continues on page two of the manifesto under the title "Maîtrise de la langue" [language mastery], an expression which the Ministry of Education was to use for the first time in its official instructions only in 1990 (Vigner 2011, 21). It states that the study of language must not end at "*troisième*", the final year of middle school before entering the *lycée* where the discipline of "French" officially becomes the study of "literature"; conversely, the study of literature as such must begin in as early as primary school, in order to cultivate the students' "freedom and authenticity" (2), presumably by providing them with the control over the means of linguistic production necessary to exercise agency. In a further erosion of disciplinary barriers between literature and non-literature that would (much) later be termed "*décloisonnement*" [decompartmentalization], the discipline of "literature" is redefined to encompass cinema, television, popular music, foreign language texts, the press, advertisements, and broadcast commercials (2–3); "language" itself encompasses non-verbal communication and non-linguistic signs, as a consequence of the growth of semiotics. By thus removing the walls that had previously confined inherited literary culture, the school replaced the goal of assimilation into a national community with "une capacité à comprendre le monde" [an ability to understand the world] (8), reflecting a desire to make good on the republican promise to replace aristocratic values with democratic ones. The AFPF, to their credit, recognized that an unprecedented degree of attention to and respect for the socially and culturally determined habitus of each student was the logical consequence. That included, for example, validating the students' sociolinguistic practices with "une attitude d'accueil...immédiate" [an attitude of immediate welcome/acceptance] (18) on the part of the teacher, in other words: *to recognize the legitimacy of cultural practices that students themselves bring to the henceforth deconsecrated classroom*. Such removal of the symbolic wall separating the school from the rest of society, and the resulting demystification of the pedagogical process, defy any attempt to compare what is gained in the process, with what is lost. Consciously or not, the Charbonnières militants reproduced the question faced by the Church after the Second Vatican Council, that had concluded three years earlier, eliminated the Latin Mass: is the gain in openness and transparency able to compensate for the loss in authority and mystique?

Other recommendations included that all French teachers must think of themselves as language teachers and not simply teachers of literature, up to and including the university level; that they must provide students access to different "forms of expression", "sans limiter les formes écrites à la littérature" [without limiting written forms to literature] (2); in addition to "literary reading", the teacher must provide "un apprentissage de la lecture critique de documents écrits, parlés, filmés (presse, publicité, etc.)" [training in the critical reading of written, spoken, filmed documents (such as) the news media, advertising, etc.] (3). In the following revolutionary statement, literature is to be demystified: "le maître de français n'est pas dépositaire d'une 'culture' qualitativement supérieure à celle des autres disciplines" [the French teacher is not the custodian of a "culture" that is qualitatively superior to those of other disciplines] (3).

The purpose of such radical statements is clear: literature must be removed from the sacred space where it has been protected for use by the privileged class at the risk, so far unrecognized, of losing its very identity. Is literature still literature if it is no longer on an altar, covered by veils, and surrounded by walls? In this ideological context, the answer is yes. Even at the university level, students must read literature in its relations to other kinds of document, "written forms" of language that include far more than the printed word, even such previously unrecognized genres as print advertisements and broadcast commercials. The statement that the French teacher must not think of him- or herself as the "custodian of a culture that is qualitatively superior to those of other disciplines" provides us with valuable insight into the atmosphere in educational institutions in France in the 1960s, where the discipline of "French" enjoyed a recognized and, in this account, wholly unjustified superiority over the others. Literary education is relativized, and therefore considered equal in importance, and perhaps also, to a degree, in purpose to other disciplines. But what does that mean? What is a literary pedagogy that is no longer culturally "superior" to math, science, history, or geography?

All of these disciplines have in common the potential to emancipate the individual from dependencies that interfere with the realization of one's humanity. Before we dismiss this sentence as a cliché, we must remember that this document is informed by a revolutionary ideology that gives a very specific meaning to the term "realization of humanity". The liberated human being, in that context, is one whose position in society is no longer determined by unequal economic power relations. As such, the individual is not held back from exercising autonomy, either economically, socially, or intellectually, as the member of a society of unmediated, and therefore just and authentic human relationships. How can the teaching of literature contribute to the development of such autonomy? The disappearance of economic inequality, even brought about through revolutionary violence, is easier to imagine than the disappearance of cultural inequality: a world where everybody stands in the same, autonomous relationship to culture both as active producer and consumer, and where nobody enjoys a privileged relationship either to reading or to writing, either to consuming or producing art. In such a world, there would no longer be associations of scholars who have special insight into the literary corpus, especially its most obscure corners. In other words, the corporation of teachers of literature would be voluntarily weakened, amputated of its mission as guardian of the sacred texts, and its function would be reduced to creating autonomous readers, writers, and speakers of language.[8] We must consider the possibility that, in fact, our purpose as literature teachers is exactly what the manifesto says it is: to debunk textual authority, whether it be that of a Mallarmé poem or a cigarette advertisement, and facilitate an unmediated relationship to language in all its forms. Instead of focusing on ways to make ourselves needed or wanted by talking about the contradictory practical and spiritual benefits of humanist education, and other forms of marketing, perhaps literature teachers should concentrate on making ourselves unnecessary, just as revolutionaries are unnecessary once class privileges have finally been abolished.

The manifesto expanded the concept of "liberation pedagogy" further to include science's promise of an escape from ideology. It states that teachers must make use of the scientific rigor enabled by the advances in applied linguistics, but "Un appareil aussi rigoureux ne se justifie que dans la mesure où il peut donner aux enfants, aux adolescents, les moyens d'une plus grande maîtrise de l'instrument linguistique et par conséquent d'une plus grande liberté de parole, c'est-à-dire d'une utilisation créatrice de la langue." [Such a rigorous apparatus is justifiable only insofar as it can give children and adolescents the means to a greater mastery of the linguistic instrument, and therefore a greater freedom of speech, that is to say a creative use of language] (7). It so happens that the year 1969 in France saw the adoption in teacher-training schools (*écoles normales*) of structuralism and applied linguistics, several years after they had taken hold in university departments of literature, and the Charbonnières authors lucidly described the attendant risks, at the same time as they welcomed a scientific antidote to the unreflective, ritualistic catechism that so much of literary pedagogy had become after the intellectual and political promise sparked by Lanson died out. The above quote states that science in literary pedagogy is justifiable only to the extent that it helps students acquire linguistic mastery, which is simply another way to liberate them from false consciousness by establishing them as creators, and not simply consumers, of language.

The warning was prescient, but too often ignored. The risk that scientific methods (under the guise of structuralism) that were intended to demystify can backfire, and turn into a discourse that is more formulaic and obfuscating as the one they were supposed to replace, was more than hypothetical. It is indeed ironic that educators who called for the redistribution of cultural capital away from the privileged classes, in the process also adopted a purportedly demystifying, yet ultimately cryptic scientific discourse that managed to produce a similar concentration of knowledge. Such is the conclusion reached by Tzvetan Todorov in his 2007 tract aimed at the literary pedagogical establishment, *La littérature en péril* [literature at risk], in which he looks back at the structuralist monster that he admits having helped to unleash. And yet this is no *mea culpa*. Todorov places the blame for the misuse of the new scientific discourse squarely on the excessive enthusiasm of members of the May 1968 generation, who assumed that it would deliver a liberation that such discourse never actually promised; in fact, the concepts of structuralist linguistics proved especially difficult to apply in the secondary school setting, resulting in a separate "crisis" all its own (see Eric Dumaître). In order to convince the reader that he is not responsible for the current fixation of *lycée* teachers on the tools of discourse analysis, rather than on literary texts and their relation to the world, despite the fact that he was one of the pioneers of structuralism in literary studies, Todorov quotes his younger self, who as early as 1969 had said: "Le désavantage de ce type de travail, c'est...le fait qu'il ne va pas très loin, qu'il ne sera jamais qu'une étude préliminaire, qu'il consiste...à identifier les catégories en jeu dans le texte littéraire, et non pas à nous parler du sens du texte." [The disadvantage of this type of work (the structuralist approach) is the fact that it does not go very far, that it will never be anything but a preliminary study, that it consists in identifying the categories in play in the literary text, and not in speaking to us about the meaning of the text] (29). Alas, because of "May 1968" and its materialist, scientist tendencies, the pendulum "ne s'est pas arrêté à un point d'équilibre, il est allé très loin dans la direction opposée" [did not stop at a point of equilibrium, it swung very far in the opposite direction]. (29)

Why did the pendulum keep moving? After all, the Charbonnières militants never intended linguistic science to dominate the classroom, but simply to counteract the blind worship of an assumed and unanalyzed literariness that the history-based commentary exercise had become. "Liberation pedagogy" is a lot to ask of a teacher, however, especially one who works in a hierarchical system. Plenty of teachers, even those swept up in the spirit of the counterculture, either did not change their methods, or else changed them in a manner that did not threaten the social order. Thus does the priesthood sustain the awe of the parishioners, not by explaining and demystifying the divine and rendering it accessible, but by protecting it with ever more numerous and elaborate veils. By contrast, "a creative use of language" puts the student in the role of the secular divinity itself: the author.[9] The ultimate transgression, from a religious perspective, is the satanic impulse to compete with the creator; from a pedagogical perspective, by contrast, closing the gap between "expert" author and "apprentice" reader is arguably the ultimate justification for what we do. Visionaries such as Lanson and the pioneer members of the AFPF understood that principle very well, even if they both ultimately failed to put it into practice.

The manifesto does much more than invest hope in contemporary developments in linguistic science, of course. It went on to declare that teachers must insist on "[le] refus d'une culture-somme" [the refusal of a summative (conception of) culture] (8); in other words, culture is an ongoing collective project, not a transmitted body of knowledge. Finally, the study of French literature at the university is no longer to be seen as continuous with the *lycée*, for the simple reason that the university does not serve the purpose of general education: "On réservera pour le premier cycle de l'Enseignement Supérieur l'étude systématique de l'histoire littéraire, indispensable pour des étudiants désormais spécialisés et pour eux seuls." (...) "L'ENSEIGNEMENT SECONDAIRE FRANÇAIS N'EST PAS DESTINÉ À FORMER DE FUTURS PROFESSEURS DE LETTRES OU DE FUTURS CRITIQUES LITTÉRAIRES." [The systematic study of literary history will be reserved for the first stage of higher education. FRENCH SECONDARY EDUCATION IS NOT INTENDED TO TRAIN FUTURE LITERATURE PROFESSORS OR FUTURE LITERARY CRITICS] (8–9, emphasis in the original). One can infer from such a *cri de guerre* that secondary education in literature is not to be a watered-down version of the specialized academic discipline of literary studies, but an entirely separate process.

The manifesto begins therefore by rejecting three outdated concepts of literary education: the passive absorption of an idealized literary patrimony, the subordination of literature to purely pragmatic ends, and the training of future experts. The goal of a "creative use of language" places individual agency ahead of the structuring power of an inherited culture, without substituting a relative "market value" for the absolute "cultural value" that is being rejected. There is a subtle but important distinction here between a "bad", market-based relativism and a "good", antielitist cultural relativism that sees all literature as part of a continuum instead of separating it into nonoverlapping categories of "high" and "low":

> Certes, tous les élèves n'arrivent pas au second cycle en état d'aborder Racine ou Balzac, par quelque méthode que ce soit. (...) Il convient en ce cas, de faire, dans un premier temps, un appel particulièrement large à la littérature contemporaine, même dans des formes peu élaborées; ou qualitativement inférieures (romans sentimentaux ou 'série noire', magazines) sur lesquels les élèves peuvent aisément s'exercer à trouver structures et 'lois du genre', à démonter les procédés de fabrication, à démythifier les succès dus à la mode ou à la publicité. (...) [L]'accès relativement facile aux grands textes contemporains (langue connue, idées 'dans l'air') (...) et des références aux œuvres du passé, soulignées au cours des recherches, peuvent les amener à des lectures qui ne seraient pas acceptées (ou mal faites) si on les proposait directement.
>
> [Indeed, not all students arrive at the second stage of secondary school (i.e., the *lycée*) capable of taking on Racine or Balzac, regardless of the method. In such cases, it is appropriate to begin by calling widely upon contemporary literature, even in its simpler forms, or qualitatively inferior ones (romance or detective novels, magazines) in which students can easily practice finding structures and "rules of the genre", unraveling the creative processes, demythologizing commercial successes attributable to fashion or marketing. The relative ease of access to great contemporary works (familiar language, ideas already "in the air"), and of references to works from the past emphasized during the students' research, can lead them to readings that would be rejected (or poorly done) if one presented them directly.] (14)

The term "qualitatively inferior", referring to pulp and romance fiction, or to the inclusion of advertisements into the curriculum in order to "demythologize" commercial strategies, seems to preserve the aura of absolute or "disinterested" value that traditionally characterizes inherited culture; yet the fact that such texts are even mentioned in the context of literary pedagogy is itself revolutionary. It is also responsible for an increasing suspicion that the French school has abandoned the distinction between contemporary mass culture and the heritage of "Racine or Balzac".

The manifesto goes on to question the central "canonical exercise" of literary pedagogy discussed in Chapter 3, the *dissertation* or argumentative literary essay, especially in its summative role as an official badge of proficiency via the all-powerful *bac* exam:

> La dissertation doit être maintenue pour l'effort de raisonnement logique, de synthèse auquel elle invite; à condition toutefois 1) qu'elle porte sur un problème véritable, présenté en termes directs, et soit le point d'arrivée d'une oeuvre ou d'un thème, 2) qu'elle cesse de conduire, dans une fatidique troisième partie à d'illusoires et rassurantes synthèses et qu'elle serve à une authentique mise en question, 3) qu'elle ne soit jamais exercice de mémoire, mais mise en œuvre de documents. Ces trois conditions l'excluent de l'examen du second degré.
>
> [The literature essay must be kept because of the effort of logical reasoning, of synthesis, that it demands, on the condition however 1) that it center on a real problem, expressed straightforwardly, and that it be the endpoint of a work or theme; 2) that it no longer lead, in an inevitable part three (of the traditional three-part structure of the French literature essay), to illusory and reassuring syntheses, but instead be in the service of an authentic questioning; 3) that it never be an exercise in memory, but rather a putting into practice of documents. These three conditions exclude it from the advanced secondary exam (i.e., the *bac*).] (15)

Here again we are faced with an apparent affirmation of traditional pedagogy (the intellectual value of the *dissertation*) that is actually a radical proposal: because the exercise must be based on a concrete problem, must avoid resolution, must use documents (in other words, depend on research), it can no longer function as certification, but rather as a purely formative process.

The "Charbonnières Manifesto" and the explicitly militant circumstances of its creation, its rejection of the superiority of "literary culture" and its appeal to scientific empiricism, reflected a willingness and even desire to expand the definition of literature beyond the classics without, however, denying their value – a contradiction that may well have diminished its influence. True, its concern for the diverse sociocultural backgrounds of students, and its emphasis on the liberating, rather than socializing, function of education, can still be discerned in the current editorial choices of *Le Français aujourd'hui*. At the same time, it exemplifies the persistence of conservative reflexes in the midst of radical thought: for example, the dismissal of detective novels as "inferior" literature, or the claim that contemporary literature is valid only as a "stepping stone" to less accessible, older works which remain paramount, despite the stated rejection of an inherited canon (*"culture-somme"*). These contradictions result from the almost nonexistent rate of change in literary education in 1969, ever since Lanson had participated in similar polemics more than half a century earlier, combined with the urge to refound the society itself on entirely new principles. And while the authors maintained the hierarchy of inherited culture over popular culture, the fact that the latter should serve as a stepping-stone to the former destroys the "legitimate-illegitimate" distinction that continues to impede literary pedagogy to this day. The failure of the Charbonnières militants to break with the past, in spite of their revolutionary rhetoric, may actually have been intentional. When pedagogy creates a bridge between student culture and inherited culture, between school and the outside world, the general education of texts by Racine and Balzac, or Shakespeare and Austen, becomes more possible: students take possession of what they previously could only worship at a distance.

LITERARY PEDAGOGY, CULTURAL RELATIVISM, AND *COMMUNAUTARISME*

While not all of the manifesto is uniformly radical (it was, after all, written by a committee), the cultural openness that it describes anticipates such controversial chapters in American pedagogical history as the experiment with "Ebonics" (the recognition of African-American as a separate language by the Oakland, California School Board in 1996), and bilingual education. In both the French and American examples, the school reaches out to students whose cultural background it considers to be an obstacle to the assimilation of *"culture-somme"* or "summative (canonical) culture". The American examples provoked conflicting interpretations of the purpose of such initiatives, and political battles that are yet to resolve. Bilingual education, according to some of its proponents, merely recognizes that some students begin school without knowing English, and that they will fall behind unless a substantial portion of their instruction occurs in their native language. Combined with ESL classes, bilingual instruction aims ultimately to produce students who are proficient in English while also studying at grade level in subjects such as math and science. But the enemies of bilingual education interpret it differently, saying that its true purpose, whether its advocates admit so or not, is to allow non-English-speaking communities to develop in parallel to the dominant culture, relieving them of the obligation to assimilate and furthering the ghettoization of society. The resulting dialogue of the deaf, a subset of the broader political fight over how (and whether) to address multiple types of ghettoization, has been studied by many researchers on education, such as Beatriz Arias and Ursula Casanova (*Bilingual Education: Politics, Practice, and Research*, 1993), with no solution in sight.

Ghettoization is of course an intractable political issue in France as well, though the word most often used is "*communautarisme*", usually translated as "communitarianism", yet bearing quite different connotations in French and in English. Rather than emphasizing and valorizing interpersonal relationships and civic engagement of all kinds, the French term is widely used in the negative sense of ethnic, religious, linguistic, and other types of resistance to cultural assimilation and/or to universalist republican values. In recent decades, it has served as an umbrella for a range of dysfunctions plaguing French society, from the question of the appropriate response to the Middle East refugee crisis, to the problem of homegrown Islamist terrorism. In 1969, it was impossible to predict that the concept of "*accueil immédiat*" [immediate welcome/acceptance] cited in the Charbonnières Manifesto would directly contradict the law passed thirty-five years later according to which: "Dans les écoles, les collèges et les lycées publics, le port de signes ou tenues par lesquels les élèves manifestent ostensiblement une appartenance religieuse est interdit" [In public primary schools, middle schools, and high schools, the wearing of signs or clothing by which students ostensibly express a religious affiliation is forbidden] (Article L141-5-1 of the "Code de l'éducation" of 2004, which defines the presence of signs of religious affiliation as a desecration of the school's space, and therefore belongs in any discussion of the attempted "deconsecration" of said space by the Charbonnières militants or other factions).

It is unfair to speculate on the changes that the Charbonnières militants would have made to their manifesto if they had written it after the 2004 law instead of thirty-five years prior. The concept "*attitude d'accueil*" was already hard for the conservative establishment to accept in 1969, when it implied openness to class diversity; who knows how it would have been received if "*accueil*" had also meant openness to cultural practices that in

France today are widely considered incompatible with republican values, such as "ostentatious" public displays of religious observance? The manifesto was written fifteen years before the first emergence of what has come to symbolize the limit of the "welcoming attitude" of the school toward its students: the notorious "*affaire du foulard*" [headscarf affair], a term created when several Muslim schoolgirls were forbidden to attend class in the Paris suburb of Creil unless they removed their hijab. "*Accueil*" after all implies acceptance of *all* "proximate culture", of the practices and beliefs that define one's identity and are separate from, or prior to school-based socialization processes. Those practices and beliefs naturally originate in the family, as well as in the child's exercise of freedom of choice. They include religion, language, exposure to popular culture, in short: the potentiality infinite diversity of values in which students are invested, and for which the school is not responsible. The question of the role of popular and nonverbal cultural artifacts in the literature classroom is but a variation on the question of the "right to difference" that the headscarf law denies. What relevance do the radical principles of Charbonnières have in a society in which the 2004 law has clearly rebuilt at least one of the walls surrounding the (religion-free) sanctuary of the school?

Use of the term "*communautarisme*" in popular media has exploded in the last twenty years, and almost always refers to the resistance against the full adoption of national, "republican" values expressed among particular minority subcultures that stubbornly define themselves by race, religion, national origin, and other characteristics. The practice of wearing the hijab, or the far-more-concealing burqa, is an example of "communitarian" behavior that has famously been banned: the hijab is forbidden in public schools, and the burqa is banned everywhere except the home. Of course there is an endless list of cultural practices that, while not illegal, are generally tagged as "non-French". The tension between French law and a portion of the French Muslim population is only the most visible symptom of a far deeper and more pervasive phenomenon: the perceived incompatibility between national culture that is inherited, taught in the school, and therefore legitimate, and culture that is local, individual, and taught in the home (if it is "taught" at all). Students' culture is branded as illegitimate, not only when it literally breaks the law (such as the partial or total veiling of women and girls), but also when it challenges the hegemony of the "legitimate" pedagogical canon. Therefore, the veil and headscarf are virtually as transgressive in the republican classroom as nonstandard language (argot, patois, Arabic), pop culture (television series, hip hop music, street art), and religious discourse or symbols (Catholicism in 1905, Islam today). The metaphor of the classroom as a "sanctuary" for the transmission, through worship, of canonical texts has led to its literal interpretation, such that *any* cultural manifestation that does not overlap with the pedagogical canon has the power to desecrate, and therefore must be suppressed. The school's demonization of values and practices that students and/or their families espouse is already a social problem, but it is a pedagogical one as well. In Chapter 1, I had mentioned that the greater familiarity of most American students with *The Incredible Hulk* over *Hamlet* was an advantage, pedagogically speaking. What I meant is that one can more easily teach literature (and other subjects) by building on what students already know and like, rather than immediately confronting them with the unfamiliar and often impenetrable world of canonical culture. In most schools, of course comics are more likely to be confiscated than taught.

All educational systems face the challenge of bridging the gap that usually separates the "familiar" culture of students from the "remote" culture of the school, especially now that some form of secondary education has become universal, and no longer caters exclusively to children of the cultural elite. In the United States, one does not have to read Alan Bloom or William Bennett in order to find an intolerance of students' private cultural practices that is at least as unyielding as the French school's exclusion of the veil. The American examples of Ebonics and bilingual education are excellent analogies for the challenge presented to the French school by the headscarf, popular culture, and all other practices viewed as illegitimate according to a standard that combines secular morality and nationalism. Policies such as bilingual education were supposed to create pathways between "culture of proximity" and "inherited culture" where currently too few exist; but the creation of such pathways depends on the dissolution of those same moral and national boundaries. The numerous and frequently violent reactions against such policies defend the boundaries, for example, by denying the claim that a teacher's attention to students' cultural background can be justified as an entrance ramp on the road to canonical knowledge and social integration, and not a substitute for them.

Although far less "decompartmentalization" has occurred in French education between inherited culture and culture of proximity, or between the disciplines of literature and linguistics, than its more reactionary critics have claimed, reformist programs such as the Charbonnières manifesto have managed to influence subsequent reforms to the teaching of French. Examples include the mandatory inclusion of works of children's and young adult literature in primary and middle school; "argumentation" as an exercise designed to better express one's opinion and to assess the opinions of others; attention to formal and informal levels of speech. Another item in the manifesto has had even more influence on the reforms of the last forty-five years: the desire to create "des liaisons vécues, entre les différents ordres d'enseignement d'une part, [et] innovation et recherche scientifique d'autre part..." [experiential links between the different levels of education on one side, and scientific research and innovation on the other] (4). The AFEF and its journal have consistently worked to reconcile the discourse of academic theory and classroom practice, promoting the application of structuralist linguistics to literary study. Emile Benvéniste's "theory of enunciation" found its way into textbooks, for example, a fact that one of the many conservative enemies of educational reform, Paul-Marie Conti, laments in *L'Enseignement du français aujourd'hui: Enquête sur une discipline malmenée*, 2008 (37–43). Another example of the adoption of linguistic theory is in the manifesto itself: "La linguistique substitue à la notion de faute celle de convenance" [Linguistics substitutes the notion of error with the one of propriety.] (5) The substitution of "*convenance*" for "*faute*" derives from the challenge of descriptive linguistics to prescriptive grammar, providing scientific recognition of the legitimacy of spontaneous student output, much like the recognition of African-American English as a distinct language one can call "Ebonics", rather than a litany of grammatical mistakes. It also removes the primary connotation of "*faute*" as an offense against a moral or religious law; but society takes a long time to catch up to its scientists.

Implementation of the manifesto, as suggested above, faced stiff resistance. Many saw the rejection of a "*culture-somme*" or cultural canon, in favor of open recognition of the spontaneous cultural affiliations of the student, as an attack on national unity. In a development that could not have been predicted in 1969, "immediate welcome" of the student's social and cultural background weakens the argument for protecting the classroom space from signs of religious affiliation. After all, if the teacher is expected to acknowledge the legitimacy of the students' "proximate culture" by viewing it as commensurate with the language and culture traditionally promoted by the school, it becomes difficult to justify the exclusion of *any* speech or behavior that does not directly impede learning (of course, some people insist that the headscarf does exactly that: impede learning). The manifesto's call for adopting new discoveries in literary and linguistic theory, among other radical proposals, provoked a reaction on the part of a large number of teachers (and parents), amplified by the intense media coverage that educational reforms always elicit in France, that has helped it retain its subversive power.

If the Charbonnières manifesto has influenced the teaching of French, it is due in part to a paradox, in the form of support from an unexpected and, for most of its authors, unwelcome source. I wrote earlier that resistance to educational reform in France expresses itself more as nostalgia than economic anxiety, but, it is not that simple. The argument that education should above all support growth, for example, by attending to the human resource needs of employers, is not limited to consumers of American higher education. At least since the 1970s, economic anxiety has loomed large in French education. The paradox is that the AFEF fought for the deconsecration of culture, and for the merging of literature and language, for the disinterested purpose of liberating the student's potential for self-realization. The free-market, "neo-liberal" faction, by contrast, supports similar reforms, not in order to free the individual as in 1960s, but in order to free the economy. Strange bedfellows, indeed.

One can discern an opportunity within this paradox of almost simultaneous right-wing co-option, and consequent left-wing critique, of the still-relevant reformist ambitions of the Charbonnières manifesto. In the wake of more than thirty years of high unemployment in France and the economic crisis of 2008–9, and under the guiding spirit of the OECD and other "neo-liberal" institutions, the subordination of education to economic growth has fueled both the reformist zeal of the French Ministry of Education, and the instinctive, almost violent reaction that such reforms provoke among public intellectuals, parents, and a wide segment of the teaching profession. The "neo-liberal right" has recently taken up the banner of reforms originally proposed by the revolutionary left, completely shuffling the political cards in the process. But the AFEF was not founded in order to promote public-private collaboration and economic growth, a fact that might help us to find value in its reforms that cannot be reduced simply to a return on financial investment. The manifesto's inspiration, once again, was "[une] action pédagogique pour la liberté, l'authenticité, l'épanouissement" [a pedagogical action in favor of freedom, authenticity, fulfillment] of humanity; and while such action "ne saurait être dissociée du contexte économique, social et politique" [cannot be separated from the economic, social, and political context], it is (of course) essential that the school not be defined by "une formation qui préparerait exclusivement à la vie professionnelle" [a training that prepares exclusively for professional life] (2). Because the original challenge, both to "national language" as taught in primary school, and to "national literature" as taught in secondary school, has roots in a long tradition of pedagogy of liberation, it should be possible to reform the system by returning to those roots – and not by placing general education under the authority of private interests, nor by expressing nostalgia for a past that never existed. And while the manifesto did not immediately transform the discipline, its legacy has had an impact on the general education of literature in France. It can even be found in what may be the most substantial and controversial series of reforms to French literary pedagogy since the crisis surrounding "la nouvelle Sorbonne" a century earlier.

THE REFORMS OF 1999

Plenty of changes occurred in the French educational system after 1968, a few of which were indeed foreshadowed in the Charbonnières manifesto. When it comes to the teaching of literature, however, progress was slow until late in the second term of President François Mitterrand, when a committee to study the discipline of French and make recommendations for reform was established by the Minister of Education, Jack Lang. Designated as the *Commission des programmes en Lettres* (Committee for the Literature Curriculum), it met under the leadership of the distinguished seventeenth-century literature scholar Alain Viala from 1992 to 2002. By 1999, then Minister of Education Claude Allègre had approved changes to the teaching of French literature in the *lycée* that were based on the committee's recommendations. The reaction to these reforms in the public as well as in academia was overwhelmingly negative, and spawned a movement, in print and electronic media, to "save literature" from what was (and still is) widely perceived as the misguided transformation of the school into an instrument of economic growth. During the past ten years, the reaction has achieved some degree of success: more recent proposals emanating from the ministry aim to dismantle, at least partly, the reforms of the "Viala era".

In order to understand what is controversial about these reforms, one must interpret the following excerpts from the new *programme* (curricular guidelines) for the year of *seconde* (the year preceding the separation of *lycée* students into different areas of specialization, and therefore still retaining the status of French literature as "general education" subject), as it was published by the *Bulletin Officiel de l'Education Nationale* in August of 1999:

> Trois préoccupations majeures ont guidé l'élaboration de ce programme.
>
> La première consiste à assurer une cohérence des cursus d'apprentissage de la sixième à la terminale.
>
> La deuxième est le souci de mieux assurer la formation des lycéens d'aujourd'hui en diversifiant les modes d'accès à la littérature.
>
> La troisième, consiste à tenir compte de l'évolution de la discipline dans la continuité des programmes précédents en précisant les objectifs et les contenus, notamment dans (...) l'oral et la maîtrise de la langue, dont le rôle est accru (...) la production de textes d'invention et la maîtrise des discours.
>
> [Three major concerns guided the development of this curriculum.
>
> The first was to ensure coherence in the curricula from *sixième* (the first year of middle school) to *terminale* (the final year of high school).
>
> The second was to improve the education of high school students by diversifying their means of access to literature.
>
> The third was to take into account the evolution of the discipline including previous curricula, while specifying objectives and content, especially mastery of language (including oral proficiency), which now has higher priority, as well as creative writing (*production de textes d'invention*), and mastery of modes of speech (*discours*).]

(35)

These guiding principles may not appear especially dangerous, until one interprets them through the lens of the above-mentioned hostility to economic theories of value. Simply put, such hostility rejects any link between literature and less exalted functions of language, such as the transparency of communication required for social harmony, contract law, and commerce; in other words, it rejects definitions of literary value in terms of market value. But the principles underlying the reforms tend to erase the literary-nonliterary distinction, reducing all texts to documents. "Continuity" of the curriculum from *sixième* to *terminale*, for example, implies eliminating the barrier between the teaching of French language for communicative purposes (primary level) and the teaching of literature (secondary level)[10]; "diversifying means of access to literature" similarly implies that literature is not *sui generis*, and can be compared to other forms of discourse, so that one can "access" it by asking the same questions one can ask of other texts ("what information does it convey?" and "what is the author trying to persuade us of?" would be examples, especially relevant if one seeks to defend against religious or political manipulation); "mastery of language" and of "modes of speech" (formal, informal, and so on) are utilitarian goals, to which literature is now subordinated; "creative writing" makes the wok of the student independent of the literary text that he or she studies. Each principle, as we shall see, has become a target for the defenders of literature.

The "rubrics" by which these goals were to be met are the following:

1 – Genres et registres
2 – Histoire littéraire et culturelle- Un mouvement ou un phénomène littéraire et culturel du XIXe ou du XXe siècle (français ou francophone) 8
3 – Production, diffusion et réception des textes
4 – Argumentation

[1 – Genres and levels of discourse
2 – Literary and cultural history; a literary or cultural movement or phenomenon from the nineteenth or twentieth century, either French or Francophone
3 – The production, distribution, and reception of texts
4 – Argumentation]
(38–9)

While "*genres et registres*" are concepts that describe literature "in itself", history, the production and reception of literature, and "argumentation" are extrinsic. Critics repeatedly singled out "argumentation" as a devious substitution of polemical skill for literary appreciation, overlooking the fact that the description of "argumentation" as "*démontrer, convaincre, et persuader*" [to demonstrate, convince, and persuade] (39), far from being a concession to modern utilitarian values, is yet another echo of the rhetorical literary pedagogy of Jesuit education that continues to hold sway long after its purported demise, just like the unexamined assumption of the absolute value of the canonical text (see Chapter 3).

LITERATURE IN FRENCH SCHOOLS AFTER 1968   145

After this description of the content of the curriculum, the proposal continues with the types of activity to be assigned in class:

1 – Lecture

[O]n vise à développer leur capacité et leur goût de lire, en les confrontant cependant à des œuvres plus éloignées de leur univers culturel familier. Pour cela, on utilise deux formes de lecture:
– La lecture cursive: elle est la forme libre, directe, courante de la lecture; il convient de la développer et d'en donner le goût et l'usage familier, afin d'inciter à la lecture, des élèves qui n'en ont pas toujours l'habitude (...)
– La lecture analytique: elle a pour but l'examen méthodique d'un texte (...). Il s'agit d'une pratique d'interprétation. Elle vise à développer la capacité de lectures autonomes (...).

[1 – Reading
The aim is to develop (students') ability and desire to read, and to have them read works that are distant from their familiar cultural universe. In order to do so, two types of reading will be used:
– Cursive reading (of longer texts, as opposed to close reading of short ones): that is the free, direct, everyday form of reading; one needs to help students that are not always used to (this type of reading) develop a desire and regular practice of it.
– Analytical reading: its purpose is the methodical examination of a text. It is an interpretive practice that aims to develop the ability to read independently.]
(39)

Reading "cursively", which is no more than a recognition that in order to read a lot, one must learn the skill of reading quickly (a point that Fareed Zakaria made in his 2015 book *In Defense of a Liberal Education*), is demonized for being a technique that is not "*une pratique d'interprétation*", which appears to be a confusion of "*lecture cursive*" and "speed reading".[11] The guidelines for writing are as follows:

2 – Écriture

(...) Ils seront entraînés progressivement à produire trois types d'écrits:
– des écrits visant à fixer des connaissances (prise de notes, résumé, fiche de synthèse); à construire et restituer des savoirs, en français et dans les autres disciplines; à initier les élèves à l'écriture d'une lettre et du compte rendu;
– des écrits visant à convaincre ou à persuader;
– des écrits d'imagination, en liaison avec les rubriques du programme....

[-Writing
(Students) will gradually be trained in three types of writing:
– writing intended to provide knowledge (note taking, summarizing, and synthesizing information); to construct and reconstruct knowledge in French as well as other disciplines; to introduce students to letter-writing and keeping records;
– writing intended to convince or persuade;
– creative writing connected to the subjects in the curriculum.]
(39–40)

In other words, writing as well as oral expression are no longer to be exclusively interpretive activities, but are to be broken down into three functions: information assimilation, argumentation, and self-expression. The activities listed above were attacked for instrumentalizing literature, substituting linguistic skills for literary knowledge and sensibility. In conclusion, the emphasis on communication, logic, the ability to recognize, and even to use historical and social variations of language contribute to transparency, to fluency, to linguistic efficiency, all have come to represent a new, debased form of "anti-literature".

"LITERATURE IS BEING ASSASSINATED"

The negative reactions summarized above took many forms, one of the most dramatic of which was an open letter published in *Le Monde* on March 4, 2000. Authored by Michel Jarrety of the Sorbonne and Michel Zink of the Collège de France,[12] it carried the signatures of almost seventy professors as well as more than fifty writers, philosophers, and other public intellectuals, and was titled: *"C'est la littérature qu'on assassine rue de Grenelle"* [It's Literature that is Being Assassinated in the *Rue de Grenelle*]. Even by the hyperbolic standards of French intellectual polemics, the accusation was startling: the Ministry of National Education (located in the *rue de Grenelle*) was guilty of nothing less than murdering literature itself. Among the signatories are distinguished academics in the field of literature, many of whom are well known in the United States, and some of whom regularly teach in American universities, who are not known for gratuitous provocation, such as Antoine Compagnon, Béatrice Didier, Frank Lestringant, Stéphane Michaud, Jean-Pierre Richard, and Jean-Yves

Tadié. While some of the authors and other intellectuals signing the letter are known for taking controversial stands on public issues, they are without exception highly respected, including: Maurice Agulhon, Elisabeth Badinter, Yves Bonnefoy, Françoise Chandernagor, Andrée Chedid, Régis Debray, Michel Deguy, Louis-René des Forêts (a few months before his death at the age of ninety-four), Alain Finkielkraut, Philippe Jaccottet, Emmanuel Le Roy Ladurie, Geneviève Page, Danièle Sallenave, Philippe Sollers, and Anne de Staël.

The text of the letter concerned more than simply the recent reforms to the teaching of French literature. It also mentioned the simultaneous reform of the *Certificat d'aptitude au professorat de l'enseignement du second degré* or CAPES (the recruitment exam for secondary school teachers) in foreign languages, that prioritized language proficiency over literary knowledge: "l'étouffement des littératures étrangères au CAPES recentré sur la seule pratique de la langue" [the suffocation of foreign literatures on the CAPES, now centered entirely on language proficiency]; and the lowering of standards on the dictation portion of the national exam given at the end of *troisième* (just prior to the *lycée*) "la dictée désormais allégée du brevet des collèges" [the dictation exercise, henceforth watered-down, of the middle school certificate]. The authors lamented what they saw as the continuation of a trend that had started at least since the late 1960s, when opportunity for Latin instruction was moved from *sixième* to *quatrième* (in American terms, from middle school to high school), and also when the texts studied in the French class of the *lycée* began to include "[des] '*textes d'idées*', qu'on demandait aux élèves de résumer et commenter sans aucune expérience des questions de société qu'ils pouvaient évoquer" ["texts of ideas" (such as editorials) that students were asked to summarize and comment on without having any experience of the societal issues they might refer to]. The consequence of this long evolution, including the promotion of the oral part of the CAPES at the expense of the written, is that:

[L]e filtre de l'écrit où se repèrent l'aptitude à penser et construire sa pensée, la solidité de la culture et la qualité de l'écriture ne compte plus; c'est décider clairement que les professeurs de demain ne seront plus les maîtres chargés de transmettre un savoir et toute la rigueur de méthode qu'il suppose, mais des animateurs qui ne parleront plus d'une littérature qui sera pour eux chose passée, mais se contenteront au mieux d'enseigner ce langage ordinaire que Mallarmé comparait à une pièce de monnaie, plate transmission de la plus élémentaire pensée.

[The filter of writing, where one can discern the ability to think and to construct one's thought, the substance of culture and the quality of writing, no longer matters; one has clearly decided that tomorrow's instructors will no longer be teachers responsible for transmitting knowledge, with all the methodical rigor it implies, but entertainers who will no longer talk about literature, which for them will be a thing of the past, but rather will at best be content to teach that ordinary language that Mallarmé compared to a coin, the mere transmission of the most basic thought.]

In summary, the primary concerns of the signatories are the shift from a literary to a nonliterary conception of the French discipline as it is taught in the *collège, lycée*, and in the training of their teachers who are recruited through the *concours* of the CAPES, as well as a similar decline of the role of literature in the teaching of foreign languages. The final reference to Mallarmé illustrates the professors' belief that literature is defined as a non-communicative, and therefore exalted, function of language, radically separate from the system of linguistic exchange represented by the metaphor of the coin. A postromantic declaration of literature's aloofness from the "language of the tribe" clearly motivates the defensive reaction to the reforms by these distinguished intellectuals.

It is not surprising that famous professors and authors, all firm believers in the cult of literature, should decry what they perceive as its loss of authority in the school: the substitution of clarity of communication and argumentation for the subtler, deeper pleasures of close literary reading.[13] More surprising, given the leftist political leaning of most (but not all) of the signatories, is the assumption that students, upon entering the school, are not in possession of any valid cultural heritage. Presenting the teaching of literature as a gift that will enable the poor and the marginalized to enter into the kingdom of true (national) culture is a proof of the surprising compatibility of republican social progressivism with aristocratic cultural regressivism; what Bertrand Daunay, one of the best scholars working today in the field of French literary pedagogy, calls "disqualification" of the student by the educational system. In the following passage, Daunay links the reactionary arguments of Agathon (see Chapter 4), to those of critic Michel Picard, who developed a theory of "literary reading" that sharply distinguishes the expert from the novice, as well as to those of the open letter in *Le Monde*:

> [L]e discours méprisant (Agathon), condescendant (Picard), compassionnel (nos modernes) sont des formes différentes d'un même discours de négation de l'altérité, au nom de valeurs culturelles jamais interrogées. Dans tous les cas, les auteurs décrètent la littérature étrangère à certaines classes sociales, pour se scandaliser soit que ces dernières accèdent au niveau d'apprentissage qui l'enseigne, soit que l'on pose la question de l'adéquation de son enseignement à ces élèves.
>
> [The discourses of contempt (Agathon), condescension (Picard), and compassion (our contemporaries [e.g., signatories of the letter]) are different forms of a same discourse, the negation of otherness in the name of cultural values that are never questioned. In every case, the authors decree that literature is alien to certain social classes, only to become indignant, either when these social classes accede to the educational levels where it is taught, or when one questions the adequacy of its teaching to such students.] (Daunay 2006)

In the above passage, Daunay succinctly explains why literary education is perpetually in crisis: not because of the difficulty of founding the discipline on a legitimate basis, though that problem still remains to be solved, but because of the persistent gap the institution of general education continues to insert between the object of study, which is literature, and its students, who are everybody. "How dare the people presume to defile the temple of culture?" asks the aristocrat; "How dare the reformers of education deny the people access to the temple of culture?" ask the progressive republicans. The problem, in both cases, is precisely that culture is not a "temple", but a common legacy and, more importantly, a common project.

What is most surprising of all is that the ever-recurring opposition to the refounding of the French discipline invariably spreads far beyond the intellectuals who occupy the upper strata of the literary field. Strong reaction against the reforms occurred throughout society, and was reflected in a wide range of media. As often happens in France, though with decreasing frequency, the position of the intelligentsia on issues of the day finds an echo all the way down the social ladder.

"*C'est la littérature qu'on assassine rue de Grenelle*" was therefore only one among many hostile reactions to the Allègre reforms based on the report of the Viala commission. During the same month that the letter appeared, a militant collective of teachers and concerned citizens was created: *Sauver les lettres* ("save literature"), which continues to be very active in print and web publishing. Another major attack occurred after the reforms had been in place for several years, in the May–August 2005 issue of the influential journal *Le Débat*, founded by historian Pierre Nora and edited by philosopher Marcel Gauchet. Although the issue begins with an interview of Viala in which he defends the work of his committee ("Former la personne et le citoyen: entretien" [educating the person and the citizen: interview] 7–21), the majority of contributions attack the reforms, often in dismissive terms. In the opening interview, Viala patiently revisited the goals that his committee had hoped to achieve. First, he says that change was long overdue: the previous major revisions to the French discipline occurred during the creation of the "*collège unique*", or combined middle school curriculum for all, in 1973 (implemented in 1975); since then, a new universe of discourse had emerged, influenced by social and technological changes such as the internet, requiring the school to rethink its purpose, to consider an "*offre nouvelle*", a renewed pedagogical "supply" to satisfy an evolving demand, based on input gleaned from an unprecedented number of consultations with teachers, ministry officials, academic experts, and others (10). Like their forebears, the equally embattled founders of the school of the Third Republic, the members of Viala's committee, understood the discipline of French not as an introduction to the specialized academic field of literary studies so much as a means of developing citizenship through the study of French language and literature: training students to think critically, to express and defend their opinions, and to form judgments on the entire range of discourses (ideological, commercial, and perhaps especially religious[14]) that they encounter. Literature, rather than simply being the "end in itself" that justifies its existence as a specialized (as opposed to general-education) discipline, becomes in this new pedagogy "un moyen) d'ausculter et d'éclairer un peu le monde" [a means of examining and explaining the world a little] (15). The 1999 reforms are necessary in order to connect literature and civic life, and while linguistic concepts must never take over the classroom ("Il ne faut pas que l'outil remplace le travail pour lequel il doit servir" [the tool must never replace the work for which it is to be used] 17), they are nevertheless essential in order to implement a literary pedagogy that is truly inclusive, non-elitist, and empirical: "partir des besoins et de la situation des élèves pour aller vers la littérature" [to start with the needs and the situations of students in order to go toward literature] (20). Viala was not entirely alone in promoting the reforms, but it must have felt to him as if he was. One of the few sympathetic voices in the *Le Débat* issue belongs to Gilles Philippe, who had recently published an important book on the danger of the cult of "linguistic perfection" for which the educational establishment is largely responsible, titled *Sujet, verbe, complément: Le moment grammatical de la littérature française (1890–1940)* [subject, verb, complement: the grammatical moment in French literature, 1890–1940]. He at least agreed with Viala that teaching literature required radical change: "en assumant... son 'autonomie' au cours du XIXe siècle, la littérature cessait d'être aisément scolarisable" [by achieving its "autonomy" during the nineteenth century, literature ceased to be easily teachable]. (162) But such understanding and support was rare. Among the more notable diatribes that dominate the remainder of the *Le Débat* issue is the article by Mireille Grange and Michel Leroux, "La pédagogie sens dessus dessous: les programmes de français des collèges" [pedagogy upside-down: the French middle school curricula] (22–36), which explicitly links educational reform to the dehumanizing effects of the capitalist quest for profitability through efficiency: "...l'on en vient à se demander si les véritables inspirateurs de l'actuelle pédagogie, plutôt que Jean Piaget ou Pierre Bourdieu, ne seraient pas en réalité Henry Ford ou Frederick Winslow Taylor" [one ends up wondering whether the true inspiration of the current pedagogy, rather than Pierre Bourdieu or Jean Piaget, might not actually be Henry Ford and Frederick Winslow Taylor] (35). A century after the Agathon and Péguy polemics against the "new Sorbonne" (see Chapter 4), we are once again hearing accusations that literary studies are being turned into an American-style assembly line. Denis Roger-Vasselin sounds a recurring theme: "On *sacrifie* la littérature en la traitant comme *communication*" [one *sacrifices* literature by treating it as *communication*, emphasis in the original] (66). Marc Fumaroli, himself a formidable critic of state control of culture in works such as *L'Etat culturel: Essai sur une religion moderne (The Cultural State: Essay on a Modern Religion*, 1991), as well as a modern advocate for the return of classical languages in general education (most recently in an interview for Le Figaro newspaper in 2015), sees in the new methods "[L]'abrasion persévérante de la notion de chef d'œuvre et de hiérarchie esthétique" [the steady erosion of the notion of masterpiece and of esthetic hierarchy] (83). After perusing one or more textbooks produced in accordance with the new standards, philosopher-politician Régis Debray laments "la chose littéraire dissoute dans la production écrite" [the literary object dissolved into (the mass of) written production] (78), an anxiety over the weakening of literature to the point of dissolution that Marc Fumaroli echoes a few pages later: "l'art littéraire est dissous dans les 'courants socio-culturels'" [literary art is dissolved into "sociocultural currents"] (83). "Sacrifice", "erosion", "dissolution" are especially revealing terms, that say more about the anxieties of the modern intellectual than they do about the actual state of the literary field. The fear of a patrimony squandered, misspent, eroded into nothing expressed in these articles is almost pathological. Using milder language, conservative academician Jean d'Ormesson simply deplores the absence of "l'admiration . . . indispensable à la critique littéraire" [the admiration necessary for literary criticism] (91), while novelist Philippe Sollers sees in the new textbooks evidence of "une volonté de ne rien savoir" [a will to learn nothing] (104). Dissolution, lack of awe, ignorance: thus do French intellectuals in 2005 condemn the inability of reformers to prevent literature from falling off the altar and into the hands of the profane. Almost as one, they want to keep literature, when it is the subject of general education, "at a distance" from those who threaten to destroy it: the students themselves.

Turning away from the neurotic fears of erosion and dissolution, some contributors took possession of the legacy of Péguy and Agathon, and accused the new methods of succumbing to the pressures of capitalism and industrialization. Literature professor and famous critic Henri Mitterand attacked the reforms specifically for their alleged submission to the demands of the employment market, specifically calling the new exercises of *"argumentation"* and *"écriture d'invention"*, both of which were designed to give students permission to speak in their own voice, a trap for the majority of students, and a giant loophole for the others: "la majorité des élèves ahanera sur un tissu de maladresses et de platitudes, et quelques élèves effectivement doués pour 'l'invention' et 'l'écriture' pourront s'offrir au bac une note magnifique sans s'être jamais préoccupés des 'perspectives' ni des 'objets d'étude'" [most students will puff and pant over a litany of infelicities and clichés, and a small number of students who in fact are gifted at "invention" and "writing" will obtain a magnificent grade on the *bac* exam without ever having had to bother with "approaches" or "objects of study"] (44–45n.). It is impossible to challenge more clearly the claim that students of literature can themselves be producers as well as consumers of literature.

Mitterand goes on to raise the supreme objection, the charge of classism: "Sous prétexte que les enfants du peuple n'ont pas encore acquis l'aptitude à percevoir les valeurs et les raffinements de la sensibilité, de l'imagination et de la pensée, on les en prive, en somme, définitivement" [on the pretext that children of the lower classes have not yet acquired the ability to perceive the values and nuances of sensibility, imagination, and thought, one essentially deprives them of it forever] (46). A sentiment in apparent contradiction with Mitterand's desire that there should be two distinct disciplines of French in secondary schools: "techniques de l'expression" for the majority, and "littérature" for a minority, with possibility of moving from one to the other, while keeping the two groups distinct. According to him, the Viala reforms contain: "rien pour un français à usage préprofessionnel, mais qui ne serait pas dépourvu d'une formation à l'esprit analytique et critique" [nothing for a French discipline that might prepare students for a professional career without sacrificing training in analytical and critical skills], but instead promote "un enseignement de la littérature mal à l'aise, tronqué, confondu pour l'essentiel avec la rhétorique du discours, se voilant la face devant tout ce qui confère aux grands textes leur savoir" [a literary education that is awkward, truncated, mostly confused for rhetorical discourse analysis, and turns a blind eye toward everything that bestows upon great texts their knowledge] (46).

Other critics, such historian Mona Ozouf, and even Bernard Pivot, former host of the popular literary talk show *Apostrophes* discussed in Chapter 4, either focus on the reforms themselves, or else on their implementation in the form of teacher training (the notorious "*Instituts universitaires de formation des maîtres*" or IUFM) and the creation of new textbooks. Even in this lopsided debate between Alain Viala and his colleagues (the journal *Le Débat*, in this instance, does not really live up to its name), there are some dissonant voices. In the midst of a litany of mostly nostalgic refusals to re-found the French discipline so as to make it "useful" to the greatest possible number of students, some articles strike a wiser, forward-looking stance. Another seventeenth-century specialist, Hélène Merlin-Kajman, in her contribution titled "Combien de mots? 'La Maîtrise de la langue française' n'est pas un but en soi" [How many words? "Mastery of the French language" is not an end in itself] (106–22), thinks constructively about breaking the stalemate. *Contra* Bourdieu and Passeron (1964) she states outright that "high" literature no longer exists as a part of "inherited culture"; it only ever did so for the privileged classes, and today, even children raised in families where they are "gavés de lecture" [force-fed with reading] tend to reject the book (108). She claims that the evangelical fervor with which people insist on bringing literature to the masses through education relies on a mistaken belief that violence is exacerbated by linguistic and cultural deprivation, that being poorly read and inarticulate causes criminal behavior. According to this faith in elevated language, if people could learn to speak well and join the cult of literary idols, then there would simply be less crime and more social peace. Merlin-Kajman sees it differently: what society must achieve through literary pedagogy is "une reconfiguration de la parole, l'introduction à une certaine position de soi à l'égard de la langue et de la communication, plutôt que par la transmission obligée de certains contenus" [a reconfiguration of speech, the introduction to a certain stance of the self in relation to language and communication, rather than the mandatory transmission of specific content] (118). The purpose of literary pedagogy is therefore not the transmission of an aristocratic attitude toward culture, nor is it social and economic success; it is to develop one's identity, to forge tools that allow one to escape from the tyranny of *communautarisme* – identification with one's ethnic, social, and especially religious community over the national community – but, and this is crucial, without falling into the opposite tyranny of an imposed national culture. In other words, the general education of literature, like the republican value of *laïcité* itself, must free the individual from the "oscillation" between communion and hatred that traditional pedagogy, with its false choice between classical culture and ignorance, tends to promote (122).

According to Merlin-Kajman, one must relinquish the goal of mastery of language that rests on familiarity with literary usage and canonical texts. To use a contemporary example: the explanation for the continuing controversy over Nicolas Sarkozy's alleged contempt for *La Princesse de Clèves* that regularly surfaces in the French media (see Chapter 2), is that Madame de Lafayette's novel is a perfect example of traditional French literary patrimony: its origin in the neoclassical French seventeenth century, its aristocratic setting, its language difficult enough to prevent its enjoyment by anyone who is not already an accomplished and experienced talented reader, ensure that a majority will, like the former President of the Republic, find it impenetrable. Merlin-Kajman's model of "mastery" is different from turning every citizen into an expert reader of Madame de Lafayette: "A certain stance of the self in relation to language and communication" is the appropriation of language – any level of any language – by the speaking subject. It is the power derived from identification with an idiolect, and the ability to negotiate different levels of various idiolects. It is literary in the way that all registers of speech have the potential to be literary: it is not in the thrall of a particular yet "universal" shared literary patrimony. It is about expressive skill, about acquiring the authority to speak in one's own name, rather than about knowledge defined as "the mandatory transmission of specific content".

One must not make the mistake of assuming that Viala and Merlin-Kajman are on the same side in the debate: she is the author of *La Langue est-elle fasciste? Langue, pouvoir, enseignement* [Is language fascist? Language, Power, and Education] (2003), a spirited attack on well-meaning attempts by progressive educators to grant school students the status of legislators and arbiters of language, that puts her squarely in the conservative camp. Yet both are among the few forward-thinking contributors to the controversy, at least in this instance. Another agent of change is the organization responsible for the Charbonnières manifesto, the *Association Française des Enseignants de Français*; while its membership no doubt includes many adherents or sympathizers of reactionary groups such as the above-mentioned *Sauver les lettres* collective, the editorial stance of its journal, *Le Français aujourd'hui*, is still committed to reform in the spirit of the 1969 manifesto. Of course, these are the same "pedagogical scientists" who have long been under attack, especially since 1999, and whom many literary academics (including signatories of the letter in *Le Monde*) continue to view with suspicion, even hostility. Still, the consensus that the teaching of literature must change, become more student-centered, and be explicitly linked to practical considerations is well-established among the applied linguists and practicing teachers who populate the field of *didactique du français* ("pedagogy of the French discipline", an academic field at the intersection of literary studies and science of education that is described in the Conclusion). They are, however, an embattled group. Less than ten years after the reforms, the pendulum at the Ministry started to lean in the opposite direction, with proposed *programmes* that returned to a top-down, culturally conservative model of knowledge transmission, as a recent editorial by the AFEF laments:

> C'est bien à une reconfiguration générale que nous assistons. Après l'école élémentaire et le collège, le lycée risque bien d'être gagné lui aussi par l'effacement progressif des avancées de la didactique et de la pédagogie, sous le masque d'un classicisme prétendument efficace et supérieur. A moins que les enseignants ne montrent rapidement que pour eux, les progrès des

élèves passent d'abord par une prise en compte de leurs capacités d'apprentissage et de production.

[We are indeed witnessing a general reconfiguration. After primary and middle school, the *lycée* is in danger of experiencing the gradual elimination of the advances in pedagogy, behind the veil of an allegedly superior and more effective classicism. Unless teachers soon demonstrate that for them, students' progress first requires taking into account their creative and learning potentials.]

(Youx and Etienne, 2010)

It is too early to tell how far the teaching of French literature in the *lycée* will revert to the pre-Viala era. No doubt, as has been the case at least since Gustave Lanson's 1909 call for a more democratic curriculum in his speech at the Museum of Pedagogy discussed in Chapter 4, reform will stumble forward despite the hostility from departments of French literature, the media, the *Académie Française*, and a large portion of the teaching profession. The slowness of progress, however, should be an increasing cause of concern for French society.

The concern is all the more urgent, as recent changes in higher education have arguably made it more difficult for members of the profession to adapt to a changing demand. Reforms begun in 2007 under the leadership of former *Ministre de l'Enseignement supérieur et de la Recherche* [minister of higher education and research] Valérie Pécresse sparked student and faculty strikes (notably during the 2008–9 academic year), demonstrations (including the public readings of *La Princesse de Clèves* mentioned in Chapter 2), and widespread anxiety among the ranks of future French professors. It is difficult for an outsider to make sense of the complex and evolving crisis in the French educational profession today; however, among the many articles on the subject, a clear and thorough account is given by André Ouzoulias, who taught at the University of Cergy-Pontoise and at the teacher-training school, or ESPE (formerly IUFM), of Versailles: *Formation des enseignants: le cauchemar de Jules Ferry* [Teacher Training: Jules Ferry's Nightmare] published simultaneously in March 2010 on the militant websites of the collective "*Sauvons l'université*" [Save the university] and of a cumbersomely named national teachers' union, the *Syndicat National Unitaire des Instituteurs, Professeurs des écoles, et Professeurs d'enseignement général de collège.* (sauvonsluniversite.com/spip.php?article3633) As Ouzoulias pointed out, most recently the anxiety has centered on "*mastérisation*", a reform that was on its way to implementation in 2011. The term refers to the fact that all teachers must hold a master's degree combining expertise in their discipline and in pedagogy, itself not a bad thing. Yet while future French teachers will spend more time in the university acquiring their master's degrees, their practical training will be sharply reduced by the replacement of the year-long, paid internship granted to all successful candidates of the competitive recruitment exams for secondary-school teachers, the CAPES or the *agrégation*, with a more cursory, mentorship-based initiation into actual teaching. The fact that the current law places the *concours* not after, but *during* the acquisition of the master's degree further reduces the quality of training, since students will be studying for the recruitment exam and working on their degree simultaneously. In addition, the IUFM (now ESPE), already subordinated to the regular university system since 2006, became increasingly marginalized. Ouzoulias, along with many professors, teachers, and students, was convinced that these reforms, which are only a part of the deep changes currently traumatizing the teaching profession, show that the government at the time discouraged the kind of pedagogical innovation required by an increasingly alienated (and alien) student population, a situation that does not seem to have improved in the intervening years.

In France today, the argument that there is only one legitimate language, and that the key to its mastery resides in assimilating a consensus-built canon of texts, is one of the most overlooked causes of social fragmentation and unrest. It is, after all, an exclusionary argument. It has delegitimized deviations from standard French, served to "disqualify" generations of schoolchildren from taking possession of their literary patrimony (see Daunay 2004 and 2006), and contributed to the growth of *communautarisme* as a form of resistance to established norms of national identity, especially by citizens who have roots in the postcolonial diaspora. To its credit, the educational establishment, urged on by various agencies including the AFEF and departments of didactics, repeatedly attempts to change the discipline of French, and save it as a viable component of general education. And yet, as long as their critics continue to persuade the public that one must teach only *La Princesse de Clèves* and similar texts, in the same way to every citizen, so that they have equal access to the single legitimate source of expression, these efforts will not succeed. Perhaps the advent of a truly multicultural national identity, corresponding to the multicultural society that France already has become, will reverse the trend. One can only hope it does so before the term "French culture" becomes, like "Roman civilization", the sign of a glorious yet inaccessible past.

Notes

1. If one goes back several decades to the era when the *bac* was still an elite diploma (10 percent of the population in 1960 compared to 75.7 percent of the population in 2014, according to *Repères et références statistiques sur les enseignements, la forme et la recherche* 2015, 232), the "literature option" was the most popular disciplinary track. Today, while the *lycée général* still provides 50 percent of the total number of candidates for the *bac*, far more than either the technological or professional *lycées*, the "L" option is chosen by only 16 percent of these students, whereas "ES" (social science) is chosen by 32 percent) and "S" (science) by 52 percent. In short: while all *lycée* students *must* take French literature as a general education discipline, less than 8 percent of them choose it as an elective (statistics are for the year 2014, published in *Education Nationale: Baccalauréat 2014, Dossier de Presse*, 28). Just as in American higher education, the part of the population that has joined the ranks most recently is much less likely to opt for literature as an elective.
2. The "Lagarde et Michard" series was the textbook that Roland Barthes discussed in "Réflexions sur un manuel", his contribution to the 1969 conference on literary pedagogy organized by Serge Doubrovsky and Tzvetan Todorov in which he made the important claim that French schools do not teach literature, but rather a debased form of literary history. I return to it in the Conclusion.
3. Sabine Loucif described in detail how the discipline of French literature in American universities has diverged from its more conservative French counterpart in her book *A la Recherche du canon perdu: l'enseignement de la littérature française dans les universités américaines* (2001), and "French in American Universities: Toward a Reshaping of Frenchness" in *Yale French Studies* 113 (2008).
4. Violaine Houdart-Merot uses the term *"exercices canoniques"* in her study of the origins of the discipline of French literature in the *lycée* of the Third Republic *La Culture littéraire au lycée depuis 1880* (1998), discussed at length in Chapter 3.
5. The *Petit Robert* dictionary definition clearly brings out the word's ideological connotations, and the basis for its rejection by a society intent on preserving deductive, rather than empirical, notions of value: "Doctrine économique classique prônant la libre enterprise, la libre concurrence et le libre jeu des initiatives

individuelles." [Doctrine of classical economics advocating free enterprise, open competition, and the free play of individual initiatives]. Among its antonyms are "*dirigisme, étatisme, socialisme*" [interventionism, statism, socialism], in which value judgment is the prerogative of a centralized authority.

6. See Raoul Frary (1885) for early arguments for change to the teaching of literature against charges of "libéralisme", a century before the current debates reached their critical point. I discuss this important forerunner of the contemporary humanities-commerce debate in my 2004 book *Teaching the Cult of Literature in the French Third Republic*.

7. The change from "*professeurs*" to "*enseignants*" in the name of the association occurred in 1973. The reason is that "*professeurs*" referred at the time only to university and secondary school teachers, and the association wanted to represent all levels, "de la maternelle à l'université" [from nursery school to university] (AFEF website). The name has stuck, even though the term "*professeur*" now is used at all levels of education, in an attempt to reduce the perception of a disparity in rank and prestige. Today, the title of an elementary school teacher is "*professeur(e) des écoles*".

8. An important variation on this radically egalitarian concept of education is philosopher Jacques Rancière's *The Ignorant Schoolmaster: Five Lessons in Intellectual Emancipation* (1987), based on the work of Joseph Jacotot, the revolutionary early nineteenth-century pedagogue who rejected any claim of superior knowledge on the part of the teacher, or of differences in intelligence among students, viewing education as a completely collaborative and inductive process. While the AFPF did not cite Jacotot in their manifesto, it is certain that their ideology was inspired by this radical tradition.

9. By the middle of the twentieth century, the discipline of literature in French schools had adopted the myth of the divinity of the author, as Paul Bénichou recounts in his groundbreaking 1973 work *Le sacre de l'écrivain, 1750–1830: essai sur l'avènement d'un pouvoir spirituel laïque dans la France moderne* (published in English in 1999 as *The Consecration of the Writer, 1750–1830*). While many reasons explain literature's elevated status, it created a major problem for idealistic teachers who wanted to liberate their students rather than subjugate them: "the advent of a secular spiritual power" embodied by the literary author described by Bénichou had the unintended consequence of making the distance separating writers from apprentice-readers virtually impossible to cross.

10. The division of French between "communication" (taught in primary school) and "literature" (taught in secondary school) is explored by the critic Renée Balibar in many works, notably *L'Institution du français: Essai sur le colinguisme des Carolingiens à la République* (1985).

11. The importance of "*lecture cursive*" or "fast reading" as a central function of literary pedagogy is a major innovation in a discipline that for centuries

focused almost exclusively on short excerpts as the basis for canonical literary exercises. Carole Bisenius-Perrin has explained this aspect of the Viala reforms in her 2001 article "De la lecture cursive au café littéraire".

12. The authors are not identified in the letter itself, but Jarrety and Zink, two of the signatories, are cited as its authors by Denis Roger-Vasselin in his article in the May-August 2005 issue of *Le Débat* (65).
13. Roland Barthes's *The Pleasure of the Text* (1973) is relevant to this discussion, given that esthetic sensibility is a universal pedagogical value. The lack of emphasis in the present study on esthetics as a justification for the general education of literature is not to imply that it is not important. I have simply chosen to focus on the economic-utilitarian dimensions, since those are the ones that currently dominate the debate over the "value" of literature as general education.
14. It might seem anachronistic to say that the French school is still competing against religious authority, especially as far as Catholicism is concerned. But there is a fear that the growing popularity of ultraconservative Islam among young French citizens contributed to the terrorist attacks in Paris on January 7 and November 13, 2015 and Nice on July 14, 2016, and that general education must therefore immunize students against religious extremism by honing their interpretive skills, just as educators in 1969 wanted to immunize them against the rhetoric of capitalism.

CHAPTER 6

How (Not) to Teach: "Parroting" vs "Proximity" in Cinematic Representations of Literary Pedagogy

One of the symptoms of the French national obsession with educational controversies is the frequent representation, both literary and cinematic, of the school. Debates over literary pedagogy therefore play out in fiction as well as in government, academic research, and the news media, providing more evidence that the classroom contributes to the disproportionately large role that literary culture plays in French society. Not only is literary pedagogy well represented in both documentary and feature films, I argue that these media provide a unique and valuable insight into the evolution of the debate over the purpose of a general literature curriculum.

Many recent films that feature the teaching of literature use as a starting point the dominance in France of literary culture, as distinct from literary practice. The teaching of literature reproduces the schism between the practice of reading on the one hand, and the mere promotion of literary culture on the other. In the classroom, "literary reading" would consist of techniques that nurture the students' ability and desire to read literature, whereas "promoting literary culture" simply teaches them to express a reverence for literature that does not have to be nourished by actual reading. The analogy at the end of Chapter 4, that France has a "Catholic culture" that does not however depend on large percentages of the population attending Church, just as it has a "literary culture" that does not depend on them reading literary texts, applies to the school as well. Everyone is required to study literature, unlike religious practice which is entirely a matter of private choice, but not everyone is required to convert to the cult that is practiced in the literature classroom. One can, and frequently does, abandon the hard work of literary reading after obtaining the *bac*. This is also true for high school graduates in the United States, of course, with the difference that far fewer people even bother to show allegiance to literary culture once they have completed their general education, since literary culture is a more peripheral phenomenon compared to its diminished, but still central role in French society.

When French writers and filmmakers introduce the literature classroom into their creations, it is often with the purpose of exploring the same contrast between "cult" and "culture", between the initiation into literariness and the superficial habit of paying respect to it, between reading literature and talking about literature.[1] Films and novels can emphasize one or the other of these types of literary pedagogy, and by doing so they express either faith or skepticism regarding the possibility of teaching literature "in itself". In most of these fictional representations, "faith" results in an idealized representation of the practice of literary pedagogy, whereas "skepticism" exposes it as an insurmountable challenge, if not an outright delusion.

The primary focus of this chapter is on film, but of course literature itself has been a means in France of commenting on the relative compatibility of school and literature. Fictional characters are often presented as readers within a pedagogical setting, and I begin this chapter with a brief detour through the novelistic tradition with which French filmmakers often have competed.[2] Given the fraught history of literary pedagogy, it is not surprising that literary authors have regarded the classroom's role as mediator between student and text with a degree of mistrust. The belief that the school actually prevents the genuine encounter with literature, or even the world (expressed by Prévert's poem discussed in Chapter 2), goes back at least as far as Rousseau's injunction against reading in *Emile*. Another case in point is André Gide, who used scenes of literary pedagogy to attack the validity of school-sanctioned reading in *Les Faux-monnayeurs* [*The Counterfeiters*, 1925]. The novel is infused with reflections on what constitutes "authentic" reading and writing, one of which takes an explicitly pedagogical form: the two adolescents at the center of the narrative, Olivier and Bernard, discuss the written portion of the *bac* exam that Bernard has just taken, which was a commentary on some lines of a poem by La Fontaine, the "Discours à Mme de La Sablière". The excerpt begins with the famous words "Papillon du Parnasse" [butterfly of Parnassus], a metaphor for the poet as a seeker of sensual forms, randomly flitting from flower to flower. When Bernard asks Olivier how he would have approached the text if he had been the one sitting for the *bac*, Olivier argues in favor of a superficial, formalistic approach to literature, an esthetic ideology that is central to the plot of the novel in which the young men appear, and is also a parody of the "art for art's sake" doctrine: "J'aurais dit (...) que la vérité, c'est l'apparence, que le mystère, c'est la forme, et ce que l'homme a de plus profond, c'est sa peau." [I would have said that truth is appearance, that mystery is form, and that man's most profound characteristic is his skin] (Gide 1958, 1142). Olivier's reading mimics the kind of conventional, glib, ready-made judgments that teachers often reward with high grades, and that also (according to Gide) happen to be rewarded with commercial success in the literature market. Because the school treats literature as a sacred text, it is logical to think that literature and education are on the same page. In fact, according to Gide, the fetishizing of the text through the educational process is what prevents literature, insofar as it is taught, from being realized.

Gide's reference to the school in *The Counterfeiters* therefore suggests that authentic literature is incompatible with education, just as it is with commerce. The budding writers Bernard and Olivier, for example, do not learn anything of importance in their *lycée*, but rather in their homoerotic relationships with two competing mentors, Edouard and the comte de Passavant, the former a struggling and unknown (hence authentic) author, the latter a commercially successful and famous (hence inauthentic) one. Gide satirized the school as a place that authorizes itself to treat literary texts, but from which literature is excluded, inserting himself into the debate over the "crisis of French" that had begun years earlier (see Chapter 4), in reaction to the refounding of literature as a scientific general education discipline during the late nineteenth and early twentieth centuries.

The sacralization of literature that has had such an inhibiting effect on pedagogy has its origin in the consecration of the writer (see Paul Bénichou). It therefore stands to reason that the school, with its scientific culture and its vulnerability to the market, be seen by literary authors as a source of danger, if not an outright fraud. That is one reason why so many writers supported the letter to *Le Monde* that declared: "Literature is being assassinated in the *rue de Grenelle*" (Chapter 5). It is why novelist Erik Orsenna portrayed the school as an environment hostile to literature in *La Grammaire est une chanson douce* (*Grammar is a Sweet, Gentle Song*, 2001), in which a well-meaning teacher is scolded by the government inspector, "Madame Jargonos", for not indoctrinating her pupils with the latest linguistic terminology, instead of instilling in them a simple love of words and stories. The list of examples could go on indefinitely.

Some positive images of the French class of course are to be found in literature, but they are far outnumbered by negative ones. The film medium by contrast, has traditionally exhibited less concern with literature's potential incompatibility with the school. Today, the French public not only consumes novels that feature some variation on the classroom experience of literature,[3] it also supports a large market for films, both documentary and fictional, that do the same. This is not a recent phenomenon. Some of the most famous works of French cinematic history belong to this subgenre: Jean Vigo's *Zéro de conduite* (*Zero for Conduct*, 1933); Marcel Pagnol's film adaptation of his play *Topaze* (1936), which he remade in 1951 in a more famous version starring Fernandel; François Truffaut's *Les 400 coups* (*The 400 Blows*, 1959); Yves Robert's *La Guerre des boutons* (*The War of the Buttons*, 1962); André Téchiné's *Les Roseaux sauvages* (*Wild Reeds*, 1994), and many more. Classroom scenes in these classic "school" films often feature a French lesson, whether performing a dictation or recitation exercise in elementary school (Truffaut), or practicing for the literature *bac* in a *lycée* (Téchiné). Whether literary pedagogy is idealized or parodied, the popularity of the subgenre reflects the status of the discipline as a source of powerful emotional investment. The classroom in which French language and literature are taught is a "*lieu de mémoire*" or "memory space", according to historian Pierre Nora's definition of the term in the famous anthology he edited from 1984 to 1992, *Les Lieux de mémoire*, part of which was translated as *Realms of Memory* (1996), and part of which was translated as *Rethinking France* (2001). One of Nora's concerns was to explore how collective memory compensates today for the loss of a historical awareness of the national past, how the trauma of rupture with the past gets hidden under layers of memorialization. As he stated in the introduction to the 2001 translation: "... our present is being enslaved to memory, that is to the fetishism of signs, an obsession with history, an accumulation of the material remains of the national past, and to the infinite ways of expressing the national life..." (xviii). Indeed, the school is in many ways the ideal site for the idealization of the past, as well as being itself a fetishized enclosure: learning literature in school is a perfect example of transmitting patrimonial texts as sacred objects, and constructing an idealized, collective memory of intimacy with those objects that takes the place of individual lived experience. Cinema has made good use of this compensating mechanism by idealizing classroom practices, and the space in which they are fetishistically preserved. Alternatively, as we will see, some films have tried to lift the veil of memory and present scenes of literary pedagogy as problematic, and even traumatic experiences.[4]

Film has always faced doubts as to its cultural legitimacy. As such, it is an ideal vehicle for the question of cultural ownership, for the representation of the pedagogic contrast between an alien (though national) cultural patrimony on the one hand, and a familiar (though often international) "popular culture" on the other. The French genre of school-based films frequently emphasizes the "parroting" style of teaching, through traditional, ritualistic exercises of reading aloud, recitation, and dictation, sometimes in a manner that accentuates their obvious intellectual vacuity (for example, in the failed attempt by a schoolboy to recite a poem in class in Truffaut's *The 400 Blows*), and sometimes as a sentimental tribute to an authoritarian and rigid, but time-honored and quasi-sacred ritual (for example, many of the classroom scenes in Louis Malle's *Au revoir les enfants*, including a dictation in Greek).[5] The French term *"passéisme"* looms large in the idealization of the classroom through film, referring to a particular form of nostalgia. But it also refers to the founding assumptions of humanistic education defined as patrimonial transmission, according to which the true value of cultural artifacts, as distinct from their market value, is above all a function of time, and therefore of distance.

"Passéisme" implies that cultural production becomes corrupt when it responds to present demand rather than remain faithful to tradition. When artists act like a business servicing its customers, they surrender their autonomy to the short-term desires of the mob. The opposite of *passéisme* is *"présentisme"*.[6] Great works are *"passéiste"* since they are not supposed to evoke our own personal past, but emerge instead from an absolute past that is more distant, obscure, hence alien and even repellent to many. Students tend to be *"présentiste"*, consumers of the irresistible best-sellers, pop songs, blockbuster movies, and video games that traditionally do not belong in school, precisely because they are irresistible.

Are *"passéisme"* and *"présentisme"* compatible? The former term challenges the discipline of literature to preserve the opportunity to encounter alien, canonical culture (canonical in part because it is alien, usually more or less archaic, and therefore in need of being taught simply to be understood, never mind appreciated), and to do so through an increase in demand, and not merely through curricular requirements. But creating opportunities for encountering such culture is not nearly enough, and that is where the latter term comes into play. One must facilitate the integration of past culture so as to make it present, ensuring that it is not simply parroted like the "*amo, amas, amat*" and other meaningless sounds that have filled classrooms for centuries. This appropriation (as opposed to parroting) of the past, upon which the viability of literary general education depends, paradoxically requires attention to *present* culture, defined as the values and practices that students bring to the classroom. Rather than start from our privileged position as experts, in other words, we must start from where our students already stand, and work to gradually expand their cultures to include the skills and knowledge that we teach. Education can and maybe should be a process by which "remote" culture grafts itself onto "proximate" culture. To return to the religious analogy first mentioned in Chapter 4: do we conduct an old style, Catholic High Mass (during which the Priest literally turns his back on the congregation) where it is sufficient to bring the worshipers into proximity of the divine, with no concern to connect them to it on their own terms? Or do we act as a Protestant Pastor whose role is to facilitate a direct communication with God, through the worshiper's own language (not Latin), and personal experience?

Teachers who present students with a literary text and expect them to learn are like the missionary who thinks that people who have never before seen a crucifix will spontaneously kneel before it. Something else must happen first. Each student must be persuaded to learn, and often must undergo conversion to the value system under which the task we require them to perform is meaningful. That means starting with the immediate concerns of the students themselves – what they already find meaningful – and then expanding those concerns to include the subject matter of cultural transmission. It requires earning the consent of the students, creating a desire in those many individuals where it does not yet exist. It is a tall order, as anybody knows who has worked in an institution that imposes general education requirements. The issue at hand is how to make a student want to choose a subject such as literature if it is not required, or else want to learn it seriously, if it is required.

This chapter focuses on several recent films that depict the teaching of language and literature, focusing specifically on the debates over methodology. The title of this chapter "how (not) to teach", refers to two contrasting pedagogical techniques: on the one hand, a catechistic, mechanical repetition of unassimilated knowledge that Gustave Lanson condemned as *psittacisme* (see Jey 2008), that is, the ability of a parrot to mimic words without understanding them; on the other, the technique of encouraging active learning by connecting the subject matter to the student's own, spontaneously acquired knowledge. "Parroting" signifies the passive, rote memorization combined with absence of understanding and emotional investment that many students endure in the presence of taught culture, and which makes it difficult for them to assume ownership of artifacts that are nevertheless stubbornly presented as their cultural birthright. Full emotional investment and understanding, by contrast, already occur when a student spontaneously and even enthusiastically follows upon his or her preexisting cultural identifications. For most students, however, such spontaneous identification occurs not in relation to taught culture, but rather to popular culture. Adolescents already "own" the artifacts of such culture literally, because they actually purchase them with the money of which they seem to have so much in the developed world since roughly the mid-twentieth century, and figuratively, because the same artifacts reflect their language, feelings, and spontaneous desires.

The question of ownership of culture is fundamental to education. Patrimony is a form of ownership, but a problematic one because of the distance, both chronological and virtual, that separates it from the living population, especially the young. To inherit cultural capital is not the same as to inherit financial wealth. To take possession of cultural capital, one must also earn it, through an endless and difficult process of appropriation, such as attempting to learn to read literary texts that rely on values and modes of expression that no longer operate in society. The number of adolescents who have achieved s significant degree of progress in the appropriation of their cultural patrimony, typically through music lessons and other privileges available to those who are born in families already heavily invested in cultural capital, is extremely small compared to those who have not. Pessimists known in the French media as "*déclinologues*" [declinologists] will claim that their number grows smaller all the time, though the truth is that it was never that large to begin with.

One should not conclude, however, that the failed inheritors who make up most of the population are culturally destitute. Instead of inherited culture or patrimony, their capital consists of "culture of proximity", a term which encompasses the films, television shows, idiolects, pop music, graphic novels, and the like, toward which they spontaneously direct their attention, and may even help to create. As the above examples imply, "culture of proximity" still exists primarily outside the confines of the school, although the opposition between "inside" patrimonial culture and "outside" culture of proximity is gradually breaking down. It is this breakdown of the inside-outside opposition that I intend to explore in this chapter, using examples from the film genre, which has always played a mediating role between levels and types of culture.

"Culture of proximity" is a term that now occurs with increasing frequency in French discussions of literary pedagogy.[7] It is related, but not identical to the English term "cultural proximity" that has existed for some time in the field of communications and media studies. Joseph D. Straubhaar in particular has used the term to refer to the tendency of most people to consume cultural artifacts that are linguistically and culturally familiar. His work on television-viewing habits in Brazil has sought to determine what "leads audiences to prefer local and national productions over those that are global and/or American" (78). "Cultural proximity" therefore belongs to the ongoing field of research into the globalization of culture through the media marketplace, and the debate over "cultural imperialism" (especially emanating from the United States). Instead of marketing television programs in Brazil, we are concerned with marketing canonical culture in the classroom, yet the two processes are undeniably related: how does one overcome the cultural consumer's bias in favor of the familiar? The difference, of course, is that in television programming, the culture of proximity is local and national, and the imported, remote culture is global, and all of them compete for ratings. In the classroom, it tends to be the reverse, at least in countries saturated with electronic media: a national corpus of literary texts that is far removed from popular entertainment struggles to insert itself into the cultural habitus of students that often is dominated by mass-marketed products and genres, whether imported or domestic.

The questioning of the incommensurability of "inherited culture" and "culture of proximity" is a recurring theme, not only in professional debates over literary pedagogy, but also in the cinematic subgenre that is set in the classroom. Experiences such as recitation, dictation, and more advanced literary rituals provide a rich source for nostalgic reimagining of a childhood past that may in reality have been traumatic. The classic image of a teacher reading a literary passage for a dictation exercise, or of students reciting poetry, of which the above-mentioned scenes in Truffaut's *The 400 Blows* provide examples, reminds viewers of a universally shared experience more effectively than would an arithmetic or history lesson. One explanation for the power of such representations is simply the emotional associations people have with the texts they encountered in school, scenes that may fulfill the repressive function of "screen memories" (an especially apt term in this context) in those all-too-common cases where the original experience was far from pleasurable. Viewed more positively, the nostalgic potential of such classroom scenes is evidence that, in a way, the school does succeed in providing an experience of literariness, one that manifests itself not as understanding or ownership, but perhaps as an inchoate sense of awe when a child speaks or hears the poetry of La Fontaine or Verlaine: the writing or recitation of literary passages, even without any attempt at interpretation, constitutes a powerful memory event, especially for adult filmgoers who performed such tasks when they were schoolchildren.[8]

Even when stripped of nostalgia, such scenes are capable of evoking the literary. Truffaut's unsentimental portrayal of the school in *The 400 Blows* is, in fact, an almost continuous filmic ode to the ineffable power of literature. In addition to the scene in which a student struggles and fails to recite a poem by Jean Richepin, "Epitaphe pour un lièvre" ("Epitaph for a Hare", 1881), arousing the teacher's anger that takes the form of moral censure, Truffaut has his protagonist, Antoine Doinel, erect a shrine to Balzac in his bedroom in order to seek quasi-divine inspiration for a composition he is required to submit. Later, after running away from home, he spends the night in a print shop, of all places. He and his friend René steal a typewriter, the act that will land Antoine in reform school. One could go on. In each scene, Truffaut repeatedly reminds us of the precedence, both chronological and in terms of value, of literature, writing, and the print medium, in relation to film, as if he wanted to promote cinema not as the new substitute for literature, but as its natural heir. On the other hand, the harshness of the classroom scenes, and the moral tyranny of the teacher, both in the failed-recitation scene and when he accuses Antoine of having plagiarized Balzac instead of simply being inspired by him for his composition assignment, perpetuates the literary representation of the school as a place intrinsically inimical to literature itself. If Antoine is ever to become a reader, or better yet a writer, he first has to escape into *l'école buissonnière*, the French term for truancy.

In the United States, such filmic scenes of literary pedagogy in action are rare. Popular fascination with adolescent culture has produced a cinematic tradition in which high school is simply a rich backdrop for "coming of age" dramas (*Blackboard Jungle*, 1955), comedies (*Ferris Bueller's Day Off*, 1986), and horror movies (*Carrie*, 1976). Literary pedagogy, and even education in general, rarely play a role in that tradition, Peter Weir's *Dead Poets Society* (1989) being an exception. It is hard to imagine an American studio producing a film like François Ozon's recent psychodrama *Dans la maison* (*In the House*, 2012), the plot of which centers on a literature teacher deciding to mentor a student who has shown exceptional writing talent. Clearly, the representation of the literature class exerts an attraction in France that is compatible with popular entertainment, due in part to the relative success the school has had in promoting the "literary culture" described at the end of Chapter 4, reinforcing the widespread belief in literature's inherent value among the general population even as it is blamed for repressing the freedom on which literary creation depends.

The reasons for this cultural difference between France and the United States provide further evidence of the value of situating the discussion of general education of literature in France. The French cinematic tradition reflects a high degree of emotional, as well as political and intellectual investment in the literature discipline, reinforcing its status as a *lieu de mémoire* or "memory realm". It is only natural that the experience of literary pedagogy, that is both individual and collective, should find expression in the medium of film, just as it informs the entirety of French "literary culture" in which virtually everyone participates even if they have read little or no literature since the end of their school career. There is reason to think that the frequency of such representations has intensified. Over the last fifteen years, France has seen a surge in the already healthy production of popular films in which the school is much more than a backdrop for the drama of lost childhood, a surge that is undoubtedly related to the sense that the educational institution itself is in an even more acute state of crisis than usual, especially in regard to literary pedagogy.

LITERATURE AND THE CINEMA OF NOSTALGIA

Crisis is in part the symptom of a rupture with the past, and calls forth a compensating repression mechanism. That fact explains the recent popularity of a type of film that idealizes the French school of the past in a manner that bears scant resemblance to the often traumatic, lived experiences of schoolchildren. Witness the box-office success, already mentioned in the Introduction, of the movie adaptation of René Goscinny's and Jean-Jacques Sempé's *Le Petit Nicolas* in 2009, and the fact that 2011 saw the release of two remakes, not just one, of the above-mentioned classic 1962 film *La Guerre des boutons*. Iconic, quaint classroom scenes appear in each of these films, as part of a rose-tinted past. *Le Petit Nicolas* is partly set in a primary school in Paris in the early 1960s (it is important that it evokes the pre-1968 society), while the latter two remakes take place in tiny, quaint villages in the countryside. The remake of *La Guerre des boutons* directed by Christophe Barratier carries the whitewashing to an extreme by setting the action during World War II, allowing for a more humane and optimistic representation of the years of German Occupation, while the one directed by Yann Samuell remains true to Yves Robert's version by situating the plot in 1960. The autobiographical novel by Louis Pergaud from 1912 on which all of the movies are based, is actually set in the late nineteenth century in an equally nostalgia-infused, rural *Belle Epoque*. While Yves Robert's adaptation is the most famous, it was not the first, a distinction that belongs to Jacques Daroy's film from 1937. There is even an English-language version that moves the action to Ireland, directed by John Roberts in 1994. What all of these works share is sentimentality, indulged through a potent mix of childhood fantasy (the "war" involves schoolchildren stealing the buttons off the clothes of their rivals from another village), pre-industrialism (most of the families are farmers), and benign, almost saintly schoolteachers.

Such memorials to the idyllic, pre-1968 pedagogical space completely ignore the rigorous scientific underpinning of the Republican school that made it a fascinating experiment in secular, empirical, intellectual emancipation, imagining it instead as a temple for the exercise of self-evidently valuable and comforting, yet repetitive and mechanical literary exercises. Today, many believe such practices as recitation and literary dictation have been marginalized if not completely replaced by a post-1968 wave of "*pédagogisme*", the pejorative term of recent vintage defined as the excessive, consumer-focused deference to the students' interests and desires when setting the classroom agenda. The term is a hostile interpretation of "constructivism", of the inductive, student-centered approach to learning developed by Jean Piaget, affirmed by the Charbonnières manifesto discussed in Chapter 5, and further entrenched by the *loi Jospin* of 1989 that called for greater agency on the part of students in the learning process.[9] The origins of student-centered learning of course go back much further, to the very roots of Republican pedagogical theory and to Ferdinand Buisson's massive, and massively influential *Dictionnaire de Pédagogie et d'instruction primaire* (published in 1887 and revised and expanded in

1911), with its elaborate theoretical justifications for such inductive techniques as the "*leçon de choses*" (object-based learning), and other attempts to grant freedom and initiative to the student.[10] Public perception matters, however, and the critics of the institution of the discipline of French clearly view 1968 as the year that teachers officially began to surrender their authority both to students and to the progressive intellectual avant-garde of Piaget, Bourdieu, Freire, and their *pédagogiste* disciples.

The iconic images that are common to the two nearly simultaneous remakes of *La Guerre des boutons* and the adaptation of *Le Petit Nicolas* is another idealized instance of the primary school mythology rooted in the school politics of the Third Republic. The teacher and students wear smocks, knee-length for the teacher and usually waist-length for the students, a practice that had the dual purpose of protecting one's clothes against stains from the inkwells that occupied a corner of each desk (for the teacher, the danger came more from chalk dust), and instituting an atmosphere of regimented seriousness. The teacher's desk is always elevated on a small stage called the *estrade*, a practice dating to well before the Jules Ferry laws of the 1880s, and which was officially phased out in the wake of the post-1968 reforms; today, teachers and students all have their feet on the same level, a small detail that still infuriates many *passéistes* (see Noé). Finally, the students always sit in straight, parallel rows of double-sized desks, in a further display of forced solidarity and conformity to a geometric sense of order. The teacher in these films is a sometimes stern, though usually benign and even comical figure of authority who frequently fails to keep his or her unruly charges under control (the one in *Le Petit Nicolas* is particularly overwhelmed). It is disorienting to compare such sentimental images with Truffaut's visually similar, but more historically accurate and pitiless classroom scenes in *The 400 Blows*.

Among other recent French films that portray education in a warm and nostalgic light, the documentary *Etre et avoir* (*To Be and To Have* by Nicolas Philibert 2002) presents a more complicated case. The nostalgia here does not take the form of an idealized reimagining of Truffaut's dismal and traumatic classroom, but the record of a year in the life of a small, rural schoolhouse in the mountains of Central France. There, a solitary teacher, Georges Lopez, must cover the entire range of primary education, from kindergarten through fifth grade. The school has only a few students, who therefore all study in the same space even though they are of different ages and levels, because the area in which they live is so vast and empty, in a dramatic visual representation of the decline of France's rural population that began under the Third Republic. The slow and irreversible decline of village life, and the weakening of French citizens' ties to a specific *terroir*, all are symptoms of the fear of globalization, of deterritorialization, and of subsequent loss of political and cultural sovereignty that also help feed the popular resistance to school reforms. In that sense, Philibert's documentary is far more deeply involved in the debate between past and future conceptions of general education than it seems.

The film's relevance to contemporary educational crises manifests itself in at least two ways. First, the wonderful interactions between Lopez and his students, as he implements all the classic elementary school exercises across the traditional disciplines, including the reading and dictation of literary texts, while serving the entire time as a sort of secular pastor, are portrayed in a melancholy mode. The elegiac atmosphere is enhanced by the slow rhythm of the editing, the subdued soundtrack, and the harsh landscape. Second, the film ends with the scene of the older students visiting the *collège* or middle school in the nearest large town, where they will continue their education in a modern, uninviting building that could not offer a more dramatic contrast with their tiny, intimate schoolhouse. Not only will they become cogs in the great educational machine in a few short months, the nurturing Eden they are about to leave is clearly a rare, unsustainable, and vanishing instance of pedagogical success.

But there is a second, more important factor that links *Etre et avoir* to the current malaise over general education. Sadly, the nostalgic idyll that moviegoers discovered upon the release of the documentary in 2002 came to an abrupt end soon afterward when the teacher, Georges Lopez, filed a lawsuit against the director and the producers. Before filming began, he had turned down their offer of payment for his role in the documentary. But as the film started to enjoy much greater commercial success than anticipated, thanks to the wide appeal of its portrayal of the spiritual bond connecting the teacher to his students, Lopez argued that he should receive a share of the royalties. After years of litigation, his suit was dismissed on the grounds that he had never signed an employment contract, and furthermore that being the subject of a documentary is not the same as collaborating on a creative work. To many members of the French public, the hero at the front lines of the fight against the dehumanization of the educational enterprise by commercial forces became, whether justifiably or not, an incarnation of selfishness and materialism, one who placed financial profit above absolute value. The fragile illusion of a school still able, in this day and age, to protect itself from the encroachment of neo-liberalism died before it had a chance to establish itself in the collective consciousness.[11]

When Lopez attempted to obtain a share of the profits of *Etre et avoir*, he inadvertently narrowed the distance separating Philibert's documentary from the big-budget crowd-pleasers like *Le Petit Nicolas* and the twin remakes of *La Guerre des boutons*. The latter films deliberately sought to exploit commercially the collective yearning for a return to a mythical pre-1968 classroom, and did so all the more easily because the historical reality behind the myth is gradually fading from national memory.[12] The documentary, by contrast, began as an alternative to such monetization of nostalgia by showing a contemporary example of a real-life pedagogical saint. But as it became more and more commercially successful, it ended up spreading the disease of free market values instead. It is important to state that an elegy is not the same as nostalgia, in that it is less optimistic. Elegy recognizes more clearly the irrevocability of the break with the past. Even disregarding the legal case that tarnished the teacher's heroic reputation in the eyes of the public, the melancholy tone of the film by itself sufficed to foreclose any hope of returning to the mythical past. One-room schoolhouses in the middle of the countryside have very little to teach us about the best way to go forward, simply because they are an increasingly rare and irrelevant institution.

Etre et avoir has the aura of a National Geographic film on the life cycle of an endangered species. It ends on an ominous note, implicitly posing the question: what will happen to the children after they graduate from their rural schoolhouse and enter the urban or suburban middle school? It is likely to be a brutal fall to earth, symbolized by their descent from the mountains into the densely populated valley. This is precisely the moment in the educational continuum, and the place at the border between rural and urban France, where another wave of recent school-based feature films takes over. Several releases from the last two decades situate their plots squarely in the middle of those geographic and social spaces that are most immune from nostalgia and optimism, and where the teaching of French literature faces its biggest challenges. These spaces are the contemporary urban and suburban communities, often associated with some of France's most severe economic and social dysfunctions, where the purpose and method of transmitting French language and culture need to be reinvented most urgently.

Literature and the Cinema of Crisis

We now turn to three of the best-known twenty-first century French films that represent literary pedagogy in the context of economic precarity, immigration, and cultural alienation: Abdellatif Kechiche's *L'esquive* ("the dodge", released in the United States as *Games of Love and Chance*, 2004), Laurent Cantet's *Entre les murs* ("between the walls", released as *The Class*, 2008), and Jean-Paul Lilienfeld's *La journée de la jupe* (*Skirt Day*, 2009). They each pose the problem of the coercive nature of education, and of persuading students to overcome their natural resistance by recognizing meaning in the apparently arbitrary demands imposed upon them; they present a range of reactions to cultural alienation, and to the frustrations of teachers who no longer can (if they ever could) simply hold up the scripture of French literature and expect the crowd to kneel down before it. As such, they are lessons in "how (not) to teach", and in attempting to identify a legitimate purpose for bringing French language and literature to a captive, general audience. By examining a few key sequences from these films, I propose to describe several of these "lessons", and suggest how they might help better understand the general education of literature.

In *L'esquive*, several middle-school students in a *banlieue* prepare a production of Marivaux's play *Le jeu de l'amour et du hasard* (*The Game of Love and Chance*, 1730) under the direction of their teacher. The film begins abruptly with an immersion into the "proximate" linguistic environment of the students, as we see a circle of boys talking in an aggressive, fast-paced slang. Kechiche forces the "mainstream" French-speaking viewer to work hard to understand the staccato, cryptic slang of the young teens, similar to the effort most people have to make in order to follow the dialog in a classical, seventeenth- or eighteenth-century play. In fact, the more educated the viewer is, the more difficulty he or she is likely to have in understanding the characters in the film.[13] As Leon Sachs pointed out, the boys' speech is not so much a conversation as a "performance" that "seems less to transmit a direct, denotative message than to convey implicit affective information" (162). The words are therefore not really intended to be understood, but to convey a feeling, something that has also been said about Marivaux who, according to one of his contemporaries, "seems to write precisely in order not to be understood" (162). Hard as it may be for many speakers of standard French to accept, the *banlieue* dialect is, like Marivaux's prose, *artistic* in the sense that it ignores the purely utilitarian function of language as a vehicle for conventional meaning. Of course, the mystifying and quasi-literary unintelligibility of the boys' speech is most obscure precisely to those who might find Marivaux easier to understand. Such disorientation caused by hearing a language that is both "French" and "alien" is intentional, placing the middle-class viewer in the same position as a schoolchild struggling to make sense of the words in a Marivaux production, and empowering the undereducated, underprivileged child of the *banlieue* for whom the dialogue is, if not clearly denotative (since that is not its purpose, as Sachs pointed out), at least less alienating. This is a radically subversive strategy on the part of Kechiche, who thereby places on the same level "culture of proximity" (*banlieue* dialect) and, in Bourdieu's terminology, "legitimate culture" (elevated, "literary" French). The structural similarity between *banlieue* French and classical literary French lies in the way both dialects are cryptic, nondenotative, and opaque, especially mutually, but also from within.

Not long after the opening scene, a second disorientation occurs as we plunge into the opposite linguistic environment: an informal, outdoor rehearsal in which three students practice their lines. The words of Marivaux sound almost like a different language: only a trace of the Arabic-inflected accents of the students remind us of their "native dialect" as they act out the drama. Marivaux's words operate like a magic wand, transforming the bleak lives of the characters into a world of privilege and formality. When acting out their roles, they seem to assimilate into adulthood and an idealized French culture.

Of course they are merely repeating the lines of a play; as soon as they stop rehearsing, they revert to their original selves, and we are left to wonder if the rehearsals are anything more than *psittacisme*, a phenomenon that the teacher as well as the students designate by a recurring imperative: it is not enough to learn the lines, "il faut entrer dans la peau du personnage" [you must enter the character's skin]. Most of the young actors succeed at making the words their own, but not all: Krimo, who is in love with Lydia, the girl playing the role of Lisette in the play, bribes Rachid, the boy playing Arlequin, so that he can take his place. But the substitution is a disaster: Krimo as Arlequin can never go beyond a mechanical repetition of words he does not really understand. As Lydia helps him to learn his lines, he says out loud what countless adolescent students of canonical French literature are too intimidated to admit: "je ne comprends rien" and "ça entre, ça ressort" [I don't understand anything.

It goes in, it goes out]: the words for him are meaningless sounds. His *esquive*, dodge, stratagem – the attempt to insert himself into Marivaux's play to show his love for Lydia – fails; as Sachs observed, "the evasion or sentimental end run that Krimo hopes to perform through the theater requires language and literary skills that he hopelessly lacks" (157). He quits the play, giving the role of Arlequin back to Rachid. In the final sequence of the film, we see him watch the performance, not from the audience, but from outside the building where it takes place.

For Krimo, the education in French culture has failed. The chasm separating his *culture de proximité* from *culture légitime*, "culture of proximity" from legitimate (remote) culture, remains as unbridgeable as ever, a depressing outcome that Sachs sees expressed earlier by the teacher who, despite urging Krimo to "enter the skin of his character", to (figuratively and literally) "liberate himself", does not herself fully believe in the power of republican pedagogy to free the individual from his or her social and cultural confines: she repeats (parrots) the traditional interpretation according to which Marivaux's play confirms that only servants can love servants, and only masters can love masters (169). And yet Sachs reminds us that, before the end of the play, the gentleman Dorante is so in love with Silvia, the woman whom he *believes* is a servant, that he is prepared to throw social norms to the wind (where Marivaux perhaps thought they belonged). Thus, the French class is shown to have the potential of reconciling students to their education through social mobility, to fulfill the longstanding Republican promise of socioeconomic and cultural liberation through French language and literature (190–91).

In Cantet's *Entre les murs* (*The Class*), we see another middle-school teacher (François Bégaudeau, author of the autobiographical novel on which the movie is based, playing François Marin, a fictionalized version of himself) struggling to reconcile the subject he teaches with the reality of the lives of his mostly underprivileged, multiethnic students. Early in the film, there is a sequence in which students select words from their reading assignment that they do not understand, and he writes them on the board. He takes from the list the word "succulent" and, after the students fail to come up with an adequate definition, helps them out by putting it in a sentence: "Bill déguste un succulent cheeseburger" [Bill is enjoying a succulent cheeseburger]. After a brief digression on whether cheeseburgers are succulent or not, the class asks why he always uses names like "Bill" in his examples, instead of ones like "Aïssata", "Rachid", or "Ahmed". They are, in effect, asking him to draw from their experience, to improve his teaching by building on "culture of proximity" (represented in this instance by immigrant culture, rather than by commercial, pop culture). Instead of acknowledging their valid pedagogical argument, Marin defends himself by saying that "Bill" is not strange, in fact it is the name of "un président américain récent" [a recent American president]. The reference to Bill Clinton is one of several reminders in the movie that the President at the time was Bill's successor, George W. Bush; the name "Guantánamo" is mentioned whenever a student wants to point out injustices caused by the arbitrary authority of the school. But of course "Bill" is indeed a strange name in France; the conflict between "native" and "immigrant" culture that is implied by the students' challenge is displaced by the teacher's unintentional acknowledgement of the omnipresence of the real hegemonic force at work in society: not French, but American, not only cultural, but economic.

The Americanism of the phrase "Bill déguste un succulent cheeseburger" is not intended as a symptom of the globalist cultural and economic invasion of the classroom.[14] It simply is the result of the informal tone and sarcastic humor that are the teacher's defense against the constant, relentless challenges to his authority. But it goes deeper. Marin is progressive enough to deviate from the "Franco-French" norms that inhibit the education of those students who come from a marginal, economically deprived subculture, yet he resists anything that might remotely resemble pandering to them as well. He claims that if he begins using names based on the ethnic origin of everyone in the classroom, "on n'en sortira pas" [we'll never get anywhere], but of course that is far more than what his students asked him to do, which merely was to sometimes use names that would make the group feel included in his examples. So why is a teacher who easily jokes about cheeseburgers reluctant to accede to the students' demand that he sometimes, not even always, use names that are of African or Arabic origin?

Marin's intransigence regarding proper names is only the first of several instances of his refusal to grant legitimacy to the spontaneous output of his students. After his awkward defense of the name "Bill", he returns to the list of words that they did not understand. Wei, a good-natured, hard-working student from China who plays the role in the movie of the "ideal" immigrant who wants to integrate culturally (in stark contrast to Souleymane, a boy from Mali whose sometimes violent insubordination provides much of the dramatic thrust of the film), had volunteered the word "Autrichienne" [Austrian]. Another student, Esmeralda, makes fun of his rudimentary French proficiency by saying that everyone knows what the word means. In his desire to defend Wei from her teasing, Marin argues that not everyone knows, and besides, Austria is such an insignificant country that he challenges the class to come up with the name of a single famous Austrian. One bright student in the back row immediately volunteers "Mozart". Taken aback, the teacher hesitates, and the student, struggling a bit with the composer's complete name, follows up with "Wolfgang Amadeus Mozart", pronouncing "Wolfgang" to rhyme with the English word "gang" (another Americanism with which the students are only too familiar). Instead of praising him, Marin mocks the student for his mispronunciation, and doubles down on his earlier challenge by saying that if Austria disappeared from the map tomorrow, nobody would notice. In his eagerness to avoid making the Chinese student feel ashamed of his ignorance, the teacher commits the pedagogical error of failing to recognize and reward the spontaneous expression of the assimilation of "legitimate culture". He compounds the error by mocking the student's Anglicized pronunciation of "Wolfgang" even though he himself used the name "Bill", as well as the word "cheeseburger", only a few minutes previously.

In a sequence that follows closely on the one above, Marin is giving a lesson on the imperfect tense, and one student asks why he always calls it "*imparfait de l'indicatif*", imperfect indicative. He replies that it is because there is another "*imparfait*", and can anyone name it? Another student correctly answers "*l'imparfait du subjonctif*", imperfect subjunctive, and Marin asks if anyone can give an example, whereupon a student named Khoumba raises her hand and tentatively offers, with a great deal of embarrassed giggling, "*je fusse*". Marin's first reflex is to mock her for inventing a new verb, "*fusser*", before admitting that she is on the right track, but does not yet master the form. He writes on the board: "Il faut que je sois en forme" [It is necessary that I be in shape] and underneath the verbs "*faut*" and "*sois*", which are in the present indicative and subjunctive modes respectively; he then inserts the two *imparfait* forms: "*fallait*" and "*fusse*", whereupon Khoumba quite rightly, and somewhat indignantly points out, "J'avais raison!" [I was right!] – but he ignores her, just as he failed to acknowledge the validity of the response "Mozart" in the earlier sequence.

Marin is spared the embarrassment of having to admit that Khoumba was right by the ruckus that erupts when Esmeralda and others object that they are wasting time talking about the "*imparfait du subjonctif*" because nobody ever uses it. While acknowledging that those who speak that way are a bit "*snob*", Marin lies to his students by claiming that he uses the verb form frequently, whereas in fact it is virtually never used in spoken discourse: "Hier, avec des amis, on utilisait l'imparfait du subjonctif" [yesterday, with some friends, we were using the imperfect subjunctive]. Rather than engage them on their (once again, very valid) objection, he quickly hides the absurdity of his answer by shifting the topic to the importance of recognizing the various "*registres du langage*" [levels of speech] ranging from the "*courant*" [informal and spoken] to the "*soutenu*" [formal, frequently written style, including literary language], the latter of which the "*imparfait du subjonctif*" is a fine example. Indeed, one of his tasks as a teacher that is spelled out in the official instructions published by the ministry of education is to familiarize his students with *registres*, with the various levels appropriate to different contexts, especially the difference between oral and written. When a girl then asks how one decides whether to use "*registre oral*" or "*registre écrit*", she understands that it is not a matter of literally distinguishing between oral and written discourse, but among various levels, regardless of whether one is speaking or writing. The question tests Marin's pedagogical skill beyond their limit: all he can answer is that it is a matter of intuition that comes with practice. The lesson on the "*imparfait*" has therefore evolved into a lesson about linguistic mastery as a metaphor for social exclusivity, and also about "literariness", a quality of an utterance that the teacher claims can be identified only through "intuition". In the past, it was a verb form that marked the speaker as an aristocrat or other member of the cultural elite. Today, the only place one is still likely to find it is in a literary text, and in contemporary French and Francophone productions, its frequency is in decline. The "*imparfait du subjonctif*" indeed is itself a metaphor, or more precisely a synecdoche, of "literariness under siege", since it is a marker of literary discourse, but is used less and less as the gap narrows between spoken and written (literary) French. In this sequence, teacher and students struggle over nothing less than the future of literary French by arguing over the necessity of preserving the link to classical style embodied by the "*imparfait du subjonctif*": Marin clinging to past markers of legitimacy, his students rejecting them. The ultimate significance of the struggle lies in whether the break with tradition demanded by the students is an unqualified loss, or on the contrary a revitalization of French culture, the active appropriation of a living heritage rather than the passive appropriation of a dead one. The future will depend on whether one looks at

Marin's motley crew of students as justifying optimism for the future of French literature, or despair.

It is hard to imagine the harsh, slang-filled and profanity-laced speech of the young protagonists of *L'esquive* and *Entre les murs* competing with literary language such as that of Marivaux, but after all, they are only fourteen or fifteen years old; their very resistance to "taught culture" has the potential to become the foundation of the "legitimate culture" of the future. While the Kechiche film soundtrack contains no hip hop, the spectator cannot help but be reminded of the transformation of exactly such speech into art by rappers in France, the world's second largest producer of hip hop after the United States (Meghelli). In fact, the emergence of such a strong tradition of French hip hop is exactly the sign of the type of literary initiative that challenges the traditional legitimacy of inherited culture, in that it is a kind of shortcut to literariness, devoid of imperfect subjunctive, that takes place outside the walls of the school (in other words, instead of Bégaudeau's title "entre les murs" [within the walls]. French hip hop is a cultural phenomenon "au-delà des murs" [outside the walls]).[15] Kechiche and the team of Cantet and Bégaudeau express faith in the ultimate compatibility of both cultures, especially through the characters of Lydia, who understands Marivaux well in spite of her youth and underprivileged background, and Esmeralda who reveals, to Marin's astonishment, that she has been reading on her own initiative her older sister's copy of Plato's *Republic*.[16] The two girls show an ability to negotiate disparate cultures, and represent the possibility of a literary discourse that neither relies on, nor completely sidesteps the aristocratic tradition. In fact, it is the girls' skill at passing from one set of cultural expectations to another, to "switch codes", that constitutes a large part of their capacity for self-expression. As one can see in the literary production of many authors from the Francophone world, such transcultural ease has become an increasingly important part of "literariness". Like the dunce in the Prévert poem "Le cancre" discussed in Chapter 2, who is the only one in the classroom in a position to create art, these teenagers are the artists and poets of tomorrow, and their style and inspiration are more likely to come from their "culture of proximity" than they are from the "inherited culture" transmitted by the school. It is not the familiarity with one culture or the other that augurs well for their future as creators, however, but their ability to navigate between these heretofore incommensurate realms that are beginning to merge, not only in popular culture, but within the space of the school itself. In the paradigmatic case of

Kechiche, who operates as a *"passeur"* or go-between among languages, cultures, and classes in all of his films, it is an author's skill at finding the most fertile intersections of multiple, distinguishable cultures (Marivaux and teenage slang, for example, or France and North Africa) that results in successful creation. But what about Krimo, and all the students who on the contrary find it impossible to cross, and thereby negate, the cultural borders surrounding them? What is their future?

Near the end of *Entre les murs* is a disturbing sequence: Henriette, one of the quieter students, approaches Marin on the last day of school and timidly announces: "J'ai rien appris" [I didn't learn anything]. There is no rebellion or reproach in the tone of her voice, only a statement of fact. In answer to Marin's stupefaction, she can only say that she does not want to be relegated to a *lycée professionnel* after she finishes middle school. She understands that the worst possible fate is to end up in an educational system the purpose of which is simply to provide students with some kind of (under)employment, and anything other than a *lycée général* would represent a capitulation: not only surrendering to market forces, but a loss of freedom and dignity. It is as if all the editorials and books attacking the school for its alleged subservience to the neo-liberal agenda were suddenly vindicated, and now the students themselves shared their dismay, with resignation rather than anger. In the case of Henriette, her fear of vocational school is not that her education will no longer be disinterested and literary. After all, she received no benefit from it, and presumably has no emotional attachment to the "inherited culture" from which she feels excluded, like a child written out of her parents' will. She is simply terrified of social exclusion, knowing as everyone does that many students in vocational training end up filling the ranks of the underpaid, underemployed victims of the global market. Whether it is fair or not to say so, the vocational track in secondary education stands for the surrender of the school's mission, not only to promote social mobility, but also to serve as the transmitter of cultural value. Marin, unable to reassure her, seems to see in her failure a reflection of his own. Indeed, the school must teach the Henriettes as well as the Esmeraldas, and he struggles to understand how to do so. Henriette and Krimo are just as deserving of effective general education as Lydia and Esmeralda, and constitute proof that its current state leaves much to be desired.

Finally, we see a humorous yet unsettling juxtaposition of "parroting" of traditional "taught" culture against the spontaneous expression of "culture of proximity" in Jean-Paul Lilienfeld's *La journée de la jupe*

(*Skirt Day*), a caricature of the gritty realism of the other two films, as well as a more reactionary and pessimistic answer to the pedagogical questions they pose.[17] Isabelle Adjani, like François Bégaudeau and Carole Franck in the other two films, plays the role of literature teacher to a group of culturally and economically marginalized middle-school students. As in *L'esquive*, the students had been given the task of memorizing lines of a play (though not the entire text), this time Molière's *Le bourgeois gentilhomme* (*The Bourgeois Gentleman*, 1670). The teacher struggles vainly to get a pair of boys to act out (and not just "parrot") a scene, desperately urging them to identify with the characters of the play, while the other students talk, yell insults, fight, and generally enjoy their complete domination of the classroom space. At one point, two students get up and hide behind a pillar to look at the handgun that one of them, a boy named Mouss, has smuggled into school in his backpack. As Madame Bergerac (Adjani) tries to take the backpack from them, the gun falls to the floor. She picks it up and realizes that, for the first time, she is in a position of power over her students: the natural order of the classroom has been restored. She locks the door and begins teaching a class on Molière at gunpoint. Because she can kill any one of them, she enjoys a room full of relatively docile and attentive students, of the kind she was trained to teach. They repeat whatever she says, in a wonderful demonstration of *psittacisme*. She asks them, "Quel était le vrai nom de Molière?" [what was Molière's real name?], and they answer catechistically, in a collective monotone, "Jean-Baptiste Poquelin". All, that is, except for the student who brought in the gun, Mouss, who defiantly yells "J'en ai rien à foutre de Molière, moi, je veux être footballeur!" [I don't give a shit about Molière, I want to be a soccer player!] and "Va niquer ta mère la pute!" [go fuck your mother the whore!] – whereupon Bergerac head-butts the teenager in the face, points the gun at his forehead and repeats the question, clearly in the throes of sadistic rage. Fearing for his life, Mouss finally says "Jean-Baptiste Poquelin!" Cradling the gun and the Molière play in her hands as she walks away, Madame Bergerac says: "Ah! tu vois, tu peux apprendre quand tu veux" [so you see, you *are* able to learn when you want to].

The dark humor of the scene derives mostly from the words "when you want to", because of course none of the students *wants* to learn. If they learn (or rather, simply repeat like parrots, or children preparing for their First Communion), they do so out of fear. The film, intended at least in part as a satire of the laxness of the current educational system, thus betrays an inconvenient truth: traditional pedagogy is coercive, and a teacher pointing a gun at her class only literalizes the underlying threat of social exclusion that has traditionally legitimized the teaching of Molière to a roomful of underprivileged fourteen-year-olds: "learn to pretend to know and like this material, or else you will spend the rest of your lives at the bottom of society (i.e., you will be damned, to continue the parallel with the Catechism, the class in which young Catholics learn to behave as if they had faith, whether they do or not)". Mouss, incidentally, provides us with the perfect caricature of the student as a consumer of education: what possible use is there to reading Molière for somebody who wants to be a professional soccer player when he grows up (or, more to the point, only cares about financial rather than cultural capital)? Money and culture may be compatible, if by culture one means hip hop, professional sports, or even some form of contemporary wage slavery. But the culture traditionally transmitted by the school is not seen either by teachers *or* students as being relevant to the desire for wealth, or even the more modest wish for subsistence, and that is a problem.

Each of the scenes above describes a different type of failure of the school, by portraying similar situations with varying degrees of irony: the failure of the "evangelical", socially emancipatory mode of teaching that, even when it succeeds in superimposing an archaic, aristocratic love story on the bleak, violent world of the *banlieue*, does not necessarily change that world for the better; the French teacher who understands and empathizes with his students, but cannot escape from the reflexes instilled in him by a top-down pedagogical tradition; and finally, the teacher who succeeds in applying that same outdated pedagogy, but only by threatening to blow her students' brains out if they do not play along. Of the three films, the first one chronologically, *L'esquive*, is also the most farsighted and optimistic concerning the commensurability of "legitimate culture" with "culture of proximity". Not only do students try to make Marivaux their own, including even the noble failure of Krimo's attempt to win over Lydia by clumsily forcing his way into the play, their daily lives are shown to be in complex synchrony with the elaborately formal, aristocratic rituals they mimic.

One can say that it was the filmmaker who successfully brought together these two worlds, and not actual teachers. True enough. Perhaps film, a traditionally hybrid, illegitimate or bastard genre, in other words, a form of expression that itself stands outside of the line of succession and patrimonial inheritance, is best suited to show the importance of acknowledging culture of proximity (thereby acknowledging itself), in order to enlist students' voluntary participation in the educational process. Inheritance is difficult in part because of the fear of many people that the cultural patrimony of the school does not, in fact, belong to them, and that it never will. They have no right to it, despite what their teachers say to persuade them. But if it is seen as continuous with those cultural riches that they do, in fact, already possess (through "proximity" and also through their own act of production), then the fear has no basis. At least some teachers understand this radical principle, and one must not forget that Bégaudeau taught French literature before he became a well-known author, movie actor, and screenwriter.

The attempt to establish a connection between the two separate worlds inside and outside of the school walls is a growing concern of French pedagogues. One of them is Marie-Claude Penloup, who promotes "*écriture extrascolaire*" [extracurricular writing] as an example of the way in which literariness manifests itself in the spontaneous cultural practices of students, in her 1999 book *L'écriture extrascolaire des collégiens: Des constats aux perspectives didactiques* [extracurricular writing by middle-school students: from observations to potential pedagogical applications]. The strict policing of the boundary between school and home, or school and street, makes such conciliatory attempts difficult, as we have seen in the anger of those who rush to protest in France every time the inviolability of the classroom is even slightly threatened, writing letters to *Le Monde* or staging marathon readings of *La Princesse de Clèves*. Even a reformer of unimpeachable institutional credentials such as Alain Viala has felt their wrath, as we saw in the previous chapter. In North America as in France, however, the recognition of a continuity linking student culture and "taught" culture will lead to an increased demand for literature by more than a niche clientele, especially now that we live in an educational market that is less and less protected by supportive administrators, political leaders, and taxpayers. Students who recognize continuity between their lives and the subjects that we teach will be more engaged than those who feel coerced to come to our classrooms at (metaphorical) gunpoint. This will not be the result of a marketing strategy, or of unfair protectionism of a chronically under-performing segment of the educational industry. It will be the result of a recognition that passing from one culture to another, and exercising ownership of all forms of culture, past and present, national and global, are indeed the skills that all people must acquire to the best of their ability. In order to achieve that recognition, however, it is necessary to address head-on the five-hundred-pound gorilla lurking behind every discussion of general education: the fear that global economic forces will overwhelm any attempt by the educational establishment to maintain control over its future. That is the subject of the next chapter.

NOTES

1. Any discussion of the difference between "reading" and merely "talking about" literature inevitably leads one to Pierre Bayard's 2007 work, *How to Talk About Books You Haven't Read*. Indeed, as Bayard brilliantly demonstrated, literary knowledge is more about familiarity with the relations between works of literature, rather than the contents of the books themselves. Bayard even writes about revolutionizing the teaching of literature so as to legitimize various forms of non-reading (which includes the vast category of books one has in fact read, but largely forgotten), and to view books as a system within which one must learn to travel easily, rather than a list of texts one must know intimately. The "literary culture" I speak of here is slightly different. While Bayard's methods require people to have read fairly extensively in order to talk about books they haven't read, the literary culture in question here does not require any reading whatsoever. It is, quite simply, the impact on society of literature without taking into account individual acts either of reading or "non-reading", to use Bayard's term.
2. Several studies have appeared that focus exclusively on the manner in which education is represented in literature, most recently *L'école dans la littérature* [the school in literature] by Claude Pujade-Renaud (2006).
3. Some recent examples of what one might call "school-based literature", a sub-genre of *Bildungsroman* that counts Colette's *Claudine à l'école* (1900) and Alain-Fournier's *Le Grand Meaulnes* (1913) among its early masterpieces, are Daniel Pennac's *Chagrin d'école* (*School Sadness*, 2007), and Erik Orsenna's above-mentioned "young person's novel" *La Grammaire est une chanson douce* (*Grammar is a Gentle, Sweet Song*, 2001). Pennac's autobiographical novel is akin to Prévert's "Le cancre" (see Chapter 2) as it critiques the school from the point of view of a failing student. All of these present strong critiques of French literary pedagogy, and Orsenna's attack on the post-1968 "scientific turn" and its responsibility for student alienation is explained in Leon Sachs's recent study, *The Pedagogical Imagination* (2014, 81–111). Orsenna's tale is a fantasy of an ideal literary pedagogy without teachers, in which two shipwrecked siblings are stranded on an island where they experience a supernatural,

"unmediated encounter with verbal and visual facts and literary objects" (Sachs 84).
4. Pierre Nora's "realms of memory" are frequently spaces and objects (monuments, buildings), but more often texts, such as historical events translated into conventional language and imagery (such as the surrender of Vercingétorix at Alésia), or in the case of literature, textual fragments that symbolize, rather than represent, the national patrimony. Former historian Daniel Milo's contribution to Nora's work is "Les classiques scolaires" (school classics), in which he analyzes the talismanic effect of this ostensibly finite list of poems and excerpts within the general education context.
5. No longer as ritualistically omnipresent as in the past, recitation and dictation are the traditional foundation of literary pedagogy, consisting of the precise reproduction, orally or in writing, of canonical texts. Criticized for their mechanical, passive, and even repressive character, explored by Ralph Albanese in *La Fontaine à l'école républicaine* (31–4), they are paradoxically the source of great nostalgia, and lately have reemerged as tools of cultural assimilation for France's marginalized populations (see the *New York Times* article by Lilia Blaise, "In Paris Suburbs, Adopting a Dreaded School Test as a Tool of Integration").
6. The word *"présentisme"* already means "philosophical presentism", the belief that neither the past nor the future exists. For our purposes, it simply means the opposite of "nostalgia". The philosophical sense is nevertheless useful, as it gives weight to the common cultural stance of rejection of all that is not "current" or "up to date": "presentism", or the philosophy of faddism.
7. An example of the pedagogical concept that is gradually becoming known in French as *"culture de proximité"* is the 2004 article by Magali Bleuse, "Créativité et proximité avec la culture des élèves" [creativity and proximity to student culture] in the professional journal for French teachers *Recherches*. Bleuse is a middle-school teacher who has had success in teaching literature to her students by relating canonical texts to popular artifacts such as reality television shows and popular song lyrics.
8. We are talking here about classroom practices that mostly predate the changes in French education that have occurred since 1968. The more remote in time such representations are situated, the easier it is for even younger spectators, despite having little or no access to analogous memory events, to experience their mythical power. Films set in a more recent past, such as the three on which I focus the most in this chapter, portray other practices that may one day serve as new "memory realms", as ambiguous sites of pedagogical success and failure.
9. Lionel Jospin, before becoming Prime Minister in 1997, was Minister of Education from 1988 to 1992. The fact that he served under François

Mitterrand, and was the socialist candidate in the 1995 and 2002 presidential elections, illustrates the classic ideological divide that so often inhibits open-minded discussions of the school. For many conservatives, it was inevitable that a socialist would take authority out of the hands of teachers and give it to students. Thus did the "*loi Jospin*" become the *bête noire* of a certain politically as well as culturally conservative opposition to school reform, in complete disregard of the fact that the law's intentions were to return to the origins of Republican pedagogy, not to disown them.

10. The serious attempt by the French republican school to serve as an instrument of individual empowerment, rather than conformity on the model of the Catholic Catechism, and its survival in contemporary representations of the classroom, can be found in Leon Sachs's important study *The Pedagogical Imagination*, cited several times in this chapter.

11. The article "*Ça Commence aujourd'hui, Être et avoir, et Entre les murs*: Une vision diffractée de l'école républicaine française" by Annie Jouan-Westlund (2014) provides a thorough overview of the legal battle between Lopez and the filmmakers, and of the implied critique of republican education in all three of the films named in her title, two of which are discussed in this chapter.

12. Each of the technicolored, nostalgic classroom scenes that punctuate these blockbuster movies needs to be compared to the documentary-like baseline that is Antoine Doinel's classroom in Truffaut's *The 400 Blows*. In spite of some whimsical, humorous flourishes, such as the boy who repeatedly tears pages out of his notebook because his ink pen keeps making blots on the page while he tries to write out the dictation exercise, the atmosphere in these scenes is far more oppressive and bleak than the comparable ones in the more recent movies.

13. Louisa Shea compares the difficulty of Marivaux's language to the opaqueness of banlieue slang; when the characters switch from real life to acting out the play, there is a doubling of unintelligibility: Marivaux, obscure even to his contemporaries, spoken in speeded-up, Arabic-inflected, twenty-first-century French (1144).

14. If there is an invasion of globalism for which Marin is responsible, it is implied in the fact that we see the students read *The Diary of Anne Frank* instead of a work of French literature (in the novel, the students are reading John Steinbeck's *Of Mice and Men*). An early scene shows a conversation between Marin and a history teacher, who proposes that they collaborate on a sequence on the Enlightenment, perhaps centered on Voltaire's *Candide*. Marin declines, saying that the book would be too difficult for them to read. The choice of Anne Frank also reflects recent policies emanating from the ministry of education: opening the curriculum to world literature, and teaching the Holocaust.

15. It is, of course, an oversimplification to say that hip hop emerged independently of the literary pedagogy that takes place in primary and secondary education: like all new literary genres, it developed both in harmony with and opposition to existing ones. Quite a few French hip hop artists acknowledge a link to canonical literature in their pieces, and it is logical to assume that the school curriculum is one source of inspiration among others. In many cases, such as Abd al Malik, the mix of "inherited (legitimate) culture" and "illegitimate culture" is especially evident, both in the form of literary allusions, and in the ways in which his verbal inventions relate directly to experimentalism in avant-garde French and Francophone literature. Hip hop has, furthermore, started to find its way into the school curriculum, has long been a subject for literary criticism (see Martinez), but as far as I can determine, has yet to be used in the literature portion of the *bac*.
16. We can infer that if Esmeralda's sister is reading Plato for school, then she must be in the final year of *lycée*, called *terminale*, in which philosophy is a required "gen ed" subject. Or she could be a university student. Or she could simply like to read classical philosophy without anyone forcing her to, as does Esmeralda herself.
17. In France, Lilienfeld's movie was praised by reactionary voices in the education debate, such as Jean-Paul Brighelli, and attacked by a few left-wing media outlets such as *Libération* or *Les Inrockuptibles*. In a valuable article on the film's reception, Geneviève Sellier joins those critics who see the film as racist, right-wing propaganda, with pale-skinned and blue-eyed Isabelle Adjani's literature teacher portraying "a missionary (white), trying to bring civilization (Western) to a threatening horde of Barbarians (African)" (148). I would argue that the film is not so black-and-white (so to speak), insofar as Adjani's character is also a caricature, along with her mostly African hoodlum students, for example when she persists in teaching "about" Molière to her class in the most conventional way (the "Jean-Baptiste Poquelin" sequence). At the end of the film we discover that she is of Algerian origin (as is Adjani herself), which might appear to complicate the political message, but really does not, as she then simply becomes an icon of perfect cultural assimilation. Despite such nuances, it is both a far more politically conservative and less artistically ambitious work than those of Kechiche and Cantet.

CHAPTER 7

Harnessing the Neo-liberal Beast

LITERATURE, THE EDUCATION MARKET, AND PROTECTIONISM

The title of this chapter refers to a theme that has played a prominent role throughout this study: that the educational crisis of our moment consists of the fear that timeless pedagogical ideals are being contaminated, indeed replaced, by the debased, market-dependent values of the "neo-liberal" and "globalized" economy. The definition of education as an instrument for economic growth is very popular in today's Republican Party, as evidenced by Governor Scott Walker's attack on the University of Wisconsin, or Governor Matt Bevin's similar attack on the University of Kentucky,[1] but it is not just a right-wing phenomenon. It is part of the dominant discourse across the political spectrum outside of academia, and inside as well, as accreditation agencies and administrators demand proof of the value of the service we provide. The relevance of such encroachments on the teaching of literature is clear: how can the education establishment justify a general education requirement in a discipline that is not only remote from the professional goals of the vast majority of students, but also notoriously difficult to measure in terms of quantifiable outcomes? It is possible to tell if a student has attained a certain proficiency level in math, foreign languages, or natural sciences; but how does one determine proficiency in the study of literature, as opposed to, say, knowledge of literary history, which is something quite different? And even if one could quantify a student's proficiency in literature, what would be the purpose of doing so? The difficulty of answering such questions, especially in the context of a global anxiety that attempts to reduce educational goals to economic growth, and therefore privileges scientific, mathematic, and other quantifiable disciplines, has not stopped people from trying. The present chapter explores a new strategy for negotiating the abyss that separates literature as general education from the global economy: not the often-invoked argument that such study helps makes someone into a better employee, entrepreneur, or consumer, but a strategy that acknowledges the inevitability of economic determinants while still preserving the disciplinary autonomy of literature. This new strategy relies on economic concepts and categories, not in order to find a place for literature in the free market, but paradoxically in order to justify and preserve its independence from market forces.

Let us begin with the economic concept of "quantifiable outcomes". Outcomes assessment – a term with which educators are familiar – includes career placement statistics and skill measurements, since these are susceptible to quantification, and therefore constitute "proof". The desire for incontrovertible evidence of the added value of instruction in all disciplines, including literature, is nothing new, as we saw in the discussion of testing in Chapter 3, nor is the controversy that surrounds it. The traditional pushback against assessment from humanities disciplines is that we do not intend to prepare students for specific careers, and that any measurable skill or knowledge gained is of secondary importance. For example, a French literature major will undoubtedly become more proficient in the language, but that is not the primary goal of the discipline. And while it is true that by honing their critical faculties on works of literature, students presumably (and perhaps even demonstrably) become more skillful readers and writers of all sorts of texts, from office memos to newspaper editorials, that also is not the goal, since the Liberal Arts by definition are ends unto themselves. And yet here we are, fighting for market share in an environment that measures value by the number of dollars paid by students and earned by graduates.

Teachers of literature participate in at least two distinct yet related markets: the first is the one just mentioned, the market of higher education (and education in general), in which a newly empowered consumer base appears to be demanding something other than what literary pedagogy traditionally offers. Our share of the education market, as measured by staffing and enrollments (our profession's versions of supply and demand), is under threat from "growth disciplines" (industries) such as some of the STEM, disciplines, business programs, and so on. The second market in which we participate is globalized culture, in which audiovisual products, often originating in or inspired by North America, outsell most other artifacts, including works of literature. The two markets – higher education and world culture – are vastly different in scale, but similar in structure: the discipline of literature is at a competitive disadvantage within the academy, just as literature itself suffers from declining demand, at least in the United States (IBISWorld).

Much of the anxiety in academia today derives from the apparent incompatibility of the two most common responses to the challenge: either to reaffirm and protect the spiritual, disinterested role of education, or conversely, to claim that such a role is and always has been an illusion, the ideological veil that hides economic self-interest. According to the latter, higher education has always been subject to market forces, but years of unhindered growth convinced its leaders otherwise, like the Big Three automakers before VW and Toyota, or the Big Three TV networks before the advent of Cable and the Internet. Like those industries, American higher education simply forgot that it operated in a market environment until recently, when students started to behave more like consumers and began to question our market-free (as opposed to free-market) definition of value.

Faced with the return of the repressed in the form of consumerist pressures, at least three strategies are possible: 1) denial, or doubling down ("the market is a corrupting force, and we must refuse to participate"); 2) acceptance ("our field, for example literary studies, is indeed a kind of product, and we will compete happily against the departments on the other side of campus or across the hall"); or 3) a combination of denial and acceptance, analogous to the regulation of trade ("our discipline cannot compete in a free market, but we have legitimate reasons for tipping the field in our favor, for example by spending more money than we bring in, which in the world of commerce is called subsidies, or to institute general education requirements that limit the student-consumer's freedom of choice, which is called trade regulation").

Let us examine these three strategies in turn. Denial is a noble stance, and of course we must fight to defend the autonomy of our enterprise. But is it worth dying for? In other words, will it not accelerate the decline in tenured positions in the humanities, both at the secondary and tertiary levels of education? Strategy number two, full acceptance of free market forces, is admirably pragmatic, but carries risk – in every game there are losers, after all – and for many of us literature teachers, it is disingenuous. It feels as wrong to say that reading literature is a marketable skill, like writing code or bookkeeping, as it is to defend Holy Communion based on the nutritional value of bread and wine. Part of the liberal arts credo is learning for its own sake. "Yes, your employability will increase", we tell our students, "but if all you're looking for is a job, don't come to us (unless the job you're looking for happens to be professor of literature)". What I propose to explore is a "third way", rejecting both strategies, of rejection and of appeasement, when faced with the consumerist challenge. This third way is akin to "protectionism", a term full of negative connotations from a free-market perspective, but one that can have positive connotations if one does not subscribe to neo-liberal absolutism of the Ayn Rand variety.

So now we arrive at a working hypothesis: the academic discipline of literature is like an industry, albeit one that has a legitimate need for protection. Like a business, we compete for resources all the time within our schools and universities, just as those institutions themselves compete with each other. But the education market (like most others) is not truly free. What would happen if our institutions based their curricula purely on student demand? If academic programs had to generate profits in order to survive? If scientific research had to obtain funding from the private sector? If our primary purpose was to help reduce unemployment and increase the rate of economic growth? What sort of dehumanized dystopia would that be? Some say that this dystopia has already come to pass, from vouchers and standardized testing in public schools to adjunctification and pre-professionalization in universities. One can argue, however, that its triumph has yet to occur. The mere fact that general education requirements in the humanities still exist is proof that not all resource allocation is determined by commercial viability. But what is it that sustains, however precariously, educational offerings that do not respond to a specific, outside demand?

If we explore the analogy of global markets further, maybe we can derive comfort from the fact that the industry of Roquefort cheese has not been destroyed by the easy availability of cheap Danish Blue. This analogy between education and cheese, in which literature stands for Roquefort, and Danish Blue stands for those more utilitarian disciplines that students and employers desire, requires some explanation. Quite simply, it is this: in the global food market, protectionism is at work. Roquefort is indeed distinctive, and manufactured according to rigid standards, but so are many similar products. However, it is illegal for restaurants in countries linked to France through trade agreements to serve "Roquefort dressing" on their salads when it is made with some other kind of blue cheese, a law that some try to circumvent by spelling "blue" b-l-e-u on their menus. The discipline of literature also enjoys protection, as does the study of languages (a field in need of slightly less protection, since all living languages have the potential to help advance global commerce, but one that still suffers from chronically weak demand). In its most basic form, academic protectionism consists of strategies that insulate disciplines from competition, such as general education requirements that require secondary school students to study literature as part of the "English Language Arts" curriculum, whether they want to or not. Foreign languages also fall under the rubric of protectionism, insofar as language study is required for admission to most selective colleges and universities, and for graduation at a good many of them as well. Finally, protectionism exists in the form of "subsidies", that is to say any policy that results in maintaining a level of supply that is in excess of demand, such as academic departments and programs with smaller-than-average class sizes and lower faculty-student ratios.

But what is at stake? Who should care if enrollments in vocational disciplines increase, causing enrollments in literature and other arts and humanities to shrink? Is that not how markets are supposed to work? It is true that protectionism sometimes unfairly prevents those who already have market share from losing it, like the coal industry lobbying for protection against the solar and wind industries. But protectionism is not always merely a way to preserve vested interests. The one aspect of markets that provides insight into the status of literature in academia is the practice of trade regulation, the idea that open competition does not always produce optimal outcomes. Free trade absolutists abhor protectionism on principle, but there are arguments in its favor. Even basic, "fungible" commodities such as agricultural products, that seem designed for a "pure" market in which the price is determined by nothing other than the relationship of supply and demand, are sometimes protected, and rightfully so. In the current TTIP (Transatlantic Trade and Investment Partnership) negotiations, the United States and Europe disagree over genetically modified organisms (GMOs) or hormone-treated beef, as well as the legal recognition of geographic trademarks (Roquefort, Champagne, and so on). By insisting on trade restrictions, Europe seeks protection for food products as well as for cultural products, ever since

France successfully lobbied for the "cultural exception" that protects its audiovisual and publishing industries, during the Uruguay round of the GATT (General Agreement on Tariffs and Trade) negotiations in 1994. In response to European resistance to the importation of GMOs, the United States has insisted on scientific data as the only acceptable criteria for restrictions on trade. American negotiators state that "We seek to eliminate or reduce non-tariff barriers that decrease opportunities for U. S. exports, provide a competitive advantage to products of the EU, or otherwise distort trade, such as unwarranted sanitary and phytosanitary (SPS) restrictions that are not based on science". In other words, American negotiators refuse any trade restrictions unless there is scientific proof that public safety is at risk (Office of the United States Trade Representative). "SPS" policies require that trade restrictions be supported by data. Banning GMOs, for example, is a point of contention because they have not (yet) been scientifically proven to have a negative impact on public health.

The protection of geographic brand names is a different issue. Quantifiable, scientific evidence does not come into play in the laws that forbid a cheese maker in Wisconsin or Denmark from using the name "Roquefort". Something less scientific and more cultural, hence even less "provable" than the harm of GMOs, is at stake. The word "*terroir*", so important to foodies all over the world (and anathema to the U.S. trade negotiators), is where agriculture and culture overlap, usually under proper names such as "Champagne", or even "Parmesan", as the U.S. Trade website deplores: "U.S. producers are concerned by EU proposals to restrict use of 'particular designations' [...] that the EU considers location-specific, such as Feta and Parmesan cheeses and possibly Budweiser beer". Indeed, the Czech Republic, home of the original Budweiser in the town of Budvar (Budweis in German), stopped the Anheuser Busch corporation from using the name in the EU, where it is forced to sell its flagship brand under the name "Bud". The beer-drinking community arguably benefits from this instance of geography-based protectionism, thanks to which a local appellation with export potential is able to defend itself against a global, commercial juggernaut. *Terroir*, the narrowing of geographic space to the level of nation, region, town, and even domain, is therefore an apt analogy of the local resistance to globalization in terms of culture, commerce, and the intersection of the two.

Agriculture is a form of culture, and much of it relies for its existence on the belief that the more local and distinctive a product is, the more urgently it needs to be nurtured and preserved. But why? One could argue that in order to justify these protectionist measures, one must prove that products with geographic appellations like "Champagne" have unique, identifiable traits (the elusive "*terroir*" argument, once again). But in the realm of culture, no such proof is necessary. It suffices to say that local culture is distinct from global culture, a spatial argument, and that tradition trumps innovation, a temporal one. Without getting into a debate over whether the worldwide appeal of Disney movies makes them better or worse as art than objects that appeal only to a smaller number (such as a work of "serious" literature), one can agree that humanity is better off with both: artifacts that are commercially successful and unsuccessful, local and global, inherited and contemporary. But if the market alone decides which artifacts are to circulate, then Disney has a much better chance. Ergo, protectionism must be implemented. And where does the protection of literature take place? In the global market, yes, but especially in the micro-market of the school.

One does not have to be a fanatical defender of localism to believe that something is at stake in trade negotiations over food that may not be susceptible to objective quantification. Defenders of the humanities in American education, when asked why they should not be exposed to raw competition, answer with a similar declaration of faith. If one measures what a literature student learns, it will come down to reading skills and knowledge. One might end up with plenty of data; but will any of it explain how literature's benefits are different from those of other disciplines that depend on language? French trade negotiators make a similar argument that relies on faith, not data: that the survival of an autonomous culture, consisting of literature or food, art or *terroir*, depends on protection. It is not enough, for example, that French audiovisual culture exists; it must also enjoy a guarantee of commercial viability. The study of literature is in a similar position. There will always be a place for it in higher education, but it risks being nothing more than an esoteric discipline unless one grants recognition of its status as a protected commodity. Is such a status justifiable?

Rational attempts to validate faith in non-quantifiable value do exist. In an editorial published in *Le Monde* on February 8, 1995, soon after the Uruguay round of the GATT negotiations that resulted in the creation of the World Trade Organization, the Czech writer Antonin Liehm explained the European position as follows: because the United States is a nation of immigrants with no common tradition, it had to develop as quickly as possible a national culture defined by accessibility, "une culture de masse unique au monde, qui s'adresse à tous, et que son haut dénominateur commun met à la portée des couches populaires non américaines du monde entier" [a mass culture that is unique in the world, that speaks to everyone, and the high common denominator of which brings it within reach of non-American masses of the entire world]. Works of European culture, on the other hand, "ne deviendront jamais ni la vérité ni le rêve de tous. Leur dénominateur commun est faible, et toute tentative pour l'accroître est vouée à l'échec car le manque d'authenticité les rend le plus souvent ridicule" [will never become either the truth or the dream of everyone. Their common denominator is low, and any attempt to increase it is destined to fail, since their lack of authenticity will usually make them ridiculous]. Ascribing a "high common denominator" to an artifact is a questionable value judgment, and Liehm is not far from dismissing all of American culture, not just pop music and TV shows, as if it were a bland, easily assimilable product like Coca-Cola. Yet his argument that cultural products deserve protection, precisely because they do not appeal spontaneously to large numbers, needs to be taken seriously.

Educators the world over resist the tyranny of the market, as well they should, unless their disciplines tend to thrive in such an environment (pre-professional ones, and to a lesser extent, the "STEM" disciplines that are receiving a huge amount of free advertising in the media). At the same time, it is urgent to overcome the Manichaean opposition between disciplines that benefit from the free-market and those that do not. To do so, it is necessary for disciplines traditionally regarded as noncompetitive to concede that "the market" is not just a metaphor, if only because it controls the distribution of classrooms, students, and salaries. But there is hope. Like French culture itself, such disciplines may receive protection, but only if it is morally justified; in other words, if it does more than simply preserve literature's share of institutional resources in a manner that students and administrators will consider arbitrary. But how does one morally justify protectionism in the world of education?

In order to answer, let us return to the notion of "*terroir*". In its strongest sense, the word acts precisely as a moral justification. If one accepts that certain wines from a particular region or even domain are distinctive, then it follows that they deserve protection from wines of comparable value, but different origin, especially if they are in danger of disappearing from the market entirely. Linguists make a similar argument, all things being relative, in favor of endangered languages. Just as linguistic variations result in different modes of thought and representation, variations in *terroir* result in differences in *saveur* that are the only non-economic rationale for the legal principle of "appellation" that so frustrates American trade negotiators. One problem is that the claim of distinctiveness, unlike the claim of quality, is largely a matter of faith, especially to the majority of the population that cannot distinguish a Bordeaux from a Beaujolais. Although cultural artifacts such as literature do not lend themselves to scientific analysis any more than *terroir*, faith may be less important in justifying their protection. The value of cultural diversity, of which literary production across languages, time periods, and genres is a prime example, is understood. While "multiculturalism" meets resistance when established identities are threatened – "Western Civilization" is an example – even cultural purists and traditionalists recognize that cultural diversity exists, and is not a bad thing. In that sense, the mere existence of "world literature" is not under threat, and has even led to an emerging academic discipline. On the other hand, the international book market is more favorable to certain authors and languages than to others. Similarly, there are groups within the academy that question literature's status as a general education discipline on free-market principles, and they often wield direct power over the distribution of institutional resources.

So what role might exceptionalism play in the future of literary studies, in particular as a general education discipline? Does the increase in demand for STEM disciplines and pre-professional programs threaten its status as anything more than a niche discipline, with little or no market presence? When literary studies are absorbed under the aegis of cultural studies, or "global studies", as has occurred in the core curricula of many secondary and tertiary institutions, is that progress or decline? What is the best future for the discipline? The search for balance between surrender and resistance to market forces has led to advocacy initiatives such as the former President of the *American Association of Teachers of French*, Marie-Christine Weidmann Koop, who has urged that "[i]n addition to more traditional courses in advanced language, literature, and civilization, the French curriculum should offer professional courses, such as business French, scientific French, or French for tourism (hotel and restaurant management) that will provide advanced training for individuals who do not wish to become teachers" (17). Professor Weidmann Koop is one of the greatest advocates for French studies in North America today, but it is important to point out that increased enrollments in professional courses does nothing to increase the viability of traditional literary studies. Indeed, why offer such courses "in addition to" rather than "instead of" literature?

It so happens that French literary criticism has addressed this question already by promoting the value of artistic autonomy, the belief that failure to make money from one's art is the hallmark of poetic genius, a perverse sign of success. A recent example of this obsession is Christian Salmon's book *Storytelling: Bewitching the Modern Mind* (original title: *Storytelling: La machine à fabriquer des histoires et à formater les esprits* [*The Machine for Manufacturing Stories and Formatting Minds*], 2007). This timely work describes the neo-liberal corruption of literature exemplified by commercials, business manuals such as Paul Corrigan's *Shakespeare on Management*, political spin doctors, Fox News, and more. In each instance, Salmon exposes the contamination of art (in this case narrative, of which "storytelling" is the debased, Americanized version) by the laws of the market.

Such commercial misuse of literature is, of course, an important issue, now more than ever, and deserves Salmon's scrutiny. Anxiety over the disappearance of cultural spaces that are protected from the encroachment of neo-liberalism has fed popular insurrections such as "Occupy Wall Street", Spain's "Los Indignados", and France's "Nuit Debout". The presidential campaign of Bernie Sanders can be viewed as yet another such twenty-first century romantic resurgence. But there is another way to look at the dissolution of the barriers separating culture and commerce, art and politics. Instead of focusing on the misappropriation of the sacred act of storytelling (or other characteristics of literariness), one can view the co-option of literature by the market from the opposite perspective, replacing the old romantic-symbolist paradigm of art constantly threatened by commerce with the paradigm of art as an extrapolative and interpretive tool for understanding commerce. The omnipresence of literariness in everyday life, including and especially in its most meretricious aspects, is an opportunity for literary pedagogues to justify protection of our discipline within the educational marketplace. Far from being a solipsistic, esthetic experience, reading literature is essential in order to understand, and even protect against, the many ways in which market forces mimic the characteristics of literature in order to function. Instead of deploring the dominance of "storytelling", in other words, we should see it as evidence of the value of widespread awareness of the varieties of literariness and of their importance in our lives.

While literary critics such as Salmon remain faithful to the cult of art, and therefore see commerce as its evil antithesis, French specialists in literary pedagogy realized long ago that such faith has limited practical value; they ask what role it might still play in today's classrooms, and whether making the walls that protect it more permeable to the outside world will result in its increased accessibility, or disappearance. In 2015, for example, the proceedings of the annual Francophone conference of "chercheurs en didactique de la littérature" (researchers in literary pedagogy, a group to which we will return in the Conclusion) included a talk by Laetitia Perret and Emilie Remond, "De la légitimation à la patrimonialisation: destinée scolaire des fictions enfantines, du conte au jeu vidéo" [from legitimation to patrimonialization: the pedagogical fate of children's fiction, from fairy tales to video games], that points out that historically, educators always begin by claiming that authentic literature is incommensurable with popular culture, especially when it is designed for a pre-adult audience, before gradually reversing position. Fairy tales, like novels and films, were once excluded from the canon because of their spontaneous appeal to an uneducated audience, on the principle that education is reserved for texts that almost nobody wants to read. Over time, however, even the most popular art acquires legitimacy, and genres once considered unworthy of serious attention, now are one of the means by which literary study has expanded beyond its traditional borders. What does this apparent openness to the world of markets and entrepreneurship portend?

Those who believe that literariness pertains only to a limited number of recognized texts deplore the recent annexation of literature by media studies, cultural studies, and other hybrid disciplines. Others by contrast view such changes as positive. Given Roman Jakobson's insight that all utterances express literariness to some degree, the latter group has a point. Film, for example, demonstrates literariness in many ways, including the process of adaptation of preexisting narrative or dramatic works, and its reliance on language. Direct lineage between literary and nonliterary works is not the only sign of literature's relevance to popular culture: today video games, which have to count as an extreme example of commercially-debased culture, have not only gained respect as art – the French National Library now has a very large "*fonds vidéo-ludique*" or video-game archive (Perret and Remond 354) – they are even beginning to appear in French school curricula of history, art history, and even literature. They have, in effect, achieved almost the same status of "teachable objects" as novels and films; and like films, they are a hybrid genre, separate from other modes of cultural production, and yet susceptible to analysis in part by using traditional tools of literary interpretation, such as narratology. While video games may never be viewed as "literature" in the strict sense of the term, much like cinema, they might serve as a pedagogical complement to works of literature and, as Perret and Remond argued, they display literary traits including narrative, character, and dialog. Most importantly, they are a transitional object from the world of "proximate" culture to the increasingly remote world of "inherited" culture,[2] as described in the previous chapter. They are tools for exploiting the continuity between mass-cultural objects and the high cultural ones that most students resist. Finally, if a video game can transform from a purely "mercantile" to "patrimonial" object (354–5), and in the process help to understand the power of literariness over our lives, then it has a pedagogical role.

During this process of patrimonialization, it is not a matter of literature being replaced by its debased, commercialized other, but rather of literature being more effectively taught by recognizing literariness in the world, including even commerce as a site for literary practices. According to such an argument, reading literature is indeed a marketable skill, and more importantly, a "means of understanding the world", as Alain Viala argued in defense of his committee's proposed reforms to French literary pedagogy (2001, 9–10). For this analogy to be valid, it is not enough to say that proficiency in reading literature is good exercise for the mind, or that manipulating texts at a high level of complexity is a good preparation for participating in growth sectors of a postindustrial economy. Linguistic proficiency alone does not require attention to literariness, and literariness, as I have argued throughout this study, is the cornerstone of the academic discipline of literature. So how does literariness interact with and explain the world, especially a world in which the metaphor of the market has achieved such universal recognition?

The answer to the question is perhaps that literature, like a justifiably protected product, is both subject to and immunized against market forces. Protectionism means that free-market absolutists do not get to decide the rules (or in their case, to decide that there are no rules). This principle applies to trade agreements covering everything from basic commodities to audiovisual culture. The French cultural market is constrained by laws that limit the broadcast of songs in English, or that tax Hollywood movies in order to support the domestic film industry. Protectionism is therefore legitimate, though in ways that are impossible to quantify.[3] To believe in the distinctiveness of the local product is a stance that nevertheless implies comparability, and therefore commensurability, with products from other regions, cultures, time periods, and also those that aim for a different share of the market. The pejorative use of a term such as "storytelling", that applies to a Tolstoy novel just as much as it does to a sales pitch, does not so much illustrate the triumph of capitalism over art as it confirms that narrative literature helps to understand how the world functions (or dysfunctions). Culture as a whole is not an aggregate of unrelated monads, but rather an interweaving of multiple continuities that link Hollywood blockbusters to experimental art films, graphic novels to the *nouveau roman*, and primarily literary to primarily nonliterary texts. In order to save the discipline of literature in America from ghettoization (a more likely fate than extinction), we must first recognize that, in addition to providing students with marketable skills, it is a more or less close cousin to the cultures that our students have known and grown up with their entire lives. Once this connection has been exploited, we can turn to what has traditionally been the foundation of literature as an autonomous discipline: interaction with more alien texts, the hard work of taking possession of the literary inheritance, both global and local. Advocacy for literary study will ultimately depend less on its contingent benefits, which it shares with many other disciplines, than on what makes it distinct from other disciplines, and yet relevant to all of them.

Reclaiming Literature as an Economic Force

Just as the debates over the general education of literature repeatedly return to disagreements over the compatibility of literary culture with practical and financial values, post-classical French literature also addresses the incompatibility of art and commerce. It is a common Romantic trope, taken up by Alfred de Vigny in 1835, the height of the movement in France, in his theatrical adaptation of the life of the tragic, misunderstood (and financially unrewarded) poet Thomas Chatterton. Balzac, though he repeatedly and unsuccessfully tried to become rich from his creations, often narrated the corrupting influence on art of the marketplace, such as in *Illusions perdues* (*Lost Illusions*, 1837–43) in which the hero Lucien is diverted from his poetic ambitions by the easier and more lucrative career of journalism, or *Le Cousin Pons* (1847) in which the eponymous hero is an art collector whose rapacious family wants to get its hands on the fortune they know that his collection is worth. These all rely on "reverse market" conceptions of value, according to which an artifact, poem, or even figure of speech is intrinsically less valid once it carries a price tag, and even less so the more popular, hence more commercially successful and more widely circulated, it is. A popular work of art lacks legitimacy because it is like a cliché. The association of artistic value with originality (which can easily turn into hermetic impenetrability) helps to perpetuate an aristocratic disdain for the "common" in our ostensibly democratic modern societies. Today, it seems that originality and its corollary, difficulty, are losing their status as a badge of cultural legitimacy. It is not only harder to argue for the incompatibility of art and commerce, but also for maintaining the distinctions of high and low, disinterested and utilitarian, "legitimate" and "illegitimate" that are associated with pedagogical tradition.

The concept of "French cultural exceptionalism" emerged from a similar principle as did the protection of geographic names referring to specific *terroirs*. The principle is, at root, antidemocratic and even aristocratic in its hostility to commerce and to the etymologically-related term "common". General education would seem incompatible with aristocratic values, since it is intended for everyone. Yet there is no need to sacrifice such values, nor is there a need to glorify them as the only ones worth teaching. The key is to find points of articulation between the common and the aristocratic, the proximate and the remote. One such articulation is the very pragmatic policy enacted by the *Centre national du cinéma et de l'image animée* [national center for cinema and the animated image], the agency responsible since 1959 for a tax on movie tickets that subsidizes the French film industry. The biggest box-office hits, the majority of which are produced in the United States (but are sometimes domestic, such as Danny Boon's *Bienvenue chez les Ch'tis* of 2008, which has sold more tickets at the box office than any other movie in France except for James Cameron's 1997 blockbuster *Titanic*[4]), provide financing that, in theory, allows the French audiovisual industry to pay less attention to its bottom line, and more to the rigorous demands of art. In another context, it would be like taxing all new car sales and giving the proceeds to Peugeot-Citroën – except, of course, that we are not talking about cars. So, is there a category of human economic activity for which the traditional bias against protectionism must be lifted? Or, in the age of globalization, a term often conflated with Americanization, is such an exception no longer justifiable, if indeed it ever was?

When the term "transmission" is applied to education, it places familiarity with past culture above the production of contemporary culture, knowledge over skills. It is the banner of the conservative camp in the culture wars, the claim that patrimonial transmission is a deductive rather than inductive process: it is wealth that is primarily inherited, not created (as such, therefore, its nature is aristocratic, not bourgeois). Even as a metaphor, one can argue that the separation of inherited from created wealth is false. Capital is never created once and for all, it is a dynamic process, and cultural capital, like financial capital, must be produced constantly to guarantee future generations of inheritors. Inherited culture can only survive in an environment conducive to the production of new culture. And yet it is surprising to see how difficult it is for people to recognize the mutual dependence, and therefore unity, of past and present culture, to which one may add cultures high and low, indigenous and foreign, commercial (private) and subsidized (public).

The very terminology of economics reflects the permeability of the boundary separating culture from commerce. The French words for "supply and demand" are *"l'offre et la demande"*. The word *"offre"* has different connotations than the word "supply": of giving (as opposed to selling), of a sacrifice, an act that exists outside of the exchange logic of the market (like the potlatch of the Indians of the American Northwest, a form of exchange that does not determine value, but transcends it[5]). *"Offre"* is a sublimation of the rationality of commercial exchange. Morally speaking, *"offre"* and *"demande"* are as different as "sacrifice" and "greed". This important difference between the French and English terms for what is essential to all economic theory has not been overlooked by those who, like Balzac, understand the similarity of the dynamics linking suppliers (sellers and producers) to consumers both in the marketplace and the cultural field. For example, French government agencies serving the public strive to make available to the greatest number *"l'offre culturelle"* of the city, the region, the nation. In 1981, a major exhibit and conference on educational policies of the Third Republic at the *Ecole Normale* of Sèvres was titled *L'Offre d'école* (Frijhoff). In each of these contexts, the word "offer" denotes a critique, if not a sublimation of economic principles.

The French terminology gives moral precedence to supply, which is at root an offer, potentially a sacrifice, over demand. The *"offre d'école"* consequently imbues teachers with moral authority compared to the consumers of education, who are unqualified to use their position in the exchange to determine the content and methods of the educational process. This is in contrast to the market for most goods and services and its principle that "the customer is always right".[6] The term "cultural market" is seen therefore as a contradiction by those who insist that any culture that is created for the purpose of satisfying a demand is not really "culture" at all. In practice, however, such moral distinctions are hard to defend. One does not have to claim that the consumer's desires substitute themselves for those of the artist, in order to believe that artists are influenced by such desires. Literature has readers, and may even be produced with some of those readers in mind, which is not the same as saying that it is merely a market. Does this fact – the role of the consumer's desires – tend to render culture illegitimate? Should the viewer, reader, listener, be a passive partner in the exchange? Are artists morally bound to ignore the consumer's desires? Is such a disinterested stance even possible after sociocriticism and reception theory have taught us that culture emerges, not fully-grown from the brow of the artist, but from the combined actions of all players in the cultural field? The claim that the reader is a partner in the creative process has long been established law in literary theory; yet the educational system, especially in France, persists in equating recognition of students' role in the production of literariness with obedience to consumer demand.

"Reader-centered" criticism has been around a long time, and one of its challenges to traditional cultural ideologies is the undermining of the artist's authority, just as "student-centered" pedagogy subverts that of the teacher. It is not simply a matter of teaching, either. Culture of proximity violates all kinds of taboos. For example, some people are so conditioned to believe in the corrupting influence of the market that it becomes a reflex. Almost thirty years after the death of Andy Warhol, people react with shock to his answer to the question, during a 1977 interview, regarding who is the greatest living American artist. He replied "Walt Disney" (confusingly, since Disney had been dead for more than ten years). The same shock reflex occurred when Disneyland Paris was under construction in the early 1990s. French avant-garde dramatist Ariane Mnouchkine, who directed the 1978 film *Molière*, famously referred to the project as a "cultural Tchernobyl".[7] But what exactly is the danger posed to inherited culture by commercial culture that justifies such a metaphor? It stems from the belief that the cultural field is a zero-sum game. People who fall under the spell of culture that is created primarily for immediate gratification will have no time or desire to take on the never-ending responsibility of appropriation of inherited culture.

Can Warhol defend Disney against Mnouchkine? His greatest achievement may have been to challenge the inviolability of the distinction between literal and figurative, low brow and high-brow. Instead of two separate geometric forms, the curve of culture that is taught, and the straight line of culture that is consumed, perhaps it is better to imagine all artifacts, literary or other, as part of the same continuum. After all, the "culture of proximity" that most students at the secondary and tertiary levels consume is far from homogeneous. It covers the entire range of possible distance between reader and text, from the absolute identification exemplified by first-person-shooter video games, to the ironic distance imposed by a meta-comedy such as *Seinfeld*. Yet while American mass culture is perfectly capable of ironic distance, it is much harder to market (perhaps because literalness is the same everywhere, but figurative speech and irony vary from place to place – *Seinfeld* was notoriously difficult to export, though when it did succeed abroad, it did so extremely well: it was very popular, it seems, in parts of Latin America, not so much in Europe). Such variability in the range of separation between spectacle and viewer, between text and reader, reproduces the variation in level of engagement that readers experience toward "taught" literature. At one extreme is the experience that most academics had in their childhood of completely immersing themselves in the fiction and poetry of the past; at the other extreme, the lack of engagement many students experience while struggling to read *The Scarlet Letter* or *Macbeth*.

Superimposed upon this variable degree of reading engagement is another type of distancing, which is the critical modernist stance of looking at all artifacts as ultimately self-referential and ironic, which has the negative consequence of condemning as illegitimate any reading that takes the text at face value, the sort of reading that Flaubert's anti-heroine Emma Bovary commits. Flaubert's contemporary in the battle for the autonomy of literature was of course Baudelaire, whose work provides a stark, cautionary example of the grotesque lengths to which such condemnation can extend. Late in his life, after he started suffering from symptoms of mental illness, Baudelaire produced an infamous diatribe against the Belgian people, whose materialism and inability to understand figurative language was as bad as those of Americans, about whom he had already complained in the prefaces to his translations of Edgar Allan Poe. Baudelaire's notes for the (thankfully) unpublished pamphlet "Pauvre Belgique!" (Poor Belgium! 1864) contain such gems as this assessment of Belgian education: "Pas de latin. Pas de grec. Etudes professionnelles.

Haine de la poésie. Education pour faire des ingénieurs ou des banquiers. (...) Haine générale de la littérature". [No Latin. No Greek. Professional studies. Hatred of poetry. Education for producing engineers or bankers. Universal hatred of literature] (873).

Baudelaire's caricature of the Belgians seems to describe our present circumstances: a young population steeped in disposable culture who learn in school how to make money so as to continue to be ideal consumers. But there may be a solution: innovative general education strategies that recognize enthusiastic consumption as a valid model for the relationship to literature may well have the counterintuitive result of preserving and even enhancing the poet's position in the collective cultural consciousness, rather than "dissolving" it into a meaningless, relativistic, undifferentiated mass market. Flaubert's Emma Bovary was not a bad reader, as he implied, but a novice one, who failed to progress beyond the preliminary stage of gullible consumer to that of producer. The failure was her teachers', not her own.

The EU, the OECD, and Educational Policy

If the hierarchy of supply (the artist) over demand (the consumer of art) breaks down in the broader culture, can it truly be maintained in the subculture of the classroom? *L'offre d'école*, the educational "supply", is supposed to exist independently from *la demande*: education is a public trust, perhaps the most important one of all. For cultural conservatives, as well as for leftist critics of neo-liberalism, it is sacrilegious to conceive of education as a private enterprise, not only because of the danger of particular interests determining matters of universal value, but because of the inherent corruption of the business model, in which the consumer, even if he or she is not always right, still wields excessive power. Once framed as a conflict between Church and State, French public education today is more about the conflict between the profit motive (supply) and responsible cultural transmission (*"offre"*). It is a resurgence of the fear that art itself is losing its soul as it becomes more and more defined in terms of market value, which is relative, and therefore volatile, rather than intrinsic value, which is absolute, and therefore stable. The surprising extent to which the values of private enterprise have already taken over French public education explains the alarmist rhetoric.

The economic offensive, as many have rightly suspected, originated from the legal institutions of globalization. At the Lisbon Conference of March 2000, European Union representatives devised a strategy to make up for Europe's lag in economic growth compared to the United States. The report concluded that "If people arriving on the labour market are to participate in the knowledge economy, their level of education must be sufficiently high. The inverse relationship between level of education and rate of unemployment is becoming more pronounced. Europe must raise the educational level of school-leavers" (Lisbon Special European Council). This report led to the creation of a committee on education that issued its own, more detailed recommendations in February of 2001. Among its conclusions were that education cannot be separated from professional training; that competency in information technology must be emphasized at every level; that educational institutions must be more open to the world, specifically to the needs and expectations of employers, and to the increasing cultural, social, and even linguistic diversity of students (Education Council of the European Union).

The European Union's "Lisbon Strategy", adopted in 2000 and reaffirmed in 2010 under the title "Europe 2020", made the link between education and prosperity explicit in its prescription for a "knowledge-based economy" that was to guarantee European prosperity. How have these unabashedly neo-liberal forces influenced French educational policy? As it happened, the election of socialist François Hollande in 2012 did not protect France against them as well as one might think: one outcome of Minister of Education Vincent Peillon's 2013 reform, known as the "Peillon law", was the creation of the *"Conseil national éducation économie"* or CNEE. Its mission: "... animer une réflexion prospective sur l'articulation entre le système éducatif et les besoins du monde économique, ainsi qu'un dialogue permanent entre leurs représentants sur la relation entre l'éducation, l'économie et l'emploi." [to initiate a prospective reflection on the articulation between the educational system and the needs of the economic world, along with a permanent dialogue between their representatives on the relationship among education, the economy, and employment] (Peillon). The new relationship between school and private enterprise emphasizes "competency" over "knowledge", marketable skills over acquired culture (the debate over the relevance of the humanities in the United States centers on exactly those issues, as does the *"Common Core State Standards Initiative"*). The "Peillon law" explicitly called for wealth enhancement through educational reform, modeled not only on the Lisbon Strategy, but also on the educational policies of the *Organization for Economic Cooperation and Development*: "Les travaux de l'OCDE, notamment, montrent les gains considérables, en termes de croissance, liés à une amélioration du niveau des élèves... aux tests internationaux en matière éducative" [Research by the OECD in particular shows considerable gain in economic growth caused by improvement in students' level as measured by international educational tests]. The "educational tests" in question are the OECD's very own, increasingly controversial "PISA" exams that link performance in reading, math, and science by fifteen-year-olds to economic growth, and to which we will return shortly.

The educational model that carries out the French government's strategy of linking education to "the needs of the economic world" is already active. The CNEE web page describes an experiment in student entrepreneurship that recently took place in a combined *lycée général* and *professionnel* in the economically-deprived Paris suburb of Seine-Saint-Denis. The experiment was as follows: students first designed an original product, an anti-theft device for cell phones, then devised a marketing strategy for their company, which they decided to name "Peabrains". The device was designed and manufactured by students in the "micro-technology" track of the "professional" section of the school, then marketed and sold by those in the "Economics and Social Science" (ES) track of the "general" section. Their entrepreneurial experiment won a national competition organized by the ministry, which earned them the right to enter their product in a competition of schools throughout the EU (Conseil National Education-Economie). Will the CNEE and similar initiatives become the new engine of educational reform? As long as the EU and the OECD set the long-term strategy, the likely answer is yes.

The degree to which government initiatives such as the CNEE subordinate education to market demands is striking, given the continued resistance from educators and academics. Entire library shelves could be filled with accusatory books and articles published since the start of the millennium. They include Yves Careil, *Ecole libérale, école inégale* [free-market school, unequal school] (2002), who described the Lisbon summit as a victory for those who value education primarily as a means to reduce unemployment, and *L'Ecole n'est pas une entreprise: Le néolibéralisme à l'assaut de l'enseignement public* [school is not an enterprise: neo-liberalism's attack on public education]

(2003) by Christian Laval, who deplored "la diversification, [l']adaptation à la demande...[la] décentralisation" [the diversification, response to demand, decentralization] (328) of education, and warned against "la crise de légitimité de la culture quand celle-ci tend à se réduire à des impératifs d'utilité sociale et de rentabilité" [the crisis of legitimacy of culture, whenever it tends to reduce itself to the imperatives of social usefulness and profit] (328–29). The list could go on indefinitely. The sum total of published American reactions against free-market ideology in education, led by Martha Nussbaum's *Not for Profit: Why Democracy Needs the Humanities* (2010) the title of which echoes the one of Laval's book mentioned above, is small by comparison.

In the background of all these debates lurks a core issue in economic theory. Does demand determine supply, or vice versa? Should the school "give the people what they want", which today appears to be economic security? Or must it set the curriculum without factoring in the desires (often expressed as needs) of the consumers of education? This is a false choice, deceptively simple until one factors in the capacity and willingness of consumers to look beyond their immediate desires. By this I mean simply what every teacher has experienced: to many students, the inherited wealth of canonical works is, at first, well out of reach. They are capable of learning and recognizing an alien system of value, yes, but only through mediation, the slow and mysterious process of assimilation. The controversy is over the effective means of achieving this end, not over the end itself.

There are signs in France that the ideological divide between quasi-religious cultural conservatism and neo-liberal pragmatism is being negotiated. Christine Bénévent, a professor at one of France's "*Grandes Ecoles*", the *Ecole Nationale des Chartes*, and who like many French academics began her teaching career in secondary education, clearly understands that the teacher's responsibility is to be a mediator, not a gatekeeper, of inherited culture. In the 2005 issue of *Le Débat* that was published in response to the Viala reforms, and the often polemical content of which is cited at length in Chapter 5, Bénévent wrote one of the few pieces that are sympathetic to the new initiatives. She began by identifying herself as a typical literature teacher, disillusioned by the hypocrisy of the institution that had just hired her: "alors que je croyais échapper aux lois du marché libéral, je découvrais...que j'appartenais donc pleinement à un marché entretenant artificiellement son existence et sécrétant de la discrimination sociale" [whereas I thought I was escaping from the laws of the market, I discovered that I belonged fully to a market that artificially maintained itself and produced social discrimination] (125). She realized, in other words, that the school that she thought of as a sanctuary turned out to be an overly-protected industry producing instruction that reinforces existing power relationships, instead of subverting them. Literary pedagogy is not only a commodity, therefore, but a luxury over which the school has a monopoly. Bénévent went on to question why French language and literature cannot become a "*bien commun*" [common good] without becoming a "*lieu commun*" [commonplace], which is a brilliant encapsulation of one of the dilemmas motivating this entire discussion. Her recommendation for a true, democratic literary pedagogy is simple yet radical: to recognize the legitimacy of "culture of proximity". She validates the reading habits that her students bring to the classroom: "pourquoi enlever toute légitimité à cette lecture d'adhésion, de fusion, qui refuse la distance de l'analyse et de l'enseignement?" [why deny legitimacy to this voluntary, immersive reading that refuses the distance (created by) analysis and instruction?] (129) Why, indeed? Every student in the world brings his or her own private cultural legacy into the school in the form of spontaneous enthusiasm for various kinds of virtual reality, many of them in the form of texts. Such is the human condition. I would add that schools not only need to recognize student reading of non-canonical texts, but also their consumption and production of audiovisual and cyber culture, *bande dessinée* (dismissed as "comics" or hallowed as "graphic novels", depending on context), slang, and more. Is it necessary that students surrender these private accumulations of wealth at the school door? Must "true" culture be inaccessible, and accessible culture be "false"? Different periods call for different pedagogical philosophies. Bénévent identifies "*époques sourcières*" [source periods] that rely on rereading and interpreting canonical texts, and "*arboricoles*" [arboreal ones] better served by a pedagogy of textual production: we have left the "*sourcière*" period and entered the "*arboricole*". The task of general education is simple, albeit difficult: "Concilier ce qui instrumentalise la matière (sans que le terme soit forcément péjoratif, lorsque l'instrument en question est de partage et de démocratisation) et ce qui en fait la gratuité, quelque chose qui échappe aux lois du marché" [to reconcile that which instrumentalizes the academic subject (a term that is not necessarily pejorative when the instrument in question serves equity and democratization), and that which constitutes its disinterestedness, that makes it into something that escapes the laws of the market] (133).

Like Alain Viala, Hélène Merlin-Kajman, the idealistic authors of the Charbonnières Manifesto before them, and Gustave Lanson much longer before them, Christine Bénévent pointed the way toward an escape from the dualistic trap that has contributed to literary pedagogy's perennial state of crisis.[8]

Yet another pragmatic argument against the signatories of the letter to *Le Monde* comes from sociologist Dominique Pasquier, who points out that even Bourdieu and Passeron's "inheritors", the well-read initiates into the cultural values of their forebears, today are no longer willing to take possession of their legacy (a point also made by Hélène Merlin-Kajman in her already-cited article). Like the scions of rich families who reject their inheritance and insist on creating their own means of survival, less than 2 percent of all French *lycée* students admit to liking classical music (143), and the percentage among them who read patrimonial literature is higher, but not by much.[9] Such massive indifference to inherited culture, in spite of many conservative diatribes that label it as a recent phenomenon, is nothing new,[10] though it has undoubtedly grown significantly since Bourdieu and Passeron's conducted their own surveys in the 1960s.

The crisis of French literary pedagogy will no doubt last for as long as there is reflexive, protectionist resistance against multiculturalism, Americanization, and *présentisme*. Is it not possible, however, that these protectionist impulses not only oppose the exploitation of society by global capitalism, but also harm those who struggle economically? Can Christine Bénévent's openness to culture of proximity lead toward a less tragic vision of the neo-liberal attack on (or indifference to) inherited culture? At issue is not whether free-market ideology corrupts culture – it clearly does, if only by subordinating both producers and consumers to a profit imperative that neither group can control. The more pressing question is whether the space of the school can serve as the site for the transformation of market forces, neutralizing some of their corruptive power by applying it to other goals than economic growth. This requires one to look at the neo-liberal encroachment on education in a more nuanced and strategic way than the above-cited variations on Martha Nussbaum's "not for profit" rallying cry.

No better example of such encroachment can be found than the above-mentioned *Organization for Economic Cooperation and Development* (OECD), the nongovernmental body through which many of the world's industrialized nations promote economic growth, full employment, and political freedom not only for the benefit of large corporations, but for all of humanity. It develops policies in every area that can affect economic performance, including education. In 2010, in response to the economic crisis of 2008, the OECD published a report: *The OECD Innovation Strategy: Getting a Head Start on Tomorrow*, that includes the following statement: "The major policy challenge is to recognise the essential role of universities in the innovation enterprise rather [than] view them, as is all too commonly the case, simply as providers of essential public goods" (3). Universities and educational institutions more generally will therefore play a crucial role in promoting the "innovation" so desperately required to fulfill the OECD's mission of stable, long-term economic growth. To be "providers of essential public goods" is no longer sufficient. Why not? Because a "public good" can be beneficial to a society in intangible ways, without benefitting it materially. An obvious example is the subsidizing of culture, such as museums and classical music. Such institutions are financial liabilities, costing far more than they bring in. Universities need to become more active in the "innovation enterprise", a term that covers economic recovery and future stability. But are these two functions, "merely" providing public good, and producing innovation, mutually exclusive, or do they overlap? Concretely, the question is whether teaching literature, for example, has any relevance to the project of reforming education so as to adapt it to twenty-first century (economic) needs.

"Universities" are dual in nature, bringing material benefits by enhancing prosperity through technological and scientific advances, and serving as expensive instruments of "public good" through basic research and "learning for its own sake". In today's world, can we afford a "public good" that does not also directly serve material needs? Few people would simply answer "no" since almost everybody is invested in one or more of these nonproductive providers of public goods, be they houses of worship, cultural organizations, amateur sports teams, and the like. The real question is whether society as a whole should support these "public goods" through tax-subsidized education. "Should public schools and universities continue to require courses in humanities and fine arts?" is the same question as "Should public authorities support classical music, professional theater, and art museums?" To give a specific example, and to return to the question that is at the origin of this book: do organizations such as the OECD believe that everyone should study literature at various stages of their education, especially in publicly-funded institutions? Does such study have anything to do with the OECD's "innovation strategy"? Since the OECD and other organizations both public and private are, at the moment, setting much of the agenda for government agencies around the world, it is important to look at what they consider to be the value of literature.

It may surprise some to learn that literature is very much a part of the OECD vision for general education, an area to which the organization has devoted a great deal of attention. The most famous OECD education initiative is the aforementioned "*Programme for International Student Assessment*" (PISA), an exam in math, science and reading that has been administered every three years since 2000 to groups of fifteen-year-olds in both member and nonmember countries all over the world. This exam is the basis of the "rankings" that people refer to whenever they lament how poorly the United States, and therefore its system of education, performs in relation to other industrialized nations, with Finland traditionally occupying the top spot (until the 2009 round of testing, when South Korea surpassed it). In 2009, the United States ranked seventeenth overall on the reading portion of the test; France, some will be surprised to learn, ranked twenty-second (OECD, PISA 2010, 8).

But are the PISA tests a fair and accurate measure of educational success, even if success is defined primarily as serving the global economy? Another way to ask the question is, once again: can educational outcomes be measured, especially education in a subject as diffuse as reading, much less "literary reading"? Not according to a distinguished group of academics, mostly from schools of education in the United States and Great Britain, who wrote an open letter published in *The Guardian* in May 2014 to Andreas Schleicher, the director of PISA:

> Pisa has contributed to an escalation in such testing and a dramatically increased reliance on quantitative measures. For example, in the US, Pisa has been invoked as a major justification for the recent "Race to the Top" programme, which has increased the use of standardised testing for student-, teacher-, and administrator evaluations. (...)
>
> By emphasising a narrow range of measurable aspects of education, Pisa takes attention away from the less measurable or immeasurable educational objectives. (...)
>
> [P]reparing young men and women for gainful employment is not the only, and not even the main goal of public education. (...) the new Pisa regime, with its continuous cycle of global testing, harms our children and impoverishes our classrooms, as it inevitably involves more and longer batteries of multiple-choice testing, more scripted "vendor"-made lessons, and less autonomy for teachers.

(...) As Pisa has led many governments into an international competition for higher test scores, OECD has assumed the power to shape education policy around the world (...). (*The Guardian* May 6, 2014)

Quantifying the value of education, turning it into an economic strategy, usurping the power of teachers, school authorities, and even national governments: these issues inform much of the previous five chapters, and are just a fraction of the total amount of anti-PISA literature in the public arena, both scientific and political.[11] In France, however, the test has met surprisingly little resistance in academic (as opposed to journalistic) sources. Not long ago, the sociologists Christian Baudelot and Roger Establet wrote the following:

[S]es évaluations des systèmes éducatifs des trente pays de l'OCDE, et aujourd'hui d'une cinquantaine d'autres, sont d'une rare qualité et résistent à la plupart des objections qui leur sont opposées.

[PISA's] evaluations of the educational systems of the thirty OECD member nations, and today of about fifty others, are of very high quality and withstand most of the objections made against them.] (15)

What is surprising is not that some French academics promote the validity of PISA, but that so many have done so, especially these two particular academics. Baudelot and Establet are well-known critics of the educational establishment, having coauthored the radical, post-1968 critique *L'Ecole capitaliste en France* (*The Capitalist School in France*) with the Marxist bookstore *cum* publishing house Maspero in 1971. Like much of the academic establishment and even a portion of the left-wing press, and unlike Diane Ravitch and much of the Anglophone educational establishment, they have concluded that the PISA rankings, which have consistently produced bad news for France, are largely valid. Their conclusion reflects a surprising degree of consensus in France over the inadequacy of the educational system to meet the economic needs of its students, just as the creation in 2013 of the "Centre National Entreprise Education" and its above-mentioned experiments in student entrepreneurship are proof of the eagerness, even from an ostensibly left-wing government, to implement the EU recommendation that education be more responsive to the needs of the private sector. The educational policy journal *Revue de l'Association Française des Acteurs de l'Education* devoted a recent issue (March 2015) to analyses of the power of PISA in setting the terms of the debate. The editors introduced the topic by asking: "Comment...interpréter cette convergence formelle des discours politiques sur le 'choc PISA' de la part de décideurs appartenant à...des forces politiques opposées?" [how should one interpret such formal convergence of political discourses on the "PISA shock" from authorities belonging to politically opposite factions?] (Michel and Pons). Justifiably or not, PISA has become a measure of the quality of general education in the developed world, and therefore a player in policy decisions. So what role does literature play in the PISA test, and what are its effects on the future of the discipline?

HOW (AND WHY) THE OECD'S *PROGRAM FOR INTERNATIONAL STUDENT ASSESSMENT* TESTS LITERATURE

A persuasive, if cynical reason for keeping literature as a required subject in secondary education, is that the PISA test explicitly includes literature as part of its "reading" portion, making it a factor in any strategy by national educational policymakers to move up and/or stay at the top of the OECD rankings. Apparently, testing reading proficiency using only nonliterary texts is inadequate, which might come as a surprise given that PISA is far more "neo-liberal" than "liberal arts"; it is a means of assessing professional readiness, not literary sensitivity. Is it possible that the two are connected? We first have to examine how PISA uses literature, which in turn will help to understand why it does so. This might also help explain why France scored less well than the United States in this category in 2009 (and did not fare much better in the other years), even though France is a country that traditionally and, one might even say, self-evidently values literature more highly in its educational and other social practices than does the United States.

The "reading" portion of the PISA exam includes the interpretation of literary as well other kinds of text, focusing at times on literary concerns, at other times on the transmission of information. For example, the 2009 PISA reading test included a passage from Gabriel Garcia Márquez's *One Hundred Years of Solitude* (1967), in which the inhabitants of the fictional village of Macondo react to the opening of the first cinema (the test is the same across all countries, so the English-language examples cited here from the American test are also to be found in the tests given in other languages, including French):

> Dazzled by so many and such marvelous inventions, the people of Macondo did not know where their amazement began. They stayed up all night looking at the pale electric bulbs fed by the plant that Aureliano Triste had brought back when the train made its second trip, and it took time and effort for them to grow accustomed to its obsessive toom-toom. They became indignant over the living images that the prosperous merchant Don Bruno Crespi projected in the theatre with the lion-head ticket windows, for a character who had died and was buried in one film, and for whose misfortune tears of affliction had been shed, would reappear alive and transformed into an Arab in the next one. The audience, who paid two centavos apiece to share the difficulties of the actors, would not tolerate that outlandish fraud and they broke up the seats. The mayor, at the urging of Don Bruno Crespi, explained by means of a proclamation that the cinema was a machine of illusions that did not merit the emotional outburst of the audience. With that discouraging explanation many felt that they had been the victims of some new and showy gypsy business and they decided not to return to the movies, considering that they already had too many troubles of their own to weep over the acted-out misfortunes of imaginary beings. (OECD, PISA 2009 Report, 174)

First, students were asked to write out an answer to the question: "What feature of the movies caused the people of Macondo to become angry?" (175) In order to receive full credit, the students had to understand that the question "[r]efers to the fictional nature of movies or more specifically to actors reappearing after they have 'died'" (175). The level of interpretation that the fifteen-year olds had to attain was quite high, commensurate with the complexity of Garcia Márquez's text. It was not enough to say that the citizens did not like the movies, or that they did not understand them; one had to recognize that they felt defrauded by the actors who only pretended to experience tragedy in order to elicit an emotional response from the audience. This refusal on the part of the citizens to accept the conventions of cinematic fiction, and therefore exposing the work of art as a lie, is an excellent example of literary *mise en abyme*, a work of fiction reflecting on the nature of fiction. This question tests not only "reading" but "literary reading" as well. Some of the other questions on this passage were multiple-choice:

At the end of the passage, why did the people of Macondo decide not to return to the movies?
A. They wanted amusement and distraction, but found that the movies were realistic and depressing.
B. They could not afford the ticket prices.
C. They wanted to save their emotions for real-life occasions.
D. They were seeking emotional involvement, but found the movies boring, unconvincing, and of poor quality.

Choosing the correct answer, "C", required students to understand the subtle juxtaposition in the text between lived experience and representation, and the villagers' refusal to grant to the actors on the screen the right to represent characters rather than themselves. In the typical "reading comprehension" format familiar to anyone who has taken an American achievement test, the PISA exam once more focuses on the literary nature of the passage. Another question asked:

Who are the "imaginary beings" referred to in the last line of the passage?
A. Ghosts.
B. Fairground inventions.
C. Characters in the movies.
D. Actors. (177)

Once again, identifying the correct answer, "C", requires students to recognize the citizens' refusal to accept the authority of fiction. The PISA report comments that "[m]ost of those who did not select the correct alternative chose option D, apparently confusing the fictional with the real" (178). Such confusion, like the inability to distinguish between literal and figurative speech, is a matter of literary expertise. Another question asked students to write in a more narrative vein:

Do you agree with the final judgment of the people of Macondo about the value of the movies? Explain your answer by comparing your attitude to the movies with theirs. (178)

The "short essay" format of the above question asks students to elaborate on the passage's self-referential theme of fiction, and they must do so effectively, in other words by conveying ideas and opinions in language that is both clear and complex. The PISA evaluation, therefore, measures the ability to perform a fairly close reading, appropriate for a fifteen-year old, of a canonical text. Literature is not simply used as a vehicle for information, and the skills assessed are therefore not "practical". Traditionally, such skills have been deemed useful for the "liberal" professions such as law, academics, politics; in other words, the domain of social elites. From a practical, economic viewpoint, therefore, the only argument for making literary interpretation part of general education is in order to open up traditionally "elite" professions to the widest possible range of social classes. That is a very strong argument, of course: if literature is no longer part of universal, general education at every level, then only social elites will experience it in the schools and universities, and we will have lost more than a century of educational democratization. Still, it is an argument based on pragmatism, not on the unique, "disinterested" value that is inherent to literary study.

Not all of the questions on the reading portion of the PISA test are literary, of course, nor do they focus exclusively on literary texts. The test samples from which the above examples are taken also included "reading comprehension" questions centered on such widely disparate texts[12] as: a library floor plan; a series of five short argumentative texts written by students on the subject of space research; a supermarket notice warning consumers about the possible presence of peanuts in a product that does not list them in the ingredients; a simple, nine-line narrative paragraph; a graphic taken from an article on the tallest buildings in the world; a passage from Thucydides on "Democracy in Athens"; a passage from Antoine de Saint-Exupéry's *Vol de nuit* [*Night Flight*]; a "hybrid" text (print combined with graphics) on a hiking trail in South Africa and Lesotho; and a map of an urban transit system. Including the passage from *One Hundred Years of Solitude*, two of the ten texts are canonical literary fiction, one is complex nonfiction (Thucydides), one is simple fiction (the nine-line narrative), one is a brief public-service notice, one is a series of student-authored argumentative paragraphs, three are primarily or exclusively visual (the library map, the tall-building comparison, and the transit map), and one is a composite of text and graphics (the hiking trail information).

One can conclude that literary questions constitute a small part of the overall PISA reading test; mostly, students are asked to demonstrate practical literacy, such as: the ability to avoid consuming a product if one is allergic to its ingredients, to get around a large city using public transportation, to be a competent tourist, and other such tasks that, in the aggregate, enable society to function and even to prosper. In context, it is clear that the subtle interpretive questions about the "Macondo" passage are to be understood as the high end of a spectrum of reading competence, more than a test of sensitivity to literariness per se.

Is that, in fact, what the OECD considers the purpose of literature in general education to be? One extreme of a literacy continuum that differs in degree, but not in kind, from the ability to read a government form or the label on a box of cookies? If so, then the only arguments for preserving its status in the school and college "gen ed" curricula are practical ones: one can obtain ever higher badges of reading expertise, and the only objective justification for reading literary texts is to be better qualified for certain professions in which it is a relevant skill, only one of which is professor of literature, whose job it is to identify and train future professors of literature, in an absurd Sisyphean cycle. No, in order to justify literature as an irreplaceable element of *general* education, it must exist both inside and outside the literacy spectrum. The presence of literature in the PISA exam, and of at least some of the questions based on the reading of literature, have to signify something other than a test of a student's communication skills. But if we do not rely exclusively on utilitarian arguments, then what justification is there?

While the OECD is probably not the proper authority for the definition of the foundation of literature as an autonomous academic discipline in general education, the literary pedagogical establishment, which would appear to be the proper authority, has been notoriously unsuccessful at presenting its case, as it becomes further entrenched behind the borders an ever-shrinking portion of the educational supply. Perhaps the economists of the OECD are not as hostile as they appear? Let us return to the multiple-choice questions on the Garcia Márquez passage: "What feature of the movies caused the people of Macondo to become angry?"; "At the end of the passage, why did the people of Macondo decide not to return to the movies?"; "Do you agree with the final judgment of the people of Macondo about the value of the movies?" The series of questions requires students to interpret the way in which a remote, uneducated population responds to its first exposure to a new medium of communication. Rather than describe the narrative, they must consider an act of interpretation (the response to the movies) and determine the reasons why it is so different from the interpretation that they (the students) would make of the identical subject matter. Is this focus on the multiple possible interpretations of the textual representation of a cinematic artifact not quintessentially "literary"? What possible practical reason could there be for testing this degree of reading comprehension? How, in other words, does it demonstrate the greater or lesser employability, and hence economic potential, of the student taking the test? And yet, in order to score well, students had to demonstrate sensitivity "to the fictional nature of movies or more specifically to actors reappearing after they have 'died'", to the outrage of the citizens of Macondo that actors not only can impersonate reality, but that this fraud can be perpetuated through the artistic medium. The students must show that, unlike the people in the book, they are able to distinguish the literal from the figurative, the original from the image, and the value of a text that submits such questions to their interpretive skills. The PISA exam is, at least in part, a gift to the teacher of literature, because it acknowledges that what we have said for all these years is true: everybody must learn to read literature literarily, and not just as a category of particularly complex cognitive puzzles. They do not explain *why* this should be true, but perhaps it is not the task of the economists, but of the humanists, to explain not only why literary texts should be studied, but why they should be studied in a certain way, that is to say (once again) literarily.

The analysis of literature as a subset of reading competency is the subject of one of the monthly PISA reports that the OECD has published over the last six years: "Do students today read for pleasure?" (*PISA in Focus* 8, 2011) The conclusion of the analysis is that they do, and underscores the reasons why they should, though once again it provides only the briefest speculation as to why it is an important question:

> Students who are highly engaged in a wide range of reading activities are more likely than other students to be effective learners and to perform well at school. Research also documents a strong link between reading practices, motivation and proficiency among adults. Proficiency in reading is crucial for individuals to make sense of the world they live in and to continue learning throughout their lives. (1)

So, reading for pleasure on one's own correlates with successful learning in other subjects besides literature and language, though the claim that such reading "is crucial ... to make sense of the world" comes dangerously close to an article of faith. Are people with lower literacy skills less able to make sense of the world? Is "disinterested reading" one of the causes of economic success or conversely, is it merely the result of economic privilege?

The data in the report itself tends to confirm the intuition that reading for pleasure and economic success are linked, but as is so often the case, the evidence is mixed, and the difference between correlation and causation is hard to determine. What country's fifteen-year olds report reading for pleasure the most? Kazakhstan, followed by Albania, with well over 90 percent of the respondents responding that they read for pleasure. Where do they do so the least? Austria and Liechtenstein, with Japan, Belgium, Switzerland, The Netherlands, and Luxembourg close behind, all reporting well under 50 percent. France ranks forty-sixth out of the sixty-five participating countries, and the United States ranks fifty-seventh (2). "Reading for pleasure" is not quite the same as "literary reading", but the two categories overlap considerably, particularly in this age group. If Japanese schoolchildren read for pleasure at half the rate of Albanian ones (making one wonder if television and video games are not simply harder to access in Albania), does that suggest that the value of reading as a tool of economic success is overrated? Well, yes and no. The 2011 report also states that:

> a crucial difference between students who perform well in the PISA reading assessment and those who perform poorly lies in whether they read daily for enjoyment, rather than in how much time they spend reading. On average, students who read daily for enjoyment score the equivalent of one-and-a-half years of schooling better than those who do not. (2)

Finally, here is an eloquent statistic: reading for pleasure correlates so closely with success in the reading test of PISA that it is the equivalent of a year and a half of schooling. First, one has to accept on faith the OECD's claim that reading for pleasure leads to success in the global economy. Even more difficult is to claim that reading literature is one of those reading skills that matter the most. To explore that claim, it is necessary to look more closely at the PISA test itself.

Of course attempts to do this have occurred many times, probably never more often or with more seriousness than in France, where the cultural importance of literature to the society is commensurate with the intellectual firepower that has been expended to theorize and rationalize such importance. To explain the non-pragmatic, non-utilitarian relationship between literature and education, or what I call "literary pedagogy", I return to Roman Jakobson's definition of "literariness" that I explored in the Introduction. Jakobson emphasized its role as the basis for the legitimacy of literary studies as a discipline: "The *subject of literary scholarship* is not literature in its totality, but literariness (...), i.e., that which makes a given work a work of literature" (quoted in Erlich 172, emphasis mine). Jakobson's proposition: that only that which distinguishes literature from all other human enterprises can serve as the basis for the foundation of an autonomous discipline, sensible as it may have been in an academy in which each department had to stake a unique claim within the vast territory of scientific inquiry, today comes under challenge. The first of these is the dissolution, since the latter half of the twentieth century, of precisely those disciplinary boundaries founded on the "properties" of the material under their purview; just as biology and psychology increasingly overlap with one another, and with other institutional bodies both traditional (chemistry) and new (neuroscience), literary studies as an autonomous field of inquiry is ceding more and more ground to interdisciplinary cultural studies and other configurations.

The second challenge to Jakobson's foundational claim is best conveyed in economic terminology: the problem of value. "Literariness" is an avatar of value, and a very specific one at that. It defines itself *sui generis*, as a characteristic of an object (a text) that is unrelated to the object's status as a commodity. By coining the term "literariness", Jakobson and his colleagues veered away from Saussure in a manner that complicates, at the very least, the standard history of the "linguistic turn" that is supposed to have dominated literary theory, and the humanities more generally, in the twentieth century. Indeed, Saussure's insight that meaning is the product of relations among words, and not of the relation between words and nonverbal phenomena, closely resembles Adam Smith's creation of modern economic theory when he identified value as the outcome of market exchange, and not its precondition. In other words, an object acquires value only when it is placed in the market alongside competing objects, that is to say, when it becomes a commodity. Similarly, discourse depends entirely, according to Saussure, on the relationships among its parts, not on the individual status of the parts themselves (hence the claim that a sememe, for example the word "cat", functions only in relation to other sememes, and not in relation to the animal sitting in one's lap). "Literariness" is a fideistic term, in some ways a reaction against the relativizing power of Smith and Saussure's theories of value and meaning, respectively. To return to the economic sphere: "literariness", by naming a linguistic function that is distinct from any other, is an example of the human need to perceive value in absolute terms. To do so is a matter of faith (hence "fideistic"), because such value can never be quantified, or even proven to exist.

Out of all the possible responses to the free-market, neo-liberal challenge to general education, there are two that I have purposely tried to avoid. The first is to argue that literature is a refuge from the dehumanizing effect of the market, a sanctuary of "real value" in a world of debased and relativized value. Among many problems with that argument, some of which have already been discussed, are that it makes literature play the role of religious consolation from the vale of tears to which humanity is condemned, which seems to exaggerate both the transcendent dimension of the poetic enterprise, as well as the cultural poverty of our modern predicament. Besides, if we want everybody to experience in school an escape from social and economic alienation, then would it not be as effective, or more so, to require all students to learn visual arts, or music? Those are also general education disciplines, but they are under even more threat than literature, and the topic of another discussion. It suffices for now to say that literature is still a requirement for obtaining a diploma, whether high school or the *bac*, while the other arts are considered a basic component of elementary education, but nothing more.

The second response I have tried to avoid is the opposite of the "literature as sanctuary" response. It is the tendency, common among education providers, to argue that literature only appears to be a disinterested human activity with little or no relevance to professional opportunity and economic progress. According to this argument, close reading, interpretation, commentary, and focused discussion of literature give everybody who practices them in school a leg up, whatever their professional goals, simply because all of society uses language, and literature is a distillation thereof. No doubt that is true to a degree, but if one adopts the pragmatic, honing-of-linguistic-skills strategy, would it not be better to study only texts that people are more likely to encounter as they move on from general education, such as journalism, legal documents, science, or advertising? That is in fact part of the strategy of the *Common Core State Standards Initiative*, in which the ratio of literary texts to non-literary texts to be taught in "English Language Arts" diminishes, the closer one gets to high school graduation (CCSI website).

Literature, Absolute and Relative

In the previous chapters, I have tried to address the challenge to literary pedagogy that originates from the tyranny of the free market, and that has existed as long as literature has been a part of general education. In France, the exalted status of literature in the education of the elites under the *ancien régime* did not change under the system of popular education instituted by the Republic, but the justification of its status, and the methods of instruction, changed considerably. The hope is that by recounting some of the battles over the general education of literature in France since it came of age in the 1880s, a better appreciation of the causes of the crisis will emerge.

Literature as a pedagogical enterprise faces a unique challenge when it comes to drawing the boundaries of the discipline. In an era of increasing interdisciplinarity, it is no longer possible, nor is it necessary, to say exactly where biology ends and chemistry begins, or what sociology owes to history, and vice versa. But literature has always faced an even bigger problem: in the traditional taxonomy of education, it is the only discipline that has never had clear boundaries separating it from others, a clear definition of "literariness" on which to found an object of study. If one teaches literature, what exactly does one teach? One reason for the difficulty is its reliance on the self-referentiality of language itself (as distinct from the artificial self-referentiality of modernism), which means that literary study shares a paradox with Proust's famous description of memory as the mind trying to explore itself: "Grave incertitude, toutes les fois que l'esprit se sent dépassé par lui-même; quand lui, le chercheur, est tout ensemble le pays obscur où il doit chercher et où tout son bagage ne lui servira à rien" (45). [What an abyss of uncertainty, whenever the mind feels overtaken by itself; when it, the seeker, is at the same time the dark region through which it must go seeking and where all its equipment will avail it nothing] (Moncrieff, Kilmartin, and Enright 61).

In the Introduction, Jakobson's definition of "literariness" served as a crucial stage in the evolution of literary pedagogy precisely in that it made the quest for a unique foundation to the discipline irrelevant. The mistake has always been to view literature as an independent enterprise, a radically different use of language from the incomparably greater mass of "non-literary" discourse. Jakobson agreed that there is a "poetic function", but simply disagreed that such a function is unique to certain utterances. All utterances partake to some degree in literariness, therefore no clear distinction can be made between them on that basis.

The recognition that all utterances are more or less literary does not appear at first glance to be terribly original. "Ordinary speech" has long been a part of recognized literary discourse, after all, whether in the form of the demotic, the vernacular, realism (in the sense of Roland

Barthes's *"effet de réel"* or "reality effect", rather than Aristotelian mimesis), Albert Camus's rejection of the literary past tense in *L'Etranger*, Louis-Ferdinand Céline's adoption of an esthetics of vulgarity, Jacques Prévert's poetry for the people (of which "Le Cancre" in Chapter 2 is an example), and so on. Indeed, the insight that literariness can be found everywhere, even in the unlikeliest places, is one with which literary critics have long been familiar. Teachers of literature, on the other hand, whether willfully or not, have fought against the consequences of that insight for their profession. The gap that still separates the study of literature from the teaching of literature has largely been due to the persistence of the belief that literature is measured against an eternal standard (the "beautiful and the true" according to the influential 1854 work by Victor Cousin *Du vrai, du beau et du bien* [on truth, beauty, and the good]), whereas non-literature is measured against variable, contingent standards (the useful, the effective, the profitable, etc.).

Jakobson's theory of the poetic function removes the distinction between sacred and profane that many teachers of literature erroneously invoke in order to justify their activity. The answer to the question "what is literature?" like the answer to "what is art?" is: anything and everything (potentially), depending on extraneous factors. For example, it is not a categorical error to read the owner's manual for a microwave oven as if it were a literary text; there would only be an error of emphasis, if one were to read the text literally when one only wants find out how to defrost a pound of ground beef. And even if one reads the manual only in order to defrost some meat, the literariness in the text remains, ready to emerge if and when one is prepared to receive it, not as essence, but as potential. *Literature, in other words, is everywhere.* This is not simply a paradoxical challenge, like David Shrigley's monumental sculpture of a shopping list mentioned in the Introduction, or one of Marcel Duchamp's "ready-mades". The proof that literature is in no way separate from the most mundane utterance can be found in some of the most admired literary texts themselves. Writers have always exploited the ubiquity of literary-poetic potentiality, which explains, for example, the power of a poem like "This is just to say" (1934) by William Carlos Williams, which is both completely literary and completely worldly. The first two stanzas are indistinguishable from the most direct kind of communication as symbolized by the transparent panes of glass carried by Baudelaire's "Bad Glazier" in Chapter 2:

I have eaten
the plums
that were in
the icebox

and which
you were probably
saving
for breakfast

It could be a note written by a husband to his wife and left on the kitchen table, in order to explain what happened to the plums that are no longer in the icebox. It also could be, and is, a poem. The first two stanzas are informational, declarative. They could easily pass for something other than poetry if they did not appear in verse form in a book by William Carlos Williams. The third stanza accomplishes the tour de force of remaining at the level of the mundane, while also escaping it entirely:

Forgive me
they were delicious
so sweet
and so cold
(372)

Beginning with the imperative "forgive me" (what Jakobson would have placed under the category of "conative" in his taxonomy of linguistic functions), the poem concludes with the exculpatory claim that the plums were "delicious", "sweet", and "cold". The genius of Williams's poem is that the third stanza, while it provides no real additional information, is just as necessary as the first two in order to complete the note to his wife, Florence. If he had not written "forgive me" and the disarming words that follow, the note would seem borderline passive-aggressive, and threatening to matrimonial harmony. At the same time, the plums that the wife had temptingly placed in the icebox within easy reach of her husband evoke original sin, inscribing the poem in the context of a secular (literary) version of Christian redemption, veering into the emotive, metalingual, and finally, the unreservedly poetic-biblical. As a text it is both human and divine, equally plausible as routine inter-spousal communication and as poetry. While "This is Just to Say" is an especially striking example of a text that is at once entirely mundane and entirely literary, it reinforces the claim that *any* utterance whatsoever partakes of both qualities, and instead of literary versus non-literary texts, we must think in terms of shades of literariness.

The reluctance of French schools in particular to recognize that literariness is a characteristic of *all* texts, and that there is consequently no justification for the process of canonization as it has operated throughout the history of literary pedagogy means that the late arrival of "reception theory" or "reader response criticism" has affected the discipline with exceptional force. By placing the reader at the center of the literary process, it opened the door to the sociology of cultural practices, and to a much more inclusive understanding of the manner in which literariness arises from these practices, rather than being contained exclusively within the text itself.

Nowhere is the fideistic concept of value more powerful than in the cultural field, where "cultural capital" persistently denies any kinship with financial capital, in spite of Pierre Bourdieu's influential attempts to prove not only their similarity but codependence. In art forms where the physical object and the creative work are inseparable, such as painting and sculpture, the commodification of art, and hence its market value, are hard to ignore. However, the fact that the art market behaves like no other, assigning astronomical value to certain works that fetishistically stand for all of "art", merely confirms that we are in the presence of irrational value, and not relative (market) value. When a Van Gogh is auctioned for hundreds of millions of dollars, and when the same artist died destitute for lack of demand for his paintings during his lifetime, both absurdities are society's way of saying that putting any price tag on art is sacrilegious. "Literariness" is, in the field of literary studies, a word for the perhaps nostalgic desire to understand the toiling of literary authors as something other than labor (that which Romanticism called "genius", sometimes regarded as the antithesis of labor), and its product as something other than a commodity.

The need to recognize "literariness" in order to found the academic discipline of literary studies, either as a component of general education or as a specialized field of inquiry, is no longer as important as it was. The organization of academic disciplines, whether the medieval *trivium* and *quadrivium*, or the taxonomy created by the German research university in the nineteenth century, is so hard to change, largely due to institutional inertia. Nevertheless, and for some time, academia has challenged the validity of disciplinary boundaries, and when one either gives up the need for boundaries or changes their location, the very foundations of each discipline are up for renegotiation as well. "Literariness" is no longer a sign of absolute value, and cannot therefore serve as an impermeable boundary between literature and other academic disciplines. In spite of this dawning reality, we are still a long way from abandoning the fideistic definition of absolute value as it applies to culture, literary or other. Were this not the case, then the massive commodification of art represented both by popular culture and by the high end art market, would arouse neither shock nor dismay. And yet it still does. As long as a large enough number of people continue to rebel against Andy Warhol's challenging claim that Disney was the greatest artist of his time, then the belief in absolute value as a necessary attribute of cultural capital is still alive. Conversely, economic pressure on educational policy is powerful, perhaps increasingly so. It is impossible to pretend otherwise. Yet embracing its power or rejecting it outright are not solutions to the crisis. The best justification for the general education of literature, and way out of the crisis, lies elsewhere.

The better strategy is to recognize that active engagement with literariness is already all-pervasive in every social demographic, and that students are no exception. Each one is already an expert in one or more facets of literariness, whether they are already avid readers of the classics, or barely literate. The OECD has recognized both the universality and situatedness of literary expertise in its development of the PISA exam on reading. We can learn from PISA, and recognize how much our students can learn from each other, and we from them, in order to reassemble the broken vessel, and finally reunite inherited, legitimate culture with the culture of proximity that has always been the matrix of inherited culture to begin with. If we can thus demonstrate literature's ubiquity, and destroy the artificial barrier between the words of the poet and those of "the tribe", a victory will have been won, not only on behalf of the discipline of literature, but of society.

Notes

1. The governors of Wisconsin and Kentucky are at the vanguard of the trend in higher education to emphasize STEM and other disciplines considered relevant to economic growth at the expense of the traditional liberal arts, in particular the humanities. Governor Bevin of Kentucky made the point very concisely, singling out French literature as a symptom of the university's lack of responsiveness to economic anxiety: "There will be more incentives to

electrical engineers than French literature majors. There just will" (quoted in Beam 2016).
2. When Bourdieu and Passeron conducted research for their landmark book *Les Héritiers* (*The Inheritors*, 1964), a substantial percentage of upper-class children were more familiar with inherited culture, such as canonical literature or classical music, than ones from less wealthy families. As Dominique Pasquier has shown in *Cultures lycéennes. La tyrannie de la majorité* (high school cultures: the tyranny of the majority, 2008), this is no longer true. "Inherited culture" is "remote culture" for all but the tiniest minority of today's student population.
3. To return to the GATT negotiations: it is understandably frustrating for American negotiators that Europe refuses to import GMOs despite the lack (so far) of conclusive scientific evidence that they are harmful. The scientific question of "sanitary and phytosanitary" concerns is one that ultimately will be decided. But no such objective criterion can be invoked in order to stop Wisconsin from calling one of its cheeses "Roquefort". Such an injunction is based simply on the belief in radical, albeit often subtle differences between *terroirs*, which is akin to the belief that all local culture is unique and untranslatable. That is the widely-shared belief on which resistance to the growing globalization, Americanization, and commercialization of culture depends.
4. These figures come from the website cbo-boxoffice.com, which compiles statistics on movie viewership in France; as of this writing, *Star Wars: The Force Awakens* (2015) was on its way to challenging for the spot held by both of the earlier movies, but had not yet succeeded.
5. The cultural impact in France of anthropologist Marcel Mauss's 1923–4 book on the potlatch, *Essai sur le don* [*The Gift*], can be attributed at least in part to its illustration of how value can function in non-relative terms. In other words, the competing clans during the potlatch festival are not simply trading gifts; they are "out-gifting" one another in an orgy of expenditure and sacrifice that makes classical economic theory irrelevant. It therefore works well as a metaphor for the Romantic conception of art that followed the "consecration of the author" (see Bénichou), and that continues to feed the fear of contamination by the market.
6. In France, the equivalent expression is "*le client est roi*" [the customer is king].
7. Quoted by Michel Boué in his article "Robert contre Fitzpatrick" in the French communist newspaper *L'Humanité* of April 10, 1992. Boué and Mnouchkine became friends at a cultural festival organized by Robert Fitzpatrick, then president of the California Institute of the Arts, during the 1984 Los Angeles Olympics. They both were shocked that this former French professor and art historian later became the CEO of Euro Disney, a

promotion that makes more sense if one knows that Cal Arts, in yet another example of continuity between commercial and non-commercial culture, had been founded by Walt Disney himself. In a conversation with Fitzpatrick while the park was under construction, Mnouchkine accused him of collaborating in a "cultural Chernobyl". Now she is better-known for those two words, at least in the Anglophone world, than for her considerable dramatic oeuvre.

8. In another sign that France is, surprisingly, prepared to consider opening up "taught culture" to "culture of proximity" (understood primarily as commercial popular culture) is the publication in *Le français aujourd'hui* of articles such as Christine Prévost, "Quelle place pour les 'produits culturels de masse' dans la classe de français?" [what is the place for "mass 'cultural products' in French class?] (2011).

9. Pasquier's statistic that less than 2 percent of *lycée* students listen to classical music may seem low, but is consistent with other sources. A 2014 survey of *lycée* students in the Val-de-Loire region revealed that approximately 8 percent sometimes listened to classical music, and far fewer list it as their favorite genre (Hannecart 7). Pasquier's statistics are from her book *Culture lycéennes: La tyrannie de la majorité* [high school cultures: the tyranny of the majority] (2005) which includes surveys on the increasing weight of "culture of proximity" in students' lives. As far as reading is concerned, other surveys show that while more than half of *lycée* students read outside of school, a much smaller percentage read on their own the "serious" literature that their teachers would like them to (Baudelot et al. 1999).

10. Henri Bouasse, the early-twentieth century physicist quoted in Chapter 4, did not hesitate to point out to his literature colleagues that many of their students were bored stiff by the authors on the official list for the *bac* exam.

11. For just one example of the anti-PISA critique from the scientific perspective, see the anthology edited by S. T. Hopmann, G. Brinek, and M. Retzl: *PISA Zufolge PISA/PISA According to PISA. Hält PISA, was es verspricht?/ Does PISA Keep What It Promises?* (2007).

12. Once again, these examples are taken from an excerpt of the test administered to American students. However, every country received an identical set of questions translated into the local language, so that the results would be comparable. Therefore, French students not only had the same passage of *One Hundred Years of Solitude* and questions, they also had identical versions of the other examples from the PISA test mentioned in this chapter.

CHAPTER 8

Conclusion: The Future of Literary Studies in General Education

What benefit, finally, is there in examining the history of literature in the general education curriculum from the French perspective? The present study is not just an attempt to contribute to the history of French education, as worthwhile a goal as that may be. I have argued throughout that the French model, especially the debates leading up to the reforms of 1902, and the reforms of 1999, provide solutions to the stalemate in which the discussion of literature's value in general education now finds itself, in North America, Europe, and many other parts of the world. It suffices to say that literary pedagogy today is under challenge, and for reasons that are relevant wherever it exists as part of secondary education, especially when it is a required subject. Such reasons include canonical literature's role as a marker of social distinction and national identity; the chasm that separates most students from an understanding of, and an intimacy with literary texts, especially those produced in culturally remote contexts, such as the distant past; the debate over whether literary language is congruent with the language of everyday usage; and the pressure, especially during periods of economic and political anxiety, to require students to study subjects that have a direct and measurable impact on their ability to contribute to the gross national product. Rather than recapitulate the previous chapters and their descriptions of the many ways in which each of these issues has informed the debate over literary pedagogy in France, this conclusion will develop possible solutions to the stalemate that have been

© The Author(s) 2017
M.M. Guiney, *Literature, Pedagogy, and Curriculum in Secondary Education*, DOI 10.1007/978-3-319-52138-1_8

foreshadowed by Gustave Lanson and his successors. The critique of literary pedagogy as an ideology has already been made, and very effectively, by Pierre Bourdieu and Jean-Claude Passeron, of course, but also by Renée Balibar, John Guillory, Alain Viala, Philippe Meirieu, Dominique Maingueneau, Jean-Louis Chiss, Dan Savatovsky, Isabelle de Peretti, Daniel Milo, and many others, some of whom have been cited in previous chapters. The new questions that might lead out of the stalemate include: is there a justification for the inclusion of literature in the general education curriculum that does not rely on ideology? Is there a universal benefit that only literature can provide, and that cannot be reduced to humanistic pieties on the one hand, or utilitarian, market-based values on the other? Much of the historical and literary material on which the previous chapters are based suggests that there is, that Charles Baudelaire's aristocratic persona (the glazier's tormentor in "The Bad Glazier"), and Jacques Prévert's iconoclastic student (in "The Dunce"), meet one another at the spot where literature becomes universally and uniquely relevant. It should not be a surprise that the clearest sign of this breakthrough is to be found among the French and Francophone members of a new, fast-growing subfield of literary studies, "*didactique de la littérature*".

THE EMERGENCE OF "DIDACTICS OF LITERATURE" IN FRENCH HIGHER EDUCATION

Throughout the previous chapters there have been references to a meta-discipline: the theoretical and practical study of "why" and "how" literature should be taught, usually designated as "literary pedagogy", a subject of research and teacher-training that in France and the Francophone world is known as "*didactique de la littérature*". This entire book has been a reflection on this discipline, which is comparatively underdeveloped in North America, especially as it relates to the teaching of literature in secondary education.[1] While schools and departments of education include the theory and practice of teaching literature within their curricula, one must keep in mind that the general education of literature in high schools in the United States has been known as "English Language Arts" or ELA since the 1940s, and literature has been merely one component of a much larger discipline, what "*didacticien de la littérature*" Dan Savatovsky has called "*littéralangue*" [literalanguage] or the subsuming of literature within the broader field of linguistics (2008, 182). For example, when a prospective teacher in the United States undertakes a specialized course such as "Methods of Teaching in Secondary English" or "Advanced Methods of Teaching English in the Secondary School" (the titles of courses in the Masters of Education program at Johns Hopkins University and George Mason University, respectively), he or she studies the pedagogy of literature, linguistic competency, English composition, and more. "Language Arts" are self-evidently important for personal and professional advancement except for their "literary" component: its importance, as I have stated throughout, is anything but self-evident. So why include literature as a "language art" at all?

The previous chapters have explored many justifications for the general education of literature, from Pierre Bergounioux's quasi-religious proclamation of faith quoted in the Introduction, to the acknowledgment by the OECD, through its PISA test, that skill in literary interpretation at least correlates with economic growth, and may even contribute to it. It should be evident by now that I do not find any of these justifications sufficient for the requirement that virtually every member of society should acquire literary proficiency. Paul Jay, in a recent book that defends the current dominance in the literature curriculum of cultural studies and theories of interpretation, against the conservative laments over the so-called "crisis" in the humanities, provides a justification that I believe is far more promising: "What is unique about literature (...) is that it treats social and cultural issues in a *literary* way, which is to say, refracted through all of the linguistic, dramatic, and narrative devices at the disposal of poets, dramatists, and novelists" (112, emphasis in original). The difficulty is to explain why it is so important to understand the world in "a literary way", when one can already understand so much about the world without recourse to literature as such, or (what amounts to the same thing), without ever being consciously aware of the literariness inherent in one's understanding, and that Jay finds so valuable. In this final chapter, I will examine some statements on literary pedagogy that have the potential to accomplish such a task.

As stated above, literary reading is simply one subfield of "English Language Arts" in the United States, and one that is not as self-evidently legitimate, as a general education subject, as grammar, spelling, and communication. In France and much of the French-speaking world, by contrast, the much more specific discipline of "*didactique de la littérature*" is well established, and has enjoyed impressive growth since the 1990s. The institutional home of this discipline is not always clear, which itself is a sign of the tension between a traditional, still predominantly "literature-centric" approach to the teaching of French, versus one more closely resembling the multidisciplinary American "Language Arts". Its practitioners sometimes are affiliated with traditional departments of literature or *"facultés de lettres"*, sometimes with education schools, once known as *"écoles normales"*, then *"instituts universitaires de formation des maîtres"* (IUFM), and now *"écoles supérieures du professorat et de l'éducation"* (ESPE). Often, *"didacticiens de la littérature"* will have joint appointments in a *"faculté de lettres"* and an "ESPE", usually at the same university, but a gap nevertheless remains between the two disciplines, as well as mutual suspicion and misunderstanding that is well illustrated by the August 2005 issue of *Le Débat* (see Chapter 5). The growth in this specific subfield of literary studies, in spite of challenges to its legitimacy both from inside and outside of academia, attests to its decisive role in the future of literary general education. *Didactique de la littérature* will grow in importance as one of the main professional gateways in literary studies, since so many university careers begin with teaching positions in institutions of secondary education.

It is not a coincidence that the implementation of the recommendations of Alain Viala's commission in 1999 (see Chapter 5) were followed in 2000 by the first meeting of a newly-constituted group from across the Francophone world, the *"chercheurs en didactique de la littérature"* (researchers in didactics of literature/literary pedagogy). The group has been very productive both individually and collectively, publishing the proceedings of each yearly conference in book form. In March of 2007, the topic was "Enseigner et apprendre la littérature aujourd'hui, pourquoi faire?" [Teaching and learning literature today: for what purpose?]. It was organized by Jean-Louis Dufays of the University of Louvain (Belgium), a leader in the field, who wrote in his introductory essay that its contemporary practice centers on "les méthodes, le rapport au monde, et les compétences" [methods, relationship to the world, and competencies] (8). He acknowledged the validity of Tzvetan Todorov's claim in *La Littérature en péril* [Literature at Risk] (2007, see Chapter 5) that in France, the excessive formalist emphasis on "methods" of reading has relegated the "relationship to the world" to the margins, at the same time as "competencies" are emerging as the wave of the future, in part as a result of outside pressures such as international comparisons of reading proficiency (PISA et al.). Like many of his colleagues, Dufays deems that "methods", "relationship to the world", and "competencies" fall short of the requirements of a mission statement for the profession. "Methods" are inadequate because they substitute linguistic concepts for the act of reading itself. "Relationship to the world" also falls short because it avoids the question of "literariness" as a founding principle of the discipline, and risks returning to a strictly moral justification for literature (the argument that it develops "empathy" in the reader, for example). Finally, "competencies" do so because they exclude aspects of the reading experience that are not objectively quantifiable, such as the students' pleasure and creativity in both reading and writing (9). The search for a more solid foundation for a discipline that has only recently come into its own continues.

So what new directions has the discipline of literary pedagogy in France and the Francophone world discovered? The teaching of literature has come to encompass far more than the traditional concern for the transmission of belief in the absolute value of a designated corpus of patrimonial texts. Changing the focus from the text to the student, from ritualistic canon-worship to the problem of *how* one manages cultural patrimony within the context of practical literacy, has opened up the field to a much wider range of general education goals than the conversion of the population to the limited – and limiting – ideologies of linguistic transparency and literary autonomy. The literature classroom is still a place where one learns how to become a citizen; but the definition of citizenship, and the process of cultural appropriation that makes it possible, is in the process of undergoing revolutionary change. The change is as necessary as it is inevitable in a French society that has lost the illusion of cultural coherence, in which practicing Muslims may soon outnumber practicing Catholics,[2] and the educational notion of patrimonial inheritance is increasingly overshadowed by the far more dynamic model of active cultural production. The object of reading, which traditionally consisted of a national literary canon, is gradually ceding ground to the process of reading. This is the ongoing project of the embattled yet ascendant field of "*didactique de la littérature*", and the reason it has much to teach us about the future viability of the general education of literature.

What are the means by which the leaders of this new subfield of "applied literary theory" redefine the mission of literary pedagogy? This question is more easily answered now, two decades after the discipline achieved a new self-awareness and international scope. When the *didacticiens* convened at the ESPE of Toulouse in 2015 for their sixteenth annual meeting, the topic was "Les formes plurielles des écritures de la réception" [the multiple forms of the writing of reception], exposing once more the growing divide between the field of literary pedagogy and more traditional departments of literature, the "*facultés de lettres*". The word "reception" recognizes that, in the act of teaching and learning literature, phenomenology at long-last trumps ontology. In other words, defining literariness as a precondition to the teaching of literature is ceding ground to a redefinition of the pedagogical process whereby reading literature *produces* literariness. The first consequence of such an emphasis on practice is to define literary pedagogy inductively rather than deductively. Pedagogical principles evolve out of student practices, in other words, rather than the reverse. Reader-response criticism and reception theory in schools of literary pedagogy have overtaken historicism, structuralism, and other approaches, because they take the agency of the student into account. The 2015 Toulouse conference focused on the "writing of reception", or the transformation of the reading experience by the student into an act of writing that definitively breaks with the canonical exercises that emerged out of the pre-Republican, Jesuit tradition. In addition to conceptualizing reading as a form of writing, conference participants examined modes of student writing that included "reading journals", discussion forums, creative writing. Such exercises are new to French secondary education, and are attracting critical attention from "didacticiens" such as Jeanne-Antide Huyhn's article "Ecriture d'invention et 'identité'", in which she defends teaching students the means to exercise their autonomy as writers. In fact, recent innovations in student writing are largely a return to the original ideals of the Republican school, which was to cultivate independence rather than assimilation.

So far this might not sound like news, since English teachers in North America are already very familiar with such emphasis on student output. The target of emphasis, however, is quite different. Professor of English Education Janet Alsup, for example, has developed a pedagogical theory informed by cognitive science that makes identification of the reader with the text a precondition for literary reading in her recent book *A Case for Teaching Literature in the Secondary School: Why Reading Fiction Matters in an Age of Scientific Objectivity and Standardization* (2015). For literary pedagogy to succeed, in Alsup's experience, students "had to find some point of connection, something that made the characters or the book feel real for them.... Once this connection was found, the real reading experience could commence" (24). The process of identification is indeed necessary, as the discussion in the previous three chapters illustrates: the initial distance between student and text, which can be daunting indeed, must ideally disappear, which is why taking advantage of students' "culture of proximity" can serve as a tool alongside the more laborious process of making strange texts familiar through more conventional, philological techniques. So far, so good. But then Alsup argues that the purpose of such identification, no matter how it is achieved, is increased empathy expressed in everyday life. In other words, the justification for the general education of literature, and for its dependence on the process of identification between student and text, is the improvement of society. Literature, therefore, is uniquely suited to the moral purpose of education, not because of its (frequently immoral) content, but because literary reading requires an identification with the text that can subsequently be transformed into identification with other inhabitants of our world. Alsup's argument also works as a justification for the teaching of difficult (archaic, alienating) texts, not just ones that elicit spontaneous enthusiasm on the part of students, since the challenge of identifying with characters in an Elizabethan play, for example, is not unlike the challenge of encountering other forms of difference in society such as race, gender, sexual orientation, and national origin. Understanding one's fellow humans, especially those from other cultures and ethnicities (and historical periods), is a challenge for which literary reading helps one prepare.

The argument that literary reading develops empathy in a way that other types of reading do not, is indeed supported by research in cognitive science (see Kidd and Castano), and has the potential to give new life to the nineteenth-century French emphasis on literature as moral example. But is this not merely another in a long line of attempts to justify the teaching of literature by substituting it for something else, in this case community-building? Of course empathy is a worthy goal of secondary education. However, I think one can find universal benefits to literary reading that are themselves literary, as Paul Jay insisted they should be, and empathy, no matter how well literature might help to develop it, is not one of them. One needs to find practical benefits for the study of literature that help to better understand what literature is, and those benefits are most clearly enunciated in the work of French and

Francophone *didacticiens de la littérature*. Their emphasis on the agency of the student draws its power from the insight that we apprehend our entire universe linguistically. The greatest value of literature is therefore not that it allows one "to teach students useful and appropriate dispositions to live in a diverse, complex, global, and increasingly uncivil and even frightening world" (Alsup 132), but that it reveals the hidden linguistic bias in our perceptions, judgments, and decisions. Literature, by drawing one's attention to language as an end in itself and to the gratuitous literariness inherent in all utterances (Jakobson), in turn allows students to recognize that so much of what they take for granted as true and natural is, in fact, a matter of linguistic convention. Such recognition by itself is a cause for despair: if language loses its authority as a reliable representation of the world, that is a huge loss to the student, and hardly what general education is designed to achieve. But that is where literature, or rather the literariness inherent in all utterances, comes into play. Literature is what allows the initially disillusioning realization of language's autonomy to turn into an opportunity for the individual student to discover a new field in which to exercise his or her freedom. It is not just the literariness of all utterances, in other words, that justifies the teaching of literature to a general population, but the literariness in all of human *experience*, which in turn makes living itself an experience in literary reading. One goal of literary pedagogy can for example be defined as "to become the author of one's life instead of a character in someone else's life", to engage in a creative, productive process, rather than submit, often unconsciously, to various forms of cultural authority. This is the potential value of literary pedagogy that informs much of the current research in France, and on which I intend to concentrate in the rest of this Conclusion.

The Charbonnières manifesto, in a passage already cited in Chapter 5, stated that "le maître de français n'est pas dépositaire d'une 'culture' qualitativement supérieure à celle des autres disciplines" [the French teacher is not the custodian of a "culture" that is qualitatively superior to those of other disciplines] (3). That was a radical affirmation because of the prevailing belief at the time that literary culture was, in fact, superior. Such a statement, that would strike any education professional in the United States, now or in 1969, as self-evident, still is controversial in France today (though not, as we will see, in the field of literary didactics). One dared not question the means by which the "superior culture" of French literature revealed itself through the educational process, and this fear encouraged the zombie-like perpetuation of pedagogical practices that had long ago lost their purpose, repeating the pattern first set by the failure of the "French composition" exercise to emancipate itself from the Latin one until well into the twentieth century (and even then, not entirely successfully).

The premise of this study has been that the French struggle against an all-powerful tradition can teach us how best to respond to the challenges to the centrality of literary study in the curriculum, and even to its ultimate value. The *Modern Language Association* and other professional organizations periodically acknowledge that there is indeed a crisis, and sometimes even agree that France has the most experience and the best tools to attempt to solve it. One such appeal to France as a response to the decline of literature's status in education occurred in 1997, roughly at the same time that "*didactique de la littérature*" started to come into its own in the Francophone world: the MLA published a collection of articles on the topic of "The Teaching of Literature". What problems were identified then, and what solutions were proposed?

"Teaching Literature", the *Modern Language Association of America*, and Roland Barthes

For those interested in literature as a pillar of general education, the January 1997 issue of the *Publications of the Modern Language Association of America* is at first disappointing. As is to be expected from members of an organization devoted exclusively to higher education, contributors discussed the teaching of advanced undergraduates, or of graduate students who aspire to become literature teachers themselves, rather than high-school students or first-year undergraduates. To be expected, but a shame nevertheless. The result of this emphasis on specialized rather than general education is a tragically short-sighted lack of concern for the steady supply, on which university literature departments depend, of students who want to study literature: that is, literature and language classes in secondary education, and at the introductory level of higher education. In short, professors pay too little attention to the fact that most literature students are made, not born, in a process that occurs well before they enroll in our classes. To make matters worse, one of many negative consequences of the adjunctification of the teaching staff of American universities is that general education courses that involve literature, such as first-year seminars and humanities diversification requirements, if they exist at all, are increasingly being taught by nontenured, often part-time instructors. The problem is not that members of this exploited group teach less well. They can be as or even more effective than their tenured colleagues, although their inadequate working conditions and low salaries necessarily inhibit good teaching. The problem is that since permanent faculty, especially in research universities, teach relatively few general education or lower-level classes, the "why" and the "how" of general literary pedagogy are not foremost on their list of concerns. But they should be. When literature professors neglect introductory classes, they lose contact with those who could potentially enroll in advanced classes, and can easily overlook the effect of the crisis in general education on the larger discipline.

To repeat: it is understandable, yet ultimately tragic, that American academics are frequently less than able or willing to address the teaching of literature at the secondary level. In a small sign of hope, however, a few of the contributors to the 1997 *PMLA* did in fact acknowledge the general education problem. The one to do so most directly is German and Women's Studies professor (and current president of Amherst College) Biddy Martin who, in the introductory essay, reflected on her experience co-teaching a summer seminar on "Women Writers" to a select group of high school students. The class allowed her to escape from the conditions that make innovative teaching difficult, such as "the obligation to cover particular periods, authors, and canonical or non-canonical works" (13); she was free, for one summer, from the needs of "majors" and of the wider profession. Her seminar for gifted adolescents represented the liberal arts ideal of a disinterested process of pure intellectual exploration. Of course, teaching to a class of eighteen of the best-performing students in their age group hardly qualifies as "general" education. Idyllic experiences such as the Telluride Association's summer programs, or the summer "college preparatory" classes offered by prestigious universities, remind us that the kind of education that would be of greatest benefit to the general population often is available only to a privileged few. The reality is that the percentage of the population that enjoys such an intimate and pure liberal arts experience is about as small as that of the *lycée* population in France in the early 1900s. As Martin admitted: "little of what we did that summer would work as well in any other situation" (15). And yet something of that Arcadian ideal, the belief that literary pedagogy "can have positive effects that are not negated by sociological reasoning [*à la* Bourdieu] and are not predictable or controllable" (15), in a word: that are not quantifiable, is impossible to give up. What are those positive effects, and if they cannot be quantified, can they at least be described?

Although Martin and the other contributors to the *PMLA* special topic made no mention of the term "general education",[3] their discussion of the "value" of literary study to individuals who are not and may never be professional critics, suggests the possibility of universally beneficial outcomes that no other discipline besides literature can achieve. Martin herself attempts to describe such benefits in a manner that is similar, at least at the outset, to Janet Alsup's theory of empathy, saying that students should identify with the texts they read, in a kind of fusional relation that produces life-long readers. But that is only the starting point of literary pedagogy, according to Martin, not its end. She wrote that once students achieve identification through reading, which is a kind of self-recognition and validation, the task is to lead them to recognize how their own experiences and self-image are expanded, challenged, and alienated by a more attentive, secondary reading. "Seeing (...) one's experience rendered valuable *and complex* can lead to more-capacious rather than more-identitarian approaches to the world and self and to examinations of how *value is created, assigned, distributed, and appropriated* (...)" (15, emphasis added). Let us reflect for a while on Martin's brief yet multilayered formulation of literary pedagogy's "benefit". First, students experience (one hopes) the thrill of linguistic mastery through understanding, followed by identification, which amounts to finding in the text more-or-less sophisticated reflections and validations of their own experience. This may be the "first step" in literary study, but it is an extremely difficult one: the entire discussion of "culture of proximity" in previous chapters is nothing other than a strategy to conceptualize, through a common, concrete example, the fusional relationship that every individual has with some type of culture, and that one hopes to replicate in the students' relationships to an ever-expanding range of literary works that includes "remote" culture, that is, works that display relative complexity, ancientness, and other kinds of distance when compared to the proximate culture that students have at their immediate disposal.

The work of identification therefore provides the student with the means of recognizing him or herself even in a text that is written in unfamiliar language and according to expired conventions. Difficult as it is to achieve, it is only the first step. The second, all-important stage in the process (and the ultimate purpose of "teaching" according to Martin) is to complicate the self-affirmation performed by the first reading, in order to assimilate what was previously alien and unknown, allowing insight into the origins and malleability of "value". In brief, literary reading provides a means to counteract the human tendency to dismiss whatever contradicts the universal validity of one's own cultural practices. Martin's formulation therefore relates the teaching of literature to the theme of "absolute" versus "relative" value that I have explored at length in this study, by viewing literature as a means of understanding the contingency of all value, both financial and cultural. The implications of the "market metaphor" go even further. The first reading of a literary text, to use Roland Barthes's distinction in S/Z (1970), is performed by a "consumer" of texts, and the second reading (what Barthes calls "the work of literature", which one can interpret as the "true" goal of literary pedagogy), is performed by a "producer" of texts (10), in a process he names "rereading":

> La relecture, opération contraire aux habitudes commerciales et idéologiques de notre société qui recommande de "jeter" l'histoire une fois qu'elle a été consommée ("dévorée"), pour que l'on puisse alors passer à une autre histoire, acheter un autre livre, et qui n'est tolérée que chez certaines catégories marginales de lecteurs (les enfants, les vieillards et les professeurs), la relecture est ici proposée d'emblée, car elle seule sauve le texte de la répétition (ceux qui négligent de relire s'obligent à lire partout la même histoire), le multiplie dans son divers et son pluriel (...). [I]l n'y a pas de *première* lecture (...) elle n'est plus consommation, mais jeu (ce jeu qui est le retour du différent). (22–3)

> [Rereading, an operation contrary to the commercial and ideological habits of our society, which would have us "throw away" the story once it has been consumed ("devoured"), so that we can then move on to another story, buy another book, and which is tolerated only in certain marginal categories of readers (children, old people, and professors), rereading is here suggested at the outset, for it alone saves the text from repetition (those who fail to reread are obliged to read the same story everywhere), multiplies it in its variety and its plurality (...). [T]here is no *first* reading (...) rereading is no longer consumption, but play (that play which is the return of the different)]. (Translated by Richard Miller 15–6)

Barthes's distinction between "consumer" and "reader" closely maps the one between culture of proximity and taught (or remote) culture, and helps explain the comments he made elsewhere regarding the teaching of literature. In its simplest interpretation, the above passage from *S/Z* asserts a truism, namely that a reader can only recognize, or "read", in a new text, that which he or she has already read before. It is a truism, because such a form of blindness to the specificity of a given text is a common obstacle to "real" reading (what Barthes calls "rereading"), in literature as well as in life. The world-text is always interpreted through the lens of past experience, which makes the assimilation of the truly new, in other words *learning*, so difficult. A similar obstacle prevents the recognition of originality in all of culture: the history of art is filled with innovations that were either rejected or ignored when they occurred, and then became standard, or canonical, after a process of assimilation analogous to Barthes's "rereading". One might say that such rejection followed by canonization, which is simply another way to describe "paradigm shifts", is a feature of innovation in all fields. In literary pedagogy, despite Barthes's claim that the teaching of literature has always been the teaching of something other than literature, such as its history, one can nevertheless see "rereading" at work in the fact that Baudelaire was excluded from French general secondary education until the end of the nineteenth century, whereas he is now among the most frequently-studied authors from middle school onward (see Fraisse 1997 *passim*, and Fayolle 48–55).

To repeat Barthes's argument: "rereading" occurs when the reader is a producer and not a consumer of the text. Barthes battles against the consumerist approach to literature by saying that the process of rereading, of which *S/Z* is itself an illustration, is to take place *d'emblée*, "from the outset", in order to save the literary text from repetition. In other words it allows one to approach the text literarily, and not as a mere reinforcement of the already-read, such as the "identitarian" reading that novice readers of literature tend to engage in, according to Biddy Martin's similar argument cited above. Both Martin and Barthes indeed provide worthwhile pedagogical goals (rereading as the only path toward learning, that is, the inclusion/assimilation of difference) that might serve in the quest for a justification for literature's status as a general education discipline. This is a variation on, but also a departure from Alsup's theory of empathy, since the primary goal is not to better know the "other" of the text, but to exercise agency in the full knowledge that one stands in relation to the world as a creator, not simply a creature. Both Martin and Barthes are less clear as to the *methods* that might bring those goals within reach, however. While *S/Z* is a masterpiece that succeeds at warning us against the consumerist limitations of the "*lisible*" ["readerly'] as opposed to the liberating promise of the "*scriptible*" ["writerly"], it fails as pedagogy in part because it completely devalues the type of "consumerist" reading that most students already practice. It does not teach how to move from the proximate (which is where people live) to the remote (which is where education should take them).

The challenge, if we are to use the concept of "*scriptible*" as a pedagogical principle (which Barthes explicitly tried to do on several occasions), then we must pay more attention than he did to the process of disalienation, to the transition from the given position of passive consumer to the desired position of active producer. In order to do so, one must begin, once again, with culture of proximity, but with a twist. At first glance, it would indeed seem that most students are avid and un-self conscious consumers, in the sense of passive receptacles, of (mass) culture. That is why the metaphor of the market so aptly conveys the challenge faced by the teacher who introduces a general population to the autonomous, "disinterested" discipline of literature. I argue, however, that in spite of the market success of so much proximate culture, its mode of assimilation is far more complex than a process of "consumption" (Barthes) or "identitarian" appropriation (Martin). Young people, as a group, do not only "own" culture in the sense that they acquire it on the open market; they express ownership in a variety of more active, even productive ways, especially in our age of relatively wide access to digital technology. Just as popular culture underwent an economic sea change when it transitioned from local folklore to global mass culture during the twentieth century, becoming accessible not only to more consumers, but also to more producers, we are once again witnessing an accelerating rate of migration across the border separating writers from readers, producers from consumers. Rare is the person who becomes a YouTube star or a famous blogger, but at least such new media are an added, and arguably easier way to achieve artistic recognition compared to older forms of publication. They increase the access to creative expression and the dissemination of demotic art, in other words, of culture produced without the mediating obstacles of academies, guilds, and other institutions of exclusion. This tendency prevails, even though the difficulty of access to new media for much of the population has rightly become the latest battle in the war against social and economic injustice.

Already, in regard to the explosion of capitalist "youth culture" following World War II, to divide the resulting market between "producers" and "consumers" is misleading. Popular culture does not merely influence the values and cultural practices of its consumers; just as often, it reflects and is determined by them, in a dialectical process, like a customer feedback loop. A defining difference between "low" and "high" culture is that the former allows for relatively easy forms of active appropriation and production, while the latter does not. The difference in difficulty of appropriation is largely the product of time: the dialectical relationship or "feedback loop" linking contemporary society to inherited culture has been lost (its producers are all dead): Shakespeare may once have belonged to "the masses", but he no longer does. And although "mass culture" exploits human beings by treating them as consumers, it is vitally important to recognize and promote the freedom that members of society still retain to break out of that passive role. Paradoxically, it is in part what makes mass culture so appealing as a commodity – its easy appeal, its openness to appropriation – that also gives the consumer the potential to play an active, transformative role; in short to become a producer in the Barthesian sense.

The difference between levels of culture reflects the difference in degree of alienation, corresponding to positions on a spectrum between active (production) and passive (consumption). Barthes correctly states that only active rereading can produce the literariness that otherwise exists only as a potential. But he explicitly designates as "readerly" the strictly-defined corpus of inherited literature that plays the role of icon of literariness in the school, and asks only for submission on the part of students; he does not explore the potential liberation of replacing it with the infinitely larger corpus that is culture itself. He fails to mention, for example, that for the novice reader of literature, the experience of a text such as Balzac's "Sarrasine" risks being forever passive and unproductive (and reading it together with *S/Z* will not help), whereas the same person's experience of a more "proximate" text such as a pop song or television series may result more easily in something like "rereading". Spontaneous identification has the power to progress from consumption to production by making "ownership" possible from the outset (*d'emblée*). As an example, one only needs to see how active and productive the readers of J. K. Rowling's *Harry Potter* series could be, even creating their own narratives on line to fill up the time between release dates of the various volumes, an activity that certainly exceeds the limits of what we understand by the term "consumption".

Is the successful, "writerly" general education of literature therefore destined to limit itself to works to which students already "adhere", to use Christine Bénévent's term (see Chapter 7)? No, because as we saw in the films by Kechiche and Cantet in Chapter 6, the contribution of education to the production of culture consists in enabling students to move *between* past and present, high and low, proximate and remote, even in something as simple as the "code switching" so dramatically illustrated by the juxtaposition of *banlieue* dialect and archaic, aristocratic wit in the film *L'Esquive*. Simply because "popular culture", whether local and traditional (folklore) or global and modern (mass-marketed audiovisual commodities), has been historically characterized by active forms of appropriation and production on the part of its users, and not simply "consumption", it does not follow that it should now become the primary concern of "general education". On the other hand, the fact that a majority of students are already actively engaged in their culture of proximity must serve as a tool of general education, since that is exactly the sort of engagement that education strives, often in vain, to cultivate in relation to "inherited" culture. The task of general education, therefore, is to discover a way to reproduce the active role, and therefore legitimate ownership, that students display in their proximate culture, and to generalize it as far as possible to remote cultures of all kind, distant in both time and space. It entails urging students to feel as comfortable in their role as producers, when they encounter inherited culture, as they already are in their encounters with popular culture. But how? The difficulty of convincing people that they exist in a similar position of power in relation to literary texts of the past, as they already do in relation to their culture of proximity, is the primary reason literary pedagogy has been in a virtually permanent state of crisis. Difficult, however, does not mean impossible.

Barthes was already aware that the transition from "*lisible*" to "*scriptible*" could, and maybe had to, come about through literary pedagogy. His own contributions to the debate over education resulted from an awareness that once attention shifts from the author to the reader, one has entered the realm of education. It is not mere coincidence that one of the articles in the 1997 *PMLA* issue for which Biddy Martin wrote the above-cited introduction is a translation of Barthes's talk at the historic 1969 conference on *L'Enseignement de la littérature* [the teaching of literature], organized by Tzvetan Todorov and Serge Doubrovsky, titled "Reflections on a Manual".[4] Barthes's other major statement on literary pedagogy was an interview published in the pedagogical journal *Pratiques* in 1975 that was reprinted in 1981 in *Le Grain de la voix* [*The Grain of the Voice*]. In both, he argued that the teaching of literature in France has been, in practice, the teaching of alienation from literature, a kind of "history of censorship" (1997, 73) that excludes the following: literariness (always taken for granted, never explained); social class (through "classicocentrism" or the identification with aristocratic definitions of power and truth, 73); and most importantly, censoring of the students themselves. Indeed, what can be more alienating and oppressive than being told that the more remote a text is from one's own discourse, the more literary, and therefore valid it is? Most of all, how can students learn literature when they are forbidden from actively participating in its production?

The student is already a cultural agent outside of the school, both as a customer and as a producer. I argue that free agency also helps to understand Barthes's laconic yet cryptic statement in his talk at the 1969 colloquium: "La littérature est ce qui s'enseigne, un point c'est tout" [Literature is what is taught, period] (1971, 170; 1997, 72). In an earlier essay originally published in 1967, "De la science à la littérature" ["From Science to Literature"] Barthes provides a key to understanding his statement by taking up the same metaphor of transparency as Baudelaire did in his prose poem "The Bad Glazier", discussed in Chapter 2:

> Pour la science, le langage n'est qu'un instrument, que l'on a intérêt à rendre aussi transparent, aussi neutre que possible (...) [L]a littérature se retrouve seule aujourd'hui à porter la responsabilité entière du langage. [Elle] s'accomplit plus qu'elle ne se transmet (...). La science se parle, la littérature s'écrit. (Barthes 1984, 13)
>
> [For science, language is merely an instrument which it chooses to make as transparent, as neutral as possible (...). Literature thus is alone today in bearing the entire responsibility for language. Literature fulfils more than it transmits itself. Science speaks itself, literature writes itself.] (Translated by Richard Howard, 4–5)

"Literature fulfils more than it transmits itself" conveys the importance of free agency, and therefore of creativity, inherent in the learning process. Barthes would no doubt have agreed that scientific writing can be literary, just like any utterance. But the dominant ideology of science is transparency, which is in contradiction to the tendency of literariness constantly to "fulfil", accomplish, or produce itself through the reading process. Literature does not exist in the same way that science does. Literature "bears the entire responsibility for language" because it is an opportunity for the individual to act as a producer of new language, and not simply a consumer or transmitter of transparent words. In a universe of signs, humans have only literature as a remedy against alienation, which leads one to assume that Barthes was in favor of the general education of literature, albeit one that has been redeemed from its current state. It is an idea that has inspired the French and Francophone researchers in literary pedagogy, whose attempt at its implementation we will now examine.

MANAGING THE BARTHESIAN LEGACY: LITERARY PEDAGOGY IN FRANCE TODAY

Bertrand Daunay in 2007 provided a major summary of the state of research in the field of *"didactique de la littérature"* in the *Revue Française de Pédagogie*. He wrote that, while the sense of a "crisis" in literary studies has been around for decades (indeed, as the previous chapters illustrate, it has existed for well over a century), its meaning has changed. In the late twentieth century, the "crisis of French" was one of literature itself: the search for a definition of "literariness" had come up against the anti-essentialism that was a given in the humanities and social sciences of the time, especially in France, and the field as a whole faced the challenge of a seriously compromised, if not vanishing object of study.

> Les travaux sur la lecture littéraire, conçue comme substitut à l'introuvable littérarité (. . .) aideront à un renouveau des études didactiques concernant la littérature. La notion prend une réelle valeur dans le champ didactique dans les années 1990, dans la mesure où elle permet à la fois de s'adosser aux recherches littéraires les plus récentes et aux nombreuses recherches didactiques sur l'apprentissage de la lecture (. . .).
>
> [Research on literary reading, conceived as a substitute for the elusive quality of literariness, will help renew pedagogical studies on literature. (Literary reading) acquired real value in the pedagogical field in the 1990s, as it allows one to build simultaneously upon recent literary research, and pedagogical research on reading acquisition.] (166)

Following Barthes, the added value of literary pedagogy is not learning how to read (the "readerly") but learning an active mode of reading (the "writerly"), which Daunay argues is a more nuanced and less condescending distinction than the one made in the early twentieth century by critic Albert Thibaudet, between "the reader for information" (*lecteur*) and "the reader of literature" (*liseur*).[5] Thibaudet relied on the distinction between transparent and opaque language, and Barthes on the more up-to-date one between the reader who always reads the same text, and the one for whom reading is a genuine learning process.

Among other recent changes to the discipline of "*didactique de la littérature*", Daunay mentions the emergence in France of the term "document" to designate the object of study, the literary text (147). Such merging of literature into the much larger mass of "documents" predictably arouses the fear of those who obsess about the "dissolution" or at least "dilution" of literature in the pedagogical process, but Daunay minimizes the term's negative connotations, arguing that it has long been the practice in literary criticism to refer to literature as "documents", well before the dominance of "cultural studies": "Une telle décision théorique de considerer le texte comme 'document 'ne peut être entendue comme prescription d'un nouveau concept enseignable" [such a theoretical decision to view the text as a "document" cannot be understood as prescribing a new teachable concept] (147).

A third development in the field Daunay mentions is the introduction of the term "*littéracie*" (more commonly spelled "*littératie*") that has so far found its way into only a few French dictionaries. As a transliteration of the English term "literacy" it betrays the continued influence of an alleged "Anglo-Saxon" (i.e., American) tendency to erase the sacred distinction between literary and nonliterary utterances. Daunay defends the term as a means to "penser la continuité des apprentissages de la langue et de la culture" [conceptualize the continuity between the acquisition of language and of culture] (149). Proof of the intensity of the French debate is the fact that even the claim of continuity between language and culture implied by the word "*littératie*" is controversial, especially if it entails the relativization of the literary text. And while the fetishizing of literature will continue to impede its instruction to a general audience that includes a majority of "non-literarians", one cannot deny that such terms as "*littératie*" seem designed to provoke the ire of the intellectual elite. Since it is something other than "literacy" in the strict sense of the term (the basic ability to read, which in French is "*alphabétisme*"), this suspicious anglicism can be made to signify all sorts of things besides the merging of linguistic and cultural competency. In fact, the perennial bogeyman of anticapitalism, the OECD, used the brand new term (as far as the French lexicon is concerned) in its report from 2000 titled *Literacy in the Information Age* (French title: *La Littératie à l'ère de l'information*). The report defines "literacy" not as knowledge, or the actual acquisition of culture, but rather as the ability to access information (including "culture"), especially through the use of technology. The term refers to "how well adults use information to function in society and the economy. Thus, literacy is defined as a particular capacity and mode of behavior" (x).

Defining "literacy" as a "mode of behavior" creates ambiguity, since it is not clear whether it emphasizes the passive ingestion, or the active selection and transformation, of information. The same ambiguity defines the consumer, who alternates between reflexive responses to stimuli both internal (hunger, desire) and external (marketing, conformism), and the conscious exercise of free will upon which classical economic theory depends. In France, where economic metaphors applied to culture are perceived as transgressive, it is not surprising that the term "*littératie*" has yet to find a permanent home in the lexicon. How could good consumer behavior and skills have any relevance to culture, much less the reading and writing of literature? Put differently, is there any way that the free agency of the *homo economicus* is comparable, or even identical, to the "creativity" of the *homo legens*, and even more of the *homo scriptor*? In the abstract, at least, one is tempted to answer in the affirmative, for what is creativity if not a specific application of the freedom to choose?

Daunay goes on to say that there persists an age-old confrontation in literary pedagogy between the "realist" camp, open to the world (arguably first represented by Gustave Lanson) and the "specialized" one, closely aligned with the elite group of academic literary theorists (153). The concept of "*lecture littéraire*" [literary reading] promoted by Jean-Louis Dufays and others, and related to Barthes's "writerly", functions as a kind of salvation due to its potential to resolve the confrontation between critics and pedagogues (165–9). Literary reading competencies "ne font qu'exploiter au maximum les ressources" [do nothing more than exploit to the utmost the tools] of ordinary reading (170). But the real breakthrough, also foreseen by Barthes, is the merging of literary reading with writing, understood not as a history of, or commentary on, literature, but as the apparition of literariness in the world through an individual's active engagement with the text.

CONCLUSION: THE FUTURE OF LITERARY STUDIES IN GENERAL EDUCATION 253

Si l'on admet la possibilité d'un continuum entre l'écriture à fonction essentiellement d'expression et de communication et l'écriture à visée essentiellement esthétique, si l'on admet encore l'impossibilité de projeter tout uniment les deux pôles d'un tel continuum sur des catégories identifiables de scripteurs, l'effet possible d'une réflexion sur les pratiques extrascolaires des élèves dans l'approche d'un enseignement de la littérature est de penser un apprentissage qui ne se fonde pas sur la seule distance de l'élève au texte, mais sur la "tentation du littéraire" que peut receler l'écriture "ordinaire".

[If one accepts the possibility of a continuum that links writing that has essentially expressive and communicative functions to writing that has essentially esthetic purposes, and if one accepts furthermore that it is impossible to project all at once the two endpoints of such a continuum onto identifiable categories of writers, then one possible effect of thinking about the extracurricular practices of students in the context of the teaching of literature is to conceive of an education that is not simply founded on the distance between student and text, but on the "temptation of the literary" that "ordinary" writing might conceal.] (173)

The fact that Daunay's important message in the above quote is expressed in such a convoluted manner is a symptom of how controversial it still is in France to claim continuity between "writing for expression" and/or "communication", and writing for "esthetic purposes". He tempers the claim by focusing on the "extracurricular" practices of students, and the possibility that their "ordinary" writing practices might be influenced, even if ever so slightly, by the "temptation" to stray from the goal of transparent language (an idea that Daunay borrows from the work of Marie-Claude Penloup); in other words, nobody writes purely for the purposes of expression or communication all of the time, even in the most "ordinary" extracurricular genre, be it text messaging. Seizing upon the "temptation of the literary" potentially solves the problem of the extreme "distance" separating proximate and remote cultures.

There are several problems with this bold claim, beginning with the fact that it is not bold enough. To begin with, of course students who engage even occasionally in extracurricular writing are "tempted" by the "literary", if it means something as simple as cultivating a voice, playing with the sounds of words, irony, levels of discourse, and any number of characteristics that can be found in every type of utterance, and certainly are part of the messaging, journaling, poetizing, and other forms of writing in which students engage. The refusal by many people to accept that such activities are "literary", and furthermore that they might provide a means of interacting with texts by established authors whose words have obtained a certificate of legitimacy, is a political stance, and therefore subject to change. Another problem is Daunay's restriction of such writing to the "extracurricular", due in part to the fact that the research of Marie-Claude Penloup, on which he bases his claim, looks at writing practices *other* than the canonical literary exercises that French secondary education rehearses over and over. But why not introduce the "temptation of the literary" directly into the classroom itself? Almost all teenagers text, tweet, and post online, and their utterances do not escape from some degree (and a potentially high one) of literariness. What most such utterances usually lack is an awareness on the part of students of their own literariness, which would naturally come about if those utterances were seen as central to the pedagogical process, and not marginal. Writing and speaking literarily are universal skills that one can learn to improve, especially once they have been marked as "literary", allowing the student to stand at a critical distance in relation to his or her own production.

From the semiological perspective, living is akin to reading, and true reading, which is a form of rereading, is akin to writing. Living, reading, and writing: the interweaving and, on a deeper level, the interchangeability of these three functions provide legitimacy to the general education of literature, insofar as an active, "writerly" engagement with the text is also a way to live. As Leon Sachs wrote in *The Pedagogical Imagination* (cited in Chapter 6), "[r]eading for Barthes is a fundamentally democratic endeavor. (...) Since every text is "written" in the present through the act of reading (...), reading becomes a "revolutionary" activity" (50). For Sachs, the educational project of the French republic inevitably leads to Barthes, whose theories of reading are ideologically akin to, rather than incompatible with, the "object lessons" (*leçons de choses*) so dear to Third Republic pedagogues. One is reminded that by the late-nineteenth century, the teaching of French in national education had outgrown the earlier, oppressive republican project to unify the territory and create a conduit from the central government to the people (concerns expressed in the famous report to the National Convention by l'Abbé Grégoire in 1794[6]), in order to liberate the citizen by enabling him or her to adopt a critical, active approach to the text. In Sachs's formulation: "critical reading is republican reading" (179). "Democracy", a radical goal of republican pedagogy, realizes itself through a consciousness-raising practice that is "revolutionary" in its attack on the very mechanisms that allow ideology to function, unsuspected, hidden behind the mask of authority, whether derived from God or nature.

How is this so? First, let us examine the above statement that "living is indistinguishable from reading", which is nothing more than semiology writ large. The world does not emerge into human consciousness as "itself", a realization that dates back at least to Plato but is no less provocative for having become a commonplace. Instead, it manifests itself as phenomena that impinge upon consciousness as signs that can be properly interpreted only when they constitute a writerly text:

[C]e texte est une galaxie de de signifiants, non une structure de signifiés; il n'a pas de commencement; il est réversible; on y accède par plusieurs entrées dont aucune ne peut être à coup sûr déclarée principale; les codes qu'il mobilise se profilent *à perte de vue* (...); de ce texte absolument pluriel, les systèmes de sens peuvent s'emparer, mais leur nombre n'est jamais clos, ayant pour mesure l'infini du langage. (Barthes 1970, 12)

[T]his text is a galaxy of signifiers, not a structure of signifieds; it has no beginning; it is reversible; we gain access to it by several entrances, none of which can be authoritatively declared to be the main one; the codes it mobilizes extend as far *as the eye can reach* (...); the systems of meaning can take over this absolutely plural text, but their number is never closed, based as it is on the infinity of language. (Translated by Richard Miller, 1974, 5–6)

In other words, the objects and events that make up our existences are always already "a forest of symbols" according to the image in Baudelaire's sonnet "Correspondences", his manifesto on behalf of literature's esthetic universality. But the claim that a "tree" is forever closed to our consciousness except as a symbol (Baudelaire) or sign (Barthes) is a truism that is nevertheless profoundly counter-intuitive to most people, for whom the world in which they live, as well as the language they speak, feel natural instead of arbitrary. In fact, one can say that the semiological turn that Barthes developed into a system of reading provides us with the justification for *two* categories of general secondary education: one in literature, in order to learn that the world is accessible to the mind as a system of signs; and one in foreign languages, since only by learning more than one language can one fully experience the arbitrariness of what speakers otherwise take for granted. But how does the semiological turn translate not only into the "why" of literary (and second language) pedagogy, but into the "how"?

The transition from "*lisible*" to "*scriptible*", "readerly" to "writerly", is crucial for the true teaching of literature to take place. What is at stake is not just the transmission of culture, in other words, but the creation of culture, which is its true path to survival (inherited wealth is notoriously sterile and vulnerable to dissipation, as realist novels teach us).

Until now, reading literary texts in school consisted simply in accepting whatever meaning the text was already considered to represent. A typical commentary exercise for the *bac* was often to "prove", using examples and logic, an established literary interpretation, such as La Bruyère's famous quote that "Corneille portrays men as they should be, Racine portrays them as they are". In Barthes's terms, the school taught students to read, but not to reread; it has been the domain of the readerly *par excellence*. Like the alienated worker that the student of literature had become according to Agathon's 1910 argument described in Chapter 4, the reader is a victim of exploitation, a proletarian: "Can literature be anything for us other than a childhood memory?" asked Barthes (1997, 72), a question that underscores that everything that happens under the rubric of "literary pedagogy" leads students further and further away from a genuine encounter with the text. The question is especially urgent when one realizes that literature can be exploited as nostalgia and even as a created memory by popular culture, as in the "nostalgic" films discussed in Chapter 6 in which canonical exercises stand for an intimate encounter with literature that most people may never have actually experienced. The answer to Barthes's question of whether literature can be other than "a childhood memory" is "yes"; it must be, if literary pedagogy is to have meaning. But it will do so only on the condition that a pedagogical means can be found of transitioning from the readerly mode to the writerly. Such a transition involves increasing the latitude that students enjoy as writers, as opposed to readers.

A key quote from Barthes's interview from 1975 in the journal *Pratiques* is that "[i]l faudrait presque imaginer que chaque élève va faire un livre et qu'il se pose toutes les tâches nécessaires à sa réalisation" [one must almost imagine that each student will create a book, and undertake all the tasks necessary for its realization] (2002, 884). The purpose of the general education of literature is to "almost imagine", therefore, that every personal trajectory through the educational system will result in the writing of a book. The "almost" in Barthes's phrase acknowledges, not just the impracticality of replacing the already-cumbersome *bac* exam with an actual book, but also that it is sufficient to bring each student to the realization that he or she is a partner in the production of literature, and not a subject under its authority. The word "book" is a metaphor for the achievement of the writerly by everyone, not just a happy few. There is no mysterious and exclusive "license to write". Education should reveal to everyone the universality of the right, and even more importantly of the ability, to write. Unsurprisingly, Barthes's view of education is political. The aphorism in "Reflections on a Manual" that "literature is that which is taught, period" places the discipline of literature above the sciences, if only as a preparation for the kind of responsible creativity that moral engagement with a universe of signs requires. The question of whether such education prepares one for occupational and social integration, the great obsession of today's consumerist anxieties in the face of the decline of post-World War II economic and political reassurances, becomes irrelevant. Of course education facilitates all forms of integration, if Barthes is correct in saying that literature and semiology are mutually dependent keys to understanding the world; its justification, however, is much broader. "Re-reading" is the privileged means by which students become aware of their status as agents, and not victims, of social and economic structures. Lanson and his contemporaries struggled to explain how literature, so long an elitist discipline, could serve an authentically general goal of personal empowerment. They intuited that reading was the primary means by which general education would achieve its political objectives, but failed to explain why reading literature was important rather than reading in general, or even why reading mattered more than other forms of interaction with the material world, especially science. Barthes, reflecting on generations of republican failure to realize those objectives, pointed to a solution: reading literature matters because all reading, as well as writing, is potentially literary. It remains to be seen whether his work, after several decades, can provide a basis for the much-desired reaffirmation and re-foundation of general literary pedagogy.

WHAT IS TO BE DONE?

Literariness, as Jakobson demonstrated, is a characteristic of all human utterances. In explaining his point, he referred to the "poetic function" that, unlike the other linguistic functions, points back at itself; unlike them, it does not depend on social relations, modeled on the exchange, in order to achieve its goals. What does that mean? For one, it is the capacity of language to point to its own formal qualities. If literature is therefore that aspect of language that draws attention to the characteristics that are unique to language (though they may be analogous to music or other modes of expression), it accomplishes the paradoxical task of being both subject and object, pointing to its formal, some would say material aspects, by formal and material means. To take Jakobson's famous example cited in the Introduction: the slogan "I like Ike", like all utterances, fulfills multiple functions. Among these are the "denotative" and "emotive", that is, to persuade people to vote for Dwight Eisenhower, and not to confuse him with Adlai Stevenson; yet another of its functions is "poetic", raising awareness of the unique material characteristics of an aural phenomenon, made of language, that has no equivalent in nature (nonhuman creatures may communicate, but they do not speak). Literature, viewed from this angle, is therefore the solution to Proust's paradox of the mind as a "seeker" that is "at the same time the dark region through which it must go seeking", quoted in the previous chapter. Literariness is, in part, the tendency of language to draw attention to those aspects of language that are unique to itself, in a manner analogous to the tendency of paintings to refer to their painterliness, musical pieces to their musicality, plays to their theatricality, and so on. But is that enough on which to found an academic discipline, much less to require its study by the general population? In order to answer, one must decide on the degree of importance of the conscious awareness of the distinctive characteristics of language.

The primary argument in favor of the importance of the awareness of literariness is its omnipresence in human life. It manifests itself in several ways. To begin with, there is indeed a fundamental gap between science and literature. It is not caused by ignorance of science among the intelligentsia, ignorance of literature among scientists, or ignorance of both by the general population, but by something more basic: the way that science interprets the world divides the scientific method itself from the object of inquiry, "nature" (we still refer to its disciplines as the "natural sciences"). Literature, insofar as it is also a distinct method of inquiry, is not "natural". Its primary function is not to inform us about the world in the way that the scientific disciplines (including the social sciences) do; it informs us about itself. There are, of course, elements of the sciences to be found in texts that are primarily literary, just as there are literary aspects to texts that are primarily scientific. But literature as such closes itself off from nature, defined as the site in which scientific inquiry takes place. To repeat Proust's example once more: literature is language, and language is condemned to be the "seeker" and "at the same time the dark region through which it must go seeking", whereas scientists strive to distinguish between the objects and the methods of investigation – the seeker and the region are not the same.[7]

Admittedly, claims on behalf of literature as a means to investigate the world, rather than an autonomous world in itself, exist. Many texts embrace literature's hybridity by subordinating it to something outside of itself, whether to the sublime, such as neoclassical works from Nicolas Boileau to Paul Valéry, or to the materialistic, such as the socio-scientific legitimacy claimed by Balzac and Zola. It is no accident, however, that the authors who rebelled against such claims the strongest did so in the name of "pure" literature, those (often French) authors who most thoroughly explored the idea of the autonomy of literature and of literary texts through the liberation of language from the obligation to represent, to persuade, to withstand legal challenge, in short: all of the mundane responsibilities that the "language of the tribe" is called upon to fulfill. What can we learn about general education from these champions of "pure literature", especially their most urgent and heartfelt claim: that literature is, above all, useless?[8]

That is where the opposition between science and literature provides some conceptual assistance. The legitimacy of most general education disciplines, including science and history, does not in fact derive from their "usefulness". They do not lead directly to economic prosperity, just as literature does not. Unlike literature, however, such disciplines separate the "seeker" (scientific inquiry) from "the dark region through which it must go seeking" (the cosmos, the biosphere, the historical record, and so on). As Barthes correctly noted, literary pedagogy is similar to those other disciplines only if one substitutes something other than "literature" for the "dark region" or object of study. In France, literary history had become the pseudo-object of literary studies, in secondary as well as tertiary education, rendering necessary the call for a return to literature itself (which became the controversy over "nouvelle critique ou nouvelle imposture" [new criticism or new fraud], the title of Raymond Picard's 1965 attack on Barthes). The rejection of literary history in favor of literature had both positive and negative effects on the discipline. Positive, because the call for a return to literature allowed the discipline finally to claim legitimacy by emancipating itself from all other disciplines; it was no longer a sub-discipline of rhetoric or history, as it had been in France before and after Gustave Lanson (rhetoric before him, history after). Negative, because the return to literature in literary pedagogy, mimicking the autonomization of literature itself during the nineteenth century, contained the seeds of a contradiction that it so far has failed to overcome. The contradiction arose when literary study surrendered its late-nineteenth-century claim to being a science, that is to say, gave up separating methodology from the object of study. That which makes literary pedagogy unique, in other words, is also that which prevents people from recognizing its legitimate place in the general curriculum.

What is an academic discipline in which there is no distinction between the methods and the object of those methods? What is literary pedagogy, in other words, when the study of literature consists primarily of "literary reading" and "literary writing", activities in which the student not only plays the role of an autonomous agent, but actually participates actively in the realization of literariness, rather than in its discovery, in its *Erfindung* rather than its *Entdeckung*? The seeker, and the methods at his or her disposal, become indeed indistinguishable from the region being explored. The question one must ask is whether this weakness – the non-scientific status of the discipline of literature – can be turned into a strength. Children begin their formal education in language after they have already acquired the capacity to speak, and they begin their formal study of literature after they have already acquired the capacity to read and write. Not only are they already initiated into language before they study it in school, they have also experienced literature, though not necessarily in the guise of patrimonial works that the school traditionally assumes it is its responsibility to transmit. It is more accurate to say that students arrive in school having already experienced literariness, since it is not a given that every child has read texts, or has even had texts read to him or her, in this era of relatively high rates of literacy coupled with low rates of exposure to traditional literary culture.[9] And yet literariness, as distinct from the purely conventional designation "literature", is everywhere. In his book *Storytelling: Bewitching the Modern Mind* (see previous chapter), Christian Salmon exposes the insidious power of narrative to trick people into buying useless products, voting for corrupt politicians, succumbing to religious fanaticism, and other destructive behaviors. Perhaps inadvertently, he has also reaffirmed the existence of an indissoluble link between the world of social exchange and the world of literary texts. It is not simply a question of reclaiming the capacity of literature to be "about" the world, in a resurrection of realist principles that allows students to "use" literature instead of merely "interpreting" it. Instead one should approach the "relevance" question from the other extreme, by recognizing that it is the world that is already, for practical purposes, a literary text.

The previous sentence appears to throw us back into the prison-house of language, in which humankind is surrounded by "a forest of symbols" that prevents each individual from ever coming into unmediated contact with the real.[10] It would not be wrong to see, in the claim of literature's relevance, a vindication of the Symbolists' faith in language as a kind of eternal horizon. One does not need to make such a profession of faith, however, in order to find reasons to believe in literature's value as a universal object of study, because language is by nature literary, and one therefore does not have to worry, as did many of the contributors to the August 2005 issue of *Le Débat*, that literature will "dissolve" if it is not walled off from the "language of the tribe". As Sylviane Ahr reassures us in her more optimistic account of the pedagogical fate of literature, *Enseigner la littérature aujourd'hui, "disputes" françaises* [teaching literature today, French "quarrels", 2015], "la dilution des spécificités de la littérature" [the dilution of literature's specificities, 53] is nothing to worry about if there is no longer any recognized, legitimate, and impermeable boundary separating taught texts and other forms of discourse.

The general education of literature in secondary education will either survive or disappear. Either literature should be taught, in some manner, to everybody, or it should continue to exist only as one of many specialized academic subjects. In a society imagined as an open market, nobody can deny anyone the right to teach or to study literature, but neither is anybody under obligation to guarantee the conditions that allow that right to exist. "Protectionism", whereby a product or service is shielded to some degree from the vagaries of public demand, is one of the few strategies that promise to maintain a role for literature in general education. Indeed it already does so, in the sense that students are not always allowed to choose the topics that they study, whether they are working toward a high school diploma, the *bac*, or some other general education certification. As argued in the previous chapter, protectionist policies only work if they are persuasive. In other words, they must serve a general good, and not just preserve a private interest. What is the general good that only a general education in literature can bring about? It is not an oversimplification to say that all of the arguments on behalf of general literary pedagogy in France over the last 150 years are attempts to establish a justification for its protection from the harsh laws of supply and demand. In the distant past, those laws ensured that literary study was required only of a minuscule socioeconomic elite. Since the end of the nineteenth century, a steady rise in prosperity and literacy helped to transform the privilege of the few into the right of the many. But the guardians of literary pedagogy have never eliminated the suspicion that their discipline is a luxury product.

The years ahead, we are told, are going to be different. Protectionism in the form of subsidies to humanistic disciplines, including the study of literature, must rely on more than faith if it is to have any legal weight. Commercial interests, many of which have purged the production of culture of its aristocratically-inspired respect for tradition, have become bolder in their encroachment on educational policy. As a pseudo-religion, the general education of literature is not sustainable. The substitution of the economic metaphor for the religious one is a *fait accompli*. While it is true that a narrow definition of "culture" as a type of "cult" will remain for as long as there are people who invest transcendent value in certain artifacts, whether visual, auditory, or literary, it cannot be the dominant trope for literature, or any cultural product, in the context of secondary education. It cannot do so for much the same reason that there is no such a thing as mandatory "national religion" in most modern democracies. One can dispense with the transmission and cultivation of faith, however, without sacrificing the objects in which such faith is invested. The change required of the educational institution is simple, yet profound. First, the pedagogical focus must move away from fetishizing the objects of study, and toward the process by which such objects are brought to the attention of students, away from texts and toward reading. In France, Roland Barthes's crusade against the substitution of history for literature in education contributed to a salutary return to the text. Sylviane Ahr argued that a return to the text in the school has led to a focus on the reader, under the rubric "*lecture littéraire*" [literary reading], a term that helped found literary didactics when it was introduced in 1995 (126). Paul Ricoeur's *Temps et récit* [*Time and Narrative,*

1983-5] was another philosophical breakthrough following Barthes, introducing the conception of the text as an event, rather than an object of study (Ahr 141). Finally, the turn to reader-response criticism continues to serve as a counterbalance to the theorists who still hold sway in French literature university departments. Indeed, what better way to take possession of the text, and of the cultural inheritance it represents, than to conceive of inherited wealth as dependent upon the active production of new wealth?

In conclusion, let us return to the multileveled question that was posed in the Introduction. When considering general education, which is to say the sum of human practices that are to be disseminated among the greatest possible number through the educational institution, one must ask what are the practices that merit such a status, and how best to teach them. The fact that there is no consensus on any of these questions, and that the requisite prior claim that literature deserves to belong to the general education curriculum has always come under challenge, suggests that one can never resolve the "crisis". In fact, as Jean-Louis Chiss and Dan Savatosky have demonstrated, the expressions "crisis of French" and "crisis of literary pedagogy" are not really the symptoms of a sudden, grave obstacle to the pedagogical process, so much as descriptive terms that have always been, and always will be used to designate the nexus of culture wars, class distinction, empty ritual, and student alienation that is present wherever the general education of literature exists.

History has the archive, the natural sciences have the cosmos, and both disciplines belong to the category of inquiry based on empirical observation. Literature is also capable of serving as a tool for understanding the physical world, and it is important to recognize with Janet Alsup that it may well provide exclusive access to certain kinds of knowledge, for example the claims by neuropsychologists that it develops empathy. Such attempts to rebuild some of literature's scientific prestige are still in their infancy, however. Literature's relative (and perhaps temporary) lack of scientific credibility does not condemn it to be a self-enclosed, virtual reality, cut off from everyday concerns. A strong case can be and has been made, that literature is on the contrary a quintessence of everyday life, insomuch as human perception itself becomes translated through the medium of an always-poetic language. It is a matter of perspective whether Mallarmé, when he wrote that the poet gives "un sens plus pur aux mots de la tribu" [a purer meaning to the words of the tribe] in "Tombeau d'Edgar Poe" (1877), he was claiming that the poet's words are separate from those used by the rest of humanity (that their meaning is not only "more pure", but different), or that they are simply a refinement upon them. "More pure" could mean that they are of a different essence, or conversely that they are the same, yet "purified" or redeemed by their presence in a poem, like William Carlos Williams's exculpatory note to his wife ("This is Just to Say", see Chapter 7). In some cases, such "purification" involves nothing more than being placed on a pedestal, either literally or figuratively, like Marcel Duchamp's urinal (the infamous "*Fontaine*" exhibited in 1917). When it comes to pedagogical purposes, however, the latter perspective matters: literature is of a piece with all language, and therefore with life as it is lived every day by every person; poetry may refine everyday speech, but does not exist separately from it.

"Literature is that which is taught, period." As a final example of the universal, and therefore pedagogical status of literature, I will turn toward a strange object, harbinger of a new literary genre that has emerged out of the contentious intersection of literature and commerce: the poem created, not for the educated amateur or for the literary critical establishment, but purely for the purpose of testing a young person's skill at understanding literariness. Thanks to the institutions of neo-liberalism, we now have a new class of literary objects. When the developers of the PISA test looked for examples to use in the reading comprehension portion, they realized that many literary texts are just too complex for many fifteen-year-olds to understand. As we saw in Chapter 7, Garcia Márquez, Thucydides, and Saint-Exupéry provided some of the reading samples for PISA in 2009, and deciphering their writings is simply beyond the reach of those who have had little or no exposure to inherited literary culture. So the developers of PISA came up with an idea. Unlike other testing methods such as the French *bac* or the American Advanced Placement Exam, the OECD did not have to test literary reading by limiting itself to a preexisting corpus: its test-designers were not in the least concerned with "inherited culture", or any kind of knowledge for that matter, but rather with measuring students' ability to recognize the nature and proper function of a text, which is a skill, such as recognizing that an owner's manual has a primary function distinct from that of a bedtime story. So they invented an entirely new genre: the literary text composed for no other purpose than to assess a novice reader's engagement with literature. Here is an example of this new genre, a short poem titled "The Motorcycle" taken from the 2009 test, the English version of which I quote in its entirety:

> Have you ever woken up feeling that something was wrong?
> It was a day like that for me.
> I sat up in bed.
> A little later I opened the curtains.
> It was terrible weather – the rain was pouring down.
> Then I looked down into the yard.
> Yes! There it was – the motorcycle.
> It was just as wrecked as last night.
> And my leg was starting to hurt.
>
> (OECD 2009, 200)

No author or date is given because this text was created "ad hoc", instead of being lifted from the canon, and yet it is clearly a piece of literature, a poem in verse. Unlike the dense and difficult "Macondo cinema" passage and other officially-literary examples, "this short, self-contained story was included in order to target students with low reading proficiency" (200). In other words, it gives those students who were flummoxed by Garcia Márquez a second chance to demonstrate *some* level of literary reading skills. Like most literary texts, it is elliptical, allusive, and enigmatic, raising questions such as: who is speaking? How does he or she feel? What happened to him or her? Each question is easy to answer, yet each one brings us further into the cognitive process that so often distinguishes literary from other types of reading. Indeed, the first question on the test asks the reader to infer the missing information, which happens also to be the most important:

> Something had happened to the person in the story the night before. What was it?
> A. The bad weather had damaged the motorcycle.
> B. The bad weather had stopped the person from going outside.
> C. The person had bought a new motorcycle.
> D. The person had been in a motorcycle accident.

In a subsequent multiple-choice question, the student must proceed from inferring the crucial, absent information, to reflecting on the reason why so much important information is missing from the text in the first place:

> Why does the writer begin the story with a question?
> A. Because the writer wants to know the answer.
> B. To involve the reader in the story.
> C. Because the question is hard to answer.
> D. To remind the reader that this kind of experience is rare.
> (OECD 2009, 202)

The above example, to quote Barthes yet again, represents a sort of "degree zero of writing". Its style evokes the paradoxical simultaneity of transparency and opacity, straightforward description and riddle that characterize works such as Camus's *The Stranger* (one of the examples cited in Barthes's foundational essay), or Williams's "This is Just to Say" (Chapter 7). The OECD is so concerned that every fifteen-year-old, regardless of his or her degree of literacy, be able to engage in literary reading, that it created a new genre: the "PISA poem". In order to "pass" this section of the reading test, first students must understand that an absence of direct communication (the missing sentence: "last night I crashed my motorcycle and injured my leg") is *not* an absence of meaning, but on the contrary, an *intensification* of meaning. Second, they must understand that the avoidance of direct meaning has a function, such as "involving the reader in the story", that direct communication cannot achieve. Even the simplest utterance deviates from the strait line, which is the shortest distance from A to B in geometry, but not necessarily in language, and less so, the more literary it is.

There are reasons why the PISA test includes literature, and do not include the value of knowing, even to the smallest degree, an established corpus of texts. The inclusion of a text that does not belong to a pre-existing corpus, such as "The Motorcycle", confirms the advertised purpose of the OECD when it first devised the PISA rankings less than twenty years ago, "to assess to what extent students at the end of compulsory education, can apply their knowledge to real-life situations and be equipped for full participation in society" (OECD "About PISA"). Beyond assessment, of course, the goal of the OECD is to improve the ability of students to apply knowledge and participate fully in society by influencing makers of education policy. A general education curriculum that does not include literature disadvantages students who are faced with a dense and complex canonical text such as the "Macondo cinema" episode, or even a much simpler "PISA poem" such as "The Motorcycle".

The questions relevant to us are "why does the OECD care about literary competency in general education?" and "why should teachers of literature care whether the OECD cares about literature?" To begin, it is not unreasonable to imagine that future PISA tests may eventually include even fewer literary examples, or none at all, keeping only the "utilitarian" examples such as maps, warranties, instructions, safety alerts, and other texts that help cope with "real life situations". And it is also reasonable to imagine that in the future, teachers of literature will continue to actively resist, or pay little or no attention to, what the OECD says or does. Either one of these futures would be an impoverishment, not because of the power wielded by PISA (with no legitimate basis, according to its critics), but because of what the test symbolizes: the overlap of artistic and economic theories of value. Though they may not be consciously aware of the fact, the test designers who work for the OECD reinforce the principle that reality has a literary bias, and that it is important to know how literature works.

In an important sense, Baudelaire was right to accentuate the distance that separates art from utility, exchange, and to doubt its teachability. Even the populist poet Prévert, whose own works frequently appear in general education textbooks (and "French as a second language" textbooks), attacked the school as inimical to the freedom required in order to write, or even to read. Such a sense of literary "cultural exceptionalism" is lacking in the United States, where the description of literature as communication or as commodity does not have as much power to offend. Still, one must guard against the devastating consequences, for both literary culture and society at large, of using inherited culture as a means of exclusion rather than inclusion.[11]

The history of the general education of literature in France offers something more than an illustration of a long tradition of recognition of the discipline's claim to autonomy, and therefore legitimacy. From Gustave Lanson to the Charbonnières manifesto, Henri Bouasse to Alain Viala, there is a second, even more impressive tradition, also worthy of emulation, one that tirelessly reexamines and challenges the presuppositions of the first. The coherence in the perpetual challenge to the quasi-religious reflexes endemic to French literary pedagogy includes an insistence on the autonomy, not of the literary discipline or corpus, but of the student. It is a rhetorical device to argue that learning to (re-)read also teaches one to live, as Tzvetan Todorov argued in "Livres et vivre" (translated in *Yale French Studies* 113 as "Reading and Living"), his contribution to the notorious August 2005 issue of *Le Débat* that served (in Chapter 5) as such a useful compendium of the passionate reactions caused whenever pedagogical practice in France experiences reform.

The fundamental continuity between the artificial creation that is literature, and the artificial creation that is every human utterance, as well as non-linguistic signs, is simply the paradigm for another continuity on which the general education of literature depends. From the all-important perspective of the student, this second continuity is the one that matters the most: the one connecting "culture of proximity" with "inherited culture". As Vincent Jouve succinctly wrote in *Pourquoi étudier la littérature?* [why study literature?] (2010): one reads literature for pleasure, but one studies it "pour conceptualiser ce qui, dans la relation esthétique, est (...) intériorisé (...)" [in order to conceptualize that which is internalized in the esthetic relationship] (quoted in Ahr 157). The pleasure of the text is a precondition for the conceptual work of literary study, and a starting point in the pedagogical enterprise. Enthusiasm for reading must occur prior to understanding why literature is universally important. This is where Christine Bénévent's moving experience as a young *lycée* professor, cited in the previous chapter, is most relevant: one must not require students to divest themselves of their culture, whatever it may be, at the door of the school, as they do with their hijab or their yarmulke. In many cases, even at the upper end of the secondary level (age fifteen and above), such literary "culture of proximity" may not include literature at all, as it has been understood.

That is why it is necessary to replace the word "literature" with "literariness", and to recognize its presence in every aspect of students' lives, including their social media habits, video entertainment, idiolects, and musical preferences. This is not to suggest in the least that student culture should *replace* patrimonial culture in the school, nor is it a variation on the much-maligned pedagogical technique of drawing connections between highbrow and lowbrow culture, such as teaching Shakespeare "through" popular music; it is merely to claim that once the ubiquity of literariness is established as a principle, it is inevitable that many of the obstacles that prevent successful literary pedagogy in secondary education will diminish. Under such a principle, students will recognize the role that literariness already plays in their lives outside of school, and furthermore that it is not an alienating quality of sacralized texts, but the root of one's love for any cultural products, as well as a model for active ownership that can and should eventually include the corpus of inherited literature. That principle explains why the OECD includes *One Hundred Years of Solitude* in a reading test designed to evaluate one's ability to succeed in the contemporary global economy. There is no denying that it is a long and tortuous path that leads from "World of Warcraft" to *The Iliad*, but the path does exist.[12] Some students come to school with an already-developed enthusiasm for almost any type of literature, but for most, following that path may be the only opportunity to arrive at an understanding of "social and cultural issues in a *literary* way", as Paul Jay wrote in the passage already cited at the beginning of this chapter (112). In order to answer the question of "how" one should design such an education, one first must remember that it is by definition intended for the benefit of all members of society, without exception. The goal is for each student to find a path that leads to the destabilizing yet quintessentially pedagogical practice of "re-reading" in Barthes's sense of the term, with its twin goals of opening language as a space of individual autonomy and "authorship", and of learning to read every new text, not as a confirmation or repetition of those one has already assimilated, but as different from them. Otherwise, the teaching of literature will use up its increasingly-contested share of the time and resources allotted to general education for the dubious purpose of affirming the value of literature without, in the vast majority of cases, proving it.

NOTES

1. Though France has many more scholars in the field of literary pedagogy, Americans have made significant contributions, such as Dennis Sumara, *Why Reading Literature in School Still Matters: Imagination, Interpretation, Insight* (2002); and Janet Alsup, *A Case for Teaching Literature in the Secondary School: Why Reading Fiction Matters in an Age of Scientific Objectivity and Standardization* (2015), to which I will return.
2. French law prohibits the census from collecting data on religious affiliation, making estimations difficult. Statistics compiled by the *Institut français d'opinion publique* (IFOP) show that practicing Catholics in France (defined by regular attendance at Mass) made up 27 percent of the population in 1952, and only 4.5 percent in 2006 (IFOP 5), which translates to fewer than three million people. Estimates of the number of practicing Muslims in the French population vary widely; according to the Ministry of the Interior, it

stood in 2010 at two million out of a total Muslim population estimated at five to six million (Agence France Presse).
3. One of the *PMLA* articles examines literature courses at the "introductory level", and compares the problems that students have in such classes with the challenge of learning a foreign language. Other than Biddy Martin's piece, it is the only contribution that directly addresses the crucial issue of the gap between the content of most literature classes and the students' prior reading experiences ("Rereading Flaubert: Toward a Dialogue between First- and Second-Language Literature Teaching Practices" by Betsy Keller, 56–68).
4. The translation of "Reflections on a Manual" appeared in the 1997 *PMLA* issue on "teaching literature" as part of the MLA's ongoing "Criticism in Translation" series. In this case, however, there already was an English version of the essay by Richard Howard in *The Rustle of Language*, his 1986 translation of Barthes's posthumous collection *Le Bruissement de la langue* (1984). Here I am using Sandy Petrey's 1997 *PMLA* version.
5. Thibaudet developed the concept of the "*liseur*" in his 1925 essay *Le Liseur de romans* [the reader of novels]. His use of the term was both visionary and reactionary. Visionary, because it foreshadowed the shift to the role of the reader that would later emerge in the phenomenological focus of the Geneva School of literary theory, and reader-response criticism. It was reactionary in that it radically divided the act of reading into two categories, literary and nonliterary, highbrow and lowbrow, the latter having no connection to the former.
6. The title of Grégoire's 1794 report, based on a survey of the diversity of languages and dialects within the French national territory and the number and degree of fluency of French speakers, gives a fair impression of its political purpose: "Rapport sur la nécessité et les moyens d'anéantir les patois et d'universaliser l'usage de la langue française" [report on the necessity and the means of eliminating local languages and of universalizing the practice of the French language].
7. The revised dichotomy between the "two cultures", literary and scientific, that I present here is naturally an oversimplification, but I argue that it is nevertheless valid: science tends to separate the tools of observation from the object of observation, whereas in literature they tend to be one and the same.
8. Baudelaire's writings on Edgar Allan Poe provide an eloquent attack on the notion that literature (and by implication, the study of literature) has a connection to any moral, practical, or other purpose other than to exist *qua* literature.
9. Brigitte Louichon argued that there is an upside to the contemporary decline of exposure to inherited culture in the home: the fact that such exposure, since it rarely occurs even in upper-class households, can no longer serve a classist

purpose. "[Le texte patrimonial] retrouve (...) une forme de virginité puisque, objet d'aucune pratique, il ne peut être suspecté de manifester la distinction" [the patrimonial text regains a form of virginity because, as it is no longer the object of a practice, it no longer can be accused of expressing distinction] (28).

10. The image is from Baudelaire's Symbolist manifesto, the sonnet "Correspondances" [correspondences]: "La nature est un temple où de vivants piliers/Laissent parfois sortir de confuses paroles" [Nature is a temple in which living pillars sometimes let out indistinct words] (my translation). The portrayal of nature as a Delphic temple, the pillars of which are the trees of a forest, suggests that the universe manifests itself to human consciousness already in the form of artificial symbols. The fact that Baudelaire uses trees to represent the impossibility of an unmediated relationship to nature probably influenced Jean-Paul Sartre's famous passage in *Nausea* (1938) in which the narrator, Roquentin, experiences a fleeting, nausea-inducing escape from language: the revelation of a phenomenon apparently divorced from its "symbolic" status, while gazing at a tree.

11. Bertrand Daunay, whose summary of the state of the field of literary pedagogy I quote extensively at the beginning of this chapter, has spent much of his career highlighting the disastrous consequences of reinforcing the alienation many students experience upon reading canonical literature, and that "disqualifies" them from the educational process itself. "L'infini processus de disqualification du lecteur ou contre une didactique bathmologique" [the infinite process of disqualification of the reader, or against a bathmological pedagogy] (2004) and "Lecture littéraire et disqualification scolaire" [literary reading and educational disqualification] (2006). "Bathmology" is yet another Barthesian coinage, referring to the multiple levels of meaning in an utterance, such as degrees of irony. Daunay therefore wants to reclaim legitimacy for "naïve" reading as a first – and for some, final – step in the acquisition of literary skill. In short, his critique redeems Emma Bovary, the quintessential "consumer" of literature, as an archetype for the novice student of literature.

12. The film *L'enlèvement de Michel Houellebecq* [*The Kidnapping of Michel Houellebecq*, 2014] contains an allusion to this same video game, "World of Warcraft", that plays on the distance between culture of proximity and inherited culture. Houellebecq (who plays himself) is having a conversation about literature with the men who are holding him hostage. One of them has read Houellebecq's book on H. P. Lovecraft, and asks him questions that are "typical" of an uneducated, naïve reader, and also quite pertinent, though strange: the conversation degenerates into an argument over whether Houellebecq did or did not write that there was blood and saliva on Lovecraft's pillow; Houellebecq is correct in denying that he wrote it, because it was actually written by Stephen King, in his introduction to the American translation of the book. A French translation of King's

introduction was then included in subsequent French editions; hence the kidnapper's confusion. Not only does the kidnapper get his authors confused, every time he refers to "Lovecraft" he calls him "Warcraft", an understandable mistake, since it is one of the most widely-played games of all time.

BIBLIOGRAPHY

I. LITERARY AND CINEMATIC WORKS

Balzac, Honoré de. *Illusions perdues. La Comédie humaine, vol. 5* Paris: Gallimard, La Pléiade, 1977.
Balzac, Honoré de. *Le Cousin Pons. La Comédie humaine, vol. 7* Paris: Gallimard, La Pléiade, 1977.
Barratier, Christian, Director. *La Nouvelle guerre des boutons.* With Jean Texier and Ilona Bachelier. Studio 37, 2011.
Baudelaire, Charles. «Correspondances» (1857). *Les Fleurs du mal. Œuvres complètes, tome I.* Paris: Gallimard, La Pléiade, 1976, 11.
Baudelaire, Charles. «Edgar Poe: sa vie et ses ouvrages (préface)» (1852). *Œuvres complètes, tome II.* Paris: Gallimard, La Pléiade, 1976, 249–288.
Baudelaire, Charles. «Le mauvais vitrier.» *Le Spleen de Paris. Œuvres complètes, tome I.* Paris: Gallimard, La Pléiade, 1976, 285–287.
Baudelaire, Charles. «Notes nouvelles sur Edgar Poe (préface)» (1857). *Œuvres complètes,* tome II. Paris: Gallimard, La Pléiade, 1976, 319–337.
Baudelaire, Charles. «Pauvre Belgique!» (1864). *Œuvres complètes,* tome II. Paris: Gallimard, La Pléiade, 1976, 819–965.
Bégaudeau, François. *Entre les murs.* Paris: Verticales (Gallimard), 2006.
Camus, Albert. *L'Etranger.* Paris: Gallimard, 1942.
Cantet, Laurent, Director. *Entre les murs.* With François Bégaudeau and Esmeralda Ouertani. Haut et Court, 2008.
Daroy, Jacques, Director. *La Guerre des gosses.* With Jean Murat and Saturnin Fabre. Forrester-Parent, 1937.
Garcia-Márquez, Gabriel. *One Hundred Years of Solitude.* Trans. Gregory Rabassa. New York: Harper and Row, 1970 (1967).

Gide, André. *Les Faux-monnayeurs*. In *Romans, récits et soties, œuvres lyriques*. Paris: Gallimard, La Pléiade, 1958, 931–1248.
Honoré, Christophe, Director. *La Belle personne*. With Louis Garrel and Léa Seydoux. Scarlett Productions, 2008.
Kechiche, Abdellatif, Director. *L'esquive*. With Sara Forestier, Osman Elkharraz. Lola, 2004.
La Fontaine, Jean de. «Discours à Mme de La Sablière» (1684), *Œuvres complètes*, vol. II. Paris: Gallimard, La Pléiade, 1943, 644.
Lafayette, Marie Madeleine, comtesse de. *La Princesse de Clèves* (1678). In *Œuvres complètes*. Paris: Gallimard, La Pléiade, 2014.
Lilienfeld, Jean-Paul, Director. *La journée de la jupe*. With Isabelle Adjani, Denis Podalydès. Arte, 2009.
Mallarmé, Stéphane. «Tombeau d'Edgar Poe» (1877). *Œuvres complètes*. Paris: Gallimard, La Pléiade, 1998.
Malle, Louis, Director. *Au revoir les enfants*. With Gaspard Manesse, Raphaël Fejtö. MK2 Productions, 1987.
Marivaux, Pierre de. *Le Jeu de l'amour et du hasard*. In *Théâtre complet, tome I*. Paris: Gallimard, La Pléiade, 1993.
Molière (Jean-Baptiste Pocquelin). *Le Bourgeois gentilhomme*. In *Œuvres complètes, tome II*. Paris: Gallimard, La Pléiade, 2010.
Nicloux, Guillaume, Director. *L'Enlèvement de Michel Houellebecq*. With Michel Houellebecq, Françoise Lebrun. Les Films du Worso and Arte France, 2014.
Orsenna, Erik. *La grammaire est une chanson douce*. Paris: Stock, 2001.
Ozon, François, Director. *Dans la maison*. With Fabrice Luchini, Ernst Umhauer. Mandarin Films, 2012.
Pennac, Daniel. *Chagrin d'école*. Paris: Gallimard, 2007.
Pergaud, Louis. *La Guerre des Boutons, roman de ma douzième année*. Paris: Mercure de France, 1912.
Philibert, Nicolas, Director. *Etre et avoir*. With Georges Lopez. Maïa Films, 2002.
Prévert, Jacques. «The Dunce». *Selections from* Paroles *by Jacques Prévert*. Trans. Lawrence Ferlinghetti. San Francisco: City Lights Books, 1958.
Prévert, Jacques. «Le cancre» (1946). *Paroles*. Paris: Editions du Point du jour, 1949 (original edition 1946).
Proust, Marcel. *Du Côté de chez Swann*. In *A la recherche du temps perdu, tome I*. Paris: Gallimard, La Pléiade, 1954.
Proust, Marcel. *Swann's Way*. Trans. F. Scott Moncrieff and Terence Kilmartin, revised by D.J. Enright. New York: The Modern Library, 1992.
Richepin, Jean. «Epitaphe pour un lièvre» in *La Chanson des gueux*. Paris: M. Dreyfous, 1881. 48–49.
Robert, Yves, Director. *La Guerre des boutons*. With André Treton and Michel Isella. La Guéville, 1962.

Roberts, John, Director. *War of the Buttons.* With Gregg Fitzgerald and Colm Meaney. Warner Brothers, 1994.
Samuell, Yann, Director. *La Guerre des boutons.* With Vincent Bres and Salomé Lemire. One World Films, 2011.
Sartre, Jean-Paul. *La Nausée (Nausea).* In *Œuvres romanesques.* Paris: Gallimard, La Pléiade, 1981.
Sauder, Régis, Director. *Nous, Princesses de Clèves.* With Saray Yagoubi and Abou Achoumi. Nord/Ouest Documentaires, 2011.
Tirard, Laurent, Director. *Le Petit Nicolas.* With Maxime Godart and Valérie Lemercier. Wild Bunch, 2009.
Truffaut, François, Director. *Les 400 coups.* With Jean-Pierre Léaud. Les Films du Carrosse, 1959.
Vallès, Jules. *Le Bachelier.* Paris: Gallimard, 1973 (original edition 1878, 1879).
Vallès, Jules. *L'Enfant.* Paris: Gallimard, 1973 (original edition 1878, 1879).
Williams, William Carlos. "This Is Just to Say" (1934) in A. Walton Litz and Christopher McGowan, eds. *The Collected Poems of William Carlos Williams: Volume I, 1909–1939,* New York: New Directions, 1986.

II. MATERIALS ON LITERARINESS, LITERARY CURRICULUM AND PEDAGOGY, GENERAL EDUCATION, AND ASSESSMENT

A. General Sources Not Restricted to France

Alsup, Jane. *A Case for Teaching Literature in the Secondary School: Why Reading Fiction Matters in an Age of Scientific Objectivity and Standardization.* New York and London: Routledge, 2015.
American Academy of Arts and Sciences Commission on the Humanities and Social Sciences. *The Heart of the Matter: The Humanities and Social Sciences for a Vibrant, Competitive, and Secure Nation.* Cambridge, MA: American Academy of Arts and Sciences, 2013.
Arias, Beatriz and Ursula Casanova, eds. *Bilingual Education: Politics, Practice, and Research.* Chicago: National Society for the Study of Education, University of Chicago Press, 1993.
Bruns, Cristina. *Why Literature? The Value of Literary Reading and What it Means for Teaching.* New York and London: Continuum International Publishing, 2011.
College Board. *AP® English Literature and Composition: 2012 Free-Response Questions.* <https://apstudent.collegeboard.org/apcourse/ap-english-litera ture-and-composition/exam-practice> October 28, 2015.
Engell, James and David Perkins, eds. *Teaching Literature: What is Needed Now.* Cambridge: Harvard University Press, 1988.

Erlich, Victor. *Russian Formalism: History-Doctrine.* Fourth Ed. The Hague: Mouton, 1980 (1955).
Ewell, Peter T. "An Emerging Scholarship: A Brief History of Assessment" in Trudy W. Banta, ed. *Building a Scholarship of Assessment.* San Francisco: John Wiley and Sons, 2002, 3–25.
Jakobson, Roman. "Linguistics and Poetics." In Krystyna Pomorska and Stephen Rusdy, eds. *Language in Literature*, Cambridge, MA: Belknap Press, 1987.
Jay, Paul. *The Humanities "Crisis" and the Future of Literary Studies.* New York: Palgrave-Macmillan, 2014.
Keller, Betsy. "Rereading Flaubert: Toward a Dialogue between First- and Second-Language Literature Teaching Practices" *PMLA* 112: 1 (January 1997) 56–68.
Koop, Marie-Christine Weidmann. "Promoting French in Colleges and Universities." *AATF National Bulletin* 24:4 (May 1999) 17–19.
Lassonde, Stephen. "High School" in Paula S. Fass, ed. *Encyclopedia of Children and Childhood: in History and Society*, New York and London: Macmillan Reference, 2004.
Lepenies, Wolf. *Between Literature and Science: The Rise of Sociology.* Trans. R. J. Hollingdale. Cambridge: Cambridge University Press, and Paris: Editions de la Maison des Sciences de l'Homme, 1988 (original edition 1984).
Loucif, Sabine. *A la Recherche du canon perdu: l'enseignement du français dans les universités américaines.* New Orleans: Presses Universitaires du Nouveau Monde, 2001.
Loucif, Sabine. "French in American Universities: Toward a Reshaping of Frenchness." Ralph Albanese and M. Martin Guiney, eds. *French Education, Fifty Years Later. Yale French Studies* 113 (Fall 2008), 115–131.
Marghescou, Mircea. *Le Concept de littérarité: Essai sur les possibilités théoriques d'une science de la littérature.* The Hague, Paris: Mouton, 1974.
Marghescou, Mircea. *Pourquoi la littérature ?* Paris: Éditions Kimé, 2014.
Martin, Biddy. "Introduction. Teaching Literature, Changing Cultures." *PMLA* 112:1 (January 1997) 7–25.
Modern Language Association. *Report to the Teagle Foundation on the Undergraduate Major in Language and Literature*, February 2009.
National Council for the Teaching of English. *Core Values.* <http://www.ncte.org/mission/corevalues>.
National Endowment for the Arts. *Reading at Risk: A Survey of Literary Reading in America*, Research Division Report #46, June 2004.
National Endowment for the Arts. *Reading on the Rise: A New Chapter in American Literacy*, 2009.
OECD (Organization for Economic Cooperation and Development). "About PISA." <http://www.oecd.org/pisa/aboutpisa/>.

OECD (Organization for Economic Cooperation and Development). "Do Students Today Read For Pleasure?" *PISA in Focus* 8 (2011).
OECD (Organization for Economic Cooperation and Development). "Print Reading Sample Tasks" (Questions from the 2009 PISA Reading Comprehension Test) *PISA 2009 Assessment Framework—Key Competencies in Reading, Mathematics and Science.* Annex A1. Paris: OECD, 2009.
Roche, Mark William. *Why Literature Matters in the 21st Century.* New Haven: Yale University Press, 2004.
Shavelson, Richard. J. *A Brief History of Student Learning Assessment: How We Got Where We Are and a Proposal for Where to Go Next.* Association of American Colleges and Universities, 2007.
Snow, Charles Percy. *The Two Cultures.* London: Cambridge University Press, 2001 (1959).
Snyder, Thomas D., ed. *120 Years of American Education: A Statistical Portrait.* Washington, DC: U.S. Department of Education, 1993.
Sumara, Dennis J. *Why Reading Literature in School Still Matters: Imagination, Interpretation, Insight.* Mahwah, NJ: Lawrence Erlbaum Associates, 2002.
Topel, Robert. "The Private and Social Values of Education." Federal Reserve Bank of Cleveland. *Education and Economic Development.* Conference Proceedings, November 18–19, 2004. 47–57.
Zill, Nicolas and Marianne Winglee. *Who Reads Literature? The Future of the United States as a Nation of Readers.* Washington, DC: Seven Locks Press, 1990.

B. Sources on France

Adam, Jean-Michel and Noël Cordonier. «Enseigner aujourd'hui la littérature» *Le Français aujourd'hui* 121 (March 1998), 6–11.
Ahr, Sylviane. *Enseigner la littérature aujourd'hui: «disputes» françaises.* Paris: Honoré Champion, 2015.
Albanese, Ralph. *Corneille à l'école républicaine: du mythe héroïque à l'imaginaire politique en France, 1800–1950.* Paris: L'Harmattan, 2008.
Albanese, Ralph. *La Fontaine à lécole républicaine: Du poète universel au classique scolaire.* Charlottesville, VA: Rookwood Press, 2003.
Albanese, Ralph and M. Martin Guiney, eds. *French Education: Fifty Years Later. Yale French Studies* 113 (Fall 2008).
Aron, Paul. «La valeur des études littéraires» *Les Valeurs dans la littérature. Diptyque* 1. Presses de l'Université de Namur, 2004) 37–54.
Baconnet, Marc, Alain Viala and Katherine Weinland. "Eléments pour une refondation de la discipline. Table ronde. Choix théoriques et didactiques des nouveaux programmes." *Ecoles des lettres second cycle* 7 (1999).
Balibar, Renée. *Les français fictifs: le rapport des styles littéraires au français national.* Paris: Hachette, 1990.

Balibar, Renée. *L'Institution du français: essai sur le colinguisme des Carolingiens à la République.* Paris: PUF, 1985.
Barthes, Roland. «De la science à la literature.» *Essais critiques IV: Le Bruissement de la langue.* Paris: Seuil, 1984.
Barthes, Roland. «From Science to Literature» in *The Rustle of Language.* Trans. Richard Howard. New York: Farrar, Straus and Giroux, 1986 (1984), 3–10.
Barthes, Roland. «Peut-on enseigner la littérature?» *Littérature/enseignement. Pratiques,* 5 (1975), reprinted in *Oeuvres complètes,* t. 4. Paris: Seuil, 2002, 879–886.
Barthes, Roland. *The Pleasure of the Text.* Trans. Richard Miller. New York: Hill and Wang, 1975 (1973).
Barthes, Roland. «Réflexions sur un manuel» in Serge Doubrovsky and Tzvetan Todorov, eds. *L'enseignement de la littérature, Colloque de Cérisy,* July 22–29, 1969. Paris: Plon, 1971. 170–177.
Barthes, Roland. «Reflections on a Manual.» Trans. Sandy Petrey, *PMLA* 112:1 (January 1997), 69–75.
Barthes, Roland. *Sur Racine.* Paris: Seuil, 1963.
Barthes, Roland. *S/Z.* Paris: Seuil, 1970.
Barthes, Roland. *S/Z.* Trans. Richard Miller. New York: Farrar, Straus and Giroux, 1974.
Bayard, Pierre. *How to Talk About Books You Haven't Read.* Trans. Jeffrey Mehlman. New York: Bloomsbury, 2007.
Bénichou, Paul. *The Consecration of the Writer, 1750–1830.* Trans. Mark K. Jensen. Lincoln and London: University of Nebraska Press, 1999 (1973).
Bénichou, Paul. *Man and Ethics: Studies in French Classicism.* Trans. Elizabeth Hughes. Garden City, NY: Anchor Books, 1971.
Bénichou, Paul. *Morales du grand siècle.* Paris: Gallimard, 1948.
Bertucci, Marie-Madeleine. «Enseigner aujourd'hui: le discours de la crise.» *Le Français aujourd'hui* 142 (July 2003) 99–101.
Bertucci, Marie-Madeleine. «Enseigner le français: crise de la discipline ou crise de l'identité professionnelle?» in Emmanuel Fraisse and Violaine Houdart-Merot, eds. *Les enseignants et la littérature: la transmission en question, actes du colloque (Nov. 2002).* Champigny: SCEREN-CRDP, 2004, 135–152.
Bisenius-Perrin, Carole. «De la lecture cursive au café littéraire» *Le français aujourd'hui* 133 (April 2001) 85–96.
Blaise, Lilia. "In Paris Suburbs, Adopting a Dreaded School Test as a Tool of Integration" *New York Times* (May 11, 2016).
Bleuse, Magali. "Créativité et proximité avec la culture des élèves." *Recherches* 40 (2004): 201–206.
Boissinot, Alain. «Les enjeux des nouveaux programmes.» *Le Français aujourd'hui* 133 (April 2001), 33–49.
Bourdieu, Pierre. *Les Règles de l'art.* Paris: Seuil, 1992.

Bourdieu, Pierre. *The Rules of Art: Genesis and Structure of the Literary Field*. Trans. Susan Emanuel. Stanford: Stanford University Press, 1996.
Bourdieu, Pierre and Jean-Claude Passeron. *The Inheritors: French Students and Their Relation to Culture*. Trans. Richard Nice. Chicago: University of Chicago Press, 1979.
Bourdieu, Pierre and Jean-Claude Passeron. *La Reproduction. Éléments pour une théorie du système d'enseignement*. Paris: Minuit, 1970.
Bourdieu, Pierre and Jean-Claude Passeron. *Les Héritiers: les étudiants et la culture*. Paris: Minuit, 1964.
Bourdieu, Pierre and Jean-Claude Passeron. *Reproduction in Education, Society, and Culture*. Trans. Richard Nice. London: Sage Publications, 1990.
Boutan, Pierre and Dan Savatovsky. «Avant-propos» in Pierrre Boutan and Dan Savatovsky, eds. *La Crise-du-français, Etudes de linguistique appliquée* 118 (April–June 2000), 133–143.
Chaitin, Gilbert. *The Enemy Within: Culture Wars and Political Identity in Novels of the French Third Republic*. Columbus: Ohio State University Press, 2009.
Chartier, Anne-Marie and Jean Hébrard. «Genèse d'une crise: la lecture littéraire dans *Les Cahiers pédagogiques* de la Libération à mai 1968» in Pierre Boutan and Dan Savatovsky, eds. *La Crise-du-français, Etudes de linguistique appliquée* 118 (April–June 2000), 227–243.
Chervel, André. *Histoire de l'enseignement du français du XVIIe au XXe siècle*. Pari: Retz, 2008 (2006).
Chervel, André. *La composition française au XIXe siècle dans les principaux concours et examens, de l'agrégation au baccalauréat*. Paris: Vuibert-INRP, 1999.
Chervel, André. «Le baccalauréat et les débuts de la dissertation littéraire, 1874–1881.» *Histoire de l'éducation* 94 (May 2002), 103–140.
Chervel, André. «Sur l'origine de l'enseignement du français dans le secondaire.» *Histoire de l'éducation* 25 (1985): 3–10.
Chervel, André et al. *Les Auteurs français, latins et grecs au programme de l'enseignement secondaire de 1800 à nos jours*. Paris: INRP /Publications de la Sorbonne, 1986.
Chiss, Jean-Louis. «La Crise du français comme idéologie linguistique (Charles Bally, 1865–1947)» in *Historicité des débats linguistiques et didactiques. Stylistique, énonciation, crise du français*, ed. Jean-Louis Chiss. Louvain and Paris: Peeters, 2006, 233–246.
Chiss, Jean-Louis. «La linguistique et la didactique sont-elles responsables de la crise de l'enseignement du français?» *Le français aujourd'hui* 156 (March 2007) 9–14.
Citton, Yves. *L'avenir des humanités: Economie de la connaissance ou cultures de l'interprétation* ? Paris: La Découverte 2010.
Compagnon, Antoine. *La Troisième République des Lettres: de Flaubert à Proust*. Paris: Seuil, 1983.

Compère, Marie-Madeleine. «Des Humanités à la culture générale: les finalités de l'enseignement secondaire en perspective historique.» François Jacquet-Francillon and Denis Kambouchner, eds. *La Crise de la culture scolaire: Origines, interprétations, perspectives.* Paris: Presses Universitaires de France, 2005, 65–76.

Compère, Marie-Madeleine and André Chervel. «Les humanités dans l'histoire de l'enseignement français.» *Histoire de l'éducation* 74:1 (1997) 5–38.

Daunay, Bertrand. «État des recherches en didactique de la littérature.» *Revue française de pédagogie* 159 (April–June 2007), 139–189.

Daunay, Bertrand. «L'infini processus de disqualification du lecteur ou contre une didactique bathmologique» in Rouxel, Annie and Gérard Langlade, eds. *Le Sujet lecteur: Lecture subjective et enseignement de la littérature* (Conference Proceedings, Rennes, January 2004). Rennes: Presses de l'Université de Rennes, 2004, 233–243.

Daunay, Bertrand. «Lecture littéraire et disqualification scolaire.» *Lidil* 33 (2006), http://lidil.revues.org/51.

Deguy, Jacques. «Lanson, enseignant progressiste.» *L'Amitié Charles Péguy* 4: 13 (January–March 1981), 39–56.

Doubrovsky, Serge and Tzvetan Todorov, eds. *L'Enseignement de la littérature.* Paris: Plon, 1971.

Dufays, Jean-Louis. «La dialectique des valeurs: le jeu très ordinaire de l'évaluation littéraire» in Karl Canvat and Georges Legros, eds. *Les Valeurs dans la littérature. Diptyque* 1. Presses de l'Université de Namur, 2004, 103–129.

Dufays, Jean-Louis, ed. *Enseigner et apprendre la littérature aujourd'hui, pour quoi faire? Sens, utilité, évaluation.* Louvain: Presses Universitaires de Louvain, 2007.

Dufays, Jean-Louis. «Enseigner la lecture littéraire, une affaire de compétences?» *Cahiers pédagogiques* 495 (February 2012) 28–30.

Dufays, Jean-Louis, L. Gemenne and D. Ledur. *Pour une lecture littéraire. Histoire, théories, pistes pour la classe.* Brussels: De Boeck, 2005 (1996).

Dumaître, Eric. *Le structuralisme littéraire et la crise de la culture scolaire.* Doctoral Thesis, Université Paris-IV, 2006.

Falcucci Clément. *L'humanisme dans l'enseignement secondaire en France au XIXe siècle.* Paris: Didier, 1939.

Fayolle, Roger. «La Poésie dans l'enseignement de la littérature: le cas Baudelaire.» *Littérature* 7 (October 1972), 48–72.

Forestier, Christian, Claude Thélot and Jean-Claude Emin. *Que vaut l'enseignement en France? Les conclusions du Haut Conseil de l'évaluation de l'école.* Paris: Stock, 2007.

Fraisse, Emmanuel. *Les Anthologies en France.* Paris: Presses Universitaires de France, 1997.

BIBLIOGRAPHY 281

Fraisse, Emmanuel. «Valeurs littéraires, valeurs scolaires: le rôle des anthologies en France, 1900-2000» in Karl Canvat and Georges Legros, eds. *Les Valeurs dans la littérature. Diptyque* 1. Presses de l'Université de Namur, 2004, 57-71.
Freire, Paulo. *L'Éducation: pratique de la liberté*, Trans. Francisco Weffort. Paris: Editions du Cerf, 1967 (originally published in Brazil in 1964).
Frijhoff, Willem, ed. *L'Offre d'école: éléments pour une étude comparée des politiques éducatives au XIX` siècle: actes du 3e Colloque international, Sèvres, 27-30 septembre 1981*. Paris: Publications de la Sorbonne, I.N.R.P., 1983.
Gélin, Josette and Dominique Roué. «L'écriture créative, une pratique nouvelle?» *Le Français aujourd'hui* 133 (April 2001), 75-84.
Guillory, John. *Cultural Capital: The Problem of Literary Canon Formation*. Chicago and London: University of Chicago Press, 1993.
Guiney, M. Martin. *Teaching the Cult of Literature in the French Third Republic*. New York: Palgrave Macmillan, 2004.
Guyot, Gaëlle. *Latin et latinité dans l'œuvre de Léon Bloy*. Paris: Honoré Champion, 2003.
Houdart-Merot, Violaine. *La Culture littéraire au lycée depuis 1880*. Rennes: Presses universitaires de Rennes, 1998.
Houdart-Merot, Violaine. «De la critique d'admiration à la lecture scriptible» in Rouxel, Annie and Gérard Langlade, eds. *Le Sujet lecteur: Lecture subjective et enseignement de la littérature*. (Conference Proceedings, January 2004). Rennes: Presses de l'Université de Rennes, 2004, 223-232.
Huyhn, Jeanne-Antide. «Ecriture d'invention et 'identité'» in Rouxel, Annie and Gérard Langlade, eds. *Le Sujet lecteur: Lecture subjective et enseignement de la littérature*. (Conference Proceedings, January 2004). Rennes: Presses de l'Université de Rennes, 2004, 305-316.
Iser, Wolfgang. *L'acte de lecture: Théorie de l'effet esthétique*. Trans. Evelyne Sznycer. Brussels: Mardaga, 1985 (originally published in Germany in 1976).
Jacquet-Francillon, François et Denis Kambouchner, eds. *La Crise de la culture scolaire: Origines, interprétations, perspectives*. (Conference Proceedings, Sorbonne, September 2003). Paris: Presses Universitaires de France, 2005.
Jakobson, Roman. *Language in Literature*. Krystyna Pomorska and Stephen Rudy, eds. Cambridge, MA: Harvard University Press, 1987.
Jalabert, Romain. «Le latin dans l'œuvre de Rimbaud.» in A. Guyaux, ed., *Rimbaud. Des «Poésies» à la «Saison»*. Paris: Éditions Garnier, 2009, 287-299.
Jauss, Hans-Robert. *Pour une esthétique de la réception*. Trans. Claude Maillard. Paris: Gallimard, 1978 (originally published in Germany in 1972).
Jey, Martine. «Crise du français et réforme de l'enseignement secondaire (1902-1914).» in Pierre Boutan and Dan Savatovsky, eds. *La Crise-du-français, Etudes de linguistique appliquée* 118 (April-June 2000), 163-177.

Jey, Martine. «Du discours latin à la composition de français: le rôle déterminant du baccalauréat.» *Le Français aujourd'hui* 133 (April 2001), 23–30.

Jey, Martine. «Gustave Lanson et la réforme de 1902.» *Fabula, la recherche en littérature: Atelier de théorie littéraire* (www.fabula.org/atelier) August 7, 2008.

Jey, Martine. «La Lecture littéraire de 1880 à 1925.» in Petitjean, André and J. M. Privat, eds. *Histoire de l'enseignement du français et textes officiels; actes du colloque de Metz, déc. 1997.* Metz: Presses de l'Université de Metz, 1999, 119–140.

Jey, Martine. *La littérature au lycée, naissance d'une discipline (1880–1925).* Metz: Presses de l'Université de Metz, 1998.

Jouan-Westlund, Annie. «Ça commence aujourd' hui, *Être et avoir* et *Entre les murs*: Une vision diffractée de l'école républicaine française». *French Politics, Culture & Society* 32:1 (Spring 2014), 111–126.

Jouve, Vincent. *Pourquoi étudier la littérature ?* Paris: Armand Colin, 2010.

Kambouchner, Denis. «La crise de la culture scolaire comme problème philosophique.» in François Jacquet-Francillon and Denis Kambouchner, eds. *La Crise de la culture scolaire: Origines, interprétations, perspectives.* Paris: Presses Universitaires de France, 2005, 355–367.

Keck, Frédéric. «L'éducation morale, entre lettres et sciences: le moment Durkheim.» in François Jacquet-Francillon and Denis Kambouchner, eds. *La Crise de la culture scolaire: Origines, interprétations, perspectives.* Paris: Presses Universitaires de France, 2005, 179–189.

Langlade, Gérard. «Quelle théorie de lecture littéraire?» *Un enseignement littéraire malgré tout: Diptyque* 6 (2006), 17–20.

Lebrun, Marlène. "La Fontaine, un auteur pour la jeunesse?» *Le Français aujourd'hui* 121 (March 1998), 60–68.

Leroux, Georges. "La raison des études. Sens et histoire du *Ratio Studiorum*." *Études françaises,* 31: 2 (1995) 29–44.

Leroy, Michel. *Peut-on enseigner la littérature française?* Paris: Presses Universitaires de France, 2001.

Lindaman, Dana. *Becoming French: Mapping the Geographies of French Identity, 1871–1914.* Chicago: Northwestern University Press, 2016.

Lirca, Corina Alexandrina. «Generating Motivation for the Study of Literature.» *Proceedings of the Conference on Contemporary Perspectives on European Integration: Between Tradition and Modernity.* Tirgu-Mures, Romania: Editura Universitatii "Petru Maior", 2013, 692–696.

Louichon, Brigitte. «La littérature patrimoniale, un objet à didactiser.» in Jean-Louis Dufays, ed. *Enseigner et apprendre la littérature aujourd'hui pourquoi faire? Sens, utilité, évaluation.* Louvain: Presses Universitaires de Louvain, 2007, 27–34.

Maingueneau, Dominique. «Les apports de l'analyse du discours à la didactique de la littérature.» *Le français aujourd'hui* 134 (2001) 73–82.

Marcoin, Francis. *A l'école de la littérature.* Paris: Les Éditions Ouvrières, 1992.
Marcoin, Francis. «Former des lecteurs ou des lettrés.» *Le Français aujourd'hui* 121 (March 1998) 18–27.
Marlair, Sébastien. «Sens et compétences: quel enseignement de la littérature?» in Jean-Louis Dufays, ed. *Enseigner et apprendre la littérature aujourd'hui, pour quoi faire? Sens, utilité, évaluation.* Louvain: Presses Universitaires de Louvain, 2007, 161–170.
Massol, Jean-François. *De l'institution scolaire de la littérature française, 1870–1925.* Grenoble: ELLUG, 2004.
Merle, Pierre. *Les Notes, secrets de fabrication.* Paris: Presses Universitaires de France, 2007.
Merlin-Kajman, Hélène. «Enseigner la littérature?» in François Jacquet-Francillon and Denis Kambouchner, eds. *La Crise de la culture scolaire: Origines, interprétations, perspectives.* Paris: Presses Universitaires de France, 2005, 205–226.
Michel, Alain and Xavier Pons. «Editorial: Le 'choc' PISA: métaphore ou révolution?» *Revue de l'Association Française des Acteurs de l'Education,* 145 (March 2015). <http://www.education-revue-afae.fr/pagint/revue/resume.php?id_art=394>
Milo, Daniel. «Les Classiques scolaires» in Pierre Nora, ed. *Les Lieux de mémoire,* tome II: *La Nation.* Paris: Gallimard, 1984, 517–562.
Painbéni, Sandra. "La télévision française fait-elle encore vendre des romans? Le rôle prescripteur des programmes littéraires (ou culturels) post-'Apostrophes'." *Actes des Journées de recherche en Marketing de Bourgogne,* Novembre 18–19, 2010, session 4, 36–51.
Penloup, Marie-Claude. *La tentation du littéraire. Essai sur le rapport à l'écriture littéraire du scripteur «ordinaire.»* Paris: Didier, 2000.
Penloup, Marie-Claude. *L'écriture extrascolaire des collégiens: Des constats aux perspectives didactiques.* Paris: ESF, 1999.
Peretti, Isabelle de. *Histoire Littéraire, Nouvelles Critiques et scolarisation de Racine au lycée: deux études sur une discipline en quête d'identité.* Doctoral Thesis, Université de Lyon, 2001.
Peretti, Isabelle de, and Béatrice Ferrier, eds. *Enseigner les classiques aujourd'hui: Approches critiques et didactiques.* Brussels: Peter Lang, 2012.
Peretti, Isabelle de, Muriel Aubert, Jacques Crinon, Séverine Depoilly, Sophie Farcy, Monique Maeda. «Bourreaux et victimes: des élèves de lycées professionnel, polyvalent et général face à l'univers tragique.» *Un enseignement littéraire malgré tout: Diptyque* 6 (2006) 99–118.
Philippe, Gilles. *Sujet, verbe, complément: Le moment grammatical de la littérature française 1890–1940.* Paris: Gallimard, 2002.
Prévost, Christine. «Quelle place pour les 'produits culturels de masse' dans la classe de français?» *Le français aujourd'hui* 172 (2011) 103–112.

Pujade-Renaud, Claude. *L'école dans la littérature*. Paris: L'Harmatan, 2006.
Régnier, Claude. «Réceptivité des étudiants littéraires à la littérature; Enquête et commentaires.» Michel Mansuy, ed. *L'Enseignement de la littérature: crises et perspectives*. Colloque de Strasbourg (December 1975). Paris: Nathan, 1977, 71–83.
Rogers, Rebecca. *From the Salon to the Schoolroom: Educating Bourgeois Girls in Nineteenth-Century France*. University Park: Penn State University Press, 2005.
Rouxel, Annie. «De la tension entre utiliser et interpréter dans la réception des œuvres littéraires en classe: réflexion sur une inversion des valeurs au fil du cursus.» Jean-Louis Dufays, ed. *Enseigner et apprendre la littérature aujourd'hui, pour quoi faire? Sens, utilité, évaluation*. Louvain: Presses Universitaires de Louvain, 2007, 45–54.
Rouxel, Annie and Gérard Langlade, eds. *Le Sujet lecteur: Lecture subjective et enseignement de la littérature*. (Conference Proceedings, Rennes, January 2004). Rennes: Presses de l'Université de Rennes, 2004.
Sachs, Leon. *The Pedagogical Imagination: The Republican Legacy in Twenty-First-Century French Literature and Film*. Lincoln: University of Nebraska Press, 2014.
Savatovsky, Dan, ed. «La Crise-du-français.» *Etudes de linguistique appliquée* 118 (April–June 2000).
Savatovsky, Dan. «Le français, matière ou discipline?» In *Langages* 29: 120. (December 1995: *Les savoirs de la langue: histoire et disciplinarité*) 52–77.
Savatovsky, Dan and Christian Puech. «De l'usage de la crise en matière linguistique: Charles Bally et *la crise du français*» in Pierre Boutan and Dan Savatovsky, eds. *La Crise-du-français, Etudes de linguistique appliquée* 118 (April–June 2000), 211–226.
Savoie, Philippe. «Autonomie et personnalité des lycées: la réforme de 1902 et ses origines» *Histoire de l'éducation* 90 (May 2001), 169–204.
Schneegans, Nicole. «Littérature de jeunesse et nouveaux programmes des collèges.» *Le Français aujourd'hui* 121 (March 1998), 38–41.
Sciolino, Elaine. «The French Still Flock to Bookstores». *New York Times* June 20, 2012.
Shea, Louisa. "Exit Voltaire, Enter Marivaux: Abdellatif Kechiche on the Legacy of the Enlightenment." *French Review* 85.6 (May 2012): 1136–1149.
Thibaudet, Albert. *Le Liseur de romans*. Paris: G. Crès, 1925.
Viala, Alain. «Des réformes en pratiques.» *Le français aujourd'hui* 133 (April 2001), 9–22.
Viala, Alain. «Le littéraire et le social: retours sur programmes et sur théorie de fond.» *Le français aujourd'hui* 145 (April 2004), 5–14.
Viala, Alain and Paul Aron. *L'enseignement de la littérature*. Paris: PUF (Que sais-je ?), 2006.

Vibert, Anne and Isabelle Olivier. "Professeurs de lecture ou de littérature? Entre dire et faire, une enquête sur le rapport personnel des enseignants à la littérature.» Jean-Louis Dufays, ed. *Enseigner et apprendre la littérature aujourd'hui, pour quoi faire? Sens, utilité, évaluation*. Louvain: Presses Universitaires de Louvain, 2007, 381-392.
Vigner, Gérard. "La maitrise de la langue: une construction institutionnelle?". *Le français aujourd'hui* 173 (February 2011), 21-32.
Weisz, George. *The Emergence of Modern Universities in France, 1863-1914*. Princeton: Princeton University Press, 1983.

III. HISTORICAL AND CONTEMPORARY WRITING ON LITERATURE AND GENERAL EDUCATION: TESTIMONIALS, POLEMICS, JOURNALISM

A. Late Nineteenth and Early Twentieth Centuries

Agathon (Henri Massis and Alfred Tarde, pseud.). *L'esprit de la nouvelle Sorbonne; la crise de la culture classique, la crise du français*. Paris: Mercure de France, 1911.
Bergson, Henri. «Les études gréco-latines et l'enseignement secondaire.» *La Revue de Paris* 10 (May 1923), 5-18.
Bouasse, Henri. *Bachot et bachotage: étude sur l'enseignement en France*. Toulouse: A. Montlauzeur, 1910.
Brunetière, Ferdinand. *La liberté de l'enseignement*. Paris: Perrin, 1900.
Frary, Raoul. *La Question du latin*. Paris: Léopold Cerf, 1885.
Gréard, Octave. *Education et instruction*. 2 vols. Paris: Hachette, 1887.
Gréard, Octave. *Le baccalauréat et l'enseignement secondaire, mémoire présenté au Conseil académique de Paris, juillet 1885*. Paris: Imprimerie Nationale, 1885.
Lanson, Gustave. *Essais de méthode, de critique et d'histoire littéraire*. Henri Peyre, ed. Paris: Hachette, 1965.
Lanson, Gustave. «La Crise des méthodes dans l'enseignement du français.» in Gustave Lanson et al. eds., *L'Enseignement du français: Conférences du Musée Pédagogique*. Paris: Musée Pédagogique, 1909.
Lanson, Gustave. "L'étude des auteurs français dans les classes de lettres." *Revue universitaire* 2 (1894): 255-271.
Lanson, Gustave. *Méthodes de l'histoire littéraire*. Paris: Les Belles Lettres, 1925.
Lemaître, Jules. *Impressions de théâtre*. Paris: Société française d'imprimerie et de librairie, 1888-98.
Loisy, Alfred. *Y a-t-il deux sources de la religion et de la morale ?* Paris: Nourry, 1931.
Mornet, Daniel. «L'Histoire littéraire et les sciences de la nature.» *Revue Universitaire* (December 15, 1909) 389-413.

Péguy, Charles. *L'Argent* and *L'Argent, suite*. Originally published in *Les Cahiers de la Quinzaine*, 1913. *Œuvres complètes, tome iii*. Paris: Gallimard, 1992.
Ribot, Alexandre. *La réforme de l'enseignement secondaire*. Paris: A. Colin, 1900.

B. Late Twentieth- and Twenty-first Centuries

Association Française des Professeurs de Français (AFPF, now the Association Française des Enseignants du Français, AFEF). «Propositions pour une rénovation de l'enseignement du français: Manifeste de Charbonnières (10, 11, 12 Septembre 1969)» Sèvres: AFEF, 1970 (also published in *Le Français aujourd'hui* 9, February 1970).
Assouline, Pierre. «Qui veut tuer *La Princesse de Clèves*?» *La République des livres* (blog on web site of *Le Monde*), December 10, 2006. passouline.blog.lemonde. fr/2006/12/10/qui-veut-tuer-laprincesse-de-cleves/
Baudelot, Christian and Roger Establet. *L'Ecole capitaliste en France*. Paris: Maspero, 1971.
Baudelot, Christian and Roger Establet. *L'Élitisme républicain: l'école française à l'épreuve des comparaisons internationales*. Paris: Seuil, 2009.
Baudelot, Christian, M. Cartier and C. Detrez. *Et pourtant, ils lisent...* Paris: Seuil, 1999.
Bénévent, Christine. «Leçons d'incertitude.» *Le Débat*, 135 (May–August 2005), 123–133.
Bergounioux, Pierre. «De la littérature à la marchandise.» *Le Débat*, 135 (May–August 2005), 167–172.
Boissinot, Alain. «Où en est l'enseignement du français? (Entretien).» *Le Débat* 110 (May–August 2000) 156–166.
Boissinot, Alain, ed. *Perspectives actuelles de l'enseignement du français, actes du séminaire national, octobre 2000*. Paris: Education nationale, CRDP de Versailles, 2001.
Boué, Michel. «Robert contre Fitzpatrick.» *L'Humanité*, April 10, 1992.
Brighelli, Jean-Paul. *La Fabrique du crétin: la mort programmée de l'école*. Paris: Gallimard (Folio Documents), 2005.
Buttet, Michel, Agnès Joste and Robert Weiner. «Sauver les lettres.» *Revue de la MAUSS* 28 (Fall–Winter 2006), 161–166.
Careil, Yves. *Ecole libérale, école inégale*. Paris: Institut FSU-Syllepse, 2002.
Centre for Language, Linguistics, and Area Studies. "Meeting the Current Challenges: The Humanities and Employability, Entrepreneurship and Employer Engagement." London, October 23, 2009. <www.llas.ac.uk/events/archive/3226>.
Chiss, Jean-Louis. «La linguistique et la didactique sont-elles responsables de la crise de l'enseignement du français?» *Le français aujourd'hui* 156 (March 2007), 9–14.
Collin, Thibaud. "Faut-il supprimer le baccalauréat ?" *Le Figaro* (June 17, 2014).

Conti, Paul-Marie. *L'enseignement du français aujourd'hui: Enquête sur une discipline malmenée*. Paris: Editions de Fallois, 2008.
Debray, Régis. «Le département communication.» *Le Débat* 135 (May–August 2005), 78–79.
Farrenq, Emmanuelle, Henri Mitterand and Dominique Rincé. «Nouveaux programmes, nouveaux manuels» (Round table discussion) *Le Débat* 135 (May–August 2005), 71–77.
Finkielkraut, Alain. «La Révolution culturelle à l'école.» in Michel Jarrety, ed. *Propositions pour les enseignementts littéraires*. Paris: PUF, 2000.
Finkielkraut, Alain and Marc Baconnet, Mireille Grange. *Enseigner les lettres aujourd'hui*. Geneva: Editions du Tricorne, 2003.
Fize, Michel. *Le Bac inutile*. Paris: Editions de l'œuvre, 2012.
Fumaroli, Marc. «'Culture' contre éducation?» *Le Débat* 135 (May–August 2005), 80–88.
Fumaroli, Marc. *L'Etat culturel: une religion moderne*. Paris: Fallois, 1991.
Fumaroli, Marc. «Les humanités au péril d'un monde numérique.» Interview in *Le Figaro*, March 31, 2015.
Goyet, Mara. «D'une détérioration générale; voilà, c'est dit.» *Le Débat* 151 (September–October 2008), 124–136.
Grange, Mireille and Michel Leroux. «La Pédagogie sens dessus dessous: les programmes de français des collèges.» *Le Débat* 135 (May–August 2005), 22–36.
Greenblatt, Stephen. «Teaching Shakespeare.» *The New York Times Magazine* (September 13, 2015), 60–62.
Gumbel, Peter. "The Stranglehold on French Schools." *The New York Times*, September 11, 2015.
Hess, Frederick M. and Michael Q. McShane. *Common Core Meets Education Reform: What it All Means for Politics, Policy, and the Future of Schooling*. New York and London: Teachers College Press, Columbia University, 2014.
Jacquet-Francillon, François and Denis Kambouchner, eds. *La crise de la culture scolaire: origines, interprétations, perspectives*. Paris: PUF, 2005.
Jarrety, Michel, ed. *Propositions pour les enseignements littéraires, Colloque sur l'avenir des enseignements littéraires, mai 2000*. Paris: PUF, 2000.
Jarrety, Michel and Michel Zink. "C'est la littérature qu'on assassine rue de Grenelle." *Le Monde* (March 4, 2000).
Joste, Agnès. *Contre-expertise d'une trahison, la réforme du français au lycée*. Paris: Mille et Une Nuits, 2002.
Kronman, Anthony T. *Education's End: Why Our Colleges and Universities Have Given Up on the Meaning of Life*. New Haven: Yale University Press, 2007.
Lapostolle, Christine. «La Princesse de Clèves au Kärcher.» *Libération* (November 26, 2006).
Laval, Christian. *L'Ecole n'est pas une entreprise: Le néo-libéralisme à l'assaut de l'enseignement public*. Paris: La Découverte, 2003.

Lecherbonnier, Bernard. *Pourquoi veulent-ils tuer le français ?* Paris: Albin Michel, 2005.
Maingueneau, Dominique. *Contre Saint Proust ou la fin de la littérature.* Paris: Belin, 2006.
Maquaire, Monique and Yvon Logéat. «Littérature: vous pratiquez? Au lycée.» *Lettres Ouvertes.* SCEREN-CRDP de Bretagne, 2003.
Meirieu, Philippe and Marc Giraud. *L'école ou la guerre civile.* Paris: Plon, 1997.
Merlin-Kajman, Hélène. «Combien de mots? La 'maîtrise de la langue française' n'est pas un but en soi.» *Le Débat* 135 (May–August 2005), 106–122.
Merlin-Kajman, Hélène. *La Langue est-elle fasciste? Langue, pouvoir, enseignement.* Paris: Seuil, 2003.
Mitterand, Henri. «Le français au lycée: radiographie des programmes.» *Le Débat* 135 (May–August 2005), 37–49.
Noé, Jean-Baptiste. «L'importance de l'estrade dans la classe.» *Le site web d'un historien.* <http://www.jbnoe.fr/L-importance-de-l-estrade-dans-la>.
Nussbaum, Martha. *Not for Profit: Why Democracy Needs the Humanities.* Princeton: Princeton UP, 2010.
Ormesson, Jean d'. «Instruire et attirer.» *Le Débat* 135 (May–August 2005), 89–92.
Ouzoulias, André. «Formation des enseignants: le cauchemar de Jules Ferry.» *Sauvons l'université* (March 29, 2010). www.sauvonsluniversite.com/spip.php?article3633.
Ozouf, Mona. «Apprendre à ne pas lire.» *Le Débat* 135 (May–August 2005), 93–96.
Philippe, Gilles. «La langue littéraire et l'enseignement du français.» *Le Débat* 135 (May–August 2005), 161–166.
Picard, Raymond. *Nouvelle critique ou nouvelle imposture.* Paris: Jean-Jacques Pauvert, 1965.
Pivot, Bernard. «La méthode ou la magie.» *Le Débat* 135 (May–August 2005), 97–99.
Pasquier, Dominique. *Cultures lycéennes. La tyrannie de la majorité.* Paris: Autrement, 2005.
Pasquier, Dominique. «Les lycéens et la culture (Entretien).» *Le Débat* 145 (May–August 2007), 142–151.
Roels, Virginie. «Sarkozy va en bouffer, de la Princesse de Clèves.» *Marianne*, February 17 2009.
Roger-Vasselin, Denis. «L'enseignement des lettres, entre français et literature.» *Le Débat* 135 (May–August 2005), 64–69.
Romilly, Jacqueline de. *Lettre aux parents sur les choix scolaires.* Paris: Fallois, 1993.
Sallenave, Danielle. *A quoi sert la littérature? Entretien avec Philippe Petit.* Paris: Textuel, 1997.

Sauver les lettres (collective). *Sauver les lettres, des professeurs accusent.* (Fourteen teachers of French interviewed by Philippe Petit). Paris: Textuel, 2001.
Sollers, Philippe. «Le refoulement de l'histoire.» *Le Débat* 135 (May–August 2005), 100–104.
Todorov, Tzvetan. *La Littérature en péril.* Paris: Flammarion, 2007.
Todorov, Tzvetan. «Livres et vivre.» *Le Débat* 135 (May–August 2005), 53–63.
Todorov, Tzvetan. "Reading and Living." Trans. M. Martin Guiney, *Yale French Studies* 113 (Fall 2008), 194–207.
Viala, Alain. «Former la personne et le citoyen: entretien.» *Le Débat* 135 (May–August 2005), 7–21.
Youx, Viviane and Bénédicte Etienne. «Une lecture du projet sur les nouveaux programmes de français au lycée.» *La Lettre de l'AFEF* 1 (June 2010) www.afef.org/blog.
Zakaria, Fareed. *In Defense of a Liberal Education.* New York: W.W. Norton & Company, 2015.
Zerofsky, Elizabeth. "Of Presidents and Princesses." *The New Yorker* November 8, 2012.

IV. Miscellaneous Cited Materials

Agence France Presse (AFP). «5 à 6 millions de musulmans en France.» (June 28, 2010).
Beam, Adam. "Kentucky Gov. Matt Bevin Wants State Colleges and Universities to Produce More Electrical Engineers and Less French Literature Scholars." *Associated Press*. January 29, 2016.
Clark, Priscilla Parkhurst. *Literary France: The Making of a Culture.* Berkeley and Los Angeles: University of California Press, 1987.
Durkheim, Emile. *De la division du travail social, thèse présentée à la Faculté des lettres de Paris.* Paris: F. Alcan, 1893.
Durkheim, Emile. *L'Evolution et le rôle de l'enseignement secondaire en France, leçon d'ouverture à la Sorbonne (chaire de pédagogie).* Paris: Editions de la Revue Bleue et de la Revue Scientifique, 1906.
Durkheim, Emile. *Les règles de la méthode sociologique.* Paris: F. Alcan, 1895.
Education Council of the European Union. *Report from Education Council to the European Council on the Concrete Future Objectives of Education and Training Systems.* Brussels: European Network on Information Literacy, 2001.
Graff, Gerald. *Beyond the Culture Wars: How Teaching the Conflicts Can Revitalize American Education.* New York: W.W. Norton, 1992.
Graff, Gerald. *Professing Literature: An Institutional History.* Chicago and London: University of Chicago Press, 1987.

Hannecart, Claire. *Rapport des jeunes à la musique à l'ère numérique*. Nantes: Pôle de coopération des acteurs pour les musiques actuelles en Pays de la Loire, 2015.
Hopmann, Stefan Thomas, Gertrude Binek and Martin Retzl, eds. *PISA According to PISA—PISA zufolge PISA: Does PISA Keep, What It Promises?—Hält PISA, was es verspricht?.* Schulpädagogik und Pädagogische Psychologie (Book 6). Vienna, Austria: LIT Verlag, 2007.
Howard, Caroline. "America's Top Colleges 2015." *Forbes Magazine*. <http://www.forbes.com/sites/carolinehoward/2015/07/29/americas-top-colleges-2015/>.
Huret, Jules. *Enquête sur l'évolution littéraire*. Paris: Charpentier, 1894.
IbISworld. "Book Publishing in the US: Market Research Report." http://www.ibisworld.com/industry/default.aspx?indid=1233.
IFOP (Institut Français d'opinion publique). "Le Catholicisme en France en 2010." http://www.ifop.com/media/pressdocument/238-1-document_file.pdf.
Kidd, David Comer and Emanuele Castano. "Reading Literary Fiction Improves Theory of Mind." *Science* 342:6156 (18 Oct 2013) 377–380.
Lisbon Special European Council (March 2000). *Towards a Europe of Innovation and Knowledge*. Europa: EU Law and Publications, 2005. <http://europa.eu/legislation_summaries/education_training_youth/general_framework/c10241_en.htm>.
Locqueneux, Robert. «Henri Bouasse (1866–1953): savant méconnu et polémiste célèbre» in Patrice Bret et Gérard Pajonk, eds. *Savants et inventeurs entre la gloire et l'oubli*. Paris: CTHS (collection Histoire), 2014, 43–50.
Martinez, Isabelle Marc. *Le Rap français, esthétique et poétique des textes, (1990–1995)*. Bern: Peter Lang, 2008.
Marx, Karl. *Capital: A Critique of Political Economy*. Vol. I. Trans. Samuel Moore and Edward Aveling. London: Electric Book Company, 2001 (1867).
Mauss, Marcel. *Essai sur le don. Forme et raison de l'échange dans les sociétés archaïques*. Paris: Presses Universitaires de France, 1973 (1924-5).
Meghelli, Samir. "Hip-Hop à la Française." *New York Times*, October 14, 2013.
Meretoja, Hanna. *The Narrative Turn in Fiction and Theory: The Crisis and Return of Storytelling from Robbe-Grillet to Tournier*. New York: Palgrave, 2014.
National Center for Education Statistics. *Digest of Education Statistics: 2013*. (May 2015). <https://nces.ed.gov/programs/digest/d13/ch_3.asp>.
Nora, Pierre (ed.). *Les Lieux de mémoire*, 3 vols. Paris: Gallimard, 1984–1992.
Nora, Pierre (ed.). *Realms of Memory: The Construction of the French Past*, 3 vols. Trans. Arthur Goldhammer. New York: Columbia University Press, 1996.
Nora, Pierre (ed.) *Rethinking France—Les Lieux de Mémoire*, 4 vols. Trans. Mary Trouille. Chicago: University of Chicago Press, 2001.

O'Brien, Glenn. Interview with Andy Warhol, June 1977. *Interview Magazine*, December 1 2008.
Office of the United States Trade Representative. *U.S. Objectives, U.S. Benefits in the Transatlantic Trade and Investment Partnership: A Detailed View.* <https://ustr.gov/about-us/policy-offices/press-office/press-releases/2014/March/US-Objectives-US-Benefits-In-the-TTIP-a-Detailed-View> 18 Jan. 2016.
Organization for Economic Cooperation and Development. *Lessons from PISA for the United States, Strong Performers and Successful Reformers in Education.* Paris: OECD Publishing, 2011.
Organization for Economic Cooperation and Development. *Literacy in the Information Age: Final Report of the International Adult Literacy Survey.* Paris: OECD Publishing, 2000.
Organization for Economic Cooperation and Development. *PISA 2009 Results: Executive Summary.* Paris: OECD Publishing, 2010.
Organization for Economic Cooperation and Development. *PISA 2012 Results in Focus.* Paris: OECD Publishing, 2014.
Richardson, F.C., Suinn R.M., "The Mathematics Anxiety Rating Scale." *Journal of Counseling Psychology* 19 (1972), 551–554.
Salmon, Christian. *Storytelling: Bewitching the Modern Mind.* London: Verso, 2010.
Salmon, Christian. *Storytelling: La machine à fabriquer des histoires et à formater les esprits.* Paris: La Découverte 2008.
Sellier, Geneviève. "Don't Touch the White Woman: La Journée de la jupe and feminism at the Service of Islamophobia." in Sylvie Durmelat and Vinay Swamy, eds. *Screening Integration: Recasting Maghrebi Immigration in Contemporary France.* Lincoln and London: University of Nebraska Press, 2011, 144–160.
Society of Jesuits (corp. author). *The Ratio Studiorum of 1599.* Trans. and ed. Allan P. Farrell, S. J. Washington, DC: Conference of Major Superiors of Jesuits, 1970.
Society of Jesuits (corp. author). *Ratio studiorum: plan raisonné et institution des études dans la Compagnie de Jésus.* Trans. Léone Albrieux and Dolorès Pralon-Julia. Marie-Madeleine Compère, ed. Paris: Belin, 1997.
Soudais, Michel. «Camus au Panthéon: une profanation obscène.» *Politis*, November 21, 2009.
State University of New York, Albany. "General Education Requirements." <www.albany.edu/gened/requirements.shtml>.
Statista (The Statistics Portal). "Unit Sales of the U.S. Book Market from 2010 to 2014." <http://www.statista.com/statistics/240088/total-book-sales-of-the-us-book-market-by-quantity/>.

Statista (The Statistics Portal). "Book sales Volume in France from 2010 to 2013." <http://www.statista.com/statistics/420733/book-sales-france/>.
Straubhaar, Joseph D. "Choosing National TV: Cultural Capital, Language, and Cultural Proximity in Brazil." Michael G. Elasmar, ed. *The Impact of International Television: A Paradigm Shift.* London: Routledge, 2008 (2003), 75–106.
Taylor, Frederick Winslow. *The Principles of Scientific Management.* New York: Harper, 1911.
Taylor, Frederick Winslow. *Shop Management.* New York: Harper, 1903.
TNS-Sofres. «Les Français et la lecture—2009.» <http://www.tns-sofres.com/etudes-et-points-de-vue/les-francais-et-la-lecture-2009>.
University of Massachusetts, Amherst. "General Education Requirements." <www.umass.edu/registrar/registration/gened_requirements.htm>.
White House, Office of the Press Secretary. *Fact Sheet: Empowering Students to Choose the College that is Right for Them.* Released September 12, 2015. <https://www.whitehouse.gov/the-press-office/2015/09/12/fact-sheet-empowering-students-choose-college-right-them>.
Wrenn, Mary V. "The Social Ontology of Fear and Neoliberalism." *Review of Social Economy* 72:3 (2014). 337–353.

V. OFFICIAL PUBLICATIONS OF THE FRENCH MINISTRY OF NATIONAL EDUCATION (FORMERLY MINISTRY OF PUBLIC INSTRUCTION)

Boissinot, Alain, ed. *Perspectives actuelles de l'enseignement du français, actes du séminaire national octobre 2000.* Paris: Ministère de l'éducation nationale, Direction de l'enseignement scolaire. Versailles: CRDP de Versailles, 2001.
Code de l'éducation, *article L613-1.* Monopole de la collation des grades ».
Conseil National Education-Economie (CNEE). "Exemple d'une mini-entreprise en Seine-Saint-Denis." <http://www.education.gouv.fr/cid74533/le-conseil-national-education-economie.html>.
Eduscol (Portail National des professionnels de l'éducation). *Baccalauréat général.* <http://eduscol.education.fr/pid23233/baccalaureat-general.html>.
Eduscol (Portail National des professionnels de l'éducation). *Baccalauréat général série littéraire.* <http://eduscol.education.fr/cid58534/serie-l.html>.
Eduscol (Portail National des professionnels de l'éducation). *Epreuve anticipée de français, série L (vendredi 19 juin 2015).* <http://eduscol.education.fr/prep-exam/sujets/15FRLIMLR1.pdf>.
Journal Officiel de la République Française. «Loi n° 2013-595 du 8 juillet 2013 d'orientation et de programmation pour la refondation de l'école de la

BIBLIOGRAPHY 293

République.» (Known as the «Loi Peillon» after Minister of Education Vincent Peillon). *Journal Officiel de la République Française* 157 (July 9, 2013), 11379.
Ministère de l'Education Nationale (education.gouv.fr). *Le Baccalauréat 2010.* (June 11, 2010). <www.education.gouv.fr/cid52071/baccalaureat-2010>.
Ministère de l'Education Nationale (education.gouv.fr) *Repères, histoire, et patrimoine: Le ministère de l'Éducation nationale, de 1789 à nos jours.* <www.education.gouv.fr/pid289/le-ministere-de-l-education-nationale-de-1789-a-nos-jours.html>.
Ministère de l'Education Nationale (education.gouv.fr) *Bulletin officiel: «Le Programme des lycées, vol.2»* Hors-série (August 12, 1999).
Ministère de l'Education Nationale (education.gouv.fr) *Bulletin officiel: modifiant les modalités de l'oral des EAF pour la session de juin 2003.* 3 (January 16, 2003).
Ministère de l'Education Nationale (education.gouv.fr) *Bulletin officiel: «Nouveaux programmes de Seconde applicables à la rentrée 1999.»* Hors-série (August 12, 1999).
Ministère de l'Education Nationale (education.gouv.fr) *Bulletin officiel: «Nouveaux programmes de Seconde et Première amendés pour la rentrée 2001.»* 27 (July 12, 2001).
Ministère de l'Education Nationale (education.gouv.fr) *Bulletin officiel: «Nouveaux programmes de Seconde et Première applicables à la rentrée 2000.»* Hors série (August 31, 2000).
Ministère de l'Education Nationale (education.gouv.fr) *Bulletin officiel: «Nouvelles modalités des Epreuves Anticipées de Français (EAF) pour juin 2002.»* 26 (June 28, 2001).
Ministère de l'Education Nationale (education.gouv.fr) *Bulletin officiel: précisant les modalités de l'oral des EAF pour juin 2002.* 1 (January 3, 2002).
Ministère de l'Education Nationale (education.gouv.fr) Département de l'évaluation, de la prospective, et de la performance. *Le Bac a 200 ans: 1808-2008.* (2008).
Ministère de l'Education Nationale (education.gouv.fr) *Documents d'accompagnement des programmes de Seconde et de Première.* Paris: CNDP, 2001 (September).
Ministère de l'Education Nationale (education.gouv.fr). *L'Education nationale en chiffres.* <http://www.education.gouv.fr/cid57111/l-education-nationale-en-chiffres.html#Le second degré>.
Ministère de l'Education Nationale (education.gouv.fr) «Les options au baccalauréat général en 2013 ont très peu d'impact sur la réussite.» <http://www.education.gouv.fr/cid80074/les-options-au-baccalaureat-general-en-2013-tres-peu-d-impact-sur-la-reussite.html>.
Ministère de l'Education Nationale (education.gouv.fr). *Repères et références statistiques sur les enseignements, la formation et la recherche* (2013).

INDEX

A

Abd al Malik (Régis Fayette-Mikano), 189
Académie Française, 156
ACT exam, 62, 85
Adams, Charles Francis, 72
Adjani, Isabelle, 183, 189
Advanced Placement exam, 63, 85
Affordable Care Act, 16
Agathon (Henri Massis and Alfred de Tarde), 29, 103, 107, 110, 118, 148, 149, 151, 152, 256
Ahr, Sylviane, 261, 262, 268
Alain-Fournier (Henri-Albin Fournier), 186
Albanese, Ralph, 187
Allais, Gustave, 110, 111
Allègre, Claude, 142, 149
Alsup, Janet, 238–240, 243, 245, 263, 269
American Association of Colleges and Universities, 17, 84
American Association of Teachers of French (AATF), 199
American Comparative Literature Association (ACLA), 31
Amherst College, 242
Amplification, literary exercise of, 80–82, 91, 93

Année de rhétorique (former term for the penultimate year of lycée), 89
Apostrophes (French television talk show), 115, 120
Argumentation, literary exercise of, 140, 144, 146, 148, 152
Arias, Beatriz, 137
Assessment, 61–64, 68–70, 84, 192, 207, 223
Association Française des Enseignants de Français (AFEF), 127, 140, 141, 155, 157, 159
Assouline, Pierre, 37–39, 42, 57
Austen, Jane, 44, 136
Austria, reading rates in, 223

B

Baccalauréat, 61, 64, 79, 85, 86
exam in literature, 29, 61, 64, 65
Balibar, Renée, 58, 234
Balzac, Honoré de, 134, 136, 169, 203, 205, 247, 259
Barratier, Christophe, 171
Barthes, Roland, 101, 124, 158, 160, 227, 241, 244–252, 254–257, 259, 262, 263, 266, 269, 270

© The Author(s) 2017
M.M. Guiney, *Literature, Pedagogy, and Curriculum in Secondary Education*, DOI 10.1007/978-3-319-52138-1

Baudelaire, Charles, 26, 28, 51–55, 70, 110, 128, 207, 208, 227, 234, 245, 249, 255, 267
Baudelaire, "Le Mauvais vitrier" (The Bad Glazier), 52
Baudelot, Christian, 216, 272
Bauerlein, Mark, 15
Bayard, Pierre, 186
Beam, Adam, 231
Beckett, Samuel, 51
Bégaudeau, François, 177, 181, 183, 185
Bénévent, Christine, 211–213, 248, 268
Bénichou, Paul, 87, 159, 163, 231
Bennett, William, 139
Benvéniste, Emile, 140
Bergounioux, Pierre, 6, 8, 235
Bergson, Henri, 119
Bevin, Matthew (Governor of Kentucky), 191, 230
Bildungsroman, 49, 51
Bilingual education (United States), 136, 139
Bill and Melinda Gates Foundation, 1
Blaise, Lilia, 187
Bleuse, Magali, 187
Bloom, Allan, 139
Boileau, Nicolas, 128, 259
Boon, Danny, 204
Bossuet, Jacques-Bénigne, 92, 98, 99
Bouasse, Henri, 95, 97–99, 232
Boué, Michel, 231
Bourdieu, Pierre, 20, 22, 32, 77, 126, 127, 151, 153, 172, 176, 213, 229, 231, 234, 243
Bretton Woods Conference, 5
Brighelli, Jean-Paul, 189
Brunetière, Ferdinand, 84, 100
Bruns, Cristina, 122
Buisson, Ferdinand, 58, 171

C
California Institute of the Arts, 231
Cameron, James, 204
Camus, Albert, 40–42, 227, 266
Canonical literary exercise, 80
Canonical school exercise, 28
Cantet, Laurent, 30, 175, 177, 181, 189, 248
Careil, Yves, 210
Carnegie Foundation, 84
Carné, Marcel, 58
Casanova, Ursula, 137
Castano, Emanuele, 239
Catholic Church, 85
Catholicism, 2, 95, 96, 99, 102, 111, 114, 115, 120, 123, 139, 160, 161, 166, 184, 188, 237, 268
Céline, Louis-Ferdinand, 227
Centre for Languages, Linguistics, and Area Studies 2009 Conference, 17
Centre national du cinéma et de l'image animée, 204
Certificat d'aptitude au professorat de l'enseignement du second degré (CAPES), 147
"*C'est la littérature qu'on assassine rue de Grenelle*", open letter published in *Le Monde* (March 2000), 146, 148, 149, 155
Chaitin, Gilbert, 95
Charbonnières Manifesto, 29, 126–129, 131, 132, 135, 137–139, 141, 142, 155, 171, 213, 240, 267
Chartier, Anne-Marie, 123
Chatterton, Thomas, 203
Chervel, André, 76, 78, 79
Chicago, University of, 100, 122
Chiss, Jean-Louis, 234, 263
Chronicle of Higher Education, 18

Clark, Priscilla Parkhurst, 114
The Class (*Entre les murs* 2008
   film), 30
Classical languages, 107, 121, 151
Colette, Gabrielle Sidonie, 186
College Board, 62, 86
Collège de France, 146
College scorecard, 3
Collin, Thibaud, 86
Comics, 212
Commentary, literary exercise of, 66,
   74, 76, 80, 81, 83
Common Core State Standards
   Initiative, 12, 30, 56, 63, 72, 85,
   209, 225, 264
Communautarisme
   (communitarianism), 30,
   136–138, 154, 157
Compagnon, Antoine, 101, 103,
   104, 109
Compère, Marie-Madeleine, 76, 78
Composition as literary exercise, 66,
   77, 80, 82, 84, 118
Composition, literary exercise of, 81,
   89, 91–93
Concours académique, 84
Concours général, 92, 118
Conseil national éducation économie
   (CNEE), 209
Constance School, 22
Conti, Paul-Marie, 140
Core curriculum, 10
Corneille, Pierre, 256
Corrigan, Paul, 200
Cousin, Victor, 203, 227
Creative writing, literary exercise
   of, 143, 144, 146
Crise du français, 103, 108–110
Crisis of French, 2, 74, 76, 89, 104,
   109, 110, 117
Crouzet, Paul, 105

Cultural exception, 196
Cultural imperialism, 168
Culture of proximity, 167, 168, 176,
   177, 181, 184, 185, 206, 239,
   243, 244, 246, 248, 268, 271
Culture wars in the United States, 24

D
Darien, Georges, 92
Daroy, Jacques, 171
Daunay, Bertrand, 148, 149, 157,
   250–254, 271
Debray, Régis, 147, 152
Deguy, Jacques, 97
Department of Education, National
   Assessment of Educational
   Progress, 62
Department of Education, United
   States, 18, 119
Didactics of Literature, 234
Doubrovsky, Serge, 158, 234
Dreyfus Affair, 95, 118
Duchamp, Marcel, 227, 264
Dufays, Jean-Louis, 236, 237, 252
Dumaître, Eric, 132
Duras, Claire de, 124
Durkheim, Emile, 29, 101, 118
Duruy, Victor, 81, 88

E
Ebonics (in school curriculum),
   136, 139
Ecole Nationale des Chartes, 211
Ecole Normale Supérieure, 83, 91, 100,
   103, 105
Einstein, Albert, 97
Eisenhower, Dwight D., 32, 258
English Language Arts, 195, 225,
   234, 235

Enseignement spécial, non-literary secondary education, 81, 88
Entre les murs (2008 film), 30
Épreuve anticipée de français (EAF), French literature baccalauréat exam, 64
Erudition
  as distinct from rhetoric, 75, 77, 79, 81
  literary exercise of, 91
Establet, Roger, 216, 233
Etienne, Bénédicte, 156
Etre et avoir (2002 film), 30
European Union (EU), 1, 196, 208, 210, 216
Evolution in public schools, Kitzmiller v. Dover (Pennsylvania) 2005, 111
Ewell, Peter, 69
Explication, literary exercise of, 64, 74, 80–82

F
Faguet, Emile, 109–111
Falcucci, Clément, 80
Falloux, Alfred de, 95
Fayolle, Roger, 245
Federal Reserve Bank of Cleveland, 2
Fénelon, François, 92
Ferlinghetti, Lawrence, 47, 48, 50
Fernandel (Fernand Contandin), 164
Ferry, Jules, 92, 156
Finland and PISA rankings, 215
First Empire (1804-1815), 71
Fitzpatrick, Robert, 231
Fize, Michel, 85
Flaubert, Gustave, 58, 114, 207, 208, 270, 271
Forbes Magazine, 4
Fortoul, Hippolyte, 80, 82, 92

Fraisse, Emmanuel, 245
Frank, Anne, 188
Frary, Raoul, 159
Free trade, 195
Freire, Paulo, 81, 127, 172
French Revolution, 87
Frijhoff, Willem, 205
Fumaroli, Marc, 87, 119, 151, 152
Fustel de Coulanges, Numa Denis, 101, 102

G
Gallicanism, 111
Games of Love and Chance (*L'Esquive* 2004 film), 30
Garcia Márquez, Gabriel, 217, 218
Gauchet, Marcel, 150
General Agreement on Tariffs and Trade (GATT), 5, 196, 197, 231
General education, 36, 39, 40, 42–46, 48, 55, 61, 62, 191, 193, 194, 199, 203, 208, 212, 215, 217, 220–221, 225, 228, 229
General education requirements, 9, 10, 16
Genetically modified organisms (GMO), 195, 196, 231
Geneva School, 270
Geographic trademarks, and trade regulation, 195
George Mason University, 235
G.I. Bill, 14, 91
Gide, André, 162, 163
Giraudoux, Jean (*La Guerre de Troie n'aura pas lieu* 1935 play), 39
Goldstein, Joshua, 31
Goscinny, René, 30, 170
Graff, Gerald, 33, 44, 45, 72, 73, 122
Graffigny, Françoise de, 124

Graffiti, 50
Grange, Mireille, 151
Greenblatt, Stephen, 44, 45
Grégoire, Henri (l'Abbé Grégoire), 254, 270
The Guardian (daily newspaper), 215, 216
Guillory, John, 234
Guiney, M. Martin, *Teaching the Cult of Literature in the French Third Republic*, 31

H
Hannecart, Claire, 232
Harry Potter series, 247
Harvard University Press, 19
Hébrard, Jean, 123
Hirst, Damien, 32
Hollande, François, 41, 43, 209, 210
Homer (The Iliad), 40, 269
Homo economicus, 24
Honoré, Christophe, 41
Houdart-Merot, Violaine, 29, 72, 75, 79, 80, 82, 83, 91–94, 158
Houellebecq, Michel, 271
Howard, Richard, 4, 270
Hugo, Victor, 98, 115, 120
Huret, Jules, 53, 58
Hutchins, Robert Maynard, 122
Huyhn, Jeanne-Antide, 238

I
Imitation, literary exercise of, 92, 94
Invention, literary exercise of, 91, 93, 99
Iser, Wolfgang, 22
Islam, 237, 269

J
Jacotot, Joseph, 159
Jakobson, Roman, 20–23, 26, 28, 201, 223, 224, 226–228, 240, 257, 258
Jalabert, Romain, 87
Jarrety, Michel, 146, 160
Jauss, Hans-Robert, 22
Jay, Paul, 17, 235, 239, 269
Jesuit Order, 28, 72, 74–76, 79, 90, 94, 95, 144, 238
Jey, Martine, 29, 72, 79, 80, 82, 83, 97, 119, 167
Johns Hopkins University, 235
Jospin, Lionel, 171, 187
Jouan-Westlund, Annie, 188
Jouve, Vincent, 268

K
Kazakhstan, reading rates in, 223
Kechiche, Abdellatif, 30, 175, 176, 181, 182, 189, 248
Keller, Betsy, 270
Kidd, David Comer, 239
King, Stephen, 271
Koons, Jeff, 32
Kronman, Anthony T., 9, 17, 32

L
La Belle personne (*The Beautiful Person* 2008 film), 41
La Bruyère, Jean de, 256
La Croix, daily newspaper, 120
La Fontaine, Jean de, 128, 162, 169, 187
Lagarde et Michard school textbooks, 124, 158
La Guerre des Boutons (1962 film), 30

La Journée de la jupe (*Skirt Day* 2009 film), 30
Lamartine, Alphonse de, 66
Lang, Jack, 142
Langlois, Charles-Victor, 101
Language Arts, 26, 27, 122, 235
Lanson, Gustave, 29, 83, 90, 92, 95–97, 99, 101–103, 105, 109, 111, 113, 119, 123–124, 126, 131, 133, 136, 156, 166, 233, 252, 257, 260, 267
Lapostolle, Christine, 37, 38, 42, 57
La Princesse de Clèves (*Madame de Lafayette*), 28, 35–37, 40, 41, 43, 154, 156, 157, 185
Larousse, Pierre, 58
Lasserre, Pierre, 118
Lassonde, Stephen, 13
Laval, Christian, 211
Lavisse, Ernest, 108–110
Law forbidding Islamic headscarf in public schools (France 2004), 137–140
Le Bon, Gustave, 118
Le Débat, journal, 150–151, 153, 160, 211, 261, 268
Lee, Stan, 23
Le Figaro (daily newspaper), 86, 87, 151
Le Français aujourd'hui (French Today, journal of the AFEF), 29, 127, 136, 155
Lemaître, Jules, 84, 100
Le Monde (daily newspaper), 37, 38, 146, 149, 155, 163, 185, 197, 213
Lepenies, Wolf, 118
Le Petit Nicolas (2009 film), 30
Leroux, Georges, 75, 76
Leroux, Michel, 151

Leroy, Michel, 78, 89, 90
Les Inrockuptibles (magazine), 189
L'Esquive (*Games of Love and Chance* 2004 film), 30
L'Humanité (daily newspaper), 231
Liberal arts, 36, 56, 194, 217, 230, 242
as disinterested quest for knowledge, 192
Libération (daily newspaper), 37, 39, 189
Liehm, Antonin, 197, 198
Lilienfeld, Jean-Paul, 30, 175, 182, 189
Lindaman, Dana, 84
Lirca, Corina Alexandrina, 15
Lisbon Conference (March 2000), 209
Lisbon Strategy of the European Union, 209, 210
Literariness, 19, 22–24, 26, 46–49, 52, 54, 70, 73, 74, 76, 84, 200–202, 206, 221, 223, 224, 226, 227, 229–230, 235, 237, 238, 240, 247, 249, 252, 254, 257, 260, 264, 268
Literary history in French secondary school curriculum, 74, 83
Littré, Emile, 58
Language Arts, 27
Locqueneux, Robert, 97
Lopez, Georges, 172, 173, 188
Los Indignados, 200
Loucif, Sabine, 158
Louichon, Brigitte, 270
Lovecraft, Howard Philips (H. P.), 271
Lycée, 64–67, 71–73, 79–82, 85, 86, 88, 123, 125, 126, 129, 132–134, 142, 147, 148, 155, 156, 158, 210, 213, 232, 242, 268

M

Magnolia, Tiffany, 31
Maingueneau, Dominique, 234
Mallarmé, Stéphane, 20, 33, 54, 131, 148, 263
Malle, Louis, 165
Marghescu, Mircea, 22
Marianne (weekly magazine), 42
Marivaux, Pierre Carlet de, 175–177, 181, 182, 184, 188
Marketable skills, literary pedagogy as a means of acquiring, 72
Marshall Plan, 5
Martin, Biddy, 242–246, 248, 270
Martinez, Isabelle Marc, 189
Marvel Comics, 23
Marx, Karl, 5, 29, 32, 104
Maspero publishing house, 216
Massis, Henri, 29, 103–106, 108, 109, 118
Massol, Jean-François, 81, 91
Math anxiety, 15
Maurras, Charles, 118
Mauss, Marcel, 231
May 1968, 27, 29, 87, 117, 126, 132
MC Solaar (Claude M'Barali), 189
Meghelli, Samir, 181
Meirieu, Philippe, 234
Melville, Herman, 114
Mercure de France (journal), 100
Merle, Pierre, 68
Merlin-Kajman, Hélène, 153–155, 213
Michel, Alain, 217
Michelet, Jules, 101, 102
Milo, Daniel, 187, 234
Ministry of Education, France, 65, 70, 85
Ministry of National Education, France, 79, 112, 124, 146
Ministry of Public Instruction, France, 90

Ministry of the Interior, France, 269
Mise en abyme, 218
Mitterand, Henri, 152
Mitterrand, François, 142, 188
Mnouchkine, Ariane, 206, 231
Moby Dick (Herman Melville), 36
Modern Language Association (MLA), 14, 18, 117, 241, 270
Molière (Jean-Baptiste Poquelin), 183, 184, 189
Monet, Claude, 54
Monod, Gabriel, 101
Montand, Yves, 58
Montessori, Maria, 81
Mornet, Daniel, 90

N

National Council of Teachers of English, 24
National Endowment for the Arts, 15, 59
National Governors Association, 63
National Science Foundation, 33
The New Yorker magazine, 41, 44
New York Review of Books, 17
New York State Regents Exam, 62
New York Times, 18, 33, 59, 187
1905 Law of separation between Church and State, France, 27, 96
No Child Left Behind Act, 12
Noé, Jean-Baptiste, 183
Nora, Pierre, 150, 164, 187
Nous, princesses de Clèves (*We, Princesses of Clèves* 2011 film), 41
Nuit Debout, 200
Nussbaum, Martha, 7, 9, 32, 211, 213

O

Obama, Barack, 57
Occupy Wall Street, 200

302 INDEX

Office of the United States Trade Representative, 196
Oprah Winfrey Book Club, 120
Organization for Economic Cooperation and Development (OECD), 5, 11, 30, 63, 64, 85, 141, 208, 210, 213–217, 221–223, 230, 235, 252, 264–267
Ormesson, Jean d', 152
Orsenna, Erik, 163, 186
Ouzoulias, André, 156, 157
Ozon, François, 170
Ozouf, Mona, 153

P

Pagnol, Marcel, 164
Painbéni, Sandra, 120
Panthéon, 40, 42
Pasquier, Dominique, 125, 213, 231, 232
Passeron, Jean-Claude, 32, 77, 126, 127, 153, 213, 231, 234
Pasteur, Louis, 120
Pearson PLC (textbook publisher), 62
Pécresse, Valérie, 156
Péguy, Charles, 29, 102–104, 106, 118, 151, 152
Peillon, Vincent, 209
Penloup, Marie-Claude, 185, 253
Pennac, Daniel, 186
Peretti, Isabelle de, 234
Pergaud, Louis, 171
Perret, Laetitia, 201, 202
Petrey, Sandy, 270
Peyre, Henri, 101
Philibert, Nicolas, 172–174
Philippe, Gilles, 151
Piaget, Jean, 81, 151, 171
Picard, Michel, 148
Picard, Raymond, 101, 259

Pius VII, Pope, 76
Pivot, Bernard, 115, 120, 153
Planck, Max, 97
Plato, 255
Poe, Edgar Allan, 27, 33, 53, 207, 263, 270
Politis (weekly magazine), 41
Pons, Xavier, 203, 217
Potlatch, 205, 231
Pratiques (journal), 249, 256
Prévert, Jacques, 28, 45–55, 58, 115, 162, 181, 186, 227, 234, 267
Prévert, "Le cancre" (The dunce), 46, 54, 55, 58
Prévost, Christine, 232
Programme for International Student Assessment (PISA), 11, 27, 40, 63, 69, 71, 85, 210, 215–223, 230, 232, 235, 237, 264, 266, 267
Protectionism, 193–196, 198, 204, 261, 262
Proust, Marcel, 226, 258, 259
Publications of the Modern Language Association (journal), 241
Pujade-Renaud, Claude, 186
Pythia, the, 50

Q

Quadrivium, 8, 32, 75, 116, 229
Quintilian, "Institutio Oratoria", 74

R

Race to the Top, 12, 215
Racine, Jean, 124, 134–136, 256
Rancière, Jacques, 159
Rand, Ayn, 194
Ratio Studiorum (1599), 28, 74, 76, 94
Ravitch, Diane, 216

Realism, 54
Reception theory and reader-response criticism, 238, 263, 270
Reforms to French literature curriculum 1902, 89
Remond, Emilie, 201, 202
Revue de l'Association Française des Acteurs de l'Education (journal), 216
Revue des deux mondes (journal), 100
Revue Française de Pédagogie (journal), 250
Rhetoric, 24, 32, 62, 69, 70, 72–79, 84, 89, 93, 95, 97, 100, 101, 110, 112
Ribot, Alexandre, 89, 117
Richardson, F.C., 15
Richepin, Jean, 169
Ricoeur, Paul, 262
Rimbaud, Arthur, 84, 87, 118
Roberts, John, 171
Robert, Yves, 164, 171
Roche, Mark, 122
Roels, Virginie, 42
Rogers, Rebecca, 80, 87
Roger-Vasselin, Denis, 151, 160
Romilly, Jacqueline de, 119
Rousseau, Jean-Jacques, 162
Rowling, J. K., 247
Rubio, Marco, 13
Rudler, Gustave, 90, 109
Russian formalists, 19, 23

S
Sachs, Leon, 118, 175–177, 186, 188, 254
Saint-Exupéry, Antoine de, 220
Sales of literature, France and United States, 112
Salmon, Christian, 200, 201, 260
Samuell, Yann, 171
Sanders, Bernie, 200

Sarkozy, Nicolas, 27, 28, 35–37, 40–44, 48, 57, 154
Sartre, Jean-Paul, 271
SAT exam, 62, 63, 69, 70, 72, 85, 87
Sauder, Régis, 41
Saussure, Ferdinand de, 224
Sauver les lettres ("save literature" collective), 77, 150
Savatovsky, Dan, 122, 234
Scalia, Antonin, 16
Scripture, as metaphor for literature, 73
Sée, Camille, 88
Seignobos, Charles, 101
Seinfeld (TV show), 207
Semiology, 26
Sempé, Jean-Jacques, 30, 170
Sermon, as example of amplification exercise, 80
Shakespeare, William, 9, 15, 23, 44, 45, 78, 116, 136, 200, 247, 268
Shavelson, Richard J., 84
Shea, Louisa, 188
Shklovsky, Victor, 23
Shrigley, David, 23, 227
Sidney, Sir Philip, 86
Skirt Day (*La Journée de la jupe* 2009 film), 30
Smith, Adam, 224
Snyder, Thomas, 13
Société Internationale Pour l'Etude des Femmes de l'Ancien Régime, 40
Sorbonne, University of the, 29, 83, 90–92, 100, 101, 103–105, 108, 109, 111, 112, 118, 121, 123, 142, 146, 151
Soudais, Michel, 40
South Korea and PISA rankings, 215
Stanford University, 24
Steinbeck, John, 188
STEM disciplines, 193, 198, 199, 230
Stendhal (Henri Beyle), 38

Stevenson, Adlai, 258
Straubhaar, Joseph D., 168
Suinn, R.M., 15
Sumara, Dennis, 122, 269
SUNY, Albany, 16
Symbolism, 54, 261, 271

T
Tarde, Alfred de, 29, 103–106, 108, 109, 118
Taylor, Frederick Winslow, 29, 105, 118, 151
Téchiné, André, 164
Telluride Association, 242
Terroir, 173, 196–199, 204, 231
Thibaudet, Albert, 251, 270
Third Republic (1871-1940), 72, 82, 91, 101, 103, 126–127, 150, 158, 172–173, 205
Thucydides, 220
To Be and To Have, Etre et Avoir (2002 film), 30, 172
Todorov, Tzvetan, 123, 132, 158, 236, 248, 268
Topel, Robert, 2
Trade regulation, 193, 195
  protectionism, 193
Transatlantic Trade and Investment Partnership (TTIP), 195
Trivium, 8, 32, 75, 116, 229
Truffaut, François, 164, 165, 168, 169, 172, 188

U
United Nations, 5, 31
Massachusetts, University of, 16

V
Valéry, Paul, 259
Vallès, Jules, 58

Varèse, Louise, 52
Vergil (*The Aeneid*), 38, 39
Verlaine, Paul, 169
Version, literary exercise of, 61, 80, 84
Viala, Alain, 27, 30, 142, 150, 151, 153, 155, 156, 185, 202, 211, 213, 234, 236, 267
Video games, 165, 201, 223
Vigny, Alfred de, 203
Vigo, Jean, 164
Viramontes, Helena Maria, 86
Voltaire (François-Marie Arouet), *Candide*, 58, 98, 99

W
Walker, Scott (Governor of Wisconsin), 191
Walt Disney Corporation, 197, 206, 230, 232
Warhol, Andy, 32, 206, 207, 230
Weidmann Koop, Marie-Christine, 199
Weir, Peter, 170
Weisz, George, 118
Whitman, Walt, 50
Williams, Florence, 229
Williams, William Carlos, 23, 227, 229, 264, 266
Wilson, Charles E., 12
World Bank, 5
World of Warcraft (videogame), 269, 271
World Trade Organization (WTO), 5, 197
Wrenn, Mary, 5

Y
YouTube, 246
Youx, Viviane, 156

Z

Zakaria, Fareed, 17, 145
Zerofsky, Elizabeth, 41, 44
Zill, Nicolas and Marianne Winglee, *Who Reads Literature? The Future of the United States as a Nation of Readers*, 59
Zink, Michel, 146, 160
Zino, Dominique, 31
Zola, Emile, 31, 54, 259

The manufacturer's authorised representative in the EU is Springer Nature Customer Service Centre GmbH, Europaplatz 3, 69115 Heidelberg, Germany. If you have any concerns regarding our products, please contact ProductSafety@springernature.com

Printed and bound by CPI Group (UK) Ltd, Croydon, CR0 4YY
23/03/2026
02076735-0014